Contemporary Debates in Applied Ethics

Contemporary Debates in Philosophy

In teaching and research, philosophy makes progress through argumentation and debate. *Contemporary Debates in Philosophy* presents a forum for students and their teachers to follow and participate in the debates that animate philosophy today in the western world. Each volume presents pairs of opposing viewpoints on contested themes and topics in the central subfields of philosophy. Each volume is edited and introduced by an expert in the field, and also includes an index, bibliography, and suggestions for further reading. The opposing essays, commissioned especially for the volumes in the series, are thorough but accessible presentations of opposing points of view.

1. Contemporary Debates in Philosophy of Religion *edited by Michael L. Peterson and Raymond J. VanArragon*
2. Contemporary Debates in Philosophy of Science *edited by Christopher Hitchcock*
3. Applied Ethics *edited by Andrew I. Cohen and Christopher Heath Wellman*
4. Epistemology *edited by Matthias Steup and David Sosa*

Forthcoming *Contemporary Debates* are in:

Aesthetics *edited by Matthew Kieran*
Cognitive Science *edited by Robert Stainton*
Metaphysics *edited by Ted Sider, Dean Zimmerman, and John Hawthorne*
Moral Theory *edited by James Dreier*
Philosophy of Mind *edited by Brian McLaughlin and Jonathan Cohen*
Social Philosophy *edited by Laurence Thomas*

CONTEMPORARY DEBATES IN APPLIED ETHICS

Edited by

**Andrew I. Cohen and
Christopher Heath Wellman**

Blackwell
Publishing

BLACKWELL PUBLISHING
350 Main Street, Malden, MA 02148-5020, USA
108 Cowley Road, Oxford OX4 1JF, UK
550 Swanston Street, Carlton, Victoria 3053, Australia

The right of Andrew I. Cohen and Christopher Heath Wellman to be identified as
the Authors of the Editorial Material in this Work has been asserted in accordance with
the UK Copyright, Designs, and Patents Act 1988.

First published 2005 by Blackwell Publishing Ltd

Library of Congress Cataloging-in-Publication Data

Contemporary debates in applied ethics / edited by Andrew I. Cohen and Christopher
Heath Wellman.
     p. cm. − (Contemporary debates in philosophy; 4)
  Includes bibliographical references and index.
  ISBN 1-4051-1547-5 (alk. paper) − ISBN 1-4051-1548-3 (pbk. : alk. paper)   1.
Applied ethics. I. Cohen, Andrew I. II. Wellman, Christopher Heath. III. Series.
  BJ1031.C597 2005
  170 − dc22
                                     2004016921

A catalogue record for this title is available from the British Library.

Set in 10/12$\frac{1}{2}$ pt Rotis serif
by SNP Best-set Typesetter Ltd., Hong Kong
Printed and bound in the United Kingdom
by TJ International, Padstow, Cornwall

The publisher's policy is to use permanent paper from mills that operate a sustainable
forestry policy, and which has been manufactured from pulp processed using acid-free
and elementary chlorine-free practices. Furthermore, the publisher ensures that the text paper
and cover board used have met acceptable environmental accreditation standards.

For further information on
Blackwell Publishing, visit our website:
www.blackwellpublishing.com

Contents

Acknowledgments

We are grateful to Bernard R. Boxill, Dorothy Denning, R. G. Frey, Deborah G. Johnson, Hugh LaFollette, and Jeffrey Rosen for advice in the early stages. Jeff Dean and Nirit Simon at Blackwell have been immensely supportive and patient. Most importantly, we would like to thank Adam Adler, Brad Champion, and Ryan McWhorter for providing crucial research and editorial assistance throughout the project.

Notes on Contributors

Andrew Altman is Professor of Philosophy at Georgia State University. He specializes in legal and political philosophy and applied ethics. Professor Altman's publications include *Critical Legal Studies: A Liberal Critique* (Princeton University Press, 1989) and *Arguing About Law: An Introduction to Legal Philosophy*, 2nd edn. (Wadsworth, 2001). His articles have appeared in *Philosophy and Public Affairs* and *Ethics*, among other leading philosophy journals. Currently he is working on issues of international criminal law.

Susan J. Brison is Associate Professor of Philosophy at Dartmouth College and has held visiting appointments at Tufts, New York University, and Princeton. She is author of *Aftermath: Violence and the Remaking of a Self* (Princeton University Press, 2002) and *Speech, Harm, and Conflicts of Rights* (Princeton University Press, forthcoming) and co-editor of *Contemporary Perspectives on Constitutional Interpretation* (Westview Press, 1993).

Daniel Callahan a cofounder of the Hastings Center, is now its Director of International Programs and a Senior Fellow at the Harvard Medical School. He has a Ph.D. in philosophy, and is the author, most recently, of *What Price Better Health: Hazards of the Research Imperative* (University of California Press, 2003).

J. Baird Callicott is Professor of Philosophy and Religion Studies in the Institute of Applied Sciences at the University of North Texas. From 1997 to 2000 he served as President of the International Society for Environmental Ethics. He is author of *Earth's Insights: A Multicultural Survey of Ecological Ethics from the Mediterranean Basin to the Australian Outback* (University of California Press, 1994), *In Defense of the Land Ethic: Essays in Environmental Philosophy* (State University of New York Press, 1989), *Beyond the Land Ethic: More Essays in Environmental Philosophy* (State University of New York Press, 1999), *American Indian Environmental Ethics: An Ojibwa Case Study* (Pearson Prentice Hall, 2004), and more than a hundred book chapters, journal articles, encyclopedia entries, and book reviews. Callicott's research proceeds on four major fronts: theoretical environmental ethics, land ethics, the philosophy of ecology and conservation, and comparative environmental philosophy.

Andrew I. Cohen is Associate Director of the Jean Beer Blumenfeld Center for Ethics and teaches in the philosophy department at Georgia State University. He specializes in ethics and political philosophy and has published papers on topics such as Hobbesian moral and political theory, the ethics of friendship, and rights theory.

Amitai Etzioni is the author of 20 books, including *Genetic Fix: The Next Technological Revolution* (Macmillan, 1973), *The Moral Dimension: Toward a New Economics* (Free Press, 1988), *The New Golden Rule: Community and Morality in a Democratic Society* (Basic Books, 1996), *My Brother's Keeper: A Memoir and a Message* (Rowman & Littlefield, 2003), and most recently, *From Empire to Community* (Palgrave Macmillan 2004). He served as a Senior Advisor to the White House on domestic affairs; he taught at Columbia University, Harvard Business School, University of California at Berkeley, and was named the first University Professor at George Washington University, where he is the Director of the Institute for Communitarian Policy Studies.

R. G. Frey is Professor of Philosophy at Bowling Green State University. He specializes in ethical and political philosophy and is the author of numerous books and articles on applied ethics, normative theory, and the history of eighteenth-century British moral philosophy. His latest books are *Euthanasia and Physician-Assisted Suicide* (with Gerald Dworkin and Sissela Bok; Cambridge University Press, 1998), *A Companion to Applied Ethics* (with Christopher Heath Wellman; Blackwell, 2003), and *Ethics, Animals, and Medicine* (Cambridge University Press, 2005).

David D. Friedman is a Professor of Law at Santa Clara University; his specialty is the economic analysis of law and his current interests include the effect of technology on the world over the next few decades. His most recent book is *Law's Order: What Economics has to do with Law and Why It Matters* (Princeton University Press, 2000). You can learn more than you want to know about both him and his ideas at <www.daviddfriedman.com>.

Robert P. George is McCormick Professor of Jurisprudence and Director of the James Madison Program in American Ideals and Institutions at Princeton University. He is a member of the President's Council on Bioethics, and served from 1993 to 1998 as a presidential appointee to the United States Commission on Civil Rights. He is a former Judicial Fellow at the Supreme Court of the United States, where he received the 1990 Justice Tom C. Clark Award. Among his books are *In Defense of Natural Law* (Clarendon Press, 1998) and *Making Men Moral: Civil Liberties and Public Morality* (Clarendon Press, 1993). His articles have appeared in the *Harvard Law Review*, the *Yale Law Journal*, the *Columbia Law Review*, the *University of Chicago*

Law Review, the *Review of Politics*, the *Review of Metaphysics*, *Law and Philosophy*, and the *American Journal of Jurisprudence*. He is a graduate of Swarthmore College and Harvard Law School, and holds a doctorate in philosophy of law from Oxford University.

John Harris is a member of the UK Human Genetics Commission and the Ethics Committee of the British Medical Association. He is the author or editor of 15 books and more than 150 papers, including *Clones, Genes, and Immortality: The Future of Human Reproduction* (Oxford University Press, 1998) and *Bioethics* (Oxford University Press, 2001). Harris is the founder and a general editor of the "Issues in Biomedical Ethics" series published by Oxford University Press. He was elected a Fellow of the United Kingdom Academy of Medical Sciences in 2001, the first philosopher to have been elected to this select group of medical scientists.

Chandran Kukathas holds the Neal A. Maxwell Chair in Political Theory, Public Policy, and Public Service in the Department of Political Science at the University of Utah. He is the author of numerous articles and books, including *The Liberal Archipelago* (Oxford University Press, 2003).

Patrick Lee is Professor of Philosophy at Franciscan University of Steubenville. He received his Ph.D. at Marquette University in 1980. Lee's book, *Abortion and Unborn Human Life* was published in 1996 (Catholic University of America Press), and he has written for various scholarly journals, including *Philosophy, Bioethics, Faith and Philosophy,* and *American Catholic Philosophical Quarterly*. He is now working on a book tentatively entitled *Dualism and Contemporary Ethical Issues*.

Margaret Olivia Little is an Associate Professor in the Philosophy Department, and a Senior Research Scholar in the Kennedy Institute of Ethics, at Georgetown University. She is co-editor (with Brad Hooker) of *Moral Particularism* (Clarendon Press, 2000) and is currently finishing a book on abortion entitled *Intimate Duties: Re-Thinking Abortion, Law, and Morality* for Oxford University Press.

David Miller is Professor of Political Theory at the University of Oxford and an Official Fellow of Nuffield College. His books include *On Nationality* (Clarendon Press, 1995), *Principles of Social Justice* (Harvard University Press, 1999), *Citizenship and National Identity* (Polity Press, 2000), and *Political Philosophy: A Very Short Introduction* (Oxford University Press, 2003). He is currently working on national responsibility and international justice, and on problems of social justice in multicultural societies.

Albert Mosley is Professor of Philosophy at Smith College. In addition to writing numerous articles and book chapters, he is the author of *Affirmative Action: Social Justice or Unfair Preference?* (with Nicholas Capaldi; Rowman & Littlefield, 1996) and *An Introduction to Logic: From Everyday Life to Formal Systems* (with Eulalio Baltazar; Ginn Press, 1984). He is also the editor of *African Philosophy: Selected Readings* (Prentice Hall, 1995).

Notes on Contributors

Stephen Nathanson is Professor of Philosophy at Northeastern University. He is the author of *An Eye for an Eye? The Immorality of Punishing by Death* (Rowman & Littlefield, 1987), *The Ideal of Rationality* (Open Court, 1994), *Should We Consent to be Governed? A Short Introduction to Political Philosophy* (Wadsworth, 1992), *Patriotism, Morality, and Peace* (Rowman & Littlefield, 1993), and *Economic Justice* (Prentice Hall, 1998), and he is the editor of an abridgement of John Stuart Mill's *Principles of Political Economy* (Hackett, 2004).

Bryan G. Norton is Professor of Philosophy, Science, and Technology in the School of Public Policy at the Georgia Institute of Technology. He has combined work in environmental ethics, environmental policy, and environmental science, and has written widely on environmental values, environmental valuation methods, and on biodiversity policy. He is author of *Why Preserve Natural Variety?* (Princeton University Press, 1987), *Toward Unity among Environmentalists* (Oxford University Press, 1991), and *Searching for Sustainability* (Cambridge University Press, 2002). He has also co-edited interdisciplinary volumes on environmental policy and animal welfare policy, and published in journals in philosophy, economics, biology, ecology, planning, and policy. He is a member of the Board of Directors of Defenders of Wildlife and of the Governing Board of the Society for Conservation Biology.

Louis P. Pojman is Professor of Philosophy at the US Military Academy. He is the author of several works in social and political philosophy.

Tom Regan is Emeritus Professor of Philosophy at North Carolina State University. He is the author of hundreds of articles and more than 20 books, including: *The Case for Animal Rights* (Routledge & Kegann Paul, 1983), *The Struggle for Animal Rights* (International Society for Animal Rights, 1987), *Defending Animal Rights* (University of Illinois Press, 2001), *Animal Rights, Human Wrongs: An Introduction to Moral Philosophy* (Rowman & Littlefield, 2003), and *Empty Cages: Facing the Challenge of Animal Rights* (Rowman & Littlefield, 2003). Upon his retirement in 2001, he received the Alexander Quarles Holladay Medal, the highest honor North Carolina State University can bestow on one of its faculty.

Jeremy Rifkin is the author of *The Biotech Century* (Tarcher Putnam, 1998). He is also President of the Foundation on Economic Trends in Washington, DC.

Michael Tooley is Professor of Philosophy at the University of Colorado. His is co-editor (with Ernest Sosa) of *Causation* (Oxford University Press, 1993) the editor of the five-volume anthology *Analytical Metaphysics* (Garland 1999), and the author of *Abortion and Infanticide* (Clarendon Press, 1983), *Causation: A Realist Approach* (Clarendon Press, 1987), and *Time, Tense, and Causation* (Clarendon Press, 1996).

Christopher Heath Wellman teaches in the Department of Philosophy at Washington University in St. Louis. He works in ethics, specializing in political and legal philosophy. He is the author of *A Theory of Secession: The Case for Political Self-*

Determination (Cambridge University Press, 2005) and (with John Simmons) *For &
Against: Is There a Duty to Obey the Law?* (Cambridge University Press, 2005).

Celia Wolf-Devine is Associate Professor of Philosophy at Stonehill. She earned her
BA from Smith College and her Ph.D. from the University of Wisconsin, Madison. In
addition to numerous articles and book chapters, she is the author of *Descartes on
Seeing: Epistemology and Visual Perception* (Southern Illinois University Press, 1993)
and *Diversity and Community in the Academy: Affirmative Action in Faculty Appointments* (Rowman & Littlefield, 1997), and is co-editor (with Philip Devine) of *Sex and
Gender: A Spectrum of Views* (Wadsworth, 2003).

Introduction

Andrew I. Cohen and Christopher Heath Wellman

Contemporary Debates in Applied Ethics presents 11 pairs of newly commissioned essays by some of the leading theorists working in the field today. Philosophers, social theorists, and legal scholars take opposing sides on issues of enduring and special contemporary importance such as abortion, affirmative action, animals, capital punishment, cloning, euthanasia, immigration, pornography, privacy in civil society, values in nature, and world hunger. The authors draw on recent developments in moral and political theory, economics, science, and public policy. Their essays are written in plain, jargon-free language so as to be accessible to introductory students, but they also feature cutting-edge, rigorous arguments that will demand the attention of scholars currently working on these important issues.

Patrick Lee and Robert P. George argue that abortion often wrongly kills a human being. A fetus, they claim in "The Wrong of Abortion," is a morally significant and distinct entity who is internally programmed to become an independent and mature human being – unless stopped by some disease or act of violence. A fetus is the same *kind* of thing as you are, but only at an earlier developmental stage. The authors discuss how we are living bodily entities, and as such we come to be long before birth. We become morally significant at the moment of conception; at that point each of us becomes the sort of entity who has the potential to develop and exercise higher mental functions. We do not find such capacities among mere parts of human beings or among nonhuman animals. Human beings enjoy rights in virtue of being a certain *kind* of entity, but their moral status is not a function of the extent to which they exhibit certain qualities. Lee and George consider a "bodily rights argument," which holds that women are not required to give the use of their bodies to gestating fetuses. But the authors reject this view, holding that nonconsensual relationships sometimes generate moral responsibilities. Except in cases where a mother's life is threatened, the sacrifice a mother must perform when carrying a fetus to term is far less serious than the harm involved in killing a fetus.

Margaret Olivia Little defends abortion as often morally permissible, but not because developing embryos are morally inert bundles of cells. In her essay, "The Moral Permissibility of Abortion," Little discusses how morality – and the reasons it furnishes – should not be forced into metaphysical views that regard steady states as the only possible explanatory categories. Rather, a more nuanced metaphysics acknowledges scalar qualities and ongoing development as key to an adequate picture of the world. Little notes that arguments investing moral significance in fetal potential are often importantly misleading. We must acknowledge that any such potential crucially depends upon some woman's choices. Little argues that fetuses are not morally inert; their developing status does confer a developing moral significance. Still, on her view, aborting a fetus is sometimes a permissible withdrawal of sustenance and support for a developing life that would not have existed but for a woman's active support in the first place. This is part of the reason why some abortions do not violate any rights. Little then proposes reframing the abortion discussion into one of the *ethics of gestation*. Gestating a child and becoming a mother are momentous projects with profound moral implications. Besides entailing considerable medical risks and physical burdens, these projects involve significant reformulations of one's practical identity. In order to protect the intimacy crucial to personal identity and meaningfulness, Little argues, gestation and motherhood are and must be an individual's significant moral prerogative. Acknowledging such a prerogative no more diminishes the value of motherhood and babies than acknowledging sexual prerogatives diminishes the value of marriage and family. Even with a moral prerogative to terminate a pregnancy, however, there may still be important moral reasons not to abort in certain circumstances. Little then considers issues regarding the ethics of *creation* and how they relate to an ethics of *gestation*.

In "A Defense of Affirmative Action," Albert Mosley defends policies that take race into account as a means of increasing the ability of minorities to take advantage of employment, educational, and investment opportunities. Mosley considers and rejects in turn several arguments by critics of affirmative action policies: racial minorities are owed nothing by the innocent beneficiaries of racial injustices, aptitude and IQ tests prove that racial minorities are less competent on the average, race is a bogus concept, and race-conscious policies are a form of reverse discrimination prohibited by the constitution. He argues that measures to increase racial diversity are morally justified as steps to undo entrenched unjust norms and to promote a better justified distribution of goods and services to underserved communities. Celia Wolf-Devine's main disagreement with Mosley concerns the merits of *preferential* affirmative action policies. Such policies privilege some applicants simply in virtue of their being members of certain historically underrepresented groups. In "Preferential Policies Have Become Toxic," Wolf-Devine considers some key contemporary arguments for such policies and finds them all inadequate. Preferential affirmative action policies might be cast as *compensation* for past injustices, but, she argues, such policies are often misguided and poorly targeted. She also cautions against devising policies to bring about proportionate representation of all groups in all professions, since, as she points out, there might be important cultural differences (independently of the effects of past oppression) that explain why particular racial and ethnic groups gravitate toward certain careers. *Corrective* defenses of preferential affirmative action hope to fix current bias, but, Wolf-Devine claims, we should be wary of generalizing findings of bias from one situation to others. Wolf-Devine then considers various *forward-looking* defenses of preferential affirmative action, but she worries about their unintended consequences, such as: fostering perverse pressures toward group conformity on some beneficiaries of the policies, further confusing race and class in remedial social policies, increasing the drop-out rate for black college students, and perpetuating negative racial stereotypes. Wolf-Devine ultimately argues that preferential policies are "divisive because they are zero-sum." She applauds recent evidence of the withering of racial categories, and defends social policies that target poverty instead of race.

In "Empty Cages: Animal Rights and Vivisection," Tom Regan argues against research on animals – whether for education, medical studies, or product testing. Many uses of animals, he notes, are unnecessary or otherwise gratuitous. Even in cases where the use of animals *seems* crucial, Regan argues that a key moral principle – moral rights – typically blocks us from using animals for our benefit. He then presents a series of arguments to show that animals possess moral rights. He discusses and rejects views that morally privilege human beings over other animals. Logical consistency demands that nonhuman animals enjoy certain fundamental rights in just the way that human beings do. R. G. Frey, on the other hand, believes using animals for some research purposes is permissible. In "Animals and Their Medical Use," he stakes out a position between an animal rights view that would forbid any experimentation on animals and an "anything goes" view that permits all but gratuitously cruel uses of animals. Against the former, Frey argues that regarding animals as bearers of rights protects them from experimental use with claims so strong that it would no longer be possible to state a defense of animal research. Their rights would cut off from the start any appeal to prospective human benefit – no matter how large the benefit. Against the "anything goes" position, Frey argues that we go to great lengths to justify inflicting suffering on animals, precisely because we rightly think that they count morally. But, not all living creatures have the same moral value. *If* experiments on living creatures are crucial for advancing human welfare, then we should "use the life of lower quality in preference to the life of higher quality." Just as there can be better or worse lives among creatures of one species, so too we can say that the life of a typical adult human is more valuable than that of an animal because a human being has more capacities for self-development, and so can have a richer life. Frey focuses particularly on how human *agency* adds moral value to a life. He then develops two accounts of moral community and applies his model to determining how and to what extent animals are morally considerable.

In "A Defense of the Death Penalty," Louis P. Pojman employs both *forward-looking* and *backward-looking* arguments. Forward-looking arguments maintain that capital punishment deters commission of murder and so helps ensure the best consequences overall in the long run. Pojman also discusses how several forms of evidence support the deterrent effects of the death penalty. Backward-looking arguments see punishment as a form of proportionate retribution. Such arguments do not appeal to the consequences in any straightforward sense but hold that murderers violate the dignity of their victims and so *deserve* to die. When responding to several objections to capital punishment, Pojman distinguishes retribution from vengeance and explains how the state has authority to inflict the death penalty. Pojman also responds to worries about mistaken death sentences and overrepresentation of certain groups among those sentenced to die.

By arguing that the "factual and moral beliefs on which death penalty support depends are mistaken," Stephen Nathanson maintains that neither deterrence nor retribution justify capital punishment. Deterrence alone is an inadequate justification, Nathanson writes in "Why We Should Put the Death Penalty to Rest," because it can license barbarically draconian punishments and the use of force on innocent persons. Standard "eye for an eye" arguments also fail because they are committed to reciprocating barbarity with barbarity. Such arguments, Nathanson worries, are also inconsistent with many of our considered moral judgments, and they give little guidance in determining appropriate punishments. We also find substantial evidence that capital punishment is unfairly applied in practice. Whether one receives the punishment is often a function of morally irrelevant factors such as one's race, class, and the quality of one's legal counsel. Maintaining the death penalty, Nathanson then argues, fosters a lack of concern about the loss of human life.

Recent technological and medical advances have made human cloning a real possibility. There are two sorts of cloning process. Reproductive human cloning aims to duplicate the genetic code of one human being in a new and separate being. Therapeutic cloning is a far less controversial procedure that focuses on microscopic cell lines and aims to improve medical treatments. In "Why I Oppose Human Cloning," Jeremy Rifkin objects to the commoditization of human cells and worries that some advancing clonal technologies may create perverse incentives for women to undergo medical procedures. Rifkin fears that using embryos for experimental purposes may invite us to harvest tissues from more developmentally advanced fetuses. He notes that reproductive cloning would cut against timeless traditions of treating conception as "a moment of utter surrender to forces outside of our control." Mainstreaming such technologies threatens to turn conception and childbirth into "the ultimate shopping experience" and to confer on corporations inappropriate control over human evolutionary destiny by giving them the chance to patent or copyright life or its genetic code. John Harris, on the other hand, defends cloning technologies – including reproductive cloning – against objections from critics such as Rifkin. In "The Poverty of Objections to Human Reproductive Cloning," Harris argues that if appeals to safety justify restricting such technologies, then they justify forbidding the introduction of *any* new technology or medical procedure. Critics may worry that cloned children will be victimized by oppressive parental expectations, but, as Harris discusses, such expectations will likely be substantially altered by the autonomy and life circumstances of the developing child. Critics must also steer clear of saying that cloned children are harmed in virtue of their origins since the alternative for any cloned child is never to have existed at all. Genetics is not destiny. Nor will reproductive cloning diminish human genetic variability, since people tend to prefer more traditional ways of conceiving children. Harris warns that we should not restrict human liberty without sufficient warrant, and absent compelling arguments against cloning technologies, there is inadequate justification for forbidding them. Against Rifkin, Harris argues that refusing to pursue certain biotechnologies dooms present and future persons to needless suffering from diseases that we might otherwise have cured or ameliorated. Harris

Andrew I. Cohen and Christopher Heath Wellman

also responds to Rifkin's patent/trademark worries by noting that ownership of cells, genes, and genetic information is not equivalent to owning human beings.

In "Defense of Voluntary Active Euthanasia and Assisted Suicide," Michael Tooley writes that euthanasia refers to "any action where a person is intentionally killed or allowed to die because it is believed that the individual would be better off dead than alive – or else, as when one is in an irreversible coma, at least no worse off." Tooley surveys several key distinctions relevant to discussions of euthanasia and proceeds to defend as morally permissible voluntary active euthanasia. Under certain circumstances, a person may be justified in committing suicide. In such cases, others would be justified in assisting that person to commit suicide. Where assisted suicide would be permissible, Tooley argues, so too would voluntary active euthanasia. Tooley considers various possible objections and finds that appeals to God or religious authority are unhelpful, and if suicide is in one's interests and violates no one's rights, then assisting someone in taking her life is morally permissible. Voluntary active euthanasia should also be legally permitted; slippery slope arguments against legalization often rest on poorly drawn distinctions and clash with empirical evidence. Allowing such euthanasia would also provide more skilled aid and comfort for those with the greatest need for it.

In "A Case against Euthanasia," Daniel Callahan notes that euthanasia does not fit into traditional categories for the justified taking of a life. Suicide is doubtless an option for many who suffer, but few make the choice. Callahan suggests that this is commendable; pain is a necessary part of human life, and "human life is better, even nobler, when we human beings put up with the pain and travail that come our way." He rejects the idea that principles of freedom and self-determination justify protecting a choice to end one's life or seek assistance in doing so. Callahan objects to physician-assisted suicide; by enlisting a doctor's aid, euthanasia is not merely a private act. It becomes a social act by enlarging the field of permissible killings. This would have dangerous consequences: it would violate a long-established norm that those with the power to save lives should not have the power to end them. Callahan also questions defenses of euthanasia that attempt to collapse the distinction between active and passive euthanasia. Removing legal obstacles to euthanasia, Callahan further argues, would "teach the wrong kind of lesson" by changing the role of physician and generating vast enforcement problems. More sharply, legalizing euthanasia would entrench as public policy the idiosyncratic preferences of a small minority who mistakenly believe human dignity is incompatible with suffering.

Freedom of movement is clearly a basic human right, David Miller admits in his essay, "Immigration: The Case for Limits," but whether that translates into a right to move to any physical space of one's choosing is another matter. There are often important reasons for restricting a freedom of movement, and many times such restrictions do not impede any *right* to move freely. So long as individuals have access to an *adequate* range of choices for satisfying significant interests, their interest in migrating elsewhere is not protected by right. A "right of exit" may give political societies reasons not to abuse members, but given the diversity of contemporary political societies, such a right does not translate into an unlimited right to go to *any* state. Much then hinges on what Miller calls the *scope* of distributive justice. Do principles of distributive justice apply *within* or *across* societies? If global justice furnishes any moral

reasons, these reasons likely fall short of requiring equal distribution of any particular good. We should note that immigration also invariably changes the public culture
of a political community, but native people have legitimate interests in controlling
such a culture. Immigration also raises significant issues in population growth, and
given economic and ecological considerations, nations have good reason to restrict
the influx of immigrants. Miller defends refugees' rights to move elsewhere for greater
security, but he also argues for states' autonomy in deciding how to handle asylum
requests. He upholds the prerogative of political communities to admit a non-refugee
on the basis of the prospective benefit for granting entry as well as the migrant's
interest in moving.

Chandran Kukathas defends free immigration and open borders in "The Case for
Open Immigration." He discusses why states of various sorts may have interests in
limiting immigration. While some authoritarian states wish to curtail the dissent that
may challenge government authority, even liberal democratic states may have
complex economic and political reasons to restrict the influx of immigrants. Though
he admits that an open borders policy is unlikely without reconsidering the notion of
the modern state, Kukathas defends the policy by appealing to principles of freedom
and humanity. Immigration is often a crucial avenue for fulfilling moral duties, pursuing economic opportunities, fleeing injustice, or striving for the improvement of
oneself or one's family. Kukathas discusses possible consequences to open borders and
argues that, in the end, there is no compelling *economic* argument for restricting immigration. An appeal to *nationality* may suggest arguments against open borders, either
because immigration will undermine a society's distinct cultural character, undermine
natives' abilities to prosper through a distinct way of life, or jeopardize a political
community's ability to implement shared principles of social justice. But Kukathas
argues against all such considerations. Cultural transformations are often entirely beneficial, and, he argues, it is unclear that the nation-state should be the locus for social
justice or that implementing principles of social justice should take precedence over
humanitarian concerns for helping the poor and the oppressed. While security concerns may give us pause, immigration restrictions are often poorly targeted and represent significant threats to personal liberty.

In "The Right to Get Turned On: Pornography, Autonomy, Equality," Andrew
Altman defends rights to produce, sell, and view pornography – including pornography depicting sexual violence. He hinges these rights not on free speech considerations but more on what he calls "sexual autonomy." A suitably constrained right to
such autonomy confers neither a right to coerce anyone into sexual acts nor a right
to entice minors into sexual encounters. But this right does protect people who choose
to produce pornography or consume the final product. They have this right even if
(as might often be true) they are deficient in some human virtues. Altman argues that
violent pornography *might* be a candidate for prohibition *if* there were conclusive
evidence connecting it to violent imitative acts. But the evidence is far too weak to
exclude violent pornography from the protection of a right to sexual autonomy. In
the meantime, Altman calls for improved education regarding sexual violence as well
as more vigorous prosecution and serious punishment for criminals guilty of such
crimes. Some critics may still worry that pornography nevertheless fosters attitudes
contributing to the degradation and subordination of women. Altman questions the

Andrew I. Cohen and Christopher Heath Wellman

connection there, noting that the liberal democracies that protect a freedom to produce and consume pornography tend to be societies with the best opportunities for the social and economic advancement of women.

Susan J. Brison rejects the notion of a right to produce and consume degrading or violent pornography. In " 'The Price We Pay'? Pornography and Harm," Brison offers detailed accounts of the exploitation and suffering of women involved in the pornography industry. She argues that many participants in pornography cannot be understood to have offered genuine consent. But even if they have given free consent, their participation in the industry has morally significant effects on social norms regarding sex roles. The industry harms nonparticipants, both male and female, by teaching and perpetuating discriminatory attitudes and by further injuring those previously victimized by sexual violence. Indeed, pornography's connection to subordination and degradation is not incidental; as Brison notes, pornography arouses precisely because of images of subordination. Brison then considers whether there can be a moral right to pornography – especially if, as Altman concedes, exercising such a right may be a sign of some moral vice. Brison argues, against Altman, that the harms pornography causes are sufficient to deny a right to produce and consume it.

Amitai Etzioni argues in "The Limits of Privacy" that there is little evidence of a loss of privacy in the contemporary age, especially considering that people often willingly waive claims to privacy. He discusses how informal norms of civil society can foster desirable behavior. Such informal enforcement may require limitations of privacy, but the surveillance it calls for would decrease the need for oppressive scrutiny and enforcement of personal conduct by the government. Etzioni stresses, though, that in today's Western democratic societies, neither privacy nor its protections are on the wane. Technology has enhanced protections for privacy (often automatically and beneath our notice). Other recent legal measures protect citizens' privacy regarding, for instance, medical, financial, and video rental records. Etzioni acknowledges dangers to privacy from increased surveillance but argues that promoting democratic institutions will best protect individuals from abuses and ultimately best protect their privacy. In "The Case for Privacy," David D. Friedman defends privacy as a bulwark against injustice inflicted by governments and private individuals. Privacy gives individuals the discretion to disclose about themselves as much or as little as they wish. While at times it may then protect some criminals, on balance privacy "gives each of us more control over his own life – which on average, if not in every case, is likely to lead to a freer world." Technology – especially encryption – furnishes many salutary improvements to privacy, partly by offsetting the effects of other technologies aimed at learning things about us without our permission, and partly by allowing us to shield our activities from prying governments and busybodies. Friedman explores Etzioni's arguments elsewhere that some restrictions on privacy are desirable, but he finds that the cases Etzioni has in mind are not cases for restricting *privacy*. The freedom of association, properly understood, dissipates any supposed problems regarding a need to curtail privacy. And, as Friedman notes, he and Etzioni differ on how trustworthy governments are.

In "The Intrinsic Value of Nature in Public Policy: The Case of the Endangered Species Act," J. Baird Callicott explores the nuances of a distinction between various ways of valuing nature. We might treat nature as valuable *intrinsically* (for its own sake), or we might regard nature as valuable *instrumentally* (purely as a means). In contrast with Bryan Norton and other environmental pragmatists, Callicott believes this distinction is not merely of theoretical interest but also has some special practical importance. Intrinsic value, Callicott writes, refers to a special domain of value that captures much about our self-concepts and our views of our world. It is what is valuable about a person or thing when all its instrumental value has been removed. Sometimes people may have preferences that clash with according nonhumans intrinsic value, but often the realm of public debate is a forum for recognizing and institutionalizing such special value. Callicott then explores the theoretical presuppositions of the intrinsic value of nature in the 1973 US Endangered Species Act.

In "Values in Nature: A Pluralistic Approach," Bryan G. Norton discusses how environmental writers typically formulate environmental values through a theory of values that is itself shaped by pre-theoretic expectations and assumptions. Some writers put theories of environmental value in service of a particular metaphysical view of the world. (Norton sees some of J. Baird Callicott's published work showing evidence of this approach.) Other writers emphasize epistemological considerations and stress that a theory of environmental values must make room for justifying value claims. And still other writers formulate and evaluate theories of environmental value with special reference to their *practical* impact, which refers not just to how easily a theory may be applied, but to how well it facilitates constructive public dialogue in resolving environmental disputes. Norton prefers the practical over earlier metaphysical approaches; pragmatic theories of environmental values encourage a commendable "shift from thinking of natural values as abstractions to thinking of values as the driving force in an action-oriented science of environmental management." Norton worries about the theoretical cogency of varying accounts of intrinsic value by theorists such as Callicott and Holmes Rolston III. Critical of both such accounts, Norton argues that they will neither persuade those who do not regard nature as having intrinsic value nor offer a constructive basis for directing public discourse toward protecting the environment. Norton instead defends an "experimental pluralism" that recognizes and embraces the different values persons bring to discussions of environmental values. This approach, he suggests, will best provide for a reasonable accommodation of different values.

In "Famine Relief: The Duties We Have to Others," Christopher Heath Wellman argues that one has a moral duty to rescue persons in dire need when one can do so without incurring unreasonable costs. Wellman is careful to note that one's duties of rescue need not take precedence over responsibilities to those near and dear. Still, when a person must choose between devoting resources to frivolous pursuits and providing easy rescue, she has a duty to lend a hand. The *proximity* of emergency is morally irrelevant if one can provide easy rescue or solicit others to do the same. Just as we often have a duty to save babies drowning within our *sight*, so too we often have a duty to direct modest amounts of our resources toward famine relief. Indeed, needy people sometimes have "samaritan rights" of rescue against persons who can provide assistance without unreasonable sacrifice. Modern communications have so expanded our knowledge of distant conditions that persons unwilling to donate a modest amount toward famine relief are often morally no different than persons who refuse easy rescue of infants drowning at their feet. Beyond our responsibilities to

Andrew I. Cohen and Christopher Heath Wellman

offer modest aid, we should also take steps to disassociate ourselves from unjust institutions – especially those that benefit us. Part of the reason we have our wealth, Wellman argues, is that we profit from an economic system that uses natural resources bought from oppressive governments abroad – and those governments "create the political conditions that play a causal role in the world's worst famines."

Appeals to babies drowning at our feet, Andrew I. Cohen argues in "Famine Relief and Human Virtue," tell us little about our responsibilities to alleviate world hunger. Hunger is a chronic problem calling for reflection on causes and alternative solutions. Such reflection is usually inappropriate for dire emergencies immediately in front of us. Cohen then explores the place for charity in a good life. He writes that persons need a protected opportunity *not* to be charitable in order for them to have the best chance properly to develop and cultivate the virtue of charity. Charity cannot be coerced. Cohen defends a limited "right to do wrong" with respect to withholding resources that good persons would otherwise have provided in similar circumstances. Such a right is important for giving persons the space to become virtuous, and it is crucial for maximizing the chance that there will be fewer needy people in the long term. He discusses several problems with enforcing positive duties to give to the needy. Such enforcement clashes with other moral values, jeopardizes satisfying other relevant moral demands, hinders personal virtue, and is often dangerously ineffective at alleviating hunger. Cohen notes that reasonable persons disagree not only about how best to satisfy need but about what the good life is and how one ought best to strive for it. The liberty to live our own lives should take precedence over the aims of busybodies and autocrats who believe they know better how we should allocate our precious resources. Cohen further argues that a good human life is marked by moral demands from many sources, and distant human need is but one possible claim on one's resources and time. We in the West best help needy persons by curtailing misguided relief policies, eradicating government price supports that unfairly privilege the wealthy, and trading with people oversees.

ABORTION

The Wrong of Abortion

Patrick Lee and Robert P. George

Much of the public debate about abortion concerns the question whether deliberate feticide ought to be unlawful, at least in most circumstances. We will lay that question aside here in order to focus first on the question: is the choice to have, to perform, or to help procure an abortion morally wrong?

We shall argue that the choice of abortion is objectively immoral. By "objectively" we indicate that we are discussing the choice itself, not the (subjective) guilt or innocence of someone who carries out the choice: someone may act from an erroneous conscience, and if he is not at fault for his error, then he remains subjectively innocent, even if his choice is objectively wrongful.

The first important question to consider is: what is killed in an abortion? It is obvious that some living entity is killed in an abortion. And no one doubts that the moral status of the entity killed is a central (though not the only) question in the abortion debate. We shall approach the issue step by step, first setting forth some (though not all) of the evidence that demonstrates that what is killed in abortion – a human embryo – is indeed a human being, then examining the ethical significance of that point.

Human Embryos and Fetuses are Complete (though Immature) Human Beings

It will be useful to begin by considering some of the facts of sexual reproduction. The standard embryology texts indicate that in the case of ordinary sexual reproduction the life of an individual human being begins with complete fertilization, which yields a genetically and functionally distinct organism, possessing the resources and active disposition for internally directed development toward human maturity.[1] In normal conception, a sex cell of the father, a sperm, unites with a sex cell of the mother, an ovum. Within the chromosomes of these sex cells are the DNA molecules which constitute the information that guides the development of the new individual brought into being when the sperm and ovum fuse. When fertilization occurs, the 23 chromosomes of the sperm unite with the 23 chromosomes of the ovum. At the end of this process there is produced an entirely new and distinct organism, originally a single cell. This organism, the human embryo, begins to grow by the normal process of cell division – it divides into 2 cells, then 4, 8, 16, and so on (the divisions are not simultaneous, so there is a 3-cell stage, and so on). This embryo gradually develops all of the organs and organ systems necessary for the full functioning of a mature human being. His or her development (sex is determined from the beginning) is very rapid in the first few weeks. For example, as early as eight or ten weeks of gestation, the fetus has a fully formed, beating heart, a complete brain (although not all of its synaptic connections are complete – nor will they be until sometime *after* the child is born), a recognizably human form, and the fetus feels pain, cries, and even sucks his or her thumb.

There are three important points we wish to make about this human embryo. First, it is from the start *distinct* from any cell of the mother or of the father. This is clear because it is growing in its own distinct direction. Its growth is internally directed to its own survival and maturation. Second, the embryo is *human:* it has the genetic makeup characteristic of human beings. Third, and most importantly, the embryo is a *complete* or *whole* organism, though immature. The human embryo, from conception onward, is fully programmed actively to develop himself or herself to the mature stage of a human being, and, *unless prevented by disease or violence, will actually do so, despite possibly significant variation in environment* (in the mother's womb). None of the changes that occur to the embryo after fertilization, for as long as he or she survives, generates a new direction of growth. Rather, *all* of the changes (for example, those involving nutrition and environment) either facilitate or retard the internally directed growth of this persisting individual.

Sometimes it is objected that if we say human embryos are human beings, on the grounds that they have the potential to become mature humans, the same will have to be said of sperm and ova. This objection is untenable. The human embryo is radically unlike the sperm and ova, the sex cells. The sex cells are manifestly not *whole* or *complete* organisms. They are not only genetically but also functionally identifiable as parts of the male or female potential parents. They clearly are destined either to combine with an ovum or sperm or die. Even when they succeed in causing fertilization, they do not survive; rather, their genetic material enters into the composition of a distinct, new organism.

Nor are human embryos comparable to somatic cells (such as skin cells or muscle cells), though some have tried to argue that they are. Like sex cells, a somatic cell is functionally only a part of a larger organism. The human embryo, by contrast, possesses from the beginning the internal resources and active disposition to develop himself or herself to full maturity; all he or she needs is a suitable environment and nutrition. The direction of his or her growth *is not extrinsically determined*, but the embryo is internally directing his or her growth toward full maturity.

So, a human embryo (or fetus) is not something distinct from a human being; he or she is not an individual of any non-human or intermediate species. Rather, an

Patrick Lee and Robert P. George

embryo (and fetus) is a human being at a certain (early) stage of development – the embryonic (or fetal) stage. In abortion, what is killed is a human being, a whole living member of the species *homo sapiens*, the same *kind* of entity as you or I, only at an earlier stage of development.

No-Person Arguments: The Dualist Version

Defenders of abortion may adopt different strategies to respond to these points. Most will grant that human embryos or fetuses are human beings. However, they then distinguish "human being" from "person" and claim that embryonic human beings are not (yet) *persons*. They hold that while it is wrong to kill persons, it is not always wrong to kill human beings who are not persons.

Sometimes it is argued that human beings in the embryonic stage are not persons because embryonic human beings do not exercise higher mental capacities or functions. Certain defenders of abortion (and infanticide) have argued that in order to be a person, an entity must be self-aware (Singer, 1993; Tooley, 1983; Warren, 1984). They then claim that, because human embryos and fetuses (and infants) have not yet developed self-awareness, they are not persons.

These defenders of abortion raise the question: Where does one draw the line between those who are subjects of rights and those that are not? A long tradition says that the line should be drawn at *persons*. But what is a person, if not an entity that has self-awareness, rationality, etc.?

This argument is based on a false premise. It implicitly identifies the human person with a consciousness which inhabits (or is somehow associated with) and uses a body; the truth, however, is that we human persons are particular kinds of physical organisms. The argument here under review grants that the human organism comes to be at conception, but claims nevertheless that you or I, the human person, comes to be only much later, say, when self-awareness develops. But if this human organism came to be at one time, but *I* came to be at a later time, it follows that I am one thing and this human organism with which *I* am associated is another thing.

But this is false. We are not consciousnesses that *possess or inhabit* bodies. Rather, we *are* living bodily entities. We can see this by examining the kinds of action that we perform. If a living thing performs bodily actions, then it is a physical organism. Now, those who wish to deny that we are physical organisms think of *themselves*, what each of them refers to as "*I*," as the subject of self-conscious acts of conceptual thought and willing (what many philosophers, ourselves included, would say are nonphysical acts). But one can show that this "I" is identical to the subject of physical, bodily actions, and so is a living, bodily being (an organism). Sensation is a bodily action. The act of seeing, for example, is an act that an animal performs with his eyeballs and his optic nerve, just as the act of walking is an act that he performs with his legs. But it is clear in the case of human individuals that it must be the same entity, the same single subject of actions, that performs the act of sensing and that performs the act of understanding. When I know, for example, that "That is a tree," it is by my understanding, or a self-conscious intellectual act, that I apprehend what is meant by "tree," apprehending what it is (at least in a general way). But the subject of that proposition, what I refer to by the word "That," is apprehended by sensation or perception. Clearly, it must be the same thing – the same I – which apprehends the predicate and the subject of a unitary judgment.

So, it is the same substantial entity, the same agent, which understands and which senses or perceives. And so what all agree is referred to by the word "I" (namely, the subject of conscious, intellectual acts) is identical with the physical organism which is the subject of bodily actions such as sensing or perceiving. Hence the entity that I am, and the entity that you are – what you and I refer to by the personal pronouns "you" and "I" – is in each case a human, physical organism (but also with nonphysical capacities). Therefore, since you and I are *essentially* physical organisms, *we* came to be when these physical organisms came to be. But, as shown above, the human organism comes to be at conception.[2] Thus you and I came to be at conception; we once were embryos, then fetuses, then infants, just as we were once toddlers, pre-adolescent children, adolescents, and young adults.

So, how should we use the word "person"? Are human embryos persons or not? People may stipulate different meanings for the word "person," but we think it is clear that what we normally mean by the word "person" is that substantial entity that is referred to by personal pronouns – "I," "you," "she," etc. It follows, we submit, that a person is a distinct subject with the natural capacity to reason and make free choices. That subject, in the case of human beings, is identical with the human organism, and therefore that subject comes to be when the human organism comes to be, even though it will take him or her months and even years to actualize the natural capacities to reason and make free choices, natural capacities which are already present (albeit in radical, i.e. root, form) from the beginning. So it makes no sense to say that the human organism came to be at one point but the person – you or I – came to be at some later point, To have destroyed the human organism that you are or I am even at an early stage of our lives would have been to have killed you or me.

No-Person Arguments: The Evaluative Version

Let us now consider a different argument by which some defenders of abortion seek to deny that human beings in the embryonic and fetal stages are "persons" and, as such, ought not to be killed. Unlike the argument criticized in the previous section, this argument grants that the being who is you or I came to be at conception, but contends that you and I became valuable and bearers of rights only much later, when, for example, we developed the proximate, or immediately exercisable, capacity for self-consciousness. Inasmuch as those who advance this argument concede that you and I once were human embryos, they do not identify the self or the person with a non-physical phenomenon, such as consciousness. They claim, however, that being a person is an accidental attribute. It is an accidental attribute in the way that someone's being a musician or basketball player is an accidental attribute. Just as you come to be at one time, but become a musician or basketball player only much later, so, they say, you and I came to be when the physical organisms we are came to be, but we became persons (beings with a certain type of special value and bearers of basic rights) only at some time later (Dworkin, 1993; Thomson, 1995). Those defenders of abor-

Patrick Lee and Robert P. George

tion whose view we discussed in the previous section disagree with the pro-life position on an ontological issue, that is, on what *kind of entity* the human embryo or fetus is. Those who advance the argument now under review, by contrast, disagree with the pro-life position on an evaluative question.

Judith Thomson argued for this position by comparing the right to life with the right to vote: "If children are allowed to develop normally they will have a right to vote; that does not show that they now have a right to vote" (1995). According to this position, it is true that we once were embryos and fetuses, but in the embryonic and fetal stages of our lives we were not yet valuable in the special way that would qualify us as having a right to life. We acquired that special kind of value and the right to life that comes with it at some point after we came into existence.

We can begin to see the error in this view by considering Thomson's comparison of the right to life with the right to vote. Thomson fails to advert to the fact that some rights vary with respect to place, circumstances, maturity, ability, and other factors, while other rights do not. We recognize that one's right to life does not vary with place, as does one's right to vote. One may have the right to vote in Switzerland, but not in Mexico. Moreover, some rights and entitlements accrue to individuals only at certain times, or in certain places or situations, and others do not. But to have the right to life is to have *moral status at all*; to have the right to life, in other words, is to be the sort of entity that can have rights or entitlements to begin with. And so it is to be expected that *this* right would differ in some fundamental ways from other rights, such as a right to vote.

In particular, it is reasonable to suppose (and we give reasons for this in the next few paragraphs) that having moral status at all, as opposed to having a right to perform a specific action in a specific situation, follows from an entity's being the *type of thing* (or substantial entity) it is. And so, just as one's right to life does not come and go with one's location or situation, so it does not accrue to someone in virtue of an acquired (i.e., accidental) property, capacity, skill, or disposition. Rather, this right belongs to a human being at all times that he or she exists, not just during certain stages of his or her existence, or in certain circumstances, or in virtue of additional, accidental attributes.

Our position is that we human beings have the special kind of value that makes us subjects of rights in virtue of *what* we are, not in virtue of some attribute that we acquire some time after we have come to be. Obviously, defenders of abortion cannot maintain that the accidental attribute required to have the special kind of value we ascribe to "persons" (additional to being a human individual) is an *actual* behavior. They of course do not wish to exclude from personhood people who are asleep or in reversible comas. So, the additional attribute will have to be a capacity or potentiality of some sort.[3] Thus, they will have to concede that sleeping or reversibly comatose human beings will be persons because they have the potentiality or capacity for higher mental functions.

But human embryos and fetuses also possess, albeit in radical form, a capacity or potentiality for such mental functions; human beings possess this radical capacity in virtue of the kind of entity they are, and possess it by coming into being as that kind of entity (viz., a being with a rational nature). Human embryos and fetuses cannot of course *immediately* exercise these capacities. Still, they are related to these capacities differently from, say, how a canine or feline embryo is. They are the kind of being – a natural kind, members of a biological species – which, if not prevented by extrinsic causes, in due course develops by active self-development to the point at which capacities initially possessed in root form become immediately exercisable. (Of course, the capacities in question become immediately exercisable only some months or years after the child's birth.) Each human being comes into existence possessing the internal resources and active disposition to develop the immediately exercisable capacity for higher mental functions. Only the adverse effects on them of other causes will prevent this development.

So, we must distinguish two sorts of capacity or potentiality for higher mental functions that a substantial entity might possess: first, an immediately (or nearly immediately) exercisable capacity to engage in higher mental functions; second, a basic, natural capacity to develop oneself to the point where one does perform such actions. But on what basis can one require the first sort of potentiality – as do proponents of the position under review in this section – which is an accidental attribute, and not just the second? There are three decisive reasons against supposing that the first sort of potentiality is required to qualify an entity as a bearer of the right to life.

First, the developing human being does not reach a level of maturity at which he or she performs a type of mental act that other animals do not perform – even animals such as dogs and cats – until at least several months after birth. A six-week old baby lacks the immediately (or nearly immediately) exercisable capacity to perform characteristically human mental functions. So, if full moral respect were due only to those who possess a nearly immediately exercisable capacity for characteristically human mental functions, it would follow that six-week old infants do not deserve full moral respect. If abortion were morally acceptable on the grounds that the human embryo or fetus lacks such a capacity for characteristically human mental functions, then one would be logically committed to the view that, subject to parental approval, human infants could be disposed of as well.

Second, the difference between these two types of capacity is merely a difference between stages along a continuum. The proximate or nearly immediately exercisable capacity for mental functions is only the development of an underlying potentiality that the human being possesses simply by virtue of the kind of entity it is. The capacities for reasoning, deliberating, and making choices are gradually developed, or brought towards maturation, through gestation, childhood, adolescence, and so on. But the difference between a being that deserves full moral respect and a being that does not (and can therefore legitimately be disposed of as a means of benefiting others) cannot consist only in the fact that, while both have some feature, one has more of it than the other. A mere *quantitative* difference (having more or less of the same feature, such as *the development* of a basic natural capacity) cannot by itself be a justificatory basis for treating different entities in *radically* different ways. Between the ovum and the approaching thousands of sperm, on the one hand, and the embryonic human being, on the other hand, there *is* a clear difference in kind. But between the embryonic human being and that same human being at any later stage of its maturation, there is only a difference in degree.

Note that there *is* a fundamental difference (as we showed above) between the gametes (the sperm and the ovum), on the one hand, and the human embryo and

Patrick Lee and Robert P. George

fetus, on the other. When a human being comes to be, a substantial entity that is identical with the entity that will later reason, make free choices, and so on, begins to exist. So, those who propose an accidental characteristic as qualifying an entity as a bearer of the right to life (or as a "person" or being with "moral worth") are *ignoring* a radical difference among groups of beings, and instead fastening onto a mere quantitative difference as the basis for treating different groups in radically different ways. In other words, there are beings a, b, c, d, e, etc. And between a's and b's on the one hand and c's, d's and e's on the other hand, there is a *fundamental difference*, a difference in kind not just in degree. But proponents of the position that being a person is an accidental characteristic ignore that difference and pick out a mere difference in degree between, say, d's and e's, and make that the basis for radically different types of treatment. That violates the most basic canons of justice.

Third, being a whole human being (whether immature or not) is an either/or matter – a thing either is or is not a whole human being. But the acquired qualities that could be proposed as criteria for personhood come in varying and continuous degrees: there is an infinite number of degrees of the *development of* the basic natural capacities for self-consciousness, intelligence, or rationality. So, if human beings were worthy of full moral respect (as subjects of rights) only because of such qualities, and not in virtue of the kind of being they are, then, since such qualities come in varying degrees, no account could be given of why basic rights are not possessed by human beings in varying degrees. The proposition that all human beings are created equal would be relegated to the status of a superstition. For example, if developed self-consciousness bestowed rights, then, since some people are more self-conscious than others (that is, have developed that capacity to a greater extent than others), some people would be greater in dignity than others, and the rights of the superiors would trump those of the inferiors where the interests of the superiors could be advanced at the cost of the inferiors. This conclusion would follow no matter which of the acquired qualities generally proposed as qualifying some human beings (or human beings at some stages) for full respect were selected. Clearly, developed self-consciousness, or desires, or so on, are arbitrarily selected degrees of development of capacities that all human beings possess in (at least) radical form from the coming into existence of the human being until his or her death. So, it cannot be the case that some human beings and not others possess the special kind of value that qualifies an entity as having a basic right to life, by virtue of a certain degree of development. Rather, human beings possess that kind of value, and therefore that right, in virtue of what (i.e., the kind of being) they are; and *all* human beings – not just some, and certainly not just those who have advanced sufficiently along the developmental path as to be able immediately (or almost immediately) to exercise their capacities for characteristically human mental functions – possess that kind of value and that right.[4]

Since human beings are valuable in the way that qualifies them as having a right to life in virtue of what they are, it follows that they have that right, whatever it entails, from the point at which they come into being – and that point (as shown in our first section) is at conception.

In sum, human beings are valuable (as subjects of rights) in virtue of what they are. But what they are are human physical organisms. Human physical organisms come to be at conception. Therefore, what is intrinsically valuable (as a subject of rights) comes to be at conception.

The Argument that Abortion is Justified as Non-intentional Killing

Some "pro-choice" philosophers have attempted to justify abortion by denying that all abortions are intentional killing. They have granted (at least for the sake of argument) that an unborn human being has a right to life but have then argued that this right does not entail that the child *in utero* is morally entitled to the use of the mother's body for life support. In effect, their argument is that, at least in many cases, abortion is not a case of intentionally killing the child, but a choice not to provide the child with assistance, that is, a choice to expel (or "evict") the child from the womb, despite the likelihood or certainty that expulsion (or "eviction") will result in his or her death (Little, 1999; McDonagh, 1996; Thomson, 1971).

Various analogies have been proposed by people making this argument. The mother's gestating a child has been compared to allowing someone the use of one's kidneys or even to donating an organ. We are not *required* (morally or as a matter of law) to allow someone to use our kidneys, or to donate organs to others, even when they would die without this assistance (and we could survive in good health despite rendering it). Analogously, the argument continues, a woman is not morally required to allow the fetus the use of her body. We shall call this "the bodily rights argument."

It may be objected that a woman has a special responsibility to the child she is carrying, whereas in the cases of withholding assistance to which abortion is compared there is no such special responsibility. Proponents of the bodily rights argument have replied, however, that the mother has not voluntarily assumed responsibility for the child, or a personal relationship with the child, and we have strong responsibilities to others only if we have voluntarily assumed such responsibilities (Thomson, 1971) or have consented to a personal relationship which generates such responsibilities (Little, 1999). True, the mother may have voluntarily performed an act which she knew may result in a child's conception, but that is distinct from consenting to gestate the child if a child is conceived. And so (according to this position) it is not until the woman consents to pregnancy, or perhaps not until the parents consent to care for the child by taking the baby home from the hospital or birthing center, that the full duties of parenthood accrue to the mother (and perhaps the father).

In reply to this argument we wish to make several points. We grant that in some few cases abortion is not intentional killing, but a choice to expel the child, the child's death being an unintended, albeit foreseen and (rightly or wrongly) accepted, side effect. However, these constitute a small minority of abortions. In the vast majority of cases, the death of the child *in utero* is precisely the object of the abortion. In most cases the end sought is to avoid being a parent; but abortion brings that about only by bringing it about that the child dies. Indeed, the attempted abortion would be considered by the woman requesting it and the abortionist performing it to have been *unsuccessful* if the child survives. In most cases abortion *is* intentional killing. Thus,

Patrick Lee and Robert P. George

even if the bodily rights argument succeeded, it would justify only a small percentage of abortions.

Still, in some few cases abortion is chosen as a means precisely toward ending the condition of pregnancy, and the woman requesting the termination of her pregnancy would not object if somehow the child survived. A pregnant woman may have less or more serious reasons for seeking the termination of this condition, but if that is her objective, then the child's death resulting from his or her expulsion will be a side effect, rather than the means chosen. For example, an actress may wish not to be pregnant because the pregnancy will change her figure during a time in which she is filming scenes in which having a slender appearance is important; or a woman may dread the discomforts, pains, and difficulties involved in pregnancy. (Of course, in many abortions there may be mixed motives: the parties making the choice may intend both ending the condition of pregnancy and the death of the child.)

Nevertheless, while it is true that in some cases abortion is not intentional killing, it remains misleading to describe it simply as choosing not to provide bodily life support. Rather, it is actively expelling the human embryo or fetus from the womb. There is a significant moral difference between *not doing* something that would assist someone, and *doing* something that causes someone harm, even if that harm is an unintended (but foreseen) side effect. It is more difficult morally to justify the latter than it is the former. Abortion is the *act* of extracting the unborn human being from the womb – an extraction that usually rips him or her to pieces or does him or her violence in some other way.

It is true that in some cases causing death as a side effect is morally permissible. For example, in some cases it is morally right to use force to stop a potentially lethal attack on one's family or country, even if one foresees that the force used will also result in the assailant's death. Similarly, there are instances in which it is permissible to perform an act that one knows or believes will, as a side effect, cause the death of a child *in utero*. For example, if a pregnant woman is discovered to have a cancerous uterus, and this is a proximate danger to the mother's life, it can be morally right to remove the cancerous uterus with the baby in it, even if the child will die as a result. A similar situation can occur in ectopic pregnancies. But in such cases, not only is the child's death a side effect, but the mother's life is in proximate danger. It is worth noting also that in these cases *what is done* (the means) is the correction of a pathology (such as a cancerous uterus, or a ruptured uterine tube). Thus, in such cases, not only the child's death, but also the ending of the pregnancy, are side effects. So, such acts are what traditional casuistry referred to as *indirect* or *non-intentional,* abortions.

But it is also clear that not every case of causing death as a side effect is morally right. For example, if a man's daughter has a serious respiratory disease and the father is told that his continued smoking in her presence will cause her death, it would obviously be immoral for him to continue the smoking. Similarly, if a man works for a steel company in a city with significant levels of air pollution, and his child has a serious respiratory problem making the air pollution a danger to her life, certainly he should move to another city. He should move, we would say, even if that meant he had to resign a prestigious position or make a significant career change.

In both examples, (a) the parent has a special responsibility to his child, but (b) the act that would cause the child's death would avoid a harm to the parent but cause a significantly worse harm to his child. And so, although the harm done would be a side effect, in both cases the act that caused the death would be an *unjust* act, and morally wrongful *as such*. The special responsibility of parents to their children requires that they *at least* refrain from performing acts that cause terrible harms to their children in order to avoid significantly lesser harms to themselves.

But (a) and (b) also obtain in intentional abortions (that is, those in which the removal of the child is directly sought, rather than the correction of a life-threatening pathology) even though they are not, strictly speaking, intentional killing. First, the mother has a special responsibility to her child, in virtue of being her biological mother (as does the father in virtue of his paternal relationship). The parental relationship itself – not just the voluntary acceptance of that relationship – gives rise to a special responsibility to a child.

Proponents of the bodily rights argument deny this point. Many claim that one has full parental responsibilities only if one has voluntarily assumed them. And so the child, on this view, has a right to care from his or her mother (including gestation) only if the mother has accepted her pregnancy, or perhaps only if the mother (and/or the father?) has in some way voluntarily begun a deep personal relationship with the child (Little, 1999).

But suppose a mother takes her baby home after giving birth, but the only reason she did not get an abortion was that she could not afford one. Or suppose she lives in a society where abortion is not available (perhaps very few physicians are willing to do the grisly deed). She and her husband take the child home only because they had no alternative. Moreover, suppose that in their society people are not waiting in line to adopt a newborn baby. And so the baby is several days old before anything can be done. If they abandon the baby and the baby is found, she will simply be returned to them. In such a case the parents have not voluntarily assumed responsibility; nor have they consented to a personal relationship with the child. But it would surely be wrong for these parents to abandon their baby in the woods (perhaps the only feasible way of ensuring she is not returned), even though the baby's death would be only a side effect. Clearly, we recognize that parents do have a responsibility to make sacrifices for their children, even if they have not voluntary assumed such responsibilities, or given their consent to the personal relationship with the child.

The bodily rights argument implicitly supposes that we have a primordial right to construct a life simply as we please, and that others have claims on us only very minimally or through our (at least tacit) consent to a certain sort of relationship with them. On the contrary, we are by nature members of communities. Our moral goodness or character consists to a large extent (though not solely) in contributing to the communities of which we are members. We ought to act for our genuine good or flourishing (we take that as a basic ethical principle), but our flourishing involves being in communion with others. And communion with others of itself – even if we find ourselves united with others because of a physical or social relationship which precedes our consent – entails duties or responsibilities. Moreover, the contribution we are morally required to make to others will likely bring each of us some discomfort and pain. This is not to say that we should simply ignore our own good, for the sake of others. Rather, since what (and who) I am is in part constituted by various

Patrick Lee and Robert P. George

relationships with others, not all of which are initiated by my will, my genuine good includes the contributions I make to the relationships in which I participate. Thus, the life we constitute by our free choices should be in large part a life of mutual reciprocity with others.

For example, I may wish to cultivate my talent to write and so I may want to spend hours each day reading and writing. Or I may wish to develop my athletic abilities and so I may want to spend hours every day on the baseball field. But if I am a father of minor children, and have an adequate paying job working (say) in a coal mine, then my clear duty is to keep that job. Similarly, if one's girlfriend finds she is pregnant and one is the father, then one might also be morally required to continue one's work in the mine (or mill, factory, warehouse, etc.).

In other words, I have a duty to do something with my life that contributes to the good of the human community, but that general duty becomes specified by my particular situation. It becomes specified by the connection or closeness to me of those who are in need. We acquire special responsibilities toward people, not only by *consenting* to contracts or relationships with them, but also by having various types of union with them. So, we have special responsibilities to those people with whom we are closely united. For example, we have special responsibilities to our parents, and brothers and sisters, even though we did not choose them.

The physical unity or continuity of children to their parents is unique. The child is brought into being out of the bodily unity and bodies of the mother and the father. The mother and the father are in a certain sense prolonged or continued in their offspring. So, there is a natural unity of the mother with her child, and a natural unity of the father with his child. Since we have special responsibilities to those with whom we are closely united, it follows that we in fact do have a special responsibility to our children anterior to our having voluntarily assumed such responsibility or consented to the relationship.[5]

The second point is this: in the types of case we are considering, the harm caused (death) is much worse than the harms avoided (the difficulties in pregnancy). Pregnancy can involve severe impositions, but it is not nearly as bad as death – which is total and irreversible. One needn't make light of the burdens of pregnancy to acknowledge that the harm that is death is in a different category altogether.

The burdens of pregnancy include physical difficulties and the pain of labor, and can include significant financial costs, psychological burdens, and interference with autonomy and the pursuit of other important goals (McDonagh, 1996: ch. 5). These costs are not inconsiderable. Partly for that reason, we owe our mothers gratitude for carrying and giving birth to us. However, where pregnancy does not place a woman's life in jeopardy or threaten grave and lasting damage to her physical health, the harm done to other goods is not total. Moreover, most of the harms involved in pregnancy are not irreversible: pregnancy is a nine-month task – if the woman and man are not in a good position to raise the child, adoption is a possibility. So the difficulties of pregnancy, considered together, are in a different and lesser category than death. Death is not just worse in degree than the difficulties involved in pregnancy; it is worse in kind.

It has been argued, however, that pregnancy can involve a unique type of burden. It has been argued that the *intimacy* involved in pregnancy is such that if the woman must remain pregnant without her consent then there is inflicted on her a unique and serious harm. Just as sex with consent can be a desired experience but sex without consent is a violation of bodily integrity, so (the argument continues) pregnancy involves such a close physical intertwinement with the fetus that not to allow abortion is analogous to rape – it involves an enforced intimacy (Boonin, 2003: 84; Little, 1999: 300–3).

However, this argument is based on a false analogy. Where the pregnancy is unwanted, the baby's "occupying" the mother's womb may involve a harm; but the child is committing no injustice against her. The baby is not forcing himself or herself on the woman, but is simply growing and developing in a way quite natural to him or her. The baby is not performing any action that could in any way be construed as aimed at violating the mother.[6]

It is true that the fulfillment of the duty of a mother to her child (during gestation) is unique and in many cases does involve a great sacrifice. The argument we have presented, however, is that being a mother *does* generate a special responsibility, and that the sacrifice morally required of the mother is less burdensome than the harm that would be done to the child by expelling the child, causing his or her death, to escape that responsibility. Our argument equally entails responsibilities for the father of the child. His duty does not involve as direct a bodily relationship with the child as the mother's, but it may be equally or even more burdensome. In certain circumstances, his obligation to care for the child (and the child's mother), and especially his obligation to provide financial support, may severely limit his freedom and even require months or, indeed, years, of extremely burdensome physical labor. Historically, many men have rightly seen that their basic responsibility to their family (and country) has entailed risking, and in many cases, losing, their lives. Different people in different circumstances, with different talents, will have different responsibilities. It is no argument against any of these responsibilities to point out their distinctness.

So, the burden of carrying the baby, for all its distinctness, is significantly less than the harm the baby would suffer by being killed; the mother and father have a special responsibility to the child; it follows that intentional abortion (even in the few cases where the baby's death is an unintended but foreseen side effect) is unjust and therefore objectively immoral.

Notes

1 See, for example: Carlson (1994: chs. 2–4); Gilbert (2003: 183–220, 363–90); Larson (2001: chs. 1–2); Moore and Persaud (2003: chs. 1–6); Muller (1997: chs. 1–2); O'Rahilly and Mueller (2000: chs. 3–4).
2 For a discussion of the issues raised by twinning and cloning, see George and Lobo (2002).
3 Some defenders of abortion have seen the damaging implications of this point for their position (Stretton, 2004), and have struggled to find a way around it. There are two leading proposals. The first is to suggest a mean between a capacity and an actual behavior, such as a disposition. But a disposition is just the development or specification of a capacity and so raises the unanswerable question of why just that much development, and not more or

Patrick Lee and Robert P. George

less, should be required. The second proposal is to assert that the historical fact of someone having exercised a capacity (say, for conceptual thought) confers on her a right to life even if she does not now have the immediately exercisable capacity. But suppose we have baby Susan who has developed a brain and gained sufficient experience to the point that just now she has the immediately exercisable capacity for conceptual thought, but she has not yet exercised it. Why should she be in a wholly different category than say, baby Mary, who is just like Susan except she did actually have a conceptual thought? Neither proposal can bear the moral weight assigned to it. Both offer criteria that are wholly arbitrary.

4   In arguing against an article by Lee, Dean Stretton claims that the basic natural capacity of rationality also comes in degrees, and that therefore the argument we are presenting against the position that moral worth is based on having some accidental characteristic would apply to our position also (Stretton, 2004). But this is to miss the important distinction between having a basic natural capacity (of which there are no degrees, since one either has it or one doesn't), and the *development of that capacity* (of which there are infinite degrees).

5   David Boonin claims, in reply to this argument – in an earlier and less developed form, presented by Lee (1996: 122) – that it is not clear that it is impermissible for a woman to destroy what is a part of, or a continuation of, herself. He then says that to the extent the unborn human being is united to her in that way, "it would if anything seem that her act is *easier* to justify than if this claim were not true" (2003: 230). But Boonin fails to grasp the point of the argument (perhaps understandably since it was not expressed very clearly in the earlier work he is discussing). The unity of the child to the mother is the basis for this child being related to the woman in a different way from how other children are. We ought to pursue our own good *and the good of others with whom we are united in various ways*. If that is so, then the closer someone is united to us, the deeper and more extensive our responsibility to the person will be.

6   In some sense being bodily "occupied" when one does not wish to be *is* a harm; however, just as the child does not (as explained in the text), neither does the state inflict this harm on the woman, in circumstances in which the state prohibits abortion. By prohibiting abortion the state would only prevent the woman from performing an act (forcibly detaching the child from her) that would unjustly kill this developing child, who is an innocent party.

References

Boonin, David (2003). *A Defense of Abortion*. New York: Cambridge University Press.

Carlson, Bruce (1994). *Human Embryology and Developmental Biology*. St. Louis, MO: Mosby.

Dworkin, Ronald (1993). *Life's Dominion: An Argument about Abortion, Euthanasia, and Individual Freedom*. New York: Random House.

Feinberg, Joel (ed.) (1984). *The Problem of Abortion*, 2nd edn. Belmont, CA: Wadsworth, 1984.

George, Robert (2001). "We should not kill human embryos – for any reason." In *The Clash of Orthodoxies: Law, Religion, and Morality in Crisis* (pp. 317–23). Wilmington, DL: ISI Books.

George, Robert and Lobo, Gòmez (2002). "Personal statement." In *The President's Council on Bioethics* (2002, pp. 294–306).

Gilbert, Scott (2003). *Developmental Biology*, 7th edn. Sunderland, MA: Sinnauer Associates.

Larson, William J. (2001). *Human Embryology*, 3rd edn. New York: Churchill Livingstone.

Lee, Patrick (1996). *Abortion and Unborn Human Life*. Washington, DC: Catholic University of America Press.

Little, Margaret Olivia (1999). "Abortion, intimacy, and the duty to gestate." *Ethical Theory and Moral Practice*, 2: 295–312.

McDonagh, Eileen (1996). *Breaking the Abortion Deadlock: From Choice to Consent*. New York: Oxford University Press, 1996.

Moore, Keith, and Persaud, T. V. N. (2003). *The Developing Human, Clinically Oriented Embryology*, 7th edn. New York: W. B. Saunders.

Muller, Werner A. (1997). *Developmental Biology*. New York: Springer Verlag.

O'Rahilly, Ronan, and Mueller, Fabiola (2000). *Human Embryology and Teratology*, 3rd edn. New York: John Wiley & Sons.

The President's Council on Bioethics (2002). *Human Cloning and Human Dignity: the Report of the President's Council on Bioethics*. New York: Public Affairs.

Singer, Peter (1993). *Practical Ethics*, 2nd edn. Cambridge: Cambridge University Press.

Stretton, Dean (2004). "Essential properties and the right to life: a response to Lee." *Bioethics*, 18/3: 264–82.

Thomson, Judith Jarvis (1971). "A defense of abortion." *Philosophy and Public Affairs*, 1: 47–66; reprinted, among other places, in Feinberg (1984, pp. 173–87)

Thomson, Judith Jarvis (1995). "Abortion." *Boston Review*. Available at ⟨www.bostonreview. mit.edu/BR20.3/thomson.html⟩.

Tooley, Michael (1983). *Abortion and Infanticide*. New York: Oxford University Press.

Warren, Mary Ann (1984). "On the moral and legal status of abortion." In Feinberg (1984, pp. 102–19).

Further reading

Bailey, Ronald, Lee, Patrick, and George, Robert P. (2001). "Are stem cells babies?" *reasononline*. Available at ⟨http://reason.com/rb/rb080601.shtml⟩.

Beckwith, Francis (1993). *Politically Correct Death: Answering the Arguments for Abortion Rights*. Grand Rapids, MI: Baker.

Beckwith, Francis (2000). *Abortion and the Sanctity of Human Life*. Joplin, MO: College Press.

Chappell, T. D. J. (1998). *Understanding Human Goods: A Theory of Ethics*. Edinburgh: Edinburgh University Press.

Finnis, John (1999). "Abortion and health care ethics." In Helga Kuhse and Peter Singer (eds.), *Bioethics: An Anthology* (pp. 13–20). London: Blackwell.

Finnis, John (2001). "Abortion and cloning: some new evasions." Available at ⟨http://lifeissues.net/writers/fin/fin_01aborcloneevasions.html⟩.

Grisez, Germain (1990). "When do people begin?" *Proceedings of the American Catholic Philosophical Quarterly*, 63: 27–47.

Lee, Patrick (2004). "The pro-life argument from substantial identity: a defense." *Bioethics*, 18/3: 249–63.

Marquis, Don (1989). "Why abortion is immoral." *Journal of Philosophy*, 86: 183–202.

Oderberg, David (2000) *Applied Ethics: A Non-Consequentialist Approach*. New York: Oxford University Press.

Pavlischek, Keith (1993). "Abortion logic and paternal responsibilities: one more look at Judith Thomson's 'Defense of abortion'." *Public Affairs Quarterly*, 7: 341–61.

Schwarz, Stephen (1990). *The Moral Question of Abortion*. Chicago: Loyola University Press.

Stone, Jim (1987). "Why potentiality matters." *Journal of Social Philosophy*, 26: 815–30.

Stretton, Dean (2000). "The argument from intrinsic value: a critique." *Bioethics*, 14: 228–39.

The Moral Permissibility
of Abortion

Margaret Olivia Little

Introduction

When a woman or girl finds herself pregnant, is it morally permissible for her to end that pregnancy? One dominant tradition says "no"; its close cousin says "rarely" – exceptions may be made where the burdens on the individual girl or woman are exceptionally dire, or, for some, when the pregnancy results from rape. On both views, though, there is an enormous presumption against aborting, for abortion involves destruction of something we've no right to destroy. Those who reject this claim, it is said, do so by denying the dignity of early human life – and imperiling their own.[1]

I think these views are deeply flawed. They are, I believe, based on a problematic conception of how we should value early human life; more than that, they are based on a profoundly misleading view of gestation and a deontically crude picture of morality. I believe that early abortion is fully permissible, widely decent, and, indeed, can be honorable. This is not, though, because I regard burgeoning human life as "mere tissue": on the contrary, I think it has a value worthy of special respect. It is, rather, because I believe that the right *way* to value early human life, and the right way to value what is involved in and at stake with its development, lead to a view that regards abortion as both morally sober and morally permissible. Abortion at later stages of pregnancy becomes, for reasons I'll outline, multiply more complicated; but it is early abortions – say, abortions in the first half of pregnancy – that are most at stake for women.

The Moral Status of Embryos and Early Fetuses

According to one tradition, the moral case against abortion is easily stated: abortion is morally impermissible because it is murder. The fetus, it's claimed, is a *person* –

not just a life (a frog is a life), or an organism worthy of special regard, but a creature of full moral status imbued with fundamental rights. Abortion, in turn, constitutes a gross violation of one of that person's central-most such rights: namely, its right to life.

Now, for a great many people, the idea of a 2-week blastocyst, or 6-week embryo, or 12-week fetus counting as an equivalent rights-bearer to more usual persons is just an enormous stretch. It makes puzzles of widely shared intuitions, including the greater sense of loss most feel at later rather than earlier miscarriages, or again the greater priority we place on preventing childhood diseases than on preventing miscarriages. However else we may think such life worthy of regard, an embryo or early fetus is so far removed from our paradigmatic notion of a person that regarding it as such seems an extreme view.

The question is why some feel pushed to such an extreme. It's in part a reflection of just how inadequate our usual theories are when they bump up against reproduction. Surely part of the urge to cast a blastocyst as a full-fledged person, for instance, is a by-product of the impoverished resources our inherited theory has for valuing germinating human life: if the only category of moral status one has is a person or rights-holder, then the only way to capture our sense of the kind of respect or honor that embryos might deserve (the only way to capture the loss many feel at early miscarriage, for instance, or the queasiness over certain aspects of human embryo research) is to insist on fetal personhood from the moment of conception. The alternative, of course, is to challenge the assumption: instead of making the fetus match those terms of moral status, we ask what our theory of value should look like to accommodate the value of an entity like the fetus.

Or again, part of the urge to cast the embryo as a person is the worry that drawing subsequent distinctions in moral status over the course of fetal development would be fatally ad hoc. But such a worry already presupposes a certain metaphysics: it is only if one believes that discrete events and steady states are the fundamental explanatory classifications that distinctions of stages will feel troublingly arbitrary. A metaphysics that accommodates *becoming* or *continua* as fundamental explanatory classifications will be more likely to regard the distinction between zygote and matured person as inherently graduated. It wouldn't expect to find – because it wouldn't think to need – any distinction between discrete properties adequate to the job.

This is not to say that everything about moral status is degreed. But if we expand our moral categories beyond *rights* to notions of *value*, and accept *continua* as everyday phenomena rather than special puzzles, the road is paved for a picture of burgeoning human life that accords far better with the intuitions of so many: burgeoning human life has a status and worth that deepen as its development progresses.

But, it will be said, such an account misses something crucial. Unlike other inherently gradualist processes – the building of a house, say – there is here something already extant that should ground full moral status to the embryo: namely, a potential or telos for personhood. The only gradualist element in the picture is its unfolding. This, it will be urged, is what really grounds the moral standing of early human life: it's not because the embryo or early fetus *is* a person, but because the right way to value potential persons is to regard them as deserving the same deference *as* persons.

Margaret Olivia Little

Now, I think there is a very important sense in which we should regard human embryos and fetuses as potential persons. We are in part biological animals, and biology classifies organisms as the types of creature they are by giving explanatory primacy to certain trajectories over others. While there are an infinite number of trajectories that fish eggs, for instance, could take – from developing into fish, to being eaten as caviar, to being infused with sheep DNA and becoming a sheep – they are understood as the kind of biological organism they are by privileging the first as their "matured state" and expressive of their "nature." It is in this sense that a fish egg is a potential fish, while a salamander egg – which could in principle be turned into a fish with enough laboratory machinations – is only thereby a possible one. Similarly, a human embryo is understood biologically as the kind of organism it is by giving explanatory primacy to the trajectory of its developing into a matured human, i.e. a person – something that cannot be said of a given sperm or egg.[2]

Lest we hang too much on this point, though, we need to remember that biology is not the only rubric that matters here. There is no direct isomorphism from the idea of a biological potential to a normative end – something that should or must be realized. Indeed, on one view, biological potential is only a candidate for normative upshot for creatures who independently count as having moral standing – a view that grounds moral status in potentiality turns out to have things exactly backwards. More deeply, though, the particular classification at issue here carries an intrinsic tension. For the trajectory in virtue of which we connect this sort of organism with that further state is a trajectory that depends on what *another person* – the pregnant woman – is able and willing to do. That is, *unlike* most biological organisms, the trajectory we privilege as the fetus's "natural" development – against which we classify its "potential" and measure when its existence is "truncated" – depends on the actions and resources of an autonomous *agent*, not the events and conditions of a *habitat*. Knowing what to think of the fetus thus requires assessing moves that have their home in biology (classifying organisms based on privileging certain environmental counterfactuals) applied when the biological "environment" is, at one and the same time, an autonomous agent subsumable under normative, not just biological, categories.

If this is easy to miss, it's in part because of how human gestation itself tends to get depicted. Metaphors abound of passive carriage; the pregnancy is a project of nature's. The woman is, perhaps, an especially close witness to that project, or again its setting, but the project is not her own. Her agency is thus noticed when she cuts off the pregnancy but passes unnoticed when she continues it. If, though, gestation belongs to the *woman* – if its essential resources are hers – her blood, her hormones, her energy, all resources that could be going to other of her bodily projects – then the concept of potential person is a hybrid concept from the start, not something we can read off of the neutral lessons of biology. In an important sense, then, talk of the fetus as potential person is dangerously misleading. For it encourages us to think of the embryo's development as mere *unfolding* – as though all that's needed other than the passage of time is already intrinsically there, or at least there independently of the woman.

In my own view, the biological capacities of early human life provide, once again, a degreed basis for according regard. Such biological potential marks out early human life as specially *respect-worthy* – which is why we should try to avoid conception where children are not what is sought (or again, why we don't think we should tack up human embryos on the wall for art, or provide them for children to dissect at school if fertilized chicken eggs get too pricey). To say that such life is respect-worthy, though, is not the same as claiming we are charged to defer as we would those with moral status.

Abortion and Gestational Assistance

Thus far, I've argued that morally restrictive views of abortion ride atop a problematic view of how we should value early human life. I now want to argue that they also ride atop a problematic misconception of the act of aborting itself. Let me illustrate first by returning to the claim that, if the fetus *were* a person, abortion would be a violation of its right to life.

We noted above that, while certain metaphors depict gestation as passive carriage (as though the fetus were simply occupying a room until it is born), the truth is of course far different. One who is gestating is providing the fetus with sustenance – donating nourishment, creating blood, delivering oxygen, providing hormonal triggers for development – without which it could not live. For a fetus, as the phrase goes, to live *is* to be receiving aid. And whether the assistance is delivered by way of intentional activity (as when the woman eats or takes her prenatal vitamins) or by way of biological mechanism, assistance it plainly is. But this has crucial implications for abortion's alleged status as murder. To put it simply, the right to life, as Judith Thomson famously put it, does not include the right to have all assistance needed to maintain that life (Thomson, 1971). Ending gestation will, at early stages at least, certainly lead to the fetus's demise, but that does not mean that doing so would violate its right to life.

Now Thomson herself illustrated the point with an (in)famous thought experiment in which one person is kidnapped and used as life support for another: staying connected to the Famous Violinist, she points out, may be the kind thing to do, but disconnecting oneself does not violate the Violinist's rights. The details of this rather esoteric example have led to widespread charges that Thomson's point ignores the distinction between killing and letting die, and would apply at any rate only to cases in which the woman was not responsible for procreation occurring. In fact, though, I think the central insight here is broader than the example, or Thomson's own analysis, indicates.[3]

As Frances Kamm's work points out (Kamm, 1992), in the usual case of a killing – if you stab a person on the street, for instance – you interfere with the trajectory the person had independently of you. She faced a happy enough future, we'll say; your action changed that, taking away from her something she would have had but for your action. In ending gestation, though, what you are taking away from this person is something she wouldn't have had to begin with without your aid. She comes to you with a downward trajectory, as it were: but for you she would already be dead. In removing that assistance, you are not violating the person's right to life, judged in the traditional terms of a right against interference. While all killings are tragedies, then, not all are alike: some killings, as Kamm puts it, share the crucial "formal"

Margaret Olivia Little

feature of letting die, which is that they leave the person no worse off than before she encountered you. Of course, if one *could* end the assistance without effecting death, then, absent extraordinary circumstances, one should. (Part of the debate over so-called partial birth abortions is whether and when we encounter such circumstances.)[4]

The argument is not some crude utilitarian one, according to which you get to kill the person because you saved her life (as though, having given you a nice lamp for your birthday, I may therefore later steal it with impunity). The point, rather, is that where I am still in the process of saving – or sustaining or enabling – your life, and that life cannot be thusly saved or sustained by anyone else, ending that assistance, even by active means, does not violate your right to life.

Some, of course, will argue that matters change when the woman is causally responsible for procreation. In such cases, it will be said, she is responsible for introducing the person's need. She isn't like someone happening by an accident on the highway who knows CPR; she's like the person who *caused* the accident. Her actions introduced a set of vulnerabilities or needs, and we have a special duty to lessen vulnerabilities and repair harms we have inflicted on others.

But there is a deep disanalogy between causing the accident and procreating. The fact of causing a crash itself introduces a harm to surrounding drivers: they are in a worse position for having encountered that driver. But the simple act of procreating does not worsen the fetus's position: without procreation, the fetus wouldn't exist at all; and the mere fact of being brought into existence is not a bad thing. To be sure, creating a human is creating someone who comes with needs. But this, crucially, is not the same as inflicting a need *onto* someone (see Silverstein, 1987). It isn't as though the fetus already existed with one level of needs and the woman added a new one (as does happen, for instance, if a woman takes a drug after conception that increases the fetus's vulnerability to, say, certain cancers). The woman is (partially) responsible for creating a life, and it's a life that necessarily includes needs, but that is not the same as being responsible for the person being needy rather than not. The pregnant woman has not made the fetus more vulnerable than it would otherwise have been: absent her procreative actions, it wouldn't have existed at all.

Even if the fetus were a person, then, abortion would not be murder. More broadly, abortion isn't a species of *wrongful interference*. This isn't to say that abortion is thereby necessarily unproblematic. It is to argue, instead, that the crucial moral issue needs to be relocated to the question of what, if any, positive obligations pregnant women have to continue gestational assistance. The question abortion really asks us to address is a question about the *ethics of gestation*. But this is a question that takes us into far richer, and far more interesting, territory than that occupied by discussions of murder. In particular, it requires us to discuss and assess claimed grounds of obligation, and to assess the very specific kinds of burdens and sacrifice involved in rendering *this* type of assistance.

I've argued elsewhere that if or when the fetus is a person, then the question of when a woman might have some obligation to provide use of her body to save its life turns out to be a fascinatingly deep matter, and one that is ultimately deeply contextual (Little, forthcoming). The issue I want to turn my attention to here is what picture we get when we join the two views I've outlined: a view that regards burgeoning human life as respect-worthy but not endowed with substantial moral status, and a view that recognizes abortion as the ending of gestational support. Abortion, I want to argue, is both permissible and widely decent, for reasons involving what we might call *authorship* and *stewardship*. Let me take them each in turn.

Intimacy, Pregnancy, and Motherhood

When people first ask what's at stake in asking a woman to continue a pregnancy, what usually get emphasized are the physical and medical risks. And indeed, they're important to emphasize. While many pregnancies go smoothly, many do not; and the neutral language of an obstetrics text hardly captures the lived reality. I think of a friend I visited who'd been put in lock-down on the psychiatric ward from pregnancy-related psychosis (and whose physician wouldn't discuss inducing at 39 weeks because there was no "obstetrical indication"). Or my sister, whose two trimester "morning sickness" – actually gut-wrenching dry heaves every 20-minutes and three hospital-izations – was the equal of many an experience of chemotherapy. Or another acquaintance, whose sudden onset of eclampsia during delivery brought her so close to dying that it left us all breathless. Asking women to take on the *ex ante* medical risks of pregnancy is asking a lot.

Then there are the social risks pregnancy can represent for some women – risks it is very hard for those of us in more comfortable lives to fully appreciate. Pregnancy is a marker for increased domestic violence. It leads for many to abandonment by family and community, even as it can lead the woman to feel tied to a relationship she would otherwise leave.

All of these burdens are important to appreciate. But there is something incomplete in such renditions of pregnancy's stakes. For a great many women, it's another set of issues that motivate the desire to end a pregnancy – issues having to do with the extraordinarily *personal* nature of gestation.

To be pregnant is to allow another living creature to live in and off of one's body for nine months. It's to have one's every physical system shaped by its needs, rather than one's own. It is to share one's body in an extraordinarily intimate and extensive – and often radically unpredictable – way. Then there is the aftermath of the nine months: for gestation doesn't just turn cells into a person; it turns the woman into a mother. One of the most common reasons women give for wanting to abort is that they do not want to become a mother – now, ever, again, with this partner, or no reliable partner, with these few resources, or these many that are now, after so many years of mothering, slated finally to another cause. Not because motherhood would bring with it such burdens – though it can – but because motherhood would so thoroughly change what we might call one's fundamental practical identity. The enterprise of mothering restructures the self – changing the shape of one's heart, the primary commitments by which one lives one's life, the terms by which one judges one's life a success or a failure. If the enterprise is eschewed and one decides to give the child over to another, the identity of mother still changes the normative facts that are true of one, as there is now someone by whom one does well or poorly

(Ross, 1982). And either way – whether one rears the child or lets it go – to continue a pregnancy means that a piece of one's heart, as the saying goes, will forever walk outside one's body.

Gestation, in short, is not just any activity. It involves sharing one's very body. It brings with it an emotional intertwinement that can reshape one's entire life. It brings another person into one's family. Deciding whether to continue a pregnancy isn't like being asked to write a check for charity, however large; it's an enormous undertaking that has reverberations for an entire lifetime. To argue that women may permissibly decline this need not trade on a view that grants no value to early life; it is, in essence, to argue about the right way to value *pregnancy* and *parenthood*. It is to recognize a level of moral prerogative based not just on the concretely understood burdens of the activity in question, but also on its deep connection to authoring a life. To illustrate, consider the following.

Imagine that the partner of your family's dreams is wildly in love with you and asks for your hand in marriage. As it turns out, substantial utility would accrue by your accepting him: his connections would seal your father's bid for political office, raise the family profile yet higher, and add nicely to its coffers just as your eldest brother faces expensive restoration of the family estate. It would also, and not incidentally, keep the fellow himself from falling into a pit of despair, as it's clear you're the only one for him.

All of this utility notwithstanding, many will believe that you don't thereby have a moral *obligation* – even a prima facie one – to accept the proposal. You might have a responsibility to give the proposal serious thought; but if, on reflection, you realize that marriage to this man – or to any man – is not what you want, then there we are. And this, even if we stipulate that marriage would not be a setback to your happiness: the utility function you'd enjoy following acceptance might, indeed, surpass the one that would follow refusal. This, even if we think that the needs presented would have coalesced to form a duty if the assistance required had been burdensome (say, writing a big check) rather than intimate.[5] Nor, finally, need we think the resistance must trace to a conviction that it would be morally wrong to accept the proposal – that it would in some way transgress the norms governing marriage. It is, we'll imagine, quite obvious to you that you would come to have an enduring love if you accept; he understands this and relishes the prospective courtship. It isn't that you would *use* him if you accept; it's that you don't *want* to have an enduring love with him, now, or at all.

Or again, imagine that your providing sexual service would help comfort and inspire the soldiers readying for battle. Many will believe this does not ground a requirement, even prima facie, to offer intercourse. This, even if you're the only one around capable of offering such service, and even if doing so wouldn't actually be distressful to you. Such an intuition, again, needn't trade on thinking it would be wrong to give sex for such a purpose. Those with more permissive views of sexuality might well think someone who authentically and with full self-respect wanted to share her body to this purpose would be doing something generous and fine. One just doesn't want to make doing so the subject of obligation.

Now not all agree to these intuitions. If Victorian novels are to be believed, the upper classes of Regency England believed both that marriage and sex were fair candidates for obligation (especially when the family estate was at stake). But for many, there is something about marriage as a relationship, and sexual intercourse as a bodily connection, that makes them deserving of some special kind of deference when assessing moral obligation. The deference is doubtless limited: one need be absolutist here no more than elsewhere. But the defense, crucially, is not merely a function of plain utility considerations; it is the intimacy, not just the concrete welfare, that matters.

An important part of being a self is that the boundaries of one's self – the borders and use of one's body, the identity by which one knows oneself as oneself – are matters over which one deserves special moral deference. We might say it's on pain of imposing alienation. But the point is not to urge some fetishism about the evil of alienation (morality, after all, doesn't give a whit if you feel alienated when returning the borrowed library book), but to insist that some activities can have a sufficiently tight connection to self that alienation with respect to *them* is specially problematic to maintaining our status *as* selves. One's self is not always implicated in sexual intercourse and marriage; where it is, one may not care. But where it is, and you do, that fact is worthy of a deference or protection in a way that caring about how one's garden grows is not.

Gestation, like sex, is a bodily intimacy of the first order. Motherhood, like marriage, is a relational intimacy of the first order. If one believes that decisions about whether to continue a pregnancy are deserving of moral prerogative, it need not be because one believes early human life has no value – any more than assigning prerogatives over sex and marriage denies the value of one's family, the boys in fighting blue, or the relationship of marriage. Such views instead stem from the conviction that the proper way to value the relationship of motherhood and the bodily connection of pregnancy is to view them as intimacies deserving of special deference. Even if continuing a pregnancy represents *no* welfare setback to the woman, classically construed, we should recognize a strong moral prerogative over whether to continue that pregnancy.

This isn't a claim that any reason to abort is a good one. Human life, even in nascent forms, should not to be extinguished lightly; one who decides to end a pregnancy because she wants to fit into a party dress, say, is getting wrong the value of burgeoning human life. To abort for such reasons is to act indecently. But this doesn't mean that such a woman now has an obligation to continue the pregnancy. What it means, in the first instance, is that she should not regard such a reason as adequate for the conclusion; not that the conclusion is not available to her.

It's not that decency is some optional ideal. Quite to the contrary: if one realizes that an action is indecent, one mustn't do it. But the "it" in question is, as Barbara Herman puts it, an action-reason pair – it is, though it makes our deliberations sound more formal than they are – a piece of practical syllogism (1993: 147). To say that a practical syllogism is indecent means one should discard it, but that doesn't yet comment on what action one should do. More specifically, it doesn't mean one can't decently arrive at its conclusion, for there may well be decent reasons waiting in the wings.

Take a standard example. A soldier, we might well decide, doesn't have an obligation to risk death by falling on the grenade that threatens his comrades. Nonethe-

Margaret Olivia Little

less, if the reason he declines has nothing to do with wanting to live and everything with wanting his hated comrades to die, his refusal is indecent. He betrays a dreadful understanding of what is here at stake; he shouldn't refuse on that basis. But this doesn't mean he thereby faces now an obligation or imperative to fall on the grenade. For there is extant a reason the soldier can deploy as an honorable basis for declining – namely, that doing so would sacrifice his life.

Or again, to return to our fanciful examples, if the reason you decide not to marry the suitor is not because you don't want at this stage of your life to enter such a commitment, but because you don't like the wart on his big toe, or the color of the drawing-room walls in his mansion, or if you decline sexual intercourse for racist reasons, your behavior is indecent. To think these acceptable reasons – to think them adequate premises to support a practical conclusion of declining – is to fundamentally misappreciate the various values here implicated. But we don't thereby conclude that the person is now under a requirement to accept (as though it's the woman with the dreadful reasons who now has an obligation to have sex). For there is extant a reason that would be honorable to deploy as a basis for declining – that one doesn't want to have sex, or enter marriage. Similarly, the fact that a given woman might deploy a genuinely trivial or offensive basis for aborting doesn't mean she is now obliged to continue the pregnancy. For there are available reasons – about sharing her body and entering motherhood – she may deploy as a basis for honorably declining.

Norms of Responsible Creation

Now some will urge that those who are (at least jointly) responsible for procreation thereby have a heightened obligation to continue gestating. People, of course, disagree over what it takes to count as "responsible" here – whether voluntary but contracepted intercourse is different from intercourse without use of birth control, and again from intentionally deciding to become pregnant at the IVF clinic. But those who satisfy the relevant criteria, it's often said, must thereby face greater duty to "see the pregnancy through." Unease is expressed at the thought of heterosexual intercourse conducted in callous disregard of procreative potential, of creating only to let wither. If you're going to allow a new life to begin, it's thought, you'd better see it through to fruition.

I think these intuitions point to important issues, but not the ones usually thought. Let's start with that notion of sexual irresponsibility. For many people, there is something troubling about the idea of couples engaging in heterosexual intercourse in complete disregard of contraception – say, when one is highly fertile and birth control is just an arm's reach away. Such a view points to an important set of intuitions about another layer of respect, namely, respect for creation itself. Respect for burgeoning human life carries implications, not just for the accommodation we might owe such life once extant, but for the conditions under which we should undertake activities with procreative potential in the first place. To regard something as a value sometimes enjoins us to make more of it, and sometimes, as with people, to take care about the conditions under which we make any.[6]

There are, as we might put it, norms of responsible creation. Such a view seems exactly right to me. Part of what I imagine teaching my own children about sexuality is that human life as such deserves respect (whatever the metaphysical details), and respect requires that one not treat one's procreative capacities in a cavalier way. But none of this means that one has a special responsibility to gestate if one *does* get pregnant. For one thing, these norms, while very important (and far too little emphasized in our current culture), are norms about the activities that can lead to procreation, not what one owes should procreation take place. They specify, as it were, the good faith conditions one should meet for engaging in certain activities. Even if the norms are broached – one has sex in callous disregard to its potential to lead to new human life – that doesn't itself imply that one now (as punishment?) must gestate: it says one shouldn't have had that sort of sex. Indeed, for many of us, the thought that negligence here means one should continue a pregnancy has an internal disconnect: that one had irresponsible sex is no reason at all to bring a new person into the world.

This last point begins to point to a very different approach to the ethics of creation. The salience of responsibility for procreation to the responsibilities of gestation is not just complex: decisions about abortion are often located *within* the norms of responsible creation. Let me explain.

Many people have deeply felt convictions about the circumstances under which they feel it right for them to bring a child into the world – can it be brought into a decent world, an intact family, a society that can minimally respect its agency? These considerations can persist even after conception has taken place; for while the embryo has already been created, a person has not. Some women decide to abort, that is, not because they do not *want* the resulting child – indeed, they may yearn for nothing more, and desperately wish that their circumstances were otherwise – but because they do not think bringing a child into the world the right thing for them to do.

As Barbara Katz Rothman (1989) puts it, decisions to abort often represent not a decision to destroy, but a refusal to create. These are abortions marked by moral language. A woman wants to abort because she knows she couldn't give up a child for adoption but feels she couldn't give the child the sort of life, or be the sort of parent, she thinks a child *deserves*; a woman who would have to give up the child thinks it would be *unfair* to bring a child into existence already burdened by rejection, however well grounded its reasons; a woman living in a country marked by poverty and gender apartheid wants to abort because she decides it would be *wrong* for her to bear a daughter whose life, like hers, would be filled with so much injustice and hardship.

Some have thought that such decisions betray a simple fallacy: unless the child's life were literally going to be worse than non-existence, how can one abort out of concern for the future child? But the worry here isn't that one would be imposing a *harm* on the child by bringing it into existence (as though children who are in the situations mentioned have lives that aren't worth living). The claim is that bringing about a person's life in these circumstances would do violence to her ideals of creating and parenthood. She does not want to bring into existence a daughter she cannot love and care for; she does not want to bring into existence a person whose life will be marked by disrespect or rejection. In struggling with these issues, the worry is not that the child would have been better off never to have been born – as though children who are in the situations just mentioned have lives that aren't worth living;[7] it's that continuing a pregnancy in such circumstances would violate the woman's commitments of respectful creation.

Nor does the claim imply judgment on women who *do* continue pregnancies in similar circumstances – as though there were here an obligation to abort. For the norms in question need not be impersonally authoritative moral claims. Like ideals of good parenting, they mark out considerations all should be sensitive to, perhaps, but equally reasonable people may adhere to different variations and weightings. Still, they are normative for those who do have them; far from expressing mere matters of taste, the ideals one does accept carry an important kind of categoricity, issuing imperatives whose authority is not reducible to mere desire. These are, at root, issues about *integrity*, and the importance of maintaining integrity over one's participation in this enterprise precisely because it is so normatively weighty.

Some will protest the thought of our deciding such matters. We have no dominion, it will be said, to pick and chose the conditions under which human life, once started, proceeds. On what we might call a "stewardship" view of creation, in contrast, this dominion is precisely *part* of the responsibility involved in creation. It's a grave matter to end a developing human life by not nurturing it; but it can be an equally grave decision to continue a process that will result in the creation of a person. The present case, note, is thus importantly different from the other area of controversy over dominion over life, namely, actions intending to hasten death. Whatever one thinks of that matter, it diverges in a key respect from abortion. When we stand by rather than hasten death, we are allowing a trajectory independent of us to proceed without our influence. Not to abort, though, *is* to do something else – namely, to create a person.

Gestation is *itself* a creative endeavor. Not in the sense that its constitutive activities are each or mostly intentional (as if the issue were whether the pregnant woman, like an athlete, deserves credit for the bodily activity involved). But if personhood emerges through pregnancy, and one has choices about whether to continue pregnancy, then decisions to do so themselves involve norms of respect. And not all norms of respect for creation, it turn outs, tell in favor of continuing.

None of this is to say that abortion is morally neutral. Abortion involves loss. Not just loss of the hope various parties have invested in the pregnancy, but loss of something valuable in its own right. Abortion is thus a sober matter, an occasion, often, for moral emotions such as grief and regret. Given the value at stake, it is only fitting to feel grief – a sorrow that life begun is now ended – or to feel moral regret – that the actions needed to help these cells develop into a person would have compromised too significantly the life of someone who already was one. Such regret, that is, can signal appreciation of the fact, not that the action was indecent, but that decent actions sometimes involve loss.

It takes enormous investment to develop early human life into a human being. Understanding the morality of early abortion involves assessing not just welfare, but intimacy, not just destruction, but creation. As profound as the respect we should have for burgeoning human life, we should acknowledge moral prerogatives over associations such as having another inhabit and use one's body in such an extraordinarily enmeshed way, over identity-constituting commitments and enterprises as profound as motherhood, and over the weighty responsibility of bringing a new person into the world.

Notes

1 Portions of this chapter draw on my essay, "Abortion" (Little, 2003).
2 At least, one of a couple of weeks' standing: earlier blastocysts' trajectories turn out to be fascinatingly underdetermined. There is, for instance, no fact of the matter internal to its own cellular information as to whether a one-week blastocyst will be one person or more; and at very early stages there is no fact of the matter as to which cells will become the fetus and which will become the placenta.
3 RU-486, which essentially interrupts the production of progesterone needed to maintain a placenta, provides a good example of an abortion method that is more straightforwardly a "letting die" than an active killing.
4 Later abortions are thus multiply complicated: fetal status increases even as its dependencies decline. On the one hand, later fetuses are much closer to, and at some stage likely count as, persons; on the other hand, they are no longer solely and fully dependent on gestational assistance for life, hence enlarging possibilities for removing assistance without effecting death.
5 That is, the action is not simply a token that falls under an imperfect duty. It's a fascinating question how to parse the structure of imperfect duties, a question I here leave aside.
6 Of course, just how much "care" one must exert to avoid conception will be heartily contested. Those, like myself, who value spontaneity in sexual relations and have mild views about the value of burgeoning human life will advance something quite modest – urging, say, good faith attempts to use birth control if it is safe, easily obtained, and immediately convenient. Others will advance stringent principles indeed, requiring, say, that one not have sex at all until one is prepared to parent.
7 My thanks to Adrienne Asche for this way of putting the point.

References

Herman, Barbara (1993). *The Practice of Moral Judgment.* Cambridge, MA: Harvard University Press.

Kamm, Frances Myrna (1992). *Creation and Abortion: A Study in Moral and Legal Philosophy.* New York: Oxford University Press.

Little, Margaret Olivia (2003). "Abortion." In R. G. Frey and Christopher Heath Wellman (eds.), *A Companion to Applied Ethics* (pp. 313–25). Oxford: Blackwell.

Little, Margaret (forthcoming). *Intimate Duties: Re-thinking Abortion, the Law, and Morality.* Oxford: Oxford University Press.

Ross, Steven (1982). "Abortion and the death of the fetus." *Philosophy and Public Affairs*, 11: 232–45.

Rothman, Barbara Katz (1989). *Recreating Motherhood: Ideology and Technology in a Patriarchal Society.* New York: Norton.

Silverstein, H. S. (1987). "On a woman's 'responsibility' for the fetus." *Social Theory and Practice*, 13: 103–19.

Thomson, Judith Jarvis (1971) "A defense of abortion." *Philosophy and Public Affairs*, 1: 47–66.

Further Reading

Callahan, Joan C. "The fetus and fundamental rights." *Commonweal* (April 11, l986): 203–9.

Crittenden, Ann (2001). *The Price of Motherhood.* New York: Henry Holt and Co.

Denes, Magda (1976). *In Necessity and Sorrow: Life and Death in an Abortion Hospital.* New York: Basic Books, Inc.

Dworkin, Ronald (1993). *Life's Dominion: An Argument About Abortion, Euthanasia, and Individual Freedom.* New York: Alfred A. Knopf.

Dwyer, Susan and Feinberg, Joel (eds.) (1997). *The Problem of Abortion*, 3rd edn. Belmont, CA: Wadsworth Publishers.

Feinberg, Joel (1992). "Abortion." In J. Feinberg, *Freedom and Fulfillment: Philosophical Essays* (pp. 37–75). Princeton: Princeton University Press.

Hursthouse, Rosalind (1987). *Beginning Lives.* Oxford: Open University.

MacKinnon, Catharine A. (1991). "Reflections on sex equality under law." *The Yale Law Journal*, 100/5 (March 1991): 1281–328.

McDonaugh, Eileen (1996). *Breaking the Abortion Deadlock: From Choice to Consent.* New York: Oxford University Press.

Quinn, Warren (1993) "Abortion: identity and loss." In W. Quinn, *Morality and Action.* New York: Cambridge University Press.

Steinbock, Bonnie (1992). *Life Before Birth: The Moral and Legal Status of Embryos and Fetuses.* New York: Oxford University Press.

Wertheimer, Roger (1974). "Understanding the abortion argument." In M. Cohen, T. Nagel, and T. Scanlon (eds.), *The Rights and Wrongs of Abortion* (pp. 23–51). Princeton: Princeton University Press.

West, Robin (1993). "Jurisprudence and gender." In D. Kelly Weisberg (ed.), *Feminist Legal Theory: Foundations* (pp. 75–98). Philadelphia: Temple University Press.

AFFIRMATIVE ACTION

CHAPTER THREE

A Defense of
Affirmative Action

Albert Mosley

Introduction

For over 300 years in what is now the United States of America, it was socially and legally acceptable to discriminate on the basis of race. Religion and science were used to justify enslaving African Americans, and after slavery was abolished, to justify excluding them from educational, employment, and investment opportunities provided to other Americans. Since the landmark Supreme Court decisions of the 1950s declaring segregation unconstitutional, the federal government has taken the lead in guaranteeing an end to racial and sexual discrimination. In publicly available education, accommodations, employment, and investment opportunities, overt discrimination against individuals on the basis of race, sex, religion, or ethnicity in the award of public goods has been legally prohibited.

But legal prohibitions against racial and sexual discrimination have not been sufficient to erase the effects of centuries of bias. Racist and sexist stereotypes, in conjunction with long-established habits and networks, continue to exclude minorities and women from educational, employment, and investment opportunities. To address this, executive orders, legislative statutes, and judicial rulings have mandated not only that discrimination cease, but that "affirmative action" be taken to end the legacies of racism and sexism.[1] Institutions doing business with or receiving payments or grants from the federal government have been required to show a good faith effort to address racial and sexual disparities in the award of educational, employment, and investment opportunities. Affirmative action is a broad set of policies that public and private institutions have evolved in response to the need to end not just the practice but also the legacy of racial and sexual discrimination. The aim of these policies is to provide women and minorities access to positions they otherwise would be unlikely to get because of the continuing effect of historical oppression (Patterson, 1998: 10).

Affirmative Action as a Remedy for Past Injustices

Affirmative action utilizes procedures designed to reach out to women and minorities to ensure that they are informed of opportunities and are given fair consideration for those opportunities. It is a way of recognizing that in the past, many employment, educational, and investment opportunities were not made known to the public at large, but were discussed by word of mouth and awarded through personal networks. Thus, admission to select educational institutions was often on the basis of recommendations from faculty, staff, or alumni; employment opportunities and union memberships were obtained by referral from individuals already employed by the firm or already a member of the relevant union; and business opportunities were made known and awarded on the basis of connections to the right people.

As a result of such networks and practices, members of groups excluded through state-sanctioned action in the past are more likely to be excluded in the present, even when the explicit basis of exclusion is not race or sex. Like laws that allowed one to vote if one's grandfather had voted, networks and procedures established by past practices constitute neutral ways of perpetuating exclusions based on race and sex.

Affirmative action policies mandate taking extra steps to ensure that women and minorities are made aware of opportunities by public advertising and extensive searches. Nonetheless, many continue to assume that minorities and women are more naturally suited for menial positions because that is where most are found. Affirmative action has been a principal means of assuring that selection and evaluation procedures are not tainted by unnecessary qualifications and unconscious biases.

But many who support outreach and fairness measures designed to eliminate discriminatory practices oppose stronger affirmative action measures that take race and sex into account as a means of increasing the representation of minorities and women. While sexual differences may seem relevant in choosing applicants for many types of positions, using the race of an applicant as a relevant factor has proven to be more controversial. For many, if it was wrong to deny a person an opportunity because of his or her race, then it should be wrong to award a person an opportunity because of his or her race. If it was wrong for white people to get preferential treatment then it ought to be wrong for black people to get it.

But such reasoning, while appealing in its simplicity, is ahistorical and ignores the lingering effect of the past on the present. The historical fact is that when slavery was protected by the constitution of the United States, a black person could be enslaved but a white person could not be. Treated as property like horses and dogs, black people were denied the benefits of their labor, denied the right to accumulate wealth, to share it with their families, or to bequeath it to their progeny. Slavery was justified on the grounds that black people were morally and cognitively incapable of acting as responsible agents, and required the direction provided by their masters. Most whites of that era who opposed slavery did so not because they believed black people were their moral and cognitive peers, but because slave labor undermined the viability of free labor. Even after slavery, most continued to believe that black people were incapable of satisfying the duties of democratic citizenship. Such views have not disappeared (Kershnar, 2000, 2003; Levin, 1997).

Albert Mosley

After the abolition of slavery, legal segregation sought to insulate whites from contact with blacks, except where the latter provided services to the former. The intent was to guarantee that blacks received educational, employment, and investment opportunities commensurate with their inferior status. Individuals considered to be members of the inferior races of Europe were able to escape their status by immigrating to America and identifying generically as white. This, in turn, gave them the privilege to displace and exclude the progeny of slaves wherever opportunities were to be had (Ignatiev, 1995; Jacobson, 1998). The enforced inferiority of Africans and their descendants justified the assumption that they were innately less competent, and continues to be used to justify their over-representation among the least well off and under-representation among the most well off. Consider some sociological data: the incarceration rate of black men in America is six times higher than the incarceration rate of black men in South Africa at the height of apartheid (Guinier and Torres, 2002: 263); Black Americans make up 12 percent of the population but over 30 percent of the poor (Appiah and Gutmann, 1996: 147); in 2000 the unemployment rate was 3.5 percent for whites but 7.6 percent for blacks and 5.7 percent for Hispanics; in 2000, 7.5 percent of non-Hispanic whites, 22 percent of blacks, and 21 percent of Hispanics were living in poverty (US Census Bureau, 2002: 291, 368). More: schools and housing are becoming increasingly segregated, minorities are hired less often than whites with similar qualifications, earn less with similar responsibilities, and are charged more often for similar products and services (Oppenheimer, 1996).

Even when it is admitted that slavery and segregation were unjust, opponents of measures that take race into consideration in awarding opportunities emphasize that people living today were neither slaves nor slaveholders. They argue that descendants of European immigrants should not be punished for something they had nothing to do with, just as the descendants of African slaves should not be rewarded for suffering they did not experience. Some go further and argue that even if the descendants of European immigrants benefited from the sins of state-sponsored slavery and segregation, nothing is owed to the descendants of slaves for the disadvantages they have inherited. Even if the immediate ancestors of contemporary whites did commit injustices against the immediate ancestors of contemporary blacks, it does not follow that contemporary whites owe contemporary blacks. The fact that x benefits from a wrong done to y doesn't imply that x owes y compensation. To illustrate this point, Stephen Kershnar presents the following scenario:

> Jim, a white American, is the second best tennis player in the world, second only to a Chinese-American, Frank. As a result of Frank's superiority, Jim makes only one-third the money that Frank makes. One weekend, however, Frank is out on the town with his girlfriend, and is viciously beaten and stabbed by a racist Brooklyn mob. This mob has no connection to Jim. Jim, now freed of competition from Frank, wins more tennis tournaments and as a result his income triples. Jim has thus directly benefited from an injustice done to Frank. (Kershar, 1997: 354)

This example is meant to illustrate how a person may benefit from a racial injustice yet be neither morally nor legally obligated to compensate the innocent victim. As Kershnar concludes, "Merely benefiting from an unjust act is not a sufficient condition to obligate payment on the basis of compensatory justice" (1997: 355).

But the simplicity of Kershnar's example begs the question. If Frank was only a random victim of the mob, then Frank's bad luck is merely Jim's good luck, much as if a car fleeing a robbery had struck Frank. That the mob was racist might be as irrelevant as that the bank robbers were racist. But if the mob's intent was to compromise Frank's ability to compete so that a minority player would not be #1 and a white player would be, then Jim's good fortune is not the result of mere chance but is morally compromised. If Jim colluded with the mob, then he is culpable for the harm suffered by Frank and should be forced to relinquish his position. If Jim had no involvement in the mob's attack on Frank but the attack was nonetheless done with the intent of benefiting Jim – and Jim comes to know this – then I believe Jim *is* morally obligated to condemn the attack and to relinquish in some way some of the benefits of his ill-gotten gains as a way of discouraging such possibilities in the future.

Like Kershnar, Louis Pojman uses a common-sense example in arguing that the innocent beneficiary of unjust acts need not assume the liabilities caused by those acts. Suppose Albert's parents buy a growth hormone for Albert, hoping he will become a great basketball star. However, Michael's parents steal the hormone, and give it to Michael, who, instead of Albert, grows to be 6 foot 10 inches and makes millions playing basketball. Both Albert's parents and Michael's parents die. Does Michael owe Albert anything? (Pojman, 1992: 195; 1998: 102). In Pojman's estimation, Michael does not owe Albert anything, either morally or legally. And the coach, upon hearing of the incident, is not obligated to compensate Albert by giving him Michael's position on the basketball team. Pojman concludes: "If minimal qualifications are not adequate to override excellence in basketball, even when the minimality [that is, the possession of minimal qualifications] is a consequence of wrongdoing, why should they be adequate in other areas?" (1992: 195).

Pojman's remarks suggest that what is true of athletes should be equally true of pilots, military leaders, business executives, and university professors. That their skills were acquired at the cost of injustices to others may be unfortunate, but this is nevertheless morally irrelevant. For both Pojman and Kershnar, individuals can legitimately inherit the benefits of unjust acts, so long as they themselves were not complicit in the performance of those acts.

But such a position ignores the fact that the agent of injustice is benefited indirectly, because the injustice furthers the agent's aim – one of which is to provide those who inherit the agent's estate with wealth they otherwise would not likely have. This position increases the probability that mobs might engage in acts that transfer wealth to those they identify with, even if that wealth does not benefit members of the mob directly. It encourages acts of injustice by tolerating them, so long as the perpetrator is not the direct beneficiary. And it makes considerations of justice less important than effectiveness, efficiency, and utility.

Affirmative Action as a Form of Compensatory Justice

By construing persons as atomized individuals, critics of restitution ignore how the prospect of benefiting those one identifies with is often a greater source of motivation than benefiting oneself. A person may commit a great injustice and be prepared to bear the personal sacrifice it entails if it is likely that his family and progeny may benefit. If this option is not discouraged, then acquiring and bequeathing unjust benefits will be sanctioned as a morally and legally permissible strategy. But human beings are not atomized, self-serving entities. Rather, human beings typically conceive themselves as having distinct family lines and group identities, and are, more often than not, as concerned with providing benefits to those with whom they identify as they are concerned with benefiting themselves (Ridley, 1995: 253–66).

Some argue that selection procedures that take race into consideration in the awarding of opportunities are wrong because they do more harm than good; they especially harm those blacks who are provided with such consideration by reinforcing the public's belief that blacks cannot compete on a fair basis. Moreover, this argument continues, using race as a plus factor rewards members of such groups who are most qualified and, therefore, least harmed by past injustices. The end result is that society as a whole is harmed because the best-qualified candidates are not chosen, increasing the likelihood of ineptitude and inefficiency.

Such objections play on the fear that candidates whose race or sex is a factor in the award of an opportunity are likely to be less productive, if not unqualified, for the position they attain. To extend the scenario introduced by Kershnar in arguing against restitution, if Frank's arm is broken by the racist mob, he should not be given the #1 tennis ranking he probably would have retained had the mob attack not occurred. Likewise, Albert should not be given the position he is more likely to have had had Michael's parents not stolen his growth hormone. But these are not objections to the moral duty to provide restitution. At best, they are objections against providing restitution of a particular kind. If certain persons are rendered unable to perform the duties of a position they otherwise are likely to have occupied had they not been unjustly injured, restitution is not achieved by putting them where they are expected to do what they cannot do. This merely adds insult to injury.

Where possible, one of the aims of restitution is to put the injured party in the position he/she would have attained had the unjust injury not occurred. Thus, suppose Frank and Jim are playing a championship match, Jim wins by having Frank's water doped, and this is subsequently made public. Then we would expect Jim's title to be invalidated, and the title awarded instead to Frank. In this way, Frank is granted what he otherwise would probably have achieved had the doping not occurred. But where the injury renders the victim incapable of fulfilling the duties he or she likely would have capable of, an alternative aim of restitution is to provide appropriate substitutes so that the disadvantages suffered by an injured party are minimized. Thus, if Frank's arm were broken before his match with Jim, it would do no good to offer Frank the opportunity to play Jim that he otherwise would have had. On the other hand, it would be pernicious to allow Jim to gain the title by forfeit, especially if the intent of breaking Frank's arm was so that Jim would win. Even if Jim is not complicit in causing Frank's arm to be broken, he becomes complicit if, upon learning that Frank was injured in order to enrich him, he does nothing to rectify the injuries done to Frank.

One of the central concerns of compensatory justice focuses not on the costs to the victim, but on the possible rewards to the perpetrator of the injury. Consider the

A Defense of Affirmative Action

following scenario: Jim is the Great White Hope of boxing and knows he can make $10,000,000 in one year if he becomes the new champion. Frank, being the typical black boxing champion, only expects to make $1,000,000 in the subsequent year. Jim discovers a dope that can only be detected at least one year after its use, has it administered to Frank during the fight, Jim wins, and his duplicity is discovered a year and a half later. Should he only be obligated to forfeit the title and the $1,000,000 Frank expected to make? Should Jim be allowed to keep the other $9,000,000 so long as it goes to his estate but not to him? I believe most people would be uneasy with a morality that tolerated injustice for the sake of innocent beneficiaries (Ridley, 1995; Sher, 1981: 10, 17). Imposing fines, penalties, and other damages that exceed the cost to the injured is one way of guaranteeing that the injuring party does not benefit or pass on benefits from the unjust injury.

Taking race or sex into consideration is not simply reversing the historical discrimination against women and people of color, for it does not affect the ability of white males to perform in positions of status and power. Rather, taking race and sex into consideration is a practical acknowledgment that prejudices and historical practices have unjustly limited the opportunities of qualified women and people of color, and that exclusion will be maintained in many areas unless directly addressed.

Many Americans resent being asked to apologize and provide restitution for injuries they had no part in. But there are many situations in which we are expected to assume moral responsibility for actions we did not do personally. Suppose A makes B a gift of $100,000 to get started in a business. But unbeknownst to B, A has robbed C of a million dollars. If B becomes aware of the robbery, but nonetheless refuses to accept any responsibility for C's fate, then B becomes complicit in the original act and continues the injury of that act (Marino, 1998). We should not be surprised that B, acting in self interest, would explain C's injuries in such a way as to minimize the effect and the injustice of A's assault, while disavowing any personal inclination to inflict similar harms. In a similar fashion, many whites disavow any personal inclination to deny any person opportunities on the basis of race alone, but also believe that being black is highly correlated with having lower intelligence, lower morals, lower motivation, etc. By avoiding overt racist justifications and opposing the use of racial categories altogether, it is possible to condemn racial oppression while maintaining the effects of state supported racial exclusion.

Standardized Tests and Race

Some who oppose using race as a factor in the selection of candidates for opportunities argue that affirmative action should only guarantee the right to compete, not the right to succeed (Wolf-Devine, 1997: 183). But the very right to compete is compromised when selection procedures are biased. This was clearly true before the Civil Rights revolution, when being of European origin was a necessary condition to be selected for the most prestigious institutions and offices. It is also true, though less clear, that selection based on the results of standardized tests is biased as well. One of the most important factors in selecting applicants for admission to select postsecondary and professional schools is their score on the ACT, SAT, GRE, LSAT, etc., all of which are highly correlated with standard IQ tests. Typically, black, Hispanic, and Native American applicants have average scores on these tests that are lower on the average score of white applicants (Nisbett, 1998; Rosser, 1989). This has reinforced the claim that less-qualified minority applicants are replacing more-qualified white and Asian candidates.

Such claims resonate with benign justifications of slavery and segregation which held that, because Africans were less intelligent, they were prone to immoral acts and irrational beliefs, and it was the white man's burden to help save them from themselves. While few contemporary whites are prone to advocate slavery or segregation as a solution to the presence of Africans in the US, a substantial proportion of whites continue to believe that blacks are less intelligent than whites. And this is not merely a belief of the uneducated. More than half the educational psychologists in the top universities of the US believe that the difference in average IQ score between blacks and whites is due to genetic factors that are inherited, and which are resistant to social and environmental changes (Patterson, 1998: 61; Synderman, 1987: 137–44).

In *The Bell Curve*, Herrnstein and Murray (1994), for instance, attribute average socio-economic class differences to average differences in intelligence capacity (IQ), and differences in average intelligence between races to differences in genetic make-up. Because genetic information is resistant to somatic influences, they suggest that changes in social and physical environment can affect genetic differences only minimally. They acknowledge that in particular cases, a less intelligent person may be more successful than a more intelligent person, but the evidence they present suggests this is not what we should expect on the average. Similarly, one may on particular occasions find a black person who is more intelligent than a white person, but this is not what we should expect on the average. The status quo is the way it is because of innate differences between species and between races. Such a point of view appears to receive scientific support from aggregate test results that show that, even when blacks achieve a middle-class status, the average IQ of their children remains below the average IQ of the children of the lower-class whites (Hacker, 1992: 146). But such facts conceal as much as they reveal. Income parity does not mean that a middle-income black family is alike in all relevant respects to a middle-income white family. In fact, a middle-income black family has fewer assets than a lower-class white family, their children attend schools that are less well endowed, and they and their children are more likely to be denied employment and convicted of a crime (Brooks, 1990: 65; Oliver and Shapiro, 1995: 101, 111). And many recent Asian immigrants are highly educated, but accept low incomes in order to gain a foothold in America.

Like IQ tests today, in the earlier part of the twentieth century, the cephalic index was considered a reliable measure of intelligence capacity. The cephalic index measured skull shape and capacity, and was considered to be genetically determined. However, Franz Boas measured average cephalic indices for immigrants from "lower European races," and showed that averages changed dramatically between descendants born in Europe and those born in America from the same parents. Such sudden changes could not be accounted for by changes in the distribution of genes between

A Defense of Affirmative Action 49

generations. Some of the most damaging evidence to the claim that IQ differences are fixed from birth reflects the earlier work of Boas regarding the claim that the intellectual potential of lower European races was limited by genetic factors fixed from birth (Boas, 1912).

More than five years before *The Bell Curve* was published, James Flynn released data which shows that, from generation to generation, IQ scores have been rising at a faster pace than can be explained by genetic changes (1987: 171–91). Herrnstein and Murray acknowledge Flynn's results, and conclude that, "on the average, whites today may differ in IQ from whites, say, two generations ago as much as whites today differ from blacks today. Given their size and speed, the shifts in time necessarily have been due more to changes in the environment than to changes in the genes" (1994: 307–8; see also Swain, 2002: ch. 8). Many other examples from public health show how improved nutrition, health, educational opportunities, and smaller family sizes have produced dramatic changes in attributes otherwise believed to be fixed and permanent features of a group's racial essence.

There is also much evidence that intelligence and aptitude tests are culturally biased. Critics of paper-and-pencil intelligence tests have pointed to numerous assumptions built into the test and the test-taking environment that create barriers for otherwise qualified candidates. Even the manner in which questions are posed on a test has been shown to differentially influence the performance of blacks and whites (Freedle, 2003). Moreover, IQ tests are not good predictors of who will be most academically successful, and academic success is not a good predictor of professional success (Rosser, 1989). Nonetheless, a long history of racist and sexist arguments makes it easy to ignore this and other evidence of the extent to which differences in test scores are products of the social and physical environment.

Presumably, written tests eliminate selection based on birth, family connections, class, and other considerations; their role is to provide an objective yardstick for measuring qualifications, one that affords each individual an equal opportunity to demonstrate his or her individual merit. Those who score highest on the tests believe it is an indication that they have more merit and are entitled to the opportunity in question. African, Native, and Hispanic Americans are considered less qualified compared with European and Asian Americans because they tend to have lower test scores and GPAs.

But we should not enshrine test-taking scores and GPAs as the principal criteria for selection. Bowen and Bok (1998) show that students admitted to our most prestigious schools under affirmative action programs are typically as successful, and are more civically involved, than those not admitted under affirmative action. Indeed, those who scored highest on admissions tests often gave least back to their communities in terms of involvement in civic affairs. A study of Harvard Law School graduates showed an inverse relationship between entering LSAT scores and postgraduate income, community involvement, and professional satisfaction (Lempert et al., 2000: 468). If one of the objectives of higher education is to contribute to the practical good of human communities, those admitted under affirmative action have often given back as much or more than their higher scoring counterparts.

Because of their importance in admissions decisions, there is a growing trend for students to study to pass tests such as the ACT, SAT, LSAT, and GRE, and for parents who can afford it to purchase expensive test-preparation programs that guarantee higher scores on standardized tests for their children. But SAT scores are little better than chance in predicting college performance after the first year of study. Instead of providing an objective way of predicting who will do best in college and afterwards, SAT scores correlate significantly more with parental income than with success in college. Thus, it is questionable whether using SAT scores as a major factor in admissions improves a college's ability to admit those candidates who are most likely to be successful in fulfilling the mission of higher education (Crouse and Trusheim, 1988: 128). To the extent that admission to select institutions is based on scores on standardized tests, the selection procedures will exclude those whose families have traditionally been denied the opportunity to accumulate wealth.

In short, we should be wary of assuming that timed paper-and-pencil tests provide a reliable estimate of who will do best as students, workers, and citizens. Some suggest that people who do best on standardized tests may often be least prepared for real-life situations involving competing perspectives and ineliminable uncertainties. Paper-and-pencil test have been notoriously inadequate in their ability to predict an individual's capacity for creative choices and collaborative involvement (Sturm and Guinier, 2000). Limiting educational opportunities at our most select institutions by the use of paper-and-pencil tests limits participation in the workplace and in civic activities at the highest levels.

Even where professional success is our primary criterion, a survey of top executives of Fortune 1,000 companies revealed that most people considered qualities such as creativity, drive, and leadership to be more important than SAT scores. Many cautioned that multiple-choice pencil-and-paper tests were poor measures of the attributes most important for success in corporate America. Only 4 percent of the executives interviewed considered standardized tests such as the SAT and the ACT to be important for long-term success, and only 20 percent cited grades in college or graduate school as good predictors of success. The core attributes considered important for success were: integrity, will to succeed, determination, hard work, ability to motivate, and ability to overcome obstacles (National Urban League, 2001).

A more diverse classroom and workplace help to counteract habitual thinking about race and gender differences (Guinier and Sturm, 2001: 9). The fact that in the past women and minorities have not been leaders in science, commerce, and the arts should not be our guide to the choice of future leaders. This requires eliminating both the discriminatory intent of individuals and the disparate impact of institutional barriers. Selection procedures need to integrate the insight that many people learn on the job in ways that are not replicated by paper-and-pencil tests. As our world evolves and institutions change, past procedures may not be reliable guides to success in the future. Affirmative action has provided the occasion for us critically to examine the extent to which aptitude and intelligence tests are good predictors of academic and practical success. Instead of estimating capacity in order to determine who participates, it acknowledges participation as necessary for developing capacity (Sturm and Guinier, 2000).

A Defense of Affirmative Action   51

Affirmative Action and Equal Protection

The use of race in deciding to include some rather than others for benefits is severely limited by the Fourteenth Amendment and the 1964 Civil Rights Act to situations where doing so is necessary to achieve a compelling state interest. Thus, the Supreme Court has sanctioned the use of race in cases where an agency has continued a documented practice of invidious racial discrimination and is mandated, as part of a settlement, to include members of the formerly excluded group. In such a case, race is not irrelevant to achieving the designated goal of dismantling a culture of racial exclusion.

According to Justice Powell's position in *Regents of the University of California* v. *Bakke* (1978), the state has a different but equally compelling interest in producing a diverse learning environment for its future leaders. Powell argued that, for the purpose of achieving diversity, the use of race as a factor in the selection process is constitutionally valid. However, that purpose is forward-looking, not remedial, and seeks to insure that future leaders have been exposed to diverse points of view. The goal is to assemble the optimum learning environment. For Powell, "The Nation's future depends upon leaders trained through wide exposure to . . . ideas" (*Regents of the University of California* v. *Bakke*, 1978: 312). The First Amendment protection accorded the free exchange of ideas recognizes the importance of providing an arena for the exploration of different points of view. Democratic governance requires an informed citizenry that is able to explore and choose from a cross-section of ideas.

According to Justice Powell, the kind of creative play and experimentation that vitalizes higher education is best achieved with a diverse student body: "The atmosphere of speculation, experiment and creation – so essential to the quality of higher education – is widely believed to be supported by a diverse student body" (*Regents of the University of California* v. *Bakke*, 1978: 312). We would expect the farm boy from North Dakota to bring different perspectives from those of the prep school graduate from New England, and we would expect a black student from a middle-class family in Clinton, Maryland to offer a different perspective from that of a white student from a middle-class family in Chevy Chase, Maryland.

Nonetheless, any legally sanctioned use of race is suspect, and prohibited unless a strong case can be made that it is necessary to achieve a compelling state interest. Thus, Cheryl Hopwood did not sue the University of Texas Law School because she was rejected even though she had higher scores than more than 100 other white applicants who were admitted. She sued because certain students were admitted whose race was used as a factor in their assessment. She argued that her rights had been violated because the Fourteenth Amendment and the Civil Rights Bills (of, e.g., 1964, 1971, etc.) explicitly prohibit state support for institutions that make choices using racial differences a significant factor.

In making its decision in this case, the Fifth Circuit Court of Appeals explicitly rejected the claim that race may be used as a factor in choosing between applicants in order to foster diversity:

> Within the general principles of the 14th Amendment, the use of race in admissions for diversity in higher education contradicts, rather than furthers, the aim of equal protection. Diversity fosters, rather than minimizes, race [as a discriminatory factor]. It treats

minorities as a group, rather than as individuals. It may further remedial purposes [the only permissible rationale in the court's view] but, just as likely, may promote improper racial stereotypes, thus fueling racial hostility. (*Hopwood* v. *State of Texas*, 1996: 945)

But just because two individuals are treated differently because of race does not mean that one of them has been treated unfairly. Fairness and equal consideration are not always achieved by identical treatment and color blindness (Appiah and Gutman, 1996: 109). Fairness too often is construed as identical treatment. But in fact it is unfair to treat people with significantly different histories and capacities as if they were identical. To take an extreme example, treating a paraplegic as one would a normally ambient person is not being fair, and it is not fair because they are being treated identically. Fairness is best construed as providing equal concern, not identical treatment. Different people may have different needs and different potentials for producing effective solutions. Using physical strength as a measure of potential for effective policing is unfair to women because it fails to consider other capacities that may be as or more effective in resolving conflicts and defusing volatile situations (Sturm and Guinier, 2002).

The backward-looking justification for affirmative action contends that centuries of white supremacy impose historical liabilities that put people of color at greater risk. When attempting to redress a wrong or achieve diversity, a qualified candidate may be given preference over other qualified candidates because of the possession of an attribute that is connected to righting the wrong or introducing an important perspective. Equal consideration of relevant differences instead of identical treatment makes equality of opportunity a reality rather than merely an abstract principle.

We do not live in a time and place where skin color makes no difference. We are not color-blind. Color-consciousness has been an important part of American history and continues to influence our perceptual judgments. To act as if color made no difference would be to ignore the facts (Appiah and Gutman, 1996: 110, 125; Guinier and Torres, 2002: 274–5). Color may be as important a qualification for a school with few or no black members as being from the south-west may be for a school whose members would otherwise all be from the north-east.

But being color-conscious does not commit one to the position that skin color is a biological sign of predictable physical, cognitive, and behavioral differences. Like all concepts, racial categories evolve, and being identified as a person of color can change from being a mark of inferiority to being a locus of historical oppression and resistance. Most of the categories we use originated in the past, but we do not always continue to use them with their original meanings (Mosley, 1997). We continue to use the terms "sunrise" and "sunset" to distinguish our perceptual awareness of the relative motion of the earth and sun, though we no longer believe that the sun is itself moving above and then below the horizon. Likewise, continuing to use racial categories to distinguish human beings does not preclude giving those categories new and more appropriate meanings.

Racialization and racism have changed over time and appear differently in different historical eras. Before WWII, the notion of European sub-races coexisted with the distinction between European, African, Asian, and Native American races. American racism created a generic white race that enabled European immigrants to displace

African, Asian, and Native Americans from employment, education, and investment opportunities. The operation of racism within European populations has been displaced from view by the focus of attention on people of non-European origin. Many whites suppress the historical experience of their own racialization, while continuing to view "poor white trash" as a race apart, often immorally conceived and genetically marred.

Hitler and the Nazis brought general discredit to race theories of the past, giving rise to the view that race has no biological validity and is purely a social construct. Such views have been used to support the demand for race-blind policies and procedures: if the concept of race has no valid biological meaning, then it was a mistake to have used it to exclude individuals from opportunities, and it is equally a mistake to use it to include individuals for opportunities sought by the public at large. Using racial notions with benign intentions, it is argued, is just as ill-conceived as using racial notions invidiously. If there are no races, it becomes difficult to see how there can be such a thing as a meaningful quest for racial diversity.[2]

In this way, critics of affirmative action argue that eliminating all uses of racial categories is a legitimate way of banishing racism. Delegitimizing race deters individuals from banding together as members of the same or different races. People disadvantaged by state-sponsored racism in the past are dissuaded from coming together around notions of race, and are often persuaded that any reference to a racial affiliation is illegitimate.

Intended originally to protect blacks, the Equal Protection clause of the Fourteenth Amendment is now being used to protect advantages others have gained from past acts of exclusion. For some philosophers, it is better to let traditional victims bear the primary costs of the past, rather than extend those costs to innocent beneficiaries (Kekes, 1998: 886).

On the other hand, color-conscious policies acknowledge the continuing effect of slavery and segregation, and ask that those who benefit from the unjust acts of the past relinquish some of those benefits. White applicants are not asked to bear the burden of past racial and gender injustice alone, but to relinquish the increased odds of success made possible through the inheritance of unjust benefits.

Given the prospect of losing benefits, there is little wonder that many whites are motivated to believe that blacks are not as intelligent as whites, are lazier, more violent, and prefer welfare to work (Guinier and Torres, 2002: 261; Sniderman and Piazza, 1993; Swain, 2002: 149). Such beliefs resonate with beliefs of generations past, and give comfortable explanations of why higher proportions of blacks than whites are incarcerated, undereducated, impoverished, sick, injured, and likely to die younger. Explanations from the past reappear in a new guise and repeat habits of thought that maintain the practical effects of an era of white supremacy. Bringing more blacks into the professional mainstream provides more opportunities to challenge such ideas and explore solutions that take all sides into consideration.

Conclusions

Opponents of affirmative action programs that take race and gender into consideration agree that it is important that we learn to interact with individuals from diverse backgrounds. But they do not take the high percentage of blacks among the least well off and low percentage of blacks among the most well off to be primarily the products of slavery and segregation. Even if there had been no slavery and segregation, it does not follow that women and minorities would be represented in all areas in proportion to their presence in the general population. To assume that any disproportionate representation is the result of an unjust act is, they argue, overbroad. Natural and cultural differences between groups of people may predispose them to different professions and to different proportional representations within professions – without this being the effect of systemic injustices.

Louis Pojman points out that African American men are over-represented and Asian American men are under-represented in professional basketball. Should our quest for diversity lead us to insist that Asian Americans be hired until parity is reached with African Americans? Would this improve the quality of professional basketball? On the other hand, Asian Americans are over-represented in the sciences. Should we require that their numbers be limited so that African Americans can be integrated into those disciplines? Would this improve the quality of science? (Pojman, 1998: 106).

Basketball is used as an example of an arena in which anti-discrimination is sufficient to allow talent to exhibit itself, and where affirmative action could be little more than an artificial attempt to achieve proportional representation. But basketball is a bad analogy because there is no history of excluding Asian Americans in basketball. If there were such a history, we might well suspect that the low proportion of Asian American players was the result of persistent attempts to eliminate them from the competition. Because we know that the participation of women and minorities in the sciences has been historically restricted, we should be concerned whether effects of that past might not be contributing to a continuing injustice.

Carl Cohen, like so many who oppose explicit attempts to increase minority enrollments, commits himself to addressing the evil of racism. He is even prepared to accept policies that use race as a factor in determining admissions, as long as race is not "dispositive." By this, he means that between two equally qualified candidates, race cannot be used as a "tie-breaker." Cohen (1997) accused the University of Michigan of using race in this fashion and of maintaining separate tract systems. Of applicants to the law school with similar GPA and LSAT scores, 85 percent of the minority applicants but only 5 percent of the non-minorities were admitted. And in the undergraduate school, of applicants with similar GPA and SAT scores, 11.5 percent of the non-minority applicants and 100 percent of the minority applicants were admitted. Cohen believes the difference in admission rates between minorities and non-minorities (17 to 1 in the law school admissions process and 9 to 1 in undergraduate admissions) proves that race is not just a factor, but also a "dispositive" factor, and is accorded more weight than is fair.

What Cohen in fact shows is how misleading percentages can be without attention to the actual number of cases involved. In the law school example, 6 out of 124 white applicants with GPAs and LSAT scores in the low range were accepted, while 17 out of 20 black applicants in this range were accepted. If treated identically, only 1 black applicant would have been admitted and an additional 16 higher-scoring non-minority applicants. Likewise, in undergraduate admissions, whites with the lower-range scores were admitted 11.5 percent of the time but black students with similar scores were admitted 100 percent of the time. For applicants with this range of test scores and GPAs, minorities were about 9 times more likely to be accepted than non-minorities. But in terms of actual numbers, if minorities were accepted at the identical rate as non-minorities, 5 minorities would have been admitted and 56 additional majority students. Taking into consideration the small number of qualified minority applicants helps make clear how a description in terms of percentages merely distort the real situation. Contrary to the intent of equal consideration, identical treatment is more likely to perpetuate than eliminate socially determined educational disparities.

For Cohen, utilizing racial categories even for benign purposes is akin to using an evil means to achieve a good end.[3] In contrast, I have argued that the constitution does not prohibit the use of race in order to disassemble a pattern and culture of racial exclusion. Nor need we assume that the use of racial categories commits us to the meanings and theories originally attached to those terms. Anti-discrimination policies have helped us to recognize that race-blind descriptions and procedures may distribute costs and benefits selectively between blacks and whites without using racial terminology at all. Many procedures that make no mention of racial categories have nonetheless been shown to have a disparate impact on a historically excluded group.

Affirmative action works to sever the link between skin color and social destiny by placing qualified people of color in positions they otherwise would be unlikely to achieve. Many institutions see it as part of their mission to help counter the lingering effects of a racist past by accepting qualified blacks for stereotypically white positions in greater numbers than would normally be expected. As Appiah and Gutmann put it, "By hiring qualified blacks for stereotypically white positions in greater numbers than blacks would be hired by color blind employers the US will move farther and faster in the direction of providing fair opportunity to all its citizens" (1996: 131). But without an appreciation of the wrong perpetrated on people of color, and a commitment to correct that wrong, it is debatable why a concern with diversity should give special attention to the "racial" variety.

The question is whether and how America addresses the continuing effect of an era of exclusion on the basis of race. I believe all Americans – white, black, red, and yellow – have an obligation not to allow certain groups to constitute the primary victims of history, while certain other groups are its primary beneficiaries. Victims and beneficiaries of past unjust acts must be reconciled, not by banishing reference to racial ills, but by addressing them openly and directly. It remains to be seen whether the most controversial part of affirmative action, the use of race as a factor in addressing the lingering effects of state-enforced racism, will be subject to such "strict scrutiny" that racial exclusion is condemned in theory but maintained in practice.

Notes

1   Executive Orders include: Executive Order 8802 by Franklin Roosevelt (1941); Executive Order 10952 by John F. Kennedy (1961) ("take affirmative action to insure that persons are

hired without regard to race, color, or creed); Executive Order 11246 by Lyndon Johnson (1965) (establishing Office of Federal Contract Compliance); and the Philadelphia Plan (1970). Legislative statutes include: 1964 Civil Rights Act, Equal Employment Opportunity Act of 1972, and the 1990 Civil Rights Bill. Supreme Court decisions include *Brown*, *Griggs* v. *Duke Power Co.*, *Bakke*, *United Steelworkers* v. *Weber*, *Sheetmetal Workers Union* v. *EEOC*, *Richmond* v. *Crosson* (1989), *Adarand* (1995), as well as many other rulings at different levels of the judiciary.

2 The very use of racial categories is considered by some to continue a racist agenda. People who trace their disadvantages to racial injustice come to be viewed like people who blame witches for their misfortune. There are no witches, and there are no races. It is possible for certain individuals to have been harmed by the false belief in the existence of races, just as individuals have been harmed by the false belief in witches.

3 "We all aspire one day to transcend the racism that has so long pervaded American life. Difficult to achieve, that goal will certainly not be advanced by the continued reliance upon the very evil we seek to eradicate" (Cohen, 1997). We may ask how this passage is consistent with Cohen's claim that race can be used as a factor, so long as it is not "dispositive." Thanks to Ernie Alleva for this point.]

References

Appiah, K. Anthony and Gutmann, Amy (1996). *Color Conscious: The Political Morality of Race*. Princeton, NJ: Princeton University Press.

Boas, Franz (1912). *Changes in the Bodily Form of Immigrants*. Senate Document No. 208, 61st Congress, May 1912.

Bowen, William and Bok, Derek (1998). *The Shape of the River: Long Term Consequences of Considering Race in College and University Admissions*. Princeton, NJ: Princeton University Press.

Brooks, Roy (1990). *Rethinking the American Race Problem*. Berkeley: University of California Press.

Cohen, Carl (1997). "Admissions policy lawsuit: affirmative action debate – Letter from Carl Cohen, to members of the University community 10/22/97." Available at ⟨http://www.umich.edu/~rescoll/AffActDebate/affirmx2.html⟩.

Crouse, James and Trusheim, Dale (1988). *The Case Against the SAT*. Chicago: University of Chicago Press.

Flynn, James R. (1987). "Massive IQ gains in 14 nations: what IQ tests really measure." *Psychological Bulletin*, 101: 171–91.

Freedle, Roy O. (2003). "Correcting the SAT's ethnic and social-class bias: a method for re-estimating SAT scores." *Harvard Educational Review*, 73: 1–43.

Guinier, Lani and Sturm, Susan (2001). *Who's Qualified?* Boston: Beacon Press.

Guinier, Lani and Torres, Gerald (2002). *The Miner's Canary*. Cambridge, MA: Harvard University Press.

Hacker, Andrew (1992). *Two Nations*. New York: Random House.

Herrnstein, Richard, and Murray, Charles (1994). *The Bell Curve: Intelligence and Class Structure in American Life*. New York: Free Press.

Hopwood v. *State of Texas* (1996). 78 F.3d 932 (3rd Cir. 1996)

Ignatiev, Noel (1995). *How the Irish Became White*. New York: Routledge.

Jacobson, Matthew F. (1998). *Whiteness of a Different Color*. Cambridge, MA: Harvard University Press.

Kekes, John (1998). "The injustice of affirmative action involving preferential treatment." In Steven Cahn and Peter Markie (eds.), *Ethics: History, Theory, and Contemporary Issues* (pp. 879–87). New York: Oxford University Press.

Kershnar, Stephen (1997). "Strong affirmative action programs at state educational institutions cannot be justified via compensatory justice." *Public Affairs Quarterly*, 11: 345–64.

Kershnar, Stephen (2000). "Intrinsic moral value and racial differences." *Public Affairs Quarterly*, 14: 205–24.

Kershnar, Stephen (2003). "Experiential diversity and *Grutter*." *Public Affairs Quarterly*, 17: 159–70.

Lempert, Richard, Chambers, David, and Adams, Terry (2000). "The river runs through law school." *Journal of Law and Social Inquiry*, 25: 395–506.

Levin, Michael (1997). "Natural subordination, Aristotle on." *Philosophy*, 72/280: 241–57.

Marino, Gordon (1998). "Apologize for slavery facing up to the living past." *Commonweal*, 25: 11–14.

Mosley, Albert (1997). "Are Racial Categories Racist?" *Research in African Literatures*, 28: 101–11.

National Urban League (2001). *Spotting Talent and Potential in the Business World: Lessons from Corporate America for College Admissions* Available at ⟨http://cgi.nul.org/studyresults.html⟩.

Nisbett, Richard (1998). "Race, genetics, and IQ." In Christopher Jencks and Meridith Philips (eds.), *The Black–White Test Score Gap* (pp. 86–102). Washington, DC: Brookings Institution Press.

Oliver, Melvin and Shapiro, Thomas (1995). *Black Wealth/White Wealth*. New York: Routledge.

Oppenheimer, David (1996). "Understanding affirmative action." *Hastings Constitutional Law Quarterly*, 23, 948–9.

Patterson, Orlando (1998). *The Ordeal of Integration*. Washington, DC: Civitas/Counterpoint.

Pojman, Louis (1992). "Equal human worth: a critique of contemporary egalitarianism." *Public Affairs Quarterly*, 6: 181–206.

Pojman, Louis (1998). "The case against affirmative action." *International Journal of Applied Philosophy*, 12: 97–115.

Regents of the University of California v. *Bakke* (1978). 438 US 265 (1978).

Ridley, Aaron (1995). "Ill-gotten gains: on the use of results from unethical experiments in medicine." *Public Affairs Quarterly*, 9: 253–66.

Rosser, Phyllis (1989). *The SAT Gender Gap: Identifying the Underlying Causes*. Washington DC: Center for Women's Policy Studies.

Sturm, Susan and Gunier, Lani (2000). "The future of affirmative action." *The Boston Review*, 25: 6. See also ⟨http://bostonreview.net/BR25.6/sturm.html⟩.

Sher, George (1981). "Ancient wrongs and modern rights." *Philosophy and Public Affairs*, 10: 3–17.

Sniderman, Paul and Piazza, Thomas (1993). *The Scar of Race*. Cambridge, MA: Harvard University Press.

Synderman, Michael and Rothman, Stanley (1987). "Survey of expert opinion on intelligence and aptitude testing." *American Psychologist*, 42: 137–44.

Swain, Carol (2002). *The New White Nationalism in America*. New York: Cambridge University Press.

US Census Bureau (2002). *Statistical Abstract of the United States*. Text available at ⟨http://www.census.gov/prod/www/statistical-abstract-02.html⟩.

Wolf-Devine, Celia (1997). *Diversity and Community in the Academy*. Lanham, MD: Rowman & Litttlefield.

Preferential Policies Have Become Toxic

Celia Wolf-Devine

The debate over affirmative action in the United States has long been a bitter one, and the parties to the debate show no signs of drawing closer together. Many people have looked to the law for clear guidance, but in vain. The law of affirmative action is lacking in coherence, since there are three different standards deriving from different sources, and they don't fit well together.[1] The tide has turned against it, but in the recent cases involving the University of Michigan, the Supreme Court has, somewhat unexpectedly, stabilized around a consensus in favor of diversity, at least in higher education.[2] The important thing to keep in mind, however, is that virtually all affirmative action programs are currently being undertaken voluntarily.[3] What the law permits is not for that reason required; law and morality are not coextensive. As philosophers, our concern is not with how to apply existing laws or how to construct a brief for our client, but with helping people understand what the issues are so they can make up their minds about what ought to be done.

What is keeping such programs in place in spite of growing opposition to them is largely a combination of institutional inertia and a feeling on the part of many people that to favor affirmative action for women and people of color is to be on the side of the angels.[4] I don't think this is true. The arguments in favor of preferential policies do not withstand critical examination; such policies are unjust, and they are having and can be expected to continue to have very bad consequences.

Framing the Issue

The main thing Albert Mosley and I disagree about is whether we ought to engage in what I call "preferential" affirmative action (he calls this "strong" affirmative action). While "procedural" affirmative action seeks only to insure that members of target groups are encouraged to apply and receive fair consideration for jobs, preferential affirmative action, by contrast, involves selecting a woman or person of color who appears to be less well qualified by the usual criteria than some white male applicant.[5] To tell whether preferential affirmative action has occurred, ask yourself: "If another black person had applied whose credentials matched those of the rejected white candidate, would that person have gotten the job over the black candidate who was in fact chosen?" If the answer is "yes," then preferential affirmative action is at work.[6] What I am opposing is preferential affirmative action.

Preferential policies are often described in misleading ways. Even the label "affirmative action" suggests that its proponents are in favor of doing something positive, while opponents of such policies are presumed to favor doing nothing, (perhaps trusting the market to correct for discrimination). This is a false dichotomy; we are *not* forced to choose between affirmative action policies in their current form and doing nothing. There is any number of things we might do to make our society more just and to help the disadvantaged other than adopting preferential policies, and I believe we ought to undertake a number of such reforms.

Calling preferential policies "policies of inclusion" blurs the distinction between procedural and preferential affirmative action (Mosley, 1998: 161–8). It is one thing to encourage members of groups who have until now been scarce in certain work environments to apply, to welcome them, to tell them that we value their talents and will treat them in every way as members of the community. It is another to include them by giving them positions for which they are less well qualified than some white male applicant. Since preferential policies are zero sum (they do not create jobs but only redistribute them), the *inclusion* of one person necessarily involves the *exclusion* of another.

Finally, affirmative action is often presented as a continuation of the great civil rights movement of the 1950s and 1960s. But while affirmative action did indeed have its roots in the 1960s, such policies have undergone a significant change in the 40 years since the Civil Rights Act of 1964, which was designed primarily to provide black citizens the same rights white people had, and enable them to participate fully in the social, economic, and political life of their communities. The large federal agencies set up in the 1960s to oversee employment discrimination moved quickly and aggressively beyond simply trying to root out discrimination to promoting proportional representation of target groups. A number of groups emerged as beneficiaries from these policies, including women, Hispanics, Orientals, American Indians, and Asians and Pacific Islanders. For an in-depth discussion of the history of affirmative action policies in their legal, economic, and political contexts, as well as detailed analyses of the arguments for the various target groups, see my book (Wolf-Devine, 1997: 5–46).

Instituting temporary programs (such as scholarships, low-interest loans for black-owned businesses or mortgages for black people, job-training programs, and the creation of jobs for young, unemployed black men) to be financed out of tax revenues and designed to help black people move forward would at least have made sense and been doable in the political and economic climate of the sixties. What we have now makes *no* sense, and should not be allowed to feed off the moral capital of the civil rights movement – which I believe was one of our high points as a nation – when we were beginning to really try to take our own American ideals seriously.[7]

Celia Wolf-Devine

Disentangling Race and Sex

Most defenders of preferential policies, including Mosley, develop arguments tailored specifically to the situation of black people and then throw in women and other beneficiaries with little or no argument. Political action has, perhaps, required banding together to advance common interests, but the situations of the groups commonly accorded preferences differ in important ways. Hispanics, for example, are almost all recent immigrants or children of immigrants. They are disproportionably young and many do not speak fluent English. So while we should help them acquire the skills they need to enter the mainstream of American life as previous immigrant groups have done, they aren't entitled to preferences over poor non-Hispanic white people whose families have been here for generations.

The situation of women is radically different from that of either Hispanics or black people. The way in which sex and race have become interwoven in the U.S. is largely the result of historical accident. The type of feminism prevalent in the US since the 1970s was started by women who were active in the civil rights movement, and the notion of "sexism" was consciously modeled on "racism." Politically active women in other countries do not think about the problems faced by women in this sort of way (Hewlett, 1987: 164–7). On the legal front also, racial and sexual discrimination became linked by something of a fluke. A Southern opponent of black civil rights added women in an amendment to Title VII at the very last minute, hoping perhaps to secure the defeat of the Civil Rights Act itself, or at least throw a monkey wrench into its enforcement by bringing in a whole new protected class.

Women themselves were bitterly divided over the advisability of adding women to Title VII. Affluent and careerist Republican women favored this, while Democratic women active in the blue-collar and pink-collar women's unions opposed it because it was too general, and preferred "specific bills for specific ills" (such as the Equal Pay Act of 1963). Some of the reasons they opposed it were that, first, it ran together discrimination against women and that against black people, which they thought should be addressed separately because they involved very different problems; second, it would endanger the women's protective legislation which they deemed essential to protect working-class women; and, third, it would divert attention and resources away from the more pressing needs of black people.

The strongest arguments in favor of preferential treatment of black people do not hold water for women. Being female is not passed on from generation to generation; women have fathers, brothers, and sons as well as daughters. They don't live in segregated communities; their lives are closely interwoven with men. They share the social class of their fathers while growing up, and that of their husbands when married. For this reason, disadvantage is not inherited in the way it is for black people. Simple non-discrimination would be enough to ensure that they were able to attain positions commensurate with their abilities. They should of course receive equal pay for equal work,[8] but this is an entirely different issue from whether they should be given preferences over better-qualified men at the hiring level.

The state has no compelling interest in promoting proportional representation of women in all the professions. If the great majority of firefighters or mathematicians continue to be male, what difference would this make so long as the jobs are done well and those women with the motivation and ability to do the job well are not excluded unfairly? In fact, if the tests firefighters have to pass had to be changed so that more women could pass them (say, by lessening the amount of weight the firefighter must be able to carry), it would be to our *dis*advantage to have women proportionally represented among firefighters.

Unlike racial differences, the biological differences between men and women are extensive, so the likelihood that these will have some impact on their behavior and capacities is far higher. Sex-based job preferences do *not* level the playing field. They tilt it in a way that makes it harder for couples that would prefer to have the man be the primary breadwinner. I believe that much of the push toward proportional representation of women comes from those who want to eliminate traditional sex roles. But the way couples arrange their domestic lives should be up to them.

Giving women preferences has created a new minority – namely, young white men who are not well established in their careers and who are asked to bear all the burden of such policies. Finally, it has cushioned the class impact of affirmative action programs, since the job lost by a middle-class white man might go to his wife with no net gain to the worst off.

Affirmative Action for Black People: Evaluating the Arguments

When doing social philosophy, although it is important to get a sense of what sort of world we live in, caution is required when relying on statistics or polls. People can put different spins on the same statistics. For example, a widely cited Federal Reserve study of racial disparities in mortgage loan approval rates indicated that black and Hispanic applicants were rejected much more often than white ones.[9] But the study did not control for net worth, the credit histories, or the existing debts of the applicants. Subsequent studies brought to light other important considerations such as the fact that minority applicants generally had greater debt burdens, poorer credit histories, sought loans covering a larger percentage of the value of the property and were also more likely to seek to finance multiple-dwelling units. It turned out that if you looked at *approved* borrowers, the minority borrowers were approved with incomes only three-quarters as high as the approved whites, and assets worth less than half the value of the assets of the whites (Sowell, 2002: 175–6). Statistics, thus, can be very tricky to interpret properly, and polls are notoriously manipulable. I therefore encourage you to reflect about your own experiences and to question your parents and grandparents about the sorts of change they have seen in their lifetimes and use this as a check on what you read.

The compensatory (or backward–looking) argument

This argument relies on the straightforward principle that the one who wrongs another owes the other. The underlying model is that of tort law; defendant has wronged plaintiff and the court must try to restore plaintiff to the position he or she would have been in had defendant not wronged him or her. Trying to apply this

Celia Wolf-Devine

model to wrongs spanning several generations, however, generates unmanageable problems.

What makes black people's claim for compensation stronger than that of others who have suffered discrimination is the fact that their ancestors were brought here as slaves. Buying and selling a human being as property violates that person's human dignity, and as a result of slavery and the Jim Crow laws subsequently instituted to keep black people in subordinate positions, those so treated were both wronged and harmed.

There is a problem, however, for those who defend racial preferences now – i.e. early in the twenty-first century. They must establish a strong connection between a current black candidate and harms inflicted on the black community by slavery and Jim Crow laws so as to justify what at least *looks like* an unfair employment practice – namely disfavoring the other candidate because he or she is white. And it is not enough to show that the black candidate deserves compensation; it must also be shown that this particular way of compensating him or her is just.

When discussing entry-level jobs we are talking mainly about people born in the 1980s or late 1970s. Thus the black candidate has not been directly harmed by (or the white candidate benefited by) slavery, Jim Crow laws, or, for the most part, overtly racial exclusions of any kind. (Recent black immigrants are not entitled to preferences on compensatory grounds.) Attempts have been made to show that the current generation of white people has benefited materially from the unpaid labor of slaves appropriated by their owners because this was passed down through the white community (Boxill, 1972: 120). But slavery was only marginally profitable economically, only a small number of white people benefited from it (some were actually harmed), and most of those who did benefit were ruined by the war. And the enormous amount of immigration that has occurred since the abolition of slavery makes any claim that all presently living white people can be supposed to have benefited from slavery indefensible.

Even if we focus on material gains the current white job candidate's parents or grandparents might have obtained because of Jim Crow laws or overtly racial exclusions (young white men at the start of their careers are no more likely to have benefited than others, and probably less likely), we don't *know* in any given case that this occurred, and such exclusions are falling rapidly into the past in any case. The law does not allow people to collect for wrongs done their parents or grandparents (with a few exceptions such as wrongful death of a parent, or requiring the heir of a thief to return stolen property – where the victim, thief, and object stolen can be identified clearly). History is full of injustices of every kind (not just racial ones), so it would appear unfair to compensate some but not others. At some point we just need to pick up and go on if we don't want to become like the Middle East where the old angers fester for millennia.

People have different moral intuitions about the innocent beneficiaries of past wrongs. Even if many currently living white people are better off than they would have been in the absence of racism, I don't think that this obligates them to compensate black people. If you know about a wrong in advance and could have done something to prevent it, or if it was committed specifically to benefit *you*, then you owe compensation, but not otherwise. I also object to the procedure of projecting moral intuitions that concern one-on-one interactions onto a large and complex society.

Perhaps instead of focusing on material damages, we might understand the harm inflicted by slavery and Jim Crow laws on the current generation of American black people as a form of cultural damage. Being a slave is not conducive to a strong work ethic, habits of deferring gratification, saving and planning for the future, taking initiatives, and so on, and black family structure was also adversely affected in various ways by slavery. To the extent that black culture in the US has been shaped by slave experience, this is likely to make it harder for black people to hold down jobs and maintain stable families. And whatever problems immigrants faced, they did not have the cultural baggage of slavery to contend with. There are two problems, however, with using the cultural damage argument to support preferences.

First, a culture that maximizes members' capacity to succeed in an individualistic and competitive society is not necessarily better than one that does not (more strongly communal cultures may afford a more humane quality of life, for example), and features of black culture that hold them back are likely to be connected with other features that they rightly want to retain. Second, the cultural damage argument undermines itself. If black people claim that their culture has inculcated traits in them that disable them from performing certain sorts of jobs successfully, it is unreasonable to then turn around and ask to be preferentially appointed to such jobs.

Finally, there are two underlying problems with the whole compensatory project. The first is that if it were not for slavery, the current generation of American black people would not exist, since their ancestors would have remained in Africa and married different people. Mosley concedes this, but suggests that had it not been for slavery and racism, some Africans might have come here like other immigrant groups, and been successful in the same way they were (Mosley and Capaldi, 1996: 34). You can write hypothetical history any way you want, but we can only act in the present, and we are the people our biology and history have made us.

The compensatory argument also requires some sort of clear standard to determine when justice has been achieved. Otherwise preferential policies open the door to endless turf war. In practice, defenders of preferences have fallen back on the assumption that in the absence of unjust discrimination, black people would be proportionally represented in all the various professions. Mosley concedes that it's not possible to tell what level of representation they would have achieved, but says that proportional representation is "the only *fair* assumption to make" (Mosley and Capaldi, 1996: 28).[10] But there are any number of reasons other than discrimination that might cause different racial and ethnic groups to clump together in certain occupations and be absent from others – the most important being cultural differences.

Cultures vary widely in the character traits they admire and strive to inculcate among members, the professions they regard as most prestigious, and the sort of family life they aspire to and achieve. Cultural differences may not be ineradicable, but they go very deep, change very slowly, and often persist in an ethnic group over hundreds of years even when they are scattered all over the globe. Chance or the environment they originated in also affect the occupations that members of an ethnic group enter (Sowell, 2002).

Celia Wolf-Devine

There are thus enough reasons not to expect to find members of various ethnic and racial groups proportionally represented at all levels in all occupations without any appeal at all to genetic factors – which have been and still are fiercely controversial. I am skeptical about whether there are genetically based differences in capacities between different racial groups. But Mosley says, "The possibility of a selective distribution of behavioral traits causally determined by race cannot be ruled out as impossible," and that, "the concept of race has both a biological and historical legitimacy." (Mosley, 1984: 226, 234). On such premises, there would be even less reason to suppose that different racial groups would be distributed throughout the professions at all levels in a random manner in the absence of injustice.

Corrective argument

The corrective argument defends preferences not to compensate for past wrongs, but to counteract *existing* bias in the hiring process. This argument has an advantage over the compensatory argument in that it does not paint the beneficiaries in a demeaning light as victims. Preferences are viewed as a way of selecting the candidates who are in fact best qualified by correcting for the bias against them (Rachels, 1993: 220). The bias, they argue, is located either in the prejudices of those making hiring decisions, or in the standards by which candidates are evaluated.

If we restrict ourselves to specific cases where there is clear evidence of bias at work (and not just statistical disparities), then there is a good case for taking some sort of corrective action, but when the corrective argument is generalized it becomes pernicious, because bias is presumed rather than shown. White people are taken to be so infected with racism (conscious or unconscious) that they cannot fairly judge the qualifications of black people, and this stigmatizes them. Or else all the criteria used to evaluate candidates are taken to be biased against black people whenever they don't yield the proper racial mix. Since there is usually at least a reasonable fit between the sorts of test employed to screen applicants and the skills needed to perform successfully, the push to eliminate all standards that don't yield the "right" results is likely to result in increased incompetence on the job.

Forward-looking arguments

Defenders of preferential policies sometimes argue for them on consequentialist grounds by pointing to the desirable results that are hoped will be produced by them, such as providing role models for other members of the group, or creating a more diverse work force or student body.

Role models Putting black people in desirable positions, it is argued, gives other black people the message that such positions are open also to them and this will encourage them to work harder and aspire to succeed. In spite of the influence this hypothesis has had upon policy-makers, surprisingly little empirical evidence has been supplied to support it.[11] Employing *preferences* in order to provide role models, in any case, sends a mixed signal. Certainly it is a good thing that there are some highly visible, successful black people, but a few really top-notch ones in different fields are enough to send the message that the field is open to black people.

Diversity and representation   "Diversity" is not so much an argument as it is a kind of umbrella under which a variety of quite different programs take shelter, so if you find this argument confusing, the problem is not just with you. Compensatory or corrective arguments are often disguised as appeals to diversity to evade legal restrictions. And all too often what is going on under the surface of demands for greater diversity is either sheer politics – "more of us; less of you" – or else an attempt to advance some ideological agenda such as feminism or multiculturalism.

Diversity is a mixed good. Deep differences of outlook between people often generate conflict (even bloody wars), so diversity must be balanced by shared values or goals that hold the group together. In practice, no one advocates limitless diversity, of course, and the idea that we should simply "celebrate diversity" is silly. Some individuals are pedophiles or racists, and some of the diverse cultures the world has seen include features we rightly find morally horrifying, such as infanticide or the routine torture of prisoners of war.

Advocates of diversity employ a mixture of aesthetic and political rhetoric to move us to accept the type of diversity they value on other grounds. Aesthetic metaphors include things like the rainbow in which a variety of colors contribute to an overall beautiful appearance, or a stew in which the different ingredients each add their distinctive flavor. Such metaphors are highly subjective; some prefer blended soups, some prefer chunky ones, some are purists who prefer to savor the taste of each food separately. Another problem is that aesthetic metaphors treat members of the groups as interchangeable. Onions, after all, are supposed to add a distinctive onion flavor to the stew.

A black person in an elite position is often said to "represent" other black people (and so on for other groups). But, a lawyer represents clients and a senator represents voters because they are hired or elected by those whose interests they purport to represent, and can be removed if they fail to do so satisfactorily. No such mechanisms are in place for college professors, accountants, CEOs, or students. Why should we suppose that they represent anyone but themselves?

In contexts where people's ideas matter (academia, for example), using this sort of rhetoric improperly puts pressure on members of the groups in question to conform to what is taken to be the official position of their group instead of being given the same right white men have to make up their own minds. (For an in-depth discussion of ways in which the corrective, role model, mentor, and diversity arguments play themselves out in the university context, see Wolf-Devine, 1997: chs. 3 and 4.)

Which groups get special consideration is all too often a function of bureaucratic inertia. Since affirmative action policies are already in place for women and certain minority groups, it is easy to favor those same groups, regardless of whether this particular sort of diversity makes sense in relation to the activity in question and its goals.[12] Some press for special consideration of their own group in order to advance their interests and those of their friends. Some support preferences as a way to work for social justice in the broader society by bringing in more members of disadvantaged groups, or compensating those who have been victims of injustice. Since so

Celia Wolf-Devine

many Americans confuse class and race, they may see improving the situation of black people relative to white people as a way of breaking the cycle of poverty. Universities may want to include those with perspectives that we think will contribute to a better environment for learning, or enable future citizens to learn to deal with those different from them. Sometimes it is just party politics, as when students agitating for the appointment of a Hispanic professor at a prestigious law school objected to a candidate on the grounds that he was a Republican!

Assessing the Arguments

I will argue that when we disentangle the different types of motivation involved, each of the goals sought could be obtained in a better way, and further that racial preferences are exacerbating the problems they are supposed to be helping solve.

Of course if one favors a group just because it is one's own group, preferences may be the only way to go. But if black people are entitled to favor their own, there is no reason why white people may not do the same. If one's goal is breaking the cycle of poverty, this is better attained by policies directly targeting the poor. Race is not an adequate proxy for poverty; only 27.7 percent of the poor are black, 20.1 percent Hispanic, and 48.1 percent are white. Since black people are disproportionately poor, they would benefit more from such programs, but focusing on poverty rather than race has the advantage of being fair to the white poor. If one's goal is compensating black people for past injustices, one needs to invest resources and thought into black community development, healthcare, and education. Black students at age 17 are four years behind white students in reading and five years behind them in math (Thernstrom, 2003: 13). Preferential admission to college does not fix this problem.

If we are concerned about students coming into contact with those different from themselves so that they will be better able to function as citizens of a pluralistic democracy, racial diversity is only one of many sorts of diversity, and there is no reason to suppose it is the most important one. In terms of cultural differences, Asian Americans clearly bring the greatest diversity, and one that might help students function better in a global economy. The South is unknown territory to most Northerners, conservative Bible Christians are very scarce on elite campuses, and being able to deal with people from a different class background than one's own is an important skill. Studying texts from other historical periods provides another important sort of diversity.

Racial preferences confirm negative racial stereotypes. Most people form their opinions about members of groups other than their own on the basis of their own experience. When there were anti-Jewish quotas at elite colleges, Jewish students had to be brighter than gentiles to be admitted, and as a result, Jews got a reputation for being especially brainy. But under a regime of racial preferences, black students will be, on average, less well qualified than their white classmates. This artificially contrived situation will reinforce the perception that black people are less able academically, and sow seeds of self-doubt in black students.[13] The strongest advocates of racial preferences themselves seem to have a rather dim view of the capacities of black students. Bowen and Bok, for example, compare race-sensitive admissions policies with parking places for the handicapped (1998: 39).

In fact, black students in the Bowen and Bok study did underperform, winding up in the 23rd percentile of their classes (and that includes those who would have been admitted without preferences). Mosley is critical of SATs (although he suggests no alternative). They do, however, have some predictive value and in fact they over-predict the performance of black students (who did not do as well as others with the same SAT scores) (Thernstrom and Thernstrom, 1997: ch. 13; 2001). But opponents of racial preferences in admissions are not committed to their being the best, let alone the only, criterion for selecting students. The point is merely that all students should be judged by the same criteria, whatever they are.

If race were taken into account in a loose sort of way in the same manner regional diversity is, this would probably be relatively benign (especially if adequate remediation was provided for those who need it). The problem is that this is not what has been happening. The amount of preference accorded black students is extremely large. Harvard may be able to employ such preferences and still get reasonably competent students, but schools with less prestige will not.

One hidden cost of racial preferences is the drop-out rate of black students, which is characteristically three times that of white students. Another one shows up later when they have to take a race-blind test. A recent study found that 43 percent of the black students admitted to law school on the basis of race either dropped out or failed to pass a bar exam, and in 1988 51 percent of black medical students failed the required Part I exam given by the National Board of Medical Examiners (Thernstrom and Thernstrom, 2001: 195–6).

The worry that motivates those advocating racial preferences in admissions, of course, is that race-neutral policies would sharply diminish the number of black students getting college educations, thus keeping them in socially inferior positions. I do not believe that the consequences of race-neutral admissions policies would be, on balance and in the long run, bad. The number of black students admitted to the most selective colleges would diminish, at least initially, but certainly not to the vanishing point. At the University of California, for example, the initial decrease in black enrollments on the Berkeley campus (they are on the rise again now) was offset by increases at the other UC campuses, and already minority students who could only get into community colleges are increasing their transfer rate to the UC campuses. It is not even clear that fewer black students will graduate from the Berkeley campus under race-neutral admissions policies if ending preferences has the effect of reducing their drop-out rate.

If there were 3.5 percent or 4 percent of black students on some elite campuses for a while, rather than 7 percent or 8 percent, there would still be opportunities for racial interaction, and the interaction would be on a healthier footing in that all students would know the others had been admitted on their merits. Bowen and Bok overestimate the importance of attending an elite school. A careful examination of the schools attended by those in elite positions (white as well as black) indicates only a small fraction of them attended such institutions. There are a number of different pathways to satisfying and lucrative careers. Black people made some of their strongest progress economically before preferences went into effect.[14] To suppose that the progress they

Celia Wolf-Devine

have made in recent years is a result of preferences would seem to imply either that they are not competent enough to attain decent jobs on their own or that white people are so hopelessly racist that they would not have hired them without pressure.

If one is concerned about underserved minority communities, and if there is evidence that those admitted under affirmative action programs practice law or medicine more in such communities than those not (there is dispute over whether this is true), communities could be served as well or better by giving scholarships or other incentives to any student who would make a commitment to serve there after graduation for a certain number of years.

Finally, one good result that eliminating preferences might have is that such elimination would force people to confront the root problems instead of being able to paper them over. Some good and creative programs are already being instituted in those states where racial preferences in admissions have been eliminated. As Fullinwider and Lictenberg note:

> It was not until the thumb on the scale was removed that universities in Florida, Texas, and California intensified their intervention programs, and that state legislatures opened their purses and began to put real money behind intervention. Perhaps the abolition of affirmative action is required to motivate institutions of higher learning and state legislatures to address causes, not just symptoms.[15]

Conclusion

In Lewis Carroll's *Alice in Wonderland*, Alice asks the Cheshire Cat: "Would you tell me, please, which way I ought to walk from here?" and the cat replies "That depends a good deal on where you want to get to" (1946: 64). At this point, then, I will step back and say a few things about where we are now, where I would like to see us go from here, and why preferential policies are not the way to get there. Preferential policies are flawed in three ways. They do not address the root problems our society is facing. They are divisive at a time when we desperately need programs that can bring people together. And they re-entrench racial categories just when it is beginning to seem possible that they may really begin to fade in importance.

We have some very serious problems now that we did not have in the 1960s. Economically, we are faced with the continued growth of poverty (in spite of our high per capita gross domestic product), an extraordinary increase over the last 30 years in the polarization between rich and poor (Phillips, 1990, 2002), increasing job insecurity caused by downsizing, and the fact that globalization has led many businesses to close plants here and move their operations to countries where labor is cheaper. Politically, the big problems are severe distrust of government and loss of a sense of the common good.

Preferential policies do not address these root problems. As Mosley admits:

> Strong affirmative action is a conservative response to racial injustice. It does not seek to eliminate the growing gap between rich and poor. Rather, it seeks to eliminate the overrepresentation of Blacks among the least well off and their underrepresentation

among the most well off ... It does not create new jobs. Rather, it addresses how jobs already created shall be distributed. (Mosley and Capaldi, 1996: 59)

Some argue that preferential policies are better than nothing. But racial, gender, and ethnic preferences are a step in the wrong direction. They are inherently divisive because they are zero sum. They were put in place by executive orders and by large federal agencies rather than by democratic means, so continuing them alienates people further from the government (this is especially true of the white working class). Those who lose out economically are likely to suspect that affirmative action was the cause, whether or not it actually was, which fuels racial hostilities.

My suggestion is that we should focus on the plight of America's children, of whom 20 percent live below the poverty level; the earlier you intervene to break the cycle of poverty, the more successful your efforts will be. Middle-class children are also at risk in a number of ways, and family-friendly policies could do a lot to help them flourish (Hewlett, 1991). Children are our future, and programs designed to give them a chance to develop their talents and contribute to society at least stand a chance to win popular support and bring people together. Targeting poor children would help black people disproportionately since they are disproportionately poor and young.

Finally, racial categories are entrenched when important benefits and burdens are distributed on the basis of race-based preferences, and when large bureaucracies are set up to oversee such programs. Indeed, such programs have a strong emotional and material interest in preserving racial categories; if people were to stop regarding skin color as all that important, they would be out of a job. But there is considerable evidence that racial barriers are finally beginning to break down.[16] My own experience – and that of people I know from a variety of backgrounds – is that anti-black racial prejudice among whites has decreased significantly. For example, my first cousin's daughter recently married an African American, and although her grandparents were upset, none of the younger members of the family has shown any discomfort with this.

Perhaps the deepest difference between Albert Mosley and me is that he wants to see racial categories preserved, and I don't. He wants them preserved because he wants those who have been harmed through racial categories to receive compensation through these same categories, and because he believes that self-identification of black people as members of the black race can help build "a positive sense of self-identity and self pride" (Mosley, 1997: 108–9). This conjunction links black identity and being a victim to being an individual whom something is owed. To the degree that black identity is linked to a culture of "oppression and resistance," this will reinforce one of the major things that may be holding black people back – namely, the tendency to regard working hard and doing well in school as "acting white." There is no reason why black people can't move into the mainstream of American life while still having pride in their own culture, much as Irish or Italian Americans have done.

Racial attitudes in this country are complex, ambiguous, and shifting. Given that things are delicately poised, it is important to be careful not to make race relations worse by generating reactive racism. Reactive racism occurs when people are told that members of the other race dislike them or think they are inferior, stupid, racists, bigots,

Celia Wolf-Devine

or whatever. If someone tells me that another person likes me, this will dispose me to take a liking to him or her, whereas if I am told that someone dislikes me or thinks badly of me, I will approach that person differently. Expectations tend to be self-fulfilling. So, I conclude with a plea for seeking common ground and treating one another with respect as individuals.

Notes

I wish to express my gratitude to the Earhart Foundation, whose generous assistance enabled me to take time off teaching to work on this project. I also wish to thank my husband Phil Devine for helping me talk out ideas and for commenting on several drafts of this chapter.

1   For a good, clear discussion of the law of affirmative action by a noted discrimination lawyer, see Rutherglen (1997). I am indebted to subsequent informal conversations with Rutherglen for some of the points I make concerning the law.

2   The recent decisions reinforce the court's support for Justice Powell's position in *Bakke*. Astute discussions of the *Bakke* case are found in the essays by Carl Cohen and Ronald Dworkin in Cahn, *The Affirmative Action Debate* (2002) and in Fullinwider and Lichtenberg (2004: ch. 9). An amicus brief filed by the National Association of Scholars critiquing the Gurin report, which the University of Michigan relied on in its defense of the educational value of diversity, can be found at ⟨www.nas.org⟩. Another valuable amicus brief on the same subject can be found at ⟨www/iwf.org⟩. The Supreme Court rejected a system employed by the undergraduate school in which applicants were given extra points for being black, but permitted the law school's more loose and indeterminate use of race as one plus factor among many so long as it is not the determining factor. In practice, however, the distinction between being *a* factor and being *the* factor is almost impossible to draw. I am inclined to think the court was swayed by briefs from former military officers and corporations that have affirmative action policies in place, and is worried that discontinuing preferences would dry up the supply of available black candidates, and that diversity really has nothing to do with the case.

3   Legally, courts may order employers to institute affirmative action programs to remedy *their own* prior acts of discrimination, and have done so in several particularly egregious cases. But voluntarily undertaking preferential hiring programs designed to counteract general societal discrimination is not permissible because they involve racial discrimination against white people. People often undertake such programs as a defense against a possible suit for racial or gender discrimination, but in fact there is very little exposure to the threat of litigation so long as employers have at least *some* members of target groups on their staff. The one area where racial, gender, and ethnic preferences still have real clout is in the government contracts program, where there are "set-asides" for female and minority contractors. ("Set asides" in hiring are illegal, so I find it puzzling that the government employs them in contracting.)

4   On the political front, the major setback to such policies has been laws along the lines of Proposition 209 (the California Civil Rights Initiative) which stipulates: "The state shall not discriminate against, or grant preferential treatment to, any individual or group on the basis of race, sex, color, ethnicity, or national origin in the operation of public employment, public education or public contracting." Similar laws have subsequently been passed also in Texas, Florida and Washington State.

5   I am indebted for this distinction to Steven M. Cahn (2002: 71–80).

6   I owe this particularly clear way of determining when preference is at work in a hiring decision to Thomas Nagel (1979: ch. 7).

7   The ideals of the civil rights movement grew out of a shared religious heritage – Protestant, Catholic, and Jewish – that grounded demands for universal human rights and respect for the dignity of each person on a common human nature, and this foundation has been called into question by those who claim to be its heirs. For an excellent account of the disintegration of the early New Left, see Gitlin (1995).

8   See Furchtgott-Roth and Stolba (1999) for a sophisticated analysis of data on women's income and progress in the professions. They argue that the wage gap between men and women is rapidly disappearing.

9   See Sowell (2002: 175) for a discussion of "Expanded HMDA data on residential lending: one year late," Federal Reserve Bulletin, November 1992.

10 To be fair, he goes on to say that he does not believe they should be *maintained* in such positions. I don't know what to make of this. I can't believe that he is seriously proposing that we engineer proportional representation of all the current beneficiaries of preferences and then see what happens. The amount of governmental intrusion into people's lives required to attain this would be well beyond what Americans would (or should) tolerate. And if the desired proportions had been attained in this way, the result would be highly unstable, since those preferentially hired would have been set up to fail. The point about being set up to fail is made by Pojman (1998: 171).

11 For one thing, it is difficult to state the hypothesis in a way that makes it actually testable, and for another one needs to specify what counts as a "same kind" role model. I am aware of only a few empirical studies of the importance of role models (all in educational settings), and these have generally failed to find any statistically significant correlation between having a teacher of one's own race or sex and student performance (see Wolf-Devine, 1997: 81–6 for discussion and references). The only exception is a study conducted in Tennessee in the 1980s that found a small but statistically significant correlation between K-3 students' performance and their having a teacher of their own race (Thernstrom and Thernstrom, 2003: 201–2).

12 For one thing, these are the groups about which statistics are collected. I'm sure, for example, that Pentecostal Christians have lower average incomes than Episcopalians or Jews, but the census does not collect data on religious affiliation.

13 I am indebted throughout this section to the Thernstroms' critique of Bowen and Bok (Thernstrom and Thernstrom, 2001: 169–231) for arguments, statistics, and for the point about how Jewish quotas gave Jews a reputation for being especially smart, as well as to Thernstrom and Thernstrom (1997: ch. 14).

14 The 1940s, '50s and '60s was a period of growth in the black middle class. The black–white income gap hit its lowest point in 1972, and then increased again because the heavy manufacturing industries in the Midwest, where many black people were employed, began decline. A lot of the variance between racial groups, I suspect, is a function of the way in which major structural economic factors impact the regions where they live and the industries in which they are employed, rather than of racial prejudice. For excellent historical discussions of the way underlying economic trends differentially affected black and white workers, see Edsall and Edsall (1991: chs. 6 and 11) and Madrick (1995).

15 I am quoting here from a draft of Fullinwider and Lichtenberg (forthcoming: ch. 11), which the authors sent me in the spring of 2003. These sentences will not appear in the published version.

16 Polls reveal enormous shifts in racial patterns and attitudes over the past 40 years both among black people and among white people, and this is especially marked if you compare the responses of adults and teens within each group. Valuable discussions of poll data are

Celia Wolf-Devine

found in Everett Ladd's essay in Thernstrom and Thernstrom (2002) and in Thernstrom and Thernstrom (1997: ch. 17).

References

Bowen, William and Bok, Derek (1998). *The Shape of the River: Long-Term Consequences of Considering Race in College and University Admissions*. Princeton, NJ: Princeton University Press.

Boxill, Bernard (1972). "The morality of reparation." *Social Theory and Practice*, 2/1: 113–22.

Cahn, Steven M. (2002). "Two concepts of affirmative action." In Steven M. Cahn (ed.), *Puzzles and Perplexities: Collected Essays* (pp. 71–80). Lanham, MD: Rowman & Littlefield.

Cahn, Steven M. (2002). *The Affirmative Action Debate*, 2nd edn. New York: Routledge.

Carroll, Lewis (1946). *Alice in Wonderland*. Kingsport, TN: Kingsport Press for Grosset & Dunlap.

Edsall, Thomas Byrne and Edsall, Mary D. (1991). *Chain Reaction: The Impact of Race, Rights and Taxes on American Politics*. New York: W.W. Norton & Company.

Fullinwider, Robert and Lichtenberg, Judith (2004). *Leveling the Playing Field: Justice, Politics, and College Admissions*. Lanham MD: Rowman & Littlefield.

Furchtgott-Roth, Diana, and Stolba, Christine (1999). *Women's Figures: An Illustrated Guide to Women's Progress in America*. Washington, DC: American Enterprise Institute.

Gitlin, Todd (1995). *The Twilight of Common Dreams: Why America is Wracked by Culture Wars*. New York: Metropolitan Books.

Hewlett, Sylvia (1987). *A Lesser Life: The Myth of Women's Liberation in America*. New York: Warner Books.

Hewlett, Sylvia (1991). *When the Bough Breaks: The Cost of Neglecting Our Children*. New York: Basic Books.

Madrick, Jeffrey (1995). *The End of Affluence: The Causes and Consequences of America's Economic Dilemmas*. New York: Random House.

Mosley, Albert G. (1984). "Negritude, nationalism and nativism: racists or racialists?" In Albert Mosley (ed.), *African Philosophy: Selected Readings* (pp. 216–35). Englewood Cliffs, NJ: Prentice Hall.

Mosley, Albert G. (1997). "Are racial categories racist?" *Research in African Literatures*, 26/4: 101–11.

Mosley, Albert G. (1998). "Policies of straw or policies of inclusion? A review of Pojman's 'Case against affirmative action'." *International Journal of Applied Philosophy*, 12/2: 161–8.

Mosley, Albert G. and Capaldi, Nicholas (1996). *Affirmative Action: Social Justice or Unfair Preference?* Lanham MD: Rowman & Littlefield.

Nagel, Thomas (1979). *Mortal Questions*. Cambridge: Cambridge University Press.

Phillips, Kevin (1990). *The Politics of Rich and Poor: Wealth and the American Electorate in the Reagan Aftermath*. New York: Random House.

Phillips, Kevin (2002). *Wealth and Democracy: A Political History of the American rich*. New York: Broadway Books.

Pojman, Lewis (1998). "The case against affirmative action." *International Journal of Applied Philosophy*, 12/1: 97–115.

Rachels, James (1993). "Are quotas sometimes justified?" In Steven M. Cahn (ed.), *Affirmative Action and the University: A Philosophical Inquiry*. Philadelphia, PA: Temple University Press.

Rutherglen, George (1997). "Affirmative action in faculty appointments: a guide to the perplexed" Appendix to Wolf-Devine (1997: 181–204).

Sowell, Thomas (2002). "Discrimination, economics and culture." In Thernstrom and Thernstrom (2002: 167–80).

Thernstrom, Stephen and Thernstrom, Abigail (1997). *America in Black and White*. New York: Touchstone.

Thernstrom, Stephen and Thernstrom, Abigail (2001). "Racial preferences in higher education: an assessment of the evidence." In Stanley Allen Renshon (ed.), *One America* (pp. 169–231). Washington, DC: Georgetown University Press. (An earlier version of this paper can be found in *UCLA Law Review*, 46/5 (June 1999), under the title "Reflections on the shape of the river.")

Thernstrom, Abigail and Thernstrom, Stephen (eds.) (2002). *Beyond the Color Line: New Perspectives on Race and Ethnicity in America*. Stanford, CA: The Hoover Institution Press.

Thernstrom, Abigail and Thernstrom, Stephen (2003). *No Excuses: Closing the Racial Gap in Learning*. New York: Simon and Schuster.

Wolf-Devine, Celia (1997). *Diversity and Community in the Academy: Affirmative Action in Faculty Appointments*. Lanham, MD: Rowman & Littlefield.

Further reading

Cahn, Steven M. (ed.) (1993). *Affirmative Action and the University: A Philosophical Inquiry*. Philadelphia: Temple University Press.

Cohen, Carl and Sterba, James (2003). *Affirmative Action and Racial Preference: A Debate*. New York: Oxford University Press.

Steele, Shelby (1990). *The Content of Our Character: A New Vision of Race in America*. New York: St. Martin's Press.

Steele, Shelby (1998). *A Dream Deferred: The Second Betrayal of Black Freedom in America*. New York: HarperCollins Publishers Inc.

Celia Wolf-Devine

ANIMALS

CHAPTER FIVE

Empty Cages: Animal Rights and Vivisection

Tom Regan

Animals are used in laboratories for three main purposes: education, product safety testing, and experimentation – medical research in particular. Unless otherwise indicated, my discussion is limited to their use in harmful, non-therapeutic medical research (which, for simplicity, I sometimes refer to as "vivisection"). Experimentation of this kind differs from therapeutic experimentation, where the intention is to benefit the subjects on whom the experiments are conducted. In harmful, non-therapeutic experimentation, by contrast, subjects are harmed, often seriously, or put at risk of serious harm, in the absence of any intended benefit for them; instead, the intention is to obtain information that might ultimately benefit others.

Human beings, not only nonhuman animals, have been used in harmful, non-therapeutic experimentation. In fact, the history of medical research contains numerous examples of human vivisection, and it is doubtful whether the ethics of animal vivisection can be fully appreciated apart from the ethics of human vivisection. Unless otherwise indicated, however, the current discussion of vivisection and my use of the term are limited to harmful, non-therapeutic experimentation using nonhuman animals.

The Benefits Argument

There is only one serious moral defense of vivisection.[1] That defense proceeds as follows. Human beings are better off because of vivisection. Indeed, we are (we are told) much better off because of it. If not all, at least the majority of the most important improvements in human health and longevity are indebted to vivisection. Included among the advances often cited are open heart surgery, vaccines (for polio and smallpox, for example), cataract and hip-replacement surgery, and advances in rehabilitation techniques for victims of spinal cord injuries and strokes. Without these and the many other advances attributable to vivisection, proponents of the Benefits Argument maintain, the incidence of human disease, permanent disability, and premature death would be far greater than it is today.

Defenders of the Benefits Argument are not indifferent to how animals are treated. They agree that animals used in vivisection sometimes suffer both during the research itself, and because of the restrictive conditions of their life in the laboratory. That the research can harm animals, no reasonable person will deny. Experimental procedures include drowning, suffocating, starving, and burning; blinding animals and destroying their hearing; damaging their brains, severing their limbs, crushing their organs; inducing heart attacks, ulcers, paralysis, seizures; forcing them to inhale tobacco smoke, drink alcohol, and ingest various drugs, such as heroine and cocaine (Diner, 1985).

These harms are regrettable, vivisection's defenders acknowledge, and everything possible should be done to minimize animal suffering. For example, to lessen the stress caused by overcrowding, animals should be housed in larger cages. But, so the argument goes, there is no other way to secure the important human health benefits vivisection yields so abundantly, benefits that greatly exceed any harms endured by animals.

What the Benefits Argument Omits

Any argument that rests on comparing benefits and harms must not only state the benefits accurately, it must also do the same for the relevant harms. Advocates of the Benefits Argument fail on both counts. Independent of their tendency to minimize the harms done to animals and their fixed resolve to marginalize non-animal alternatives,[2] advocates overestimate the human benefits attributable to vivisection and ignore the massive human harms that are an essential part of vivisection's legacy. Even more fundamentally, they uniformly fail to provide an intelligible methodology for comparing benefits and harms across species. I address each of these three failures in turn.

The overestimation of human benefits

Proponents of the Benefits Argument would have us believe that most of the truly important improvements in human health could not have been achieved without vivisection. The facts tell a different story. Public health scholars have shown that animal experimentation has made at best only a modest contribution to public health. As a matter of fact, the vast majority of the most important health advances have resulted from improvements in living conditions (in sanitation, for example) and changes in personal hygiene and lifestyle, none of which has anything to do with animal experimentation (Greek and Greek, 2000, 2002; LaFollette and Shanks, 1996).

The underestimation of human harms

Advocates of the Benefits Argument conveniently ignore the hundreds of millions of deaths and the uncounted illnesses and disabilities that are attributable to reliance

Tom Regan

on the "animal model" in research. Sometimes the harms result from what reliance on vivisection makes available; sometimes they result from what reliance on vivisection prevents. The deleterious effects of prescription medicines are examples of the former.

Prescription drugs are first tested extensively on animals before being made available to consumers. As is well known, there are problems involved in extrapolating results obtained from studies on animals to humans. In particular, many medicines that are not toxic for test animals prove to be highly toxic for human beings. In fact, it is estimated that one hundred thousand Americans die and some two million are hospitalized annually because of the harmful effects of the prescription drugs they are taking (US General Accounting Office, 1990). That makes prescription drugs the fourth leading cause of death in America, behind only heart disease, cancer, and stroke – a fact that, without exception, goes unmentioned by the advocates of the Benefits Argument.

Worse, the Food and Drug Administration, the federal agency charged with regulating prescription drugs, estimates that physicians report only 1 percent of adverse drug reactions. In other words, for every adverse drug response reported, 99 are not. Clearly, before vivisection's defenders can reasonably claim that human benefits greatly exceed human harms, they must acknowledge how often and how much reliance on this model leads to prescribed therapies that cause massive human harm (Kessler, 1993).

Massive harm to humans is also attributable to what reliance on vivisection prevents. The role of cigarette smoking in the incidence of cancer is a case in point. As early as the 1950s, human epidemiological studies revealed a causal link between cigarette smoking and lung cancer. Nevertheless, repeated efforts, made over more than 50 years, rarely succeeded in inducing tobacco-related cancers in animals. Despite the alarm sounded by public health advocates, governments around the world for decades refused to mount an educational campaign informing smokers about the grave risks they were running. Today, one in every five deaths in the United States is attributable to the effects of smoking, and fully 60 percent of direct healthcare costs in the United States go to treating tobacco-related illnesses (American Cancer Society, 2004).

How much of this massive human harm could have been prevented if the results of vivisection had not directed government healthcare policy? It is not clear that anyone knows the answer, beyond saying, "A great deal. More than we will ever know." One thing we do know, however: advocates of the Benefits Argument contravene the logic of their argument when they fail to include these harms in their defense of vivisection.

Comparisons across species

Not to go unmentioned, finally, is the universal failure of vivisection's defenders to explain how we are to weigh benefits and harms across species. Before we can judge that vivisection's benefits for humans greatly exceed its harms to other animals, someone needs to explain how to make the relevant comparisons. For example: how much animal pain equals how much human relief from a drug that was tested on animals? It does not suffice to say – to quote the American philosopher Carl Cohen

– that "the suffering of our species does seem somehow to be more important than the suffering of other species" (Cohen and Regan, 2001: 291). Not only does this fail to explain how much more important our suffering is supposed to be, it offers no reason why anyone should think that it is.

Until those who support the Benefits Argument offer an intelligible methodology for comparing benefits and harms across species, the claim that human benefits derived from vivisection greatly exceed the harms done to animals is more in the nature of unsupported ideology than demonstrated fact.

Human Vivisection and Human Rights

The Benefits Argument suffers from an even more fundamental defect. Despite appearances to the contrary, the argument begs all the most important moral questions; in particular, it fails to address the role that moral rights play in assessing harmful, non-therapeutic research on animals. The best way to understand its failure in this regard is to position the argument against the backdrop of human vivisection and human rights.

Human beings have been used in harmful, non-therapeutic experiments for thousands of years (Annas and Grodin, 1992: chs. 1–7, 11; Homblum, 1999; Jones, 1993; Lansbury, 1985: chs. 1–4; Lederer, 1995: chs. 2, 4, 5). Not surprisingly, most human "guinea pigs" have not come from the wealthy and educated, not from the dominant race, not from those with the power to assert and enforce their rights. No, most victims of human vivisection have been coercively conscripted from, for example, the ranks of young children (especially orphans), elderly, severely developmentally disabled, insane, poor, illiterate, members of "inferior" races, homosexuals, military personnel, prisoners of war, and convicted criminals.

The scientific rationale behind vivisecting human beings needs little explanation. Using human subjects in research overcomes the difficulty of transposing results from another species to our species. If "benefits for humans" establishes the morality of animal vivisection, should we favor human vivisection instead? After all, vivisection that uses members of our own species promises even greater benefits.

No serious advocate of human rights can support such research. This judgment is not capricious or arbitrary; it is a necessary consequence of the logic of basic moral rights, including our rights to bodily integrity and to life. This logic has two key components (Regan, 1983, 2004b).

First, possession of these rights confers a unique moral status. Those who possess these rights have a kind of protective moral shield – an invisible "No Trespassing" sign, so to speak – that prohibits others from injuring their bodies, taking their life, or putting them at risk of serious harm, including death (Nozick, 1974). When people violate our rights, when they "trespass on our moral property," they do something wrong to us directly.

This does not mean that it must be wrong to hurt someone or even to take his life. When terrorists exceed their rights by violating ours, we act within our rights if we respond in ways that can cause serious harm to the violators. Still, what we are free to do when someone violates our rights does not translate into the freedom to override their rights without justifiable cause.

Second, the obligation to respect others' rights to bodily integrity and to life trumps any obligation we have to benefit others (Dworkin, 1977). Even if society in general were to benefit if the rights of a few people were violated, that would not make violating their rights morally acceptable to any serious defender of human rights. The rights of the individual are not to be sacrificed in the name of promoting the general welfare. This is what it means to affirm our rights. It is also why the basic moral rights we possess, as the individuals we are, have the moral importance that they do.

Why the Benefits Argument Begs the Question

Once we understand why, given the logic of moral rights, respect for the rights of individuals takes priority over any obligation we might have to benefit others, we can understand why the Benefits Argument fails to justify vivisection on nonhuman animals. Clearly, all that the Benefits Argument *can* show is that vivisection on non-human animals benefits human beings. What this argument *cannot* show is that vivi-secting animals for this purpose is morally justified. And it cannot show this because the benefits humans derive from vivisection are irrelevant to the question of animals' rights. We cannot show, for example, that animals have no right to life because we benefit from using them in research in which they are killed.

It does not suffice that advocates of the Benefits Argument insist that "there are no alternatives" to vivisection that will yield as many human benefits for two reasons. First, this reply is disingenuous. The greatest impediment to developing new scientif-ically valid non-animal alternatives and to using those that already exist is the hold that the ideology of vivisection currently has on medical researchers and those who fund them. Second, whether animals have rights is not a question that can be answered by saying how much vivisection benefits human beings. No matter how great the human benefits might be, the practice is morally wrong if animals have rights that vivisection violates.

But *do* animals have any rights? The best way to answer this question is to begin with an actual case of human vivisection.

The Children of Willowbrook

Now closed, Willowbrook State Hospital was a mental hospital located in Staten Island, one of New York City's five boroughs. For 15 years, from 1956 to 1971, under the leadership of New York University Professor Saul Krugman, hospital staff con-ducted a series of viral hepatitis experiments on thousands of the hospital's severely retarded children, some as young as 3 years' old. Among the research questions asked was: "Could injections of gamma globulin (a complex protein extracted from blood serum) produce long-term immunity to the hepatitis virus?" (Rothman and Rothman, 1984).

What better way to find the answer, Dr Krugman decided, than to separate the chil-dren in one of his experiments into two groups. In one, children were fed the live hepatitis virus and given an injection of gamma globulin, which Dr Krugman believed would produce immunity; in the other, children were fed the virus but received no injection. In both cases, the virus was obtained from the feces of other Willowbrook children who suffered from the disease. Parents or guardians were asked to sign a release form that would permit their children to be "given the benefit of this new preventive."

The results of the experiment were instrumental in leading Dr Krugman to conclude that hepatitis is not a single disease transmitted by a single virus; there are, he confirmed, at least two distinct viruses that transmit the disease, what today we know as hepatitis A and hepatitis B, the latter of which is the more severe of the two. Early symptoms include fatigue, loss of appetite, malaise, abdominal pain, vomiting, headache, and intermittent fever; then the patient becomes jaundiced, the urine darkens, the liver swells, and enzymes normally stored in the liver enter the blood. Death results in 1 to 10 percent of cases.

Everyone agrees that many people have benefited from this knowledge and the therapies that Dr Krugman's research made possible. Some question the necessity of his research, citing the comparable findings that Baruch Blumberg made by analyzing blood antigens in his laboratory, where no children were harmed or put at risk of grievous harm. But even if we assume that Dr Krugman's results could not have been achieved without experimenting on his uncomprehending subjects, what he did was wrong.

The purpose of his research, after all, was not to benefit each of the children. If that was his objective, he would not have withheld injections of gamma globulin from half of them. *Those* children certainly could not be counted among the intended beneficiaries. (Thus the misleading nature of the release form: not *all* the children were "given the benefit of this new preventive.")

Moreover, it is a perverse moral logic that says, "The children who received the injections of gamma globulin but who did not contract hepatitis – they were the real beneficiaries." Granted, if these children already had the hepatitis virus and failed to develop the disease because of the injections, it would make sense to say that they benefited from Dr Klugman's experiment. But these children did not already have the virus; they were given the virus by Dr Klugman and his associates. How can they be described as "beneficiaries"? If I hide a time bomb armed with an experimental device that I think will defuse the bomb before it is set to go off under your bed, and if the device works, you would not shake my hand and thank me because you benefited from my experiment. You would wring my neck for placing you in grave danger.

No serious advocate of human rights can accept the moral propriety of Dr Krugman's actions. By intentionally infecting all the children in his experiment, he put each of them at risk of serious harm. And by withholding the suspected means of preventing the disease from half the children, he violated their rights twice over: first, by willfully placing them at risk of serious physical illness; second, by risking their very lives. This grievous breach of ethics finds no justification in the benefits derived by others. To violate the moral rights of the few is never justified by adding the benefits for the many.

The Basis of Human Rights

Those who deny that animals have rights frequently emphasize the uniqueness of human beings. We not only write poetry and compose symphonies, read history and solve math problems, but we also understand our own mortality and make moral choices. Other animals do none of these things. That is why we have rights and they do not.

This way of thinking overlooks the fact that many human beings do not read history or solve math problems, do not understand their own mortality or make moral choices. The profoundly retarded children used by Dr Krugman in his research are a case in point. If possession of the moral rights to bodily integrity and life depended on understanding one's mortality or making moral choices, for example, then those children lacked these rights. In their case, therefore, there would be no protective moral shield, no invisible "No Trespassing" sign that limited what others were free to do to them. Lacking the protection of rights, there would not have been anything about the moral status of the children themselves that prohibited Dr Krugman from injuring their bodies, taking their life, or putting them at risk of serious harm. Lacking the protection of rights, Dr Krugman did not – indeed, he could not – have done anything wrong to the children. Again, this is not a position any serious advocate of human rights can accept.

But what is there about those of us reading these words, on the one hand, and the children of Willowbrook, on the other, that can help us understand how they can have the same rights we claim for ourselves? Where will we find the basis of our moral equality? Not in the ability to write poetry, make moral choices, and the like; not in human biology, including facts about the genetic make-up humans share. All humans are (in some sense) biologically the same. However, biological facts are indifferent to moral truths. Who has what genes has no moral relevance to who has what rights. Whatever else is in doubt, this we know.

But if not in some advanced cognitive capacity or genetic similarity, then where might we find the basis of our equality? Any plausible answer must begin with the obvious: the differences between the children of Willowbrook and those who read these words are many and varied. We do not denigrate these children when we say that our lives have a richness that theirs lacked. Few among us would trade our life for theirs, even if we could.

Still, as important as these differences are, they should not obscure the similarities. For, like us, these children were the subjects-of-a-life, *their* life, a life that was experientially better or worse for the child whose life it was. Like us, each child was a unique somebody, not a replaceable something. True, they lacked the ability to read and to make moral choices; nevertheless, what was done to these children – both what they experienced and what they were deprived of – mattered to them as the individuals they were, just as surely as what is done to us, when we are harmed, matters to us.

In this respect, as the subjects-of-a-life, we and the children of Willowbrook are the same; we are equal. Only in this case, our sameness – our equality – is morally important. Logically, we cannot claim that harms done to us matter morally, but that harms done to these children do not. Relevantly similar cases must be judged similarly. This is among the first principles of rational thought – a principle that has immediate application here. Logically, we cannot claim our rights to bodily integrity and to life, then deny these same rights in the case of the children. Without a doubt, if we have rights, so too did the children of Willowbrook.

Why Animals Have Rights

We routinely divide the world into animals, vegetables, and minerals. Amoebae and paramecia are not vegetables or minerals; they are animals. No one engaged in the vivisection debate thinks that the use of such simple animals poses a vexing moral question. By contrast, everyone engaged in the debate recognizes that using nonhuman primates must be assessed morally. All parties to the debate, therefore, must "draw a line" somewhere between the simplest forms of animate life and the most complex, a line that marks the boundary between those animals that do, and those that do not, clearly matter morally.

One way to avoid some of the controversies in this quarter is to follow Charles Darwin's lead. When he compares "the Mental Powers of Man and the Lower Animals," Darwin restricts his explicit comparisons to humans and other mammals (Darwin, 1976).

His reasons for doing so depend in part on structural considerations. In all essential respects, these animals are physiologically like us, and we, like them. Now, in our case, an intact, functioning central nervous system is associated with our capacity for subjective experience. For example, injuries to our brain or spinal cord can diminish our sense of sight or touch, or impair our ability to feel pain or remember. By analogy, Darwin thinks it is reasonable to infer that the same is true of animals that are most physiologically similar to us. Because our central nervous system provides the physical basis for our subjective awareness of the world, and because the central nervous system of other mammals resembles ours in all the relevant respects, it is reasonable to believe that their central nervous systems provide the physical basis for their subjective awareness.

Of course, if attributing subjective awareness to nonhuman mammals clashes with common sense, makes their behavior inexplicable, or is at odd with our best science, Darwin's position should be abandoned. But just the opposite is true. Every person of common sense agrees with Darwin. All of us understand that dogs and pigs, cats and chimps enjoy some things and find others painful. Not surprisingly, they act accordingly, seeking to find the former and avoid the latter. In addition, both humans and other mammals share a family of cognitive abilities (we both are able to learn from experience, remember the past, and anticipate the future) as well as a variety of emotions (Darwin (1976) lists fear, jealousy, and sadness). Not surprisingly, again, these mental capacities affect their behavior. For example, other mammals will behave one way rather than another because they remember which ways of acting had pleasant outcomes in the past, or because they are afraid or sad.

Moreover, that these animals are subjectively present in the world, Darwin understands, is required by evolutionary theory.[3] The mental complexity we find in humans did not arise from nothing. It is the culmination of a long evolutionary process. We should not be surprised, therefore, when Darwin summarizes his general outlook in these terms: "The differences between the mental faculties of humans and the higher animals, great as it is, is one of degree and not of kind" (Darwin, 1976: 80).

The psychological complexity of mammals (henceforth "animals," unless otherwise indicated) plays an important role in arguing for their rights. As in our case, so in theirs: they are the subjects-of-a-life, *their* life, a life that is experientially better or worse for the one whose life it is. Each is a unique somebody, not a replaceable something. True, like the children of Willowbrook, they lack the ability to read, write, or make moral choices; nevertheless, what is done to animals – both what they experience and those things of which they are deprived – matters to them, as the individuals they are, just as what was done to the children of Willowbrook, when they were harmed, mattered to them.

In this respect, as the subjects-of-a-life, other mammals are our equals. And in this case, our sameness, our equality, is important morally. Logically, we cannot maintain that harms done to us matter morally, but that harms done to these animals do not. Relevantly similar cases must be judged similarly. As was noted earlier, this is among the first principles of rational thought, and one that again has immediate application here. Logically, we cannot claim our rights to bodily integrity and life, or claim these same rights for the children of Willowbrook, and deny them when it comes to other mammals. Without a doubt, if humans have rights, so too do these animals.

Challenging Human and Animal Equality: Speciesism

The argument for animal rights sketched above implies that humans and other animals are equal in morally relevant respects. Some philosophers repudiate any form of species egalitarianism. According to Cohen (Cohen and Regan, 2001), whereas humans are equal in morally relevant respects, regardless of our race, gender, or ethnicity, humans and other animals are not morally equal in any respect, not even when it comes to suffering. Here are a few examples that will clarify Cohen's position.

First, imagine that a boy and girl suffer equally. If someone assigns greater moral weight to the boy's suffering because he is a white male from Ireland, and less moral weight to the girl's suffering because she is a black female from Kenya, Cohen would protest – and rightly so. Human racial, gender, and ethnic differences are not morally relevant differences. The situation differs, however, when it comes to differences in species. Imagine that a cat and dog both suffer as much as the boy and girl. For Cohen, there is nothing morally prejudicial, nothing morally arbitrary in assigning greater importance to the suffering of the children, because they are human, than to the equal suffering of the animals, because they are not.

Proponents of animal rights deny this. We believe that views like Cohen's reflect a moral prejudice against animals that is fully analogous to moral prejudices, like sexism and racism, that humans often have against one another. We call this prejudice speciesism (Ryder, 1975).

Empty Cages: Animals Rights and Vivisection | 85

For his part, Cohen affirms speciesism (human suffering does "somehow" count for more than the equal suffering of animals) but denies its prejudicial status. Why? Because according to him, while there are no morally relevant differences between human men and women, or between whites and blacks, "the morally relevant differences [between humans and other animals] are enormous" (Cohen and Regan, 2001: 62). In particular, human beings but not other animals are "morally autonomous"; we can, but they cannot, make moral choices for which we are morally responsible.

This defense of speciesism is no defense at all. Not only does it overlook the fact that a very large percentage of the human population (children up through many years of their life, for example) are not morally autonomous, but moral autonomy is not relevant to the issues at hand. An example will help explain why.

Imagine someone says that Jack is smarter than Jill because Jack lives in Syracuse, Jill in San Francisco. Where the two live is different, certainly, and where different people live sometimes is a relevant consideration – for example, when a census is being taken or taxes are levied. But everyone will recognize that where Jack and Jill live has no logical bearing on whether Jack is smarter. To think otherwise is to commit a fallacy of irrelevance familiar to anyone who has taken a course in elementary logic.

The same is no less true when a speciesist says that Toto's suffering counts for less than the equal suffering of Dorothy because Dorothy, but not Toto, is morally autonomous. If the question we are being asked is whether Jack is smarter than Jill, we are given no relevant reason for thinking one way or the other if we are told that Jack and Jill live in different cities. Similarly, if the question we are being asked is, "Does Toto's pain count as much as Dorothy's?" we are given no relevant reason for thinking one way or the other, even if we are told that Dorothy is morally autonomous, and Toto is not.

This is not because the capacity for moral autonomy is never relevant to our moral thinking about humans and other animals; sometimes it is. If Jack and Jill have this capacity, then they, but not Toto, will have an interest in being free to act as their conscience dictates. In this sense, the difference between Jack and Jill, on the one hand, and Toto, on the other, *is* morally relevant. But just because moral autonomy is morally relevant to the moral assessment of *some* cases, it does not follow that it is relevant in *all* cases. And one case in which it is not relevant is the moral assessment of pain. Logically, to discount Toto's pain because Toto is not morally autonomous is fully analogous to discounting Jill's intelligence because she does not live in Syracuse.

The question, then, is: can any relevant defensible reason be offered in support of the speciesist judgment that the moral importance of human and animal pain, equal in other respects, should always weigh in favor of the human being over the animal? To this question, neither Cohen nor any other philosopher, to my knowledge, offers a logically relevant answer. To persist in judging human pains (I note that the same applies to equal pleasures, benefits, harms, and so on, throughout all similar cases) as being more important than the like pains of other animals, because they are human pains, is not rationally defensible. Speciesism is a moral prejudice. Contrary to Cohen's assurances otherwise, it is wrong.

Other Objections, Other Replies

Not everyone who denies rights to animals is a speciesist. Some critics agree that human and nonhuman animals are equal in some morally relevant respects; for example, if a man and a mouse suffer equally, then their suffering should count the same, when judged morally. These critics simply draw the line when it comes to moral rights. Humans have them, other animals do not. Why this difference? The answers vary. Here, briefly, is a summary statement of some of the most common objections to animal rights together with my replies.[4] It is to be recalled that the rights in question are the moral rights to bodily integrity and life.

Objection: Animals do not understand what rights are. Therefore, they have no rights.

Reply: The children of Willowbrook, and all young children for that matter, do not understand what rights are. Yet we do not deny rights in their case, for this reason. To be consistent, we cannot deny animals rights.

Objection: Animals do not respect our rights. For example, lions sometimes kill innocent people. Therefore, they have no rights.

Reply: Children sometimes kill innocent people. Yet we do not deny rights in their case, for this reason. To be consistent, we cannot deny animals rights.

Objection: Animals do not respect the rights of other animals. For example, lions kill wildebeests. Therefore, they have no rights.

Reply: Children do not always respect the rights of other children; sometimes they kill them. Yet we do not deny rights in their case, for this reason. To be consistent, we cannot deny animals rights.

Objection: If animals have rights, they should be allowed to vote, marry, file for divorce, and immigrate, for example, which is absurd. Therefore, animals have no rights.

Reply: Yes, permitting animals to do these things is absurd. But these absurdities do not follow from claiming rights to life and bodily integrity, either in the case of animals or in that of the children of Willowbrook.

Objection: If animals have rights, then mosquitoes and roaches have rights, which is absurd. Therefore, animals have no rights.

Reply: Not all forms of animate life must have rights because some animals do. In particular, neither mosquitoes nor roaches have the kind of physiological complexity associated with being the subject-of-a-life. In their case, therefore, we have no good reason to believe that they have rights, even while we have abundantly good reason to believe that other animals, mammals in particular, do.

Objection: If animals have rights, then so do plants, which is absurd. Therefore, animals have no rights.

Reply: "Plant rights" do not follow from animal rights. We have no reason to believe, and abundant reason to deny, that carrots and cabbages are subjects-of-a-life. We have abundantly good reason to believe, and no good reason to deny, that mammals are. In claiming rights for animals, therefore, we are not committed to claiming rights for plants.

Objection: Human beings are closer to us than animals; we have a special relation to them. Therefore, animals have no rights.

Reply: Yes, we have relations to humans that we do not have to other animals. However, we also have special relations to our family and friends that we do not have to other human beings. But we do not conclude that other humans have no rights, for this reason. To be consistent, we cannot deny animals rights.

Objection: Only human beings live in a moral community in which rights are understood. Therefore, all human beings, and only human beings, have rights.[5]

Reply: Yes, at least among terrestrial forms of life, only human beings live in such a moral community. But it does not follow that only human beings have rights. Only human beings live in a scientific community in which genes are understood. From this we do not conclude that only human beings have genes. Neither should we conclude, using analogous reasoning, that only human beings have rights.

Objection: Humans have rights, and animals do not, because God gave rights to us but withheld rights from them.

Reply: No passage in any sacred book states, "I (God) give rights to humans. And I (God) withhold them from animals." We simply do not find such declarations in the Old Testament, the New Testament, the Torah, or the Koran, for example (Regan, 2004a: ch. 8; 1991: 143–58).

Objection: Animals have some rights to bodily integrity and life, but the rights they have are not equal to human rights. Therefore, human vivisection is wrong, but animal vivisection is not.

Reply: This objection begs the question; it does not answer it. What morally relevant reason is there for thinking that humans have greater rights than animals? Certainly it cannot be any of the reasons examined in the objections above. But if not in any of them, then where? The objection does not say.

The objections just reviewed have been considered because they are among the most important, not because they are the least convincing. Their failure, individually and collectively, goes some way towards suggesting the logical inadequacy of the anti-animal rights position. Morality is certainly not mathematics. In morality, there are no proofs like those we find in geometry. What we can find, and what we must live with, are principles and values that have the best reasons, the best arguments on their side. The principles and values that pass this test, whether most people accept them or not, are the ones that should guide our lives. Given this reasonable standard, the principles and values of animal rights should guide our lives.

Conclusion

As was noted at the outset, animals are used in laboratories for three main purposes: education, product safety testing, and experimentation, harmful non-therapeutic experimentation in particular. Of the three, the latter has been the object of special consideration. However, the implications for the remaining purposes should be obvious (Regan, 2004b: ch. 10). It is wrong when any animal's rights are violated in pursuit of benefits for others. It is conceivable, however, that some uses of animals for educational purposes – for example, having students observe the behavior of injured animals when they are returned to their natural habitat – may be justified. By contrast, it is not conceivable that using animals in product testing can be. Harming animals to establish what brands of cosmetics or combinations of chemicals are safe for humans is an exercise in power, not morality. In the moral universe, animals are not our tasters, and we are not their kings.

The implications of animal rights for vivisection are both clear and uncompromising. Vivisection is morally wrong. It should never have begun and, like all great

Tom Regan

speciesist evils, it ought to end, the sooner, the better. To reply that "there are no alternatives" not only misses the point, it is false. It misses the point because it assumes that the benefits humans derive from vivisection are derived morally when they are not, and it is false because, apart from using already existing and developing new non-animal research techniques, there is another, more fundamental alternative to vivisection. This is to stop doing it. When all is said and done, the only adequate moral response to vivisection is empty cages, not larger ones.[6]

Notes

1   One could attempt to justify animal vivisection by arguing that it is interesting, challenging, and yields knowledge, which is intrinsically good even when it is not useful. However, a defender of human vivisection could make the same claims, and no one (one hopes) would think that this settles any moral question in that case. Logically, there is no reason to judge animal vivisection any differently. Even if it is interesting and challenging, and even if it yields knowledge (which is intrinsically good), that would not make it right.

2   The philosopher Carl Cohen, the most strident defender of the Benefits Argument, is guilty on both counts. The most he will admit is that "some" animals "sometimes" are caused "some pain"; as for alternatives, he dismisses their validity as "specious." See his contribution (and my rejoinder) in Cohen and Regan (2001). I discuss his ideas more pointedly in the sequel.

3   Many people of good will do not believe in evolution. They believe that human existence is the result of a special creation by God, something that took place approximately 10,000 years ago. For these people, the evidence for animal minds provided by evolutionary theory is no evidence at all. Despite first impressions, the rejection of evolution need not undermine the main conclusions summarized in the previous paragraph. All of the world's religions speak with one voice when it comes to the question before us. Read the Bible, the Torah, or the Koran; study Confucianism, Buddhism, Hinduism, or Native American spiritual writings. The message is everywhere the same; mammals *most certainly* are psychologically present in the world. These animals *most certainly* have both preference and welfare interests. In these respects, all the world's religions teach the same thing. Thus, while the argument I have given appeals to the implications of evolutionary theory, the conclusions I reach are entirely consistent with the religiously based convictions of people who do not believe in evolution. And for those who believe both in God and in evolution? Well, these people have reasons of both kinds for recognizing the minds of other animals with whom we share a common habitat: the Earth.

4   I address a number of more philosophical objections in Regan (2001: 39–65).

5   Cohen (1997) favors this argument. I reply more fully in Cohen and Regan (2001: 281–4).

6   This chapter adapts material from my chapter in Cohen and Regan (2001) and Regan (2002).

References

American Cancer Society (2004). "Questions about smoking, tobacco, and health." Available at ⟨http://www.cancer.org/docroot/PED/content/PED_10_2x_Questions_About_Smoking_Tobacco_and_Health.asp⟩.

Annas, George J. and Grodin, Michael, A. (eds.) (1992). *The Nazi Doctors and the Nuremberg Code: Human Rights in Human Experimentation.* New York: Oxford University Press.

Cohen, Carl (1997). "Do animals have rights?" *Ethics and Behavior*, 7: 91–102.

Cohen, Carl and Regan, Tom (2001). *The Animal Rights Debate*. Lanham, MD: Rowman & Littlefield.

Diner, Jeff (1985). *Behind the Laboratory Door*. Washington, DC: Animal Welfare Institute.

Dworkin, Ronald (1977). *Taking Rights Seriously*. Cambridge, MA: Harvard University Press.

Darwin, Charles (1976). "Comparison of the mental powers of man and the lower animals." In Tom Regan and Peter Singer (eds.), *Animal Rights and Human Obligations* (pp. 72–81). Englewood-Cliffs, NJ: Prentice Hall.

Greek, C. Ray and Greek, Jean S. (2000). *Sacred Cows and Golden Geese: The Human Costs of Experiments on Animals*. New York: Continuum.

Greek, C. Ray and Greek, Jean S. (2002). *Specious Science: How Genetics and Evolution Reveal Why Medical Research on Animals Harms Humans*. New York: Continuum.

Homblum, Allen M. (1999). *Acres of Skin*. London: Routledge.

Jones, James (1993). *Bad Blood: The Tuskegee Syphilis Experiment*. New York: Free Press.

Kessler, D. A. (1993). "Introducing MedWatch: a new approach to reporting medication and adverse effects and product problems." *Journal of the American Medical Association*, 269: 2765–8.

LaFollette, Hugh and Shanks, Niall (1996). *Brute Science: Dilemmas of Animal Experimentation*. London: Routledge.

Lansbury, Coral (1985). *The Old Brown Dog: Women, Workers, and Vivisection in Edwardian England*. Madison, WI: University of Wisconsin Press.

Lederer, Susan E. (1995). *Subjected to Science: Human Experimentation in America Before the Second World War*. Baltimore, MD: John's Hopkins University Press.

Nozick, Robert (1974). *Anarchy, State, and Utopia*. New York: Basic Books.

Regan, Tom (1983). *The Case for Animal Rights*. Berkeley: University of California Press.

Regan, Tom (1991). *The Thee Generation: Reflections on the Coming Revolution*. Philadelphia, PA: Temple University Press.

Regan, Tom (2001). *Defending Animal Rights*. Champaigne: University of Illinois Press.

Regan, Tom (2002). "Empty cages: animals rights and vivisection." In Tony Gilland (ed.), *Animal Experimentation: Good or Bad?* (pp. 19–36). London: Hodder & Stoughton.

Regan, Tom (2004a). *Animal Rights, Human Wrongs: An Introduction to Moral Philosophy*. Lanham, MD: Rowman & Littlefield.

Regan, Tom (2004b). *Empty Cages: Facing the Challenge of Animal Rights*. Lanham, MD: Rowman & Littlefield.

Rothman, David and Rothman, Sheila (1984). *The Willowbrook Wars*. New York: Harper & Row.

Ryder, Richard (1975). *Victims of Science: The Use of Animals in Science*. London: David-Poynter.

US General Accounting Office (1990). *Report to the Chairman, Subcommittee on Human Resources and Intergovernmental Relations Committee on Government Operations, House of Representatives, FDA Drug Review, Postapproval Risk, 1976–1985*. Washington, DC: US Government Printing Office.

Further reading

Americans for Medical Advancement. Available at ⟨www.curedisease.com/⟩.

Americans for Medical Progress. Available at ⟨www.ampef.org/⟩.

The National Association for Biomedical Research. Available at ⟨www.nabr.org/⟩.

Physicians Committee for Responsible Medicine. Available at ⟨www.pcrm.org/⟩.

Animals and Their Medical Use

R. G. Frey

May we use animals in medicine, in order to enhance and to extend our lives?[1] That we do so is commonplace, and their numbers, especially given developments in genetic engineering, xenotransplantation, cloning, and the like have increased, even as questions have been raised today about their continued use. Thus – e.g., in the search for "designer" mice that exhibit just those features that we are breeding them to exhibit – vast numbers of mice as by-products are produced along the way. Again, we need only to imagine a series of successful xenotransplants to believe that a wholesale effort to produce human organs in animals would take root with a passion. Moreover, genetic engineering and cloning continue to take place in animal models, before being attempted in humans, and trial and error in this regard is likely to result in increasing numbers of animals created for these essentially human ends. In any event, it remains true today that millions of animals continue to be used in medical experiments, even if we ignore those animals used in countries about which we lack adequate information or which effectively hide their research projects from prying eyes.

Are we justified in using animals in these ways? This question must not be thought applicable only because some of our efforts at the moment result in failure. For it would apply even if, as in the case of the development of Salk vaccine for polio, we were eventually proved to be successful in eradicating a disease. If, for example, we were successful through genetic engineering and eventually gene therapy in eliminating Huntington's disease, would we have been justified in reaching this happy outcome through using animals in order to do so?

It is tempting to see this question as one pitting life enhancement and extension in humans against suffering in and the very lives of animals – tempting, in other words, to see the issue as one in which we have to decide whether it is permissible to use animal suffering and lives in order to benefit humans. Can we give a principled justification of this use (Frey, 1989, 2003)?

I believe that we can give a principled justification of this use, but I also believe that it is not easy to do so and that the kind of justification to be given exacts from us a cost that many people will not be prepared to pay. To this extent, I think the case for anti-vivisectionism is far stronger than most people suppose.

I do not have space here to give any very detailed account of how I think this case for animal experimentation goes and so for how we are to choose between animal and human lives, but I certainly can give an indication of some of the important issues that bear upon this choice.

The way I have put the central issue pits human and animal lives against each other. For it is surely wrong to maintain that the bulk of medical experimentation takes place for the benefit of animals themselves, even though it may be true, through the incorporation of discoveries into veterinary practice, that animals may indeed at times benefit from the experiments of which they are a part. Seen in this light, two obvious positions suggest themselves, namely, abolitionism on the one hand, or the view that it is always impermissible to use animals for human benefit, and, on the other, anything goes, or the view that it is always permissible so to use animals.

In the case of abolitionism, all experiments involving animals, whether invasive or not, however far advanced, whatever the likelihood of imminent or eventual success, must be stopped at once. In the case of anything goes we may do whatever we like to animals, short perhaps of excessive cruelty and wanton slaughter, in the name of medical advance, most especially if what is proposed figures in the research protocol that is subject to peer review and if it is carried out in accordance with what counts as usual levels of standard of care for the animals in question.

These two positions are, I think, too extreme. For different reasons, they strike me as objectionable; the second is objectionable in ways that take us to the very core of the choice between human and animal lives. Some more middle position strikes me as preferable, and I here set out what I take to be the first steps towards that middle position. Obviously, as with any middle position, it will be exposed to attack from the two extremes, and I will try to show how it might try to deal with some of those attacks.

The Abolitionist Appeal to Animal Rights

Abolitionism fails because the vehicle by which the case in favor is to be made cannot bear the weight that is put upon it. In the main today this vehicle is moral rights, but not just moral rights under any conception. For under most conceptions it will not follow that a case for human use of animals in experimentation will be barred. There will be merely a prima facie right on the animal's part, and such rights can have countervailing concerns arrayed against them and so possibly be outweighed. So, the theorist must come up with a conception of a right that bars precisely this effect.

Most mainstream rights theorists today either do not confer rights upon animals or do so only in some attenuated sense. Tom Regan, on the other hand, wants to confer upon animals rights in the sense of a trump, much along the lines of Ronald Dworkin's sense of certain moral rights as trumps in the human case (Regan, 2001).

R. G. Frey

That is, Regan conceptualizes rights as trumps to considerations of the general welfare. Giving animals rights in this sense disallows appeals to human benefit as a justification for the use of animals in medical research, since that would amount to using appeals to the general welfare to justify an infringement of an animal's right, say, to life. And what, other than appeal to human benefit, is animal research all about?

In Regan's picture, then, we are left with no way to raise the issue of animal research. For the only way moral perplexity registers at any deep level in Regan's picture is if some countervailing right comes into the matter, such that it then poses a conflict with the animal's right to life; then, one is on the familiar though nonetheless difficult terrain of a rights-theorist having to deal with a conflict of rights. Conflicts, of course, pose problems, and their resolution is not always easy. But in the case of medical experimentation there is no countervailing right: we do not have a right to use animals merely in order to benefit ourselves. Our convenience battles their right, and we lose. There is no way, then, to register the moral perplexity people feel between weighing and balancing human and animal lives and seeing whether there can be a case for using animals.

In Regan's picture, rights are powerful things to have, and, if animals have them, they have them in the full sense that human beings or persons do. Nothing contends against a right except another right, since anything else is not sufficiently weighty to contend; all medical research has is gain in human benefit. Thus, there is no way to portray the effects of polio vaccine as eliminating one of the scourges of human life in order to justify using monkeys in the research. All invasive (or, for that matter, non-invasive) medical research that is for our mere benefit must be stopped at once, for benefit can never trump rights. And that, basically, covers all the medical research that exists.

The problem here is that Regan has set out to endow animals with rights in so powerful a sense that nothing is able to contend with them. Certainly no argument grounded in human benefit can. Thus, to cite benefit as a ground for an argument in support of animal experimentation fails to appreciate the force of the rights that animals possess – rights that do not accept benefits to others as a reason for their infringement. It is not possible even to state the pro-research position, since all such statements inevitably run through human benefit and thus fail to grasp that, in Regan's eyes, animals have rights that trump our attempts to achieve that very benefit. It seems odd not even to be able to state the pro-research position, even if it ultimately turns out to be mistaken, which, I suspect, is one important reason why mainstream rights theorists continue to resist endowing animals with rights as trumps. But the matter seems worse than odd: to bestow upon the animal a right so strong that one thereby ensures that no case from benefit can even register and then to turn around and point to the fact that no case from benefit can overcome an animal's right (to life) seems to achieve the desired result by cooking the broth.

The "Anything Goes" View on Animals

If the abolition of animal experiments and the forgoing of all benefits in terms of the removal of illnesses and the prolongation of life that animal research confers or promises constitute an extreme position, so too does the "anything goes" position. On this position, anything we might do to animals appears justified, provided only that the benefit obtained, actually or potentially, is significant enough to offset massive animal suffering and deaths. (Obviously, what counts as "significant enough" here is contentious, and it can often appear, even to sympathetic observers to the research cause, that the benefit gained is trivial compared to the cost exacted.) This position also strikes me as extreme: to hold it on plausible philosophical grounds requires one, I think, to argue that animals do not matter morally in the sense that they are not members of the moral community. This strikes me as mistaken.

What is it about animals that does not warrant our moral concern? The usual answers are their pain and suffering and their lives. As for the former, everywhere today the medical research community has presented guidelines governing animal pain and suffering that insist that these be controlled, limited, mitigated where feasible, and justified in the research protocol and actual experiment, and the very care that researchers bestow upon their animals shows that they take animal suffering seriously, as does the insistence that animals be euthanized before they recover from certain painful experiments. If this level of care should be absent, government and funding oversight committees can challenge – indeed, close down – research projects.

On the other hand, to take seriously or to count morally animal suffering, but not animal lives, is implausible, since so much of the worry over suffering, whether in our case or theirs, is precisely owing to the way it can blight, impair, and destroy a life. If animal lives have no value, why should we care about ruining them? Why, in medical research, do we go to such great lengths to justify animal sacrifice? Why do we demand that such sacrifice be directly related to the achievement of the protocol's results? If, however, animal lives have some value, then we need to justify their destruction and the intentional diminution of their quality of life.

At bottom, adherents to the anything goes position must hold that there is a genuine moral difference between the human and animal cases, where pain and suffering and/or the destruction of valuable lives are concerned. But what is the genuine moral difference between burning a man and burning a baboon? Between infecting a man with a certain disorder and genetically engineering a baboon to be subject to that disorder? Between killing both man and baboon? What is at issue is not the claim that it is worse to do these things to the man, but that, according to the anything goes view, doing these things to the baboon is of no moral concern whatever, even though – as in the man's case – suffering occurs, the quality of life is drastically lowered, and killing takes place. If done to the man, these things are wrong; if done to the baboon, they are not. How can species membership make this difference? For it is not easy to see how species membership can constitute a moral difference between two relevantly similar acts of killing or lowering of quality of life; in the case of pain and suffering, I cannot see how they constitute a moral difference at all. Nor is my view any different if we substitute a rat for a baboon. If, in other words, we use something other than a primate by way of contrast, for, as will be seen below, my views of moral standing and the comparative value of lives assigns both to the lives of rats.

It should be obvious that these issues involved in the anything goes position take us to the very center of the debate on the choice between human and animal lives. I

R. G. Frey

will now elaborate on some of these issues, with an eye towards indicating how, if we must choose to use certain creatures in medical experimentation (since fully developed alternatives are not yet in existence), we are to choose those creatures (Frey, 1996b, 1997a, 1997b, 2002).

In my view, moral standing or considerability turns upon whether a creature is an experiential subject with an unfolding series of experiences that, depending upon their quality, can make that creature's life go well or badly. Such a creature has a welfare that can be positively and negatively affected; with a welfare that can be enhanced and diminished, a creature has a quality of life. In this guise, rodents and baboons are experiential subjects, with a welfare and a quality of life that our actions can affect, and this is so whether or not they are agents (which we think they are not) and whether or not they are the bearers of rights (which most of us think they are not). (Thus, agency and rights to my mind are irrelevant to the issue of moral standing.) Such creatures have lives that consist in the unfolding of experiences and so have a welfare and a quality of life, and while there may be some creatures about which I am uncertain of these things, the usual experimental subjects in laboratories are not among them. Thus, to my mind, these laboratory creatures have moral standing, and are, therefore, part of the moral community on the same basis that we are.

I reject, then, the central claims of the anything goes position. I see no reason to deny that rats and baboons feel pain, and I can see no moral difference between burning a man and burning a rat or a baboon. Pain is pain, and species strikes me as irrelevant; what matters is that a creature is an experiential one, and pain typically represents an evil in the lives of all such creatures, if only instrumentally, with respect to quality of life. But if pain and suffering count morally, it is hard to see why animal lives do not; as what concerns us so much about pain and suffering in our case is how these things can impair and significantly diminish the quality of life, they can also, it seems reasonable to believe, in the cases of all creatures who can experience them. No one takes intense pain or prolonged suffering, other things equal, to indicate a high or desirable quality of life, and animals, just as we ourselves, are living creatures with experiential lives, and thus beings with a quality of life. For these reasons, I think animal lives have value.

Thus, I reject abolitionism and the anything goes position. And I am not a speciesist. I do not think we can justify animal experimentation by citing species as a morally relevant reason for using animals in experiments. Nor do I deny that animals are members of the moral community; they are. So how is mine a position that can support some animal research?

The Value of Lives and Quality of Life

In my view, not all members of the moral community have lives of equal value, and where sacrificing life is concerned the threshold for taking lives of lesser value is lower than it is for taking lives of higher value.

It is deeply unpalatable to many to think that some lives are less valuable than others; they would dearly love it to be true that at least all human lives are equally valuable. But when I speak of not all lives being equally valuable I am not referring only to the difference between animal and normal adult human lives; I refer also to human lives themselves. A quality of life view of the value of a life makes the value of a life a function of its quality, and it is commonplace in the medical world today that not all human lives are of equal quality. Indeed, some people lead lives of such a quality that even they themselves seek release from them, as some cases involving a right to die and physician-assisted suicide make clear, and it seems somewhat bizarre to tell such people that, after all, according to some abstraction or other that one happens to believe, they really do have lives as valuable as normal adult human lives. There are some lives we would not wish upon even our worst enemies, and it seems mere pretense to claim that these are as valuable as normal adult human lives. Of course, no one can deny that some may find comfort in such abstractions that substitute for, or, indeed, may even reflect the old adage that all lives are equal in the eyes of God; but I take it to be equally obvious today that many people no longer find this venerable adage comforting.

What is at issue, then, is the comparative value of human and animal life. If we think that not all human lives have the same value, and if we think about the depths to which human life can tragically plummet, then it may well turn out that some animal lives have a higher quality than some human lives. And if we have to use lives in experiments (if, I emphasize, we *have* to), then surely we are here also to use the life of lower quality in preference to the life of higher quality. (Here, I allude only to the logic of the position, not to any side-effects that might easily bar one from acting on that logic.)

My account of how we are to decide the comparative value of human and animal life must be subject to scrutiny; that is, at the very least, I must have something to say, in addition to trying to assess the comparative value of these lives, for going about assessing it in the way I do.

One of the strengths of my position on the value of human and animal life, I think, is that it coheres nicely with recent discussions of the value of life in medical ethics and allied areas. In a word, what matters is not life but quality of life. The value of a life is a function of its quality, its quality of its richness, and its richness of its capacities and scope for enrichment; it matters, then, what a creature's capacities for a rich life are. The question is not, say, whether a rat's life has value; I agree that it does. The rat has an unfolding series of experiences and can suffer, and it is perfectly capable of living out a life appropriate to its species. The question is whether the rat's life approaches normal adult human life in quality (and so value) given its capacities and the life that is appropriate to its species, and this is a matter of the comparative value of such lives. Here, the claim is that normal adult human life is more valuable than animal life, based on greater richness and greater potentialities for enrichment. Autonomy or agency can help augment that value. How?

The claim is not that autonomy will inevitably or certainly enhance the value of a life; rather, it is that autonomy can be used for that purpose. In my view, autonomy is instrumentally, not intrinsically, valuable; its value depends upon the uses made of it, and, in the case, at least, of normal adult humans, those possible usages significantly enrich a life. To direct one's own life to secure what one wants; to make one's own choices in the significant affairs of life; to assume responsibility over a

R. G. Frey

domain of one's life and so acquire a certain sense of freedom to act; to decide how one will live, and to mold and shape one's life accordingly: these are the sorts of thing that open up areas of enrichment in a life with consequent effect upon that life's quality and value. Equally, however, it is possible that nothing of the sort will issue from the exercise of one's autonomy: just because a life's value can be augmented through the exercise of autonomy in no way shows that it is inevitably or always so augmented. The point behind all this, of course, is that these ways of augmenting the value of our lives are, arguably, not available to animals. It does not follow that animal life has no value (indeed, exactly the opposite is my view) or that an animal life cannot have greater value than some human life (again, it is my view that it can). Rather, what is centrally at issue is the comparative value of normal adult human life and animal life and how we go about deciding the matter.

Certainly, were we to adopt some Eastern religion or some form of quasi-religious metaphysic, it is possible that we might come to have a different view of animals and of how we stand to them. Indeed, we might come to take a different view of our relations to the animal kingdom (and to the inanimate environment), without any specifically religious impulses at all. This much is clear through poetry, through cultural differences we encounter among the individuals that make up our society, and through exposure to the art of different ages and cultures. From these different possible views of our relations to animals different possible accounts of the comparative value of human and animal lives may flow. But from the mere fact that different possible accounts of this comparative value may arise nothing follows per se about the adequacy of any single one. Argument must establish the soundness of such accounts, and if, e.g., one's claims about comparative value turn upon one's adoption of an Eastern religion, some religious metaphysic, or some abstraction (such as the claim that all life, whatever its quality, has the same "intrinsic" or "inherent" or "innate" value), then it is that religion, metaphysic, or abstraction that must be subjected to scrutiny.

As I have indicated, since not all human lives have the same richness and potentialities for enrichment, not all human lives are equally valuable. In fact, some human lives can be so blighted, with no or so little prospect for enrichment that the quality of such lives can fall well below that of ordinary, healthy animals.

It might be claimed that we can know nothing of the richness of animal lives, but ethologists and animal behaviorists, including some sympathetic to the "animal rights" cause, certainly think otherwise. How else, for example, could the claim that certain rearing practices blight animal lives be sustained? That we cannot know everything about the inner lives of animals, of course, in no way implies that we cannot know a good deal.

Quality of life views turn upon richness, and if we are to answer the question of the comparative value of human and animal life we must inquire after the richness of their respective lives. Intra-species comparisons are sometimes difficult, as we know in our own cases in, say, medical ethics; but such comparisons are not completely beyond us. Inter-species comparisons of richness and quality of life are likely to be even more difficult, though again not impossible. To be sure, as we descend from the "higher" animals, we lose behavioral correlates that we use to gain access to animals' interior states. Yet scientific work that gives us a glimpse into animal lives continues to appear, though it is hard as yet to make out much of a case for extensive richness (or so it appears).

Again, we must not simply think that criteria for assessing the richness of human lives apply straightforwardly to animals. Rather, we must use all that we know about animals, especially those closest to us, to try to gauge the quality of their lives in terms appropriate to their species. Then we must try to gauge what a rich, full life looks like to an animal of that species, and, subsequently, try to gauge the extent to which this approaches what we should mean in the human case when we say of someone that they had led a rich, full life. A rich, full life for the rat, science seems to suggest, does not approach a rich, full life for a human; the difference in capacities is just too great. However, if one is going to suggest otherwise, we need evidence of what in the rat's case compensates for its apparent lack of certain capacities, since by its behavior alone we do not normally judge it to have comparable richness.

In order to adopt a quality of life view of the value of a life of a rat, we must try to place ourselves in the rat's position, adopting the capacities and life of the rat. This may be difficult, but it does not appear impossible, and in the case of primates, or animals closer to ourselves, we may well be able to overcome many difficulties that impede our doing this with rats, chickens, or birds.

Can one drop the provision that quality be determined by richness and so avoid the judgment of reduced richness and quality in the animal case? However, richness does not determine quality of life – i.e., by the extent, variety, and quality of experiences – so what else can determine it?

Of course, one might just want to claim that humans and animals have different capacities and lives, and that each leads a rich and full though different life. But this makes it appear that we are barred from comparative judgments, when, in fact, the central ingredients of the respective lives – namely, experiences – appear remarkably alike. Surely I can know something of the lives of animals? Ethologists and animal behaviorists support this. But I have no reason to believe that the rat's life possesses anything like the variety and depth of ways of enrichment that normal adult human life possesses, and I need evidence to make me believe that, for example, one of the rat's capacities so enriches its life that it approaches normal adult human life in richness. The rat has a keener sense of smell, but how does this fact transform the richness of its life to approximate the richness that all the variety and depth of human capacities typically confer upon us? We need evidence to think this.

Two Senses of Moral Community

The ultimate problem over vivisection should now be obvious: we cannot be sure that human life will always and in every case be of higher quality than animal life. And if we are to use the life of lower quality in preference to the life of higher quality, assuming that some life or other has to be used, then we seem committed to using the human life of lower quality in this case. To be sure, this thought might (or will) outrage people, and adverse side-effects might (or will) make us choose otherwise. And I am not advocating that we use humans. What I am doing is trying to point out the logic of the position. Today, in medical ethics, we appeal constantly to con-

R. G. Frey

cerns of quality of life, and we treat quality as if it determines the value of a life. What can be cited that guarantees that human life will be more valuable than animal life? I cannot think of any such thing.

Well, it might be said, this just goes to show the problem with using quality of life talk in this kind of context; perhaps. But it seems a peculiar reason to, say, believe in God or to endorse some abstraction about the (greater) inherent value of all human life because one has thought through the logic of the position on animal experimentation and can find no argument that enables us to continue to only use animals for our benefit.

Finally, I think we must draw a distinction between two different senses of the moral community and show how this distinction fits the earlier discussion.

No one will deny that the patient in the final throes of Alzheimer's disease or the severely mentally enfeebled are members of the moral community in the sense of having moral standing, since they remain experiential subjects with a welfare and quality of life that can be augmented or diminished by what we do to them. This is true of all kinds of human beings who presently, as the result of disease or illness, have had the quality of their lives radically diminished, from those seriously in the grip of amyotrophic lateral sclerosis to those with Huntington's disease. All kinds of human beings presently live lives of massively reduced quality – reduced from the quality of life we find in healthy, normal, adult humans. Yet, they remain members of the moral community.

On the other hand, patients in a permanently vegetative state or anencephalic infants are more problematic candidates for membership in the moral community in this first sense. For though what happens to them may well affect the welfare and quality of life of other people, such as their parents, it is not obvious that they have experiential states that would include them as members of the moral community in their own right.

This first sense of moral community, then, is that in which the creatures that figure within it are all those who are morally considerable in their own right. I have indicated how I think (the "higher") animals get into this sense of the moral community, but it does not matter if one thinks that sentience in one of its senses encompasses animals, and so admits them. For all accounts of moral community in this first sense are accompanied by disclaimers that animals are moral agents – are capable, in the sense of agency that matters for the assessment of moral responsibility, of acting for and weighing reasons. They are not morally responsible for what they do, not because they fall outside the moral community in this first sense, but because they do not weigh reasons for action.

Animals, then, are morally considerable; what befalls them as patient or as the object of actions on our part that affect their welfare counts morally. This is no mean consideration, since, heretofore, many have insisted that animals are not morally considerable. But all the creatures that fall within the class of morally considerable beings are not alike: some are included as agents, some as patients, and there is a (further) sense of moral community in the case of the former that is not present in the case of the latter.

In this second sense of moral community, members have duties to each other, reciprocity of action occurs, standards for the assessment of conduct figure, reasons for action – especially where deviation from standards occurs – are appropriately offered and received. The absence of agency – the absence of the proffering and receiving of standards and reasons – matters because those who cannot do these things are not appropriately regarded as moral beings in the sense of being held accountable for their actions. To be accountable for what one does in a community of others who are accountable for what they do is not the same thing as being considerable in one's own right.

Plainly, some humans are not members of the moral community in this second sense: they are incapable of adducing standards for the evaluation of conduct, of conforming their conduct to those standards, and of receiving and weighing reasons for action. Disease and illness, for example, can undo agency in this sense. Equally, perfectly normal children and many of the very severely mentally enfeebled are not members of the moral community in this second sense. In this sense, many more humans can fall outside the moral community as a community of agents than fall outside the moral community as a community of morally considerable beings.

Some humans, such as those in permanently vegetative states and anencephalic infants, fall outside the moral community in both senses. (Hence, much of the controversy about, say, whether the former may permissibly be removed from respirators or whether the latter may permissibly be used as organ donors.) On the other hand, while a great many, if not all, animals arguably fall outside the moral community in the second sense, a great many fall inside the moral community in the first sense. Thus, there are some humans outside the moral community altogether, even while some animals are within the moral community in the first sense, and if one were going to select a creature upon which to experiment, this consideration, at least to morally serious beings, would seem to be relevant.

(I do not here address the question of whether creatures that fall outside the scope of both senses of moral community can be more easily killed than creatures that fall without the second but within the first sense. In fact, given some argument from potentiality that encompasses children, if it works, I do think the threshold for killing is lower in the cases of those in a permanently vegetative state and anencephalic infants. But the facts that affect this case for a lower threshold are too numerous and complex to go into on the present occasion.)

Membership in the moral community in this second sense has nothing to do with whether a being is morally considerable. Agency construed as acting and weighing reasons for action in the light of proffered standards is not required in order to be morally considerable in one's own right. So to what is it relevant? The answer, I believe, is that it *can* be relevant – note, the absence of any necessity in the matter – to augmenting and helping to determine the value of a life.

On a quality of life view of the value of a life, being a member of the moral community in the second sense can enrich one's life and, therefore, enhance its quality. It does this by informing the relations in which we stand to others and thus affecting how we live and judge our lives (Frey, unpublished).[2]

The moral relations in which we stand to each other are part of the defining characteristics of who we are. We are husbands, fathers, sons, brothers, friends, etc. These are important roles we play in life, and they are informed by a view of the moral

R. G. Frey

burdens and duties they impose on us, as well as the opportunities for action they allow us. Seeing ourselves in these relations is often integral to whom we take ourselves to be, from the point of view of the son as well as that of the father. In these relations, we come to count on others to entwine ourselves with the fate of at least some others, to be moved by what befalls these others, and to be motivated to affect the fates of these others to the extent that we can. Our lives, and how we live them, are affected in corresponding ways. Though there is no necessity in any of this, being a functioning member of a unit of this kind can be one of the great goods of life – enriching the very texture of the life one lives.

Again, binding ourselves to others, pledging ourselves to perform within the moral relations in which we stand to others, and holding ourselves responsible for shortcomings in this regard are all part of what we mean by being a functioning member of a moral community, within which we live our lives with other members. We come to count on others and they on us: the reciprocity of action and regard so characteristic of fully functioning moral communities find their root in these moral relations.

Part of the richness conferred on our lives by being a functioning member of a community characterized by these moral relations is that we come to take certain reasons for action almost for granted. We come to take the standards to be at least prima facie ones that it is appropriate by which to judge our own and others' actions. Again, there is no necessity about any of this, for we can come to reject the standards implied in the usual understanding of these moral relations in our societies in favor of others. But that these standards take a normative form by which we can evaluate reasons and actions, whatever their substance, is the crucial point; it is a normative understanding of these roles that seems crucial (1) to how we see ourselves within them, (2) to how we live our lives and judge many of our actions within those lives, and so (3) to how we judge how well or badly those lives are going.

Participation in such a community can enrich our lives; even in a minimal form, it achieves this by enabling us to cooperate over extensive areas of our lives with at least some others to achieve those of our ends that can only be achieved through cooperation. Put differently, the relations in which we stand to each other aid us in the pursuit of our ends and projects, many of which require the cooperation of others to achieve, and the pursuit of these ends and projects. The pursuit, as some philosophers would have it, of one's own conception of the good, adds enormously to how well we take our lives to be going. Since our welfare is, to a significant extent, bound up in these kinds of pursuits, to ignore this fact is to give a radically impoverished account of a "characteristically" human life. Since all these ends and projects can vary between persons, there is, in this sense, no life "appropriate" to our species, no single way of living to which every one of us "has" to conform. Agency, of course, enables us to select different ends and projects, to mold and shape our lives differently, and to achieve and accomplish different things.

But, beyond any such minimal form, we should note that the very way we live our lives as, for instance, fathers and sons – in order to fulfill what we see as our obligations within these moral relations – forms part of the texture and richness of our lives. We often cannot explain who we are and what we take some of our prized ends in life to be except in terms of these relationships in a moral community, and we often find it difficult to explain why we did something that obviously was at great cost to ourselves except through citing how we see ourselves linked to certain others. Thus, the fact that most humans are members of the moral community in the second sense is a powerful and important feature of their lives: they can live out lives of their own choosing, molded and shaped in the ways they want, in order to reflect and capture the ends and projects they want to pursue. More than this, they can live out these lives in a normative understanding, e.g., of the relationships that characterize their interactions with others, relationships in terms of which they see themselves as linked to these others. Here, also, the normative understanding of these relationships enables us to see our lives as going well or badly depending upon how these relationships are affected by what we do to others and by what they do to us. The reciprocity so characteristic of a fully functioning moral community is not the mere reciprocity of action; it is the reciprocity of judging actions from a normative point of view that sees something like enhancing the welfare of another as a reason for action.

Of course, much that we do mirrors the animal case, but agency enables us to fashion a life for ourselves, to live a life molded and shaped by choices that are of our own making and reflect, presumably, how we want to live. Achievement or accomplishment of ends so chosen in this regard is one of the great goods of human life and is one of the factors that can – again, there is no necessity in the matter – enrich individual human lives.

Conclusion

When we seek to compare human and animal life, then, in order to make judgments about the comparative richness of lives, account must be taken of this fashioning of a life for ourselves in a community of shared moral relations. Nothing I have said has implied that there may not be to animal lives features that enable them to make up in richness what agency can confer on ours. We should need evidence of this, of course, thus we have added reason to take seriously the subjective experiences of animals. All I am claiming is that agency can enable normal adult humans to enhance the quality and value of their lives in ways that no account of the activities that we share with animals comprehends (as best we know), and in seeking to give some account of the comparative value of human and animal lives, this kind of difference is obviously both relevant and important.

Notes

1 For a sample of my other writings on this issue, which I draw upon in this chapter, see Frey (1996a, 1997a, 1997b, 1998, 2001, and 2003).
2 What follows draws upon material referenced earlier, especially material from Frey (1997b, 2003, and unpublished manuscript).

R. G. Frey

References

Frey, R. G. (1989). "Vivisection, medicine, and morals." In T. Regan and P. Singer (eds.), *Animal Rights and Human Obligations* (pp. 223–6). Englewood Cliffs, NJ: Prentice-Hall.

Frey, R. G. (1995). "The ethics of using animals for human benefit." In T. B. Mepham, G. A. Tucker, and J. Wiseman (eds.), *Issues in Agricultural Bioethics* (pp. 335–44). Nottingham: University of Nottingham Press.

Frey, R. G. (1996a). "Medicine, animal experimentation, and the moral problem of unfortunate humans." *Social Philosophy and Policy*, 13: 181–211.

Frey, R. G. (1996b). "Autonomy, animals, and conceptions of the good life." *Between the Species*, 12: 8–14.

Frey, R. G. (1997a). "Moral community and animal research in medicine." *Ethics and Behavior*, 7: 123–36.

Frey, R. G. (1997b). "Moral standing, the value of lives, and speciesism." In H. Lafollette (ed.), *Ethics in Practice* (pp. 139–52). Oxford: Blackwell.

Frey, R. G. (1998). "Organs for transplant: animals, moral standing, and one view of the ethics of xenotransplantation." In A. Holland and A. Johnson (eds.), *Animal Biotechnology and Ethics* (pp. 190–208). London: Chapman and Hall.

Frey, R. G. (2001). "Justifying animal experimentation: the starting point." In E. F. Paul and J. Paul (eds.), *Why Animal Experimentation Matters* (pp. 197–214). New Brunswick, NJ: Transaction Publishers.

Frey, R. G. (2002). "Ethics, animals, and scientific inquiry." In J. Gluck, T. DiPasquale, and F. B. Orlans (eds.), *Applied Ethics in Animal Research* (pp. 13–24). West Lafayette, IN: Purdue University Press.

Frey, R. G. (2003). "Animals." In H. LaFollette (ed.), *Oxford Handbook to Practical Ethics* (pp. 151–86). New York: Oxford University Press.

Frey, R. G. (unpublished manuscript). "Lives within the moral community."

Regan, Tom (2001). *Defending Animal Rights*. Urbana: University of Illinois Press.

CAPITAL PUNISHMENT

A Defense of the
Death Penalty

Louis P. Pojman

Who so sheddeth man's blood, by man shall his blood be shed.

Genesis 9: 6

There is an ancient tradition, going back to biblical times but endorsed by the main-stream of philosophers, from Plato to Thomas Aquinas, from Thomas Hobbes to Immanuel Kant, Thomas Jefferson, John Stuart Mill, and C. S. Lewis, that a fitting punishment for murder is the execution of the murderer. One prong of this tradition, the *backward-looking* or deontological position, epitomized in Aquinas and Kant, holds that because human beings, as rational agents, have dignity, one who with malice aforethought kills a human being, forfeits his or her right to life and deserves to die. The other, the *forward-looking* or consequentialist tradition, exemplified by Jeremy Bentham, Mill, and Ernest van den Haag, holds that punishment ought to serve as a deterrent, and that capital punishment is an adequate deterrent to prospective murderers. Abolitionists such as Hugo Adam Bedau (1982, 1980) and Jeffrey Reiman (1998) deny both prongs of the traditional case for the death penalty. They hold that long prison sentences are a sufficient retributive response to murder and that the death penalty probably does not serve as a deterrent. I will argue that both traditional defenses are sound and together they make a strong case for retaining the death penalty. That is, I hold a combined theory of punishment: a backward-looking judgment that the criminal has committed a heinous crime plus a forward-looking judgment that a harsh punishment will deter would-be murderers are sufficient to justify the death penalty. I turn first to the retributivist theory in favor of capital punishment. Then I will examine the deterrence theory. Finally, I will present four of the major objections to the death penalty along with the retributivist's response to each of them.

In Favor of the Death Penalty

Retribution

The small crowd that gathered outside the prison to protest the execution of Steven Judy softly sang: "We Shall Overcome." But it didn't seem quite the same hearing it sung out of concern for someone who, on finding a woman with a flat tire, raped and murdered her and drowned her three small children, then said that he hadn't been "losing any sleep" over his crimes.

I remember the grocer's wife. She was a plump, happy woman who enjoyed the long workday she shared with her husband in their ma-and-pa store. One evening, two young men came in and showed guns, and the grocer gave them everything in the cash register.

For no reason, almost as an afterthought, one of the men shot the grocer in the face. The woman stood only a few feet from her husband when he was turned into a dead, bloody mess.

She was about 50 when it happened. In a few years her mind was almost gone, and she looked 00. They might as well have killed her too.

Then there was the woman I got to know after her daughter was killed by a wolf-pack gang during a motoring trip. The mother called me occasionally, but nothing that I said could ease her torment. It ended when she took her own life.

A couple of years ago I spent a long evening with the husband, sister and parents of a fine young woman who had been forced into the trunk of a car in a hospital parking lot. The degenerate who kidnapped her kept her in the trunk, like an ant in a jar, until he got tired of the game. Then he killed her.[1]

Human beings have dignity as self-conscious rational agents who are able to act morally. One could maintain that it is precisely their moral goodness or innocence that bestows dignity and a right to life on them. Intentionally taking the life of an innocent human being is so evil that the perpetrator forfeits his own right to life. He or she deserves to die.

The retributivist holds three propositions: (1) that all the guilty deserve to be punished; (2) that only the guilty deserve to be punished; and (3) that the guilty deserve to be punished in proportion to the severity of their crime. Thomas Jefferson supported such a system of proportionality of punishment to crime:

> Whosoever shall be guilty of rape, polygamy, sodomy with man or woman, shall be punished, if a man, by castration, if a woman by cutting through the cartilage of her nose a hole of one half inch in diameter at the least. [And] whosoever shall maim another, or shall disfigure him . . . shall be maimed, or disfigured in the like sort: or if that cannot be, for want of some part, then as nearly as may be, in some other part of at least equal value. (Quoted in van den Haag, 1975: 193)

One need not accept Jefferson's specific penalties to concur with his central point of some equivalent harm coming to the criminal.

Criminals such as Steven Judy, Timothy McVeigh, Ted Bundy (who is reported to have raped and murdered more than 100 women), and the two men who gunned down the grocer (mentioned in the quotation by Royko, above) have committed capital

Louis P. Pojman

offenses and deserve nothing less than capital punishment. No doubt malicious acts like the ones committed by these criminals deserve a worse punishment than death, but at a minimum, the death penalty seems warranted.

People often confuse retribution with revenge. While moral people will feel outrage at acts of heinous crimes, such as those described above by Royko, the moral justification of punishment is not vengeance, but desert. Vengeance signifies inflicting harm on the offender out of anger because of what he has done. Retribution is the rationally supported theory that the criminal deserves a punishment fitting to the gravity of his crime.

The nineteenth-century British philosopher James Fitzjames Stephens thought vengeance was a justification for punishment, arguing that punishment should be inflicted "for the sake of ratifying the feeling of hatred – call it revenge, resentment, or what you will – which the contemplation of such [offensive] conduct excites in healthily constituted minds" (1967: 152). But retributivism is not based on hatred for the criminal (though a feeling of vengeance may accompany the punishment). Retributivism is the theory that the criminal *deserves* to be punished and deserves to be punished in proportion to the gravity of his or her crime – whether or not the victim or anyone else desires it. We may all deeply regret having to carry out the punishment, but consider it warranted.

On the other hand, people do have a sense of outrage and passion for taking revenge on criminals for their crimes. Stephens was correct in asserting that "[t]he criminal law stands to the passion for revenge in much the same relation as marriage to the sexual appetite" (1863: 80). Failure to punish would no more lessen our sense of vengeance than the elimination of marriage would lessen our sexual appetite. When a society fails to punish criminals in a way thought to be proportionate to the gravity of the crime, the danger arises that the public would take the law into its own hands, resulting in vigilante justice, lynch mobs, and private acts of retribution. The outcome is likely to be an anarchistic, insecure state of injustice. As such, legal retribution stands as a safeguard for an orderly application of punitive desert.

Our natural instinct is for vengeance, but civilization demands that we restrain our anger and go through a legal process, letting the outcome determine whether, and to what degree, to punish the accused. Civilization demands that we not take the law into our own hands, but the laws should also satisfy our deepest instincts when they are consonant with reason. Our instincts tell us that some crimes, such as McVeigh's, Judy's, and Bundy's, should be severely punished, but we refrain from personally carrying out those punishments, committing ourselves to the legal processes. The death penalty is supported by our gut animal instincts as well as our sense of justice as desert.

The death penalty reminds us that there are consequences to our actions, and that we are responsible for what we do, so that dire consequences for immoral actions are eminently appropriate. The death penalty is such a fitting response to evil.

Deterrence

The second tradition justifying the death penalty is the forward-looking utilitarian theory of deterrence. This holds that by executing convicted murderers we will deter would-be murderers from killing innocent people. The evidence for deterrence is controversial. Some scholars, such as Sellin (1967) and Bedau, argue that the death penalty is not such a superior deterrent of homicides as long-term imprisonment. Others, such as Ehrlich (1975), make a case for the death penalty as a significant deterrent. Granted, the evidence is ambiguous and honest scholars can differ on the results. However, one often hears abolitionists claiming that the evidence shows that the death penalty fails to deter homicide. This is too strong a claim. The sociological evidence doesn't show either that the death penalty deters or that it fails to deter. The evidence is simply inconclusive. But a common-sense case can be made for deterrence.

Imagine that every time someone intentionally killed an innocent person he was immediately struck down by lightning. When mugger Mike slashed his knife into the neck of the elderly pensioner, lightning struck, killing Mike. His fellow muggers witnessed the sequence of events. When burglar Bob pulled his pistol out and shot the bank teller through her breast, a bolt leveled Bob, and his compatriots beheld the spectacle. Soon men with their guns lying next to them were found all across the world in proximity to the corpses of their presumed victims. Do you think that the evidence of cosmic retribution would go unheeded?

We can imagine the murder rate in the USA and everywhere else plummeting. The close correlation between murder and cosmic retribution would surely serve as a deterrent to would-be-murderers. If this thought-experiment is sound, we have a prima facie argument for the deterrent effect of capital punishment. In its ideal, prompt performance, the death penalty would likely deter most rational, criminally minded people from committing murder. The question then becomes: how do we institute the death penalty in a manner that would have the maximal deterrent effect without violating the rights of the accused?

The accused would have to be brought to trial more quickly, and the appeals process of those found guilty "beyond reasonable doubt" limited. Having DNA evidence should make this more feasible than hitherto. Furthermore, public executions of the convicted murderer would serve as a reminder that crime does not pay. Public executions of criminals seem an efficient way to communicate the message that if you shed innocent blood, you will pay a high price. Hentoff (2001: 31) advocated that Timothy McVeigh be executed in public so that the public themselves would take responsibility for such executions. I agree with Hentoff on the matter of accountability, especially if such publicity would serve to deter homicide.

Abolitionists sometimes argue that because the statistical evidence in favor of the deterrent effect of capital punishment is indecisive, we have no basis for concluding that it is a better deterrent than long prison sentences. If I understand these abolitionists, their argument presents us with an exclusive disjunct. Either we must have conclusive statistical evidence (i.e., a proof) for the deterrent effect of the death penalty, or we have no grounds for supposing that the death penalty deters. Many people accept this argument. Recently, a colleague said to me, "There is no statistical evidence that the death penalty deters," as if to dismiss the argument from deterrence altogether. This confuses the proposition "there is no statistical proof for the deterrence-effect" with the proposition "there is statistical proof against the deterrence-effect." This is a fallacious inference, for it erroneously supposes that only two

Louis P. Pojman

opposites are possible. There is a middle position that holds that while we cannot prove conclusively that the death penalty deters, the weight of evidence supports its deterrent effect. Furthermore, I think there are too many variables to hold constant for us to prove via statistics the deterrence hypothesis, and even if the requisite statistics were available, we could question whether they were cases of mere correlation versus causation. On the other hand, common-sense or anecdotal evidence may provide insight into the psychology of human motivation, providing evidence that fear of the death penalty deters some types of would-be criminals from committing murder. Granted, people are sometimes deceived about their motivation. But usually they are not deceived, and, as a rule, we should presume that they know their motives until we have evidence to the contrary. The general common-sense argument goes like this:

1 What people (including potential criminals) fear more will have a greater deterrent effect on them.
2 People (including potential criminals) fear death more than they do any other humane punishment.
3 The death penalty is a humane punishment.
4 Therefore, people (including criminals) will be deterred more by the death penalty than by any other humane punishment.

Since the purpose of this argument is to show that the death penalty very likely deters more than long-term prison sentences, I am assuming it is humane – that is, acceptable to the moral sensitivities of the majority in our society. Torture might deter even more, but it is not considered humane.

Common sense informs us that most people would prefer to remain out of jail, that the threat of public humiliation is enough to deter some people, that a sentence of 20 years will deter most people more than a sentence of 2 years, and that a life sentence will deter most would-be criminals more than a sentence of 20 years. I think that we have common-sense evidence that the death penalty is a better deterrent than long prison sentences. For one thing, as Wilson and Herrnstein (1986) have argued, a great deal of crime is committed on a cost-benefit schema, wherein the criminal engages in some form of risk assessment as to his or her chances of getting caught and punished in some manner. If he or she estimates the punishment to be mild, the crime becomes inversely attractive, and vice versa. The fact that those who are condemned to death generally do everything in their power to get their sentences postponed or reduced to long-term prison sentences, in the way lifers do not, shows that they fear death more than life in prison.

The point is this: imprisonment constitutes one evil, the loss of freedom, but the death penalty imposes a more severe loss, that of life itself. If you lock me up, I may work for a parole or pardon. I may learn to live stoically with diminished freedom, and I can plan for the day when my freedom has been restored. But if I believe that my crime may lead to death, or loss of freedom followed by death, then I have more to fear than mere imprisonment. I am faced with a great evil plus an even greater evil. I fear death more than imprisonment because it alone takes from me all future possibility.

A Defense of the Death Penalty

I am not claiming that the fear of legal punishment is all that keeps us from criminal behavior. Moral character, good habit, fear of being shamed, peer pressure, fear of authority, or the fear of divine retribution may have a greater influence on some people. However, many people will be deterred from crime, including murder, by the threat of severe punishment. The abolitionist points out that many would-be murderers simply do not believe they will be caught. Perhaps this is true for some. While the fantastic egoist has delusions of getting away with his crime, many would-be criminals are not so bold or delusionary.

Former Prosecuting Attorney for the State of Florida, Richard Gernstein, has set forth the common sense case for deterrence. First of all, he claims, the death penalty certainly deters the murderer from any further murders, including those he or she might commit within the prison where he is confined. Secondly, statistics cannot tell us how many potential criminals have refrained from taking another's life through fear of the death penalty. He quotes Judge Hyman Barshay of New York: "The death penalty is a warning, just like a lighthouse throwing its beams out to sea. We hear about shipwrecks, but we do not hear about the ships the lighthouse guides safely on their way. We do not have proof of the number of ships its saves, but we do not tear the lighthouse down" (Gernstein, 1960: 253).

Some of the common-sense evidence is anecdotal, as the following quotation shows. British Member of Parliament Arthur Lewis explains how he was converted from an abolitionist to a supporter of the death penalty:

One reason that has stuck in my mind, and which has proved [deterrence] to me beyond question, is that there was once a professional burglar in [my] constituency who consistently boasted of the fact that he had spent about one-third of his life in prison. . . . He said to me "I am a professional burglar. Before we go out on a job we plan it down to every detail. Before we go into the boozer to have a drink we say 'Don't forget, no shooters' – shooters being guns." He adds: "We did our job and didn't have shooters because at that time there was capital punishment. Our wives, girlfriends and our mums said, 'Whatever you do, do not carry a shooter because if you are caught you might be topped [executed].' If you do away with capital punishment they will all be carrying shooters." (British Parliamentary Debates, 1982)

It is difficult to know how widespread this reasoning is. My own experience corroborates this testimony. Growing up in the infamous Cicero, Illinois, home of Al Capone and the Mafia, I had friends, including a brother, who drifted into crime, mainly burglary and larceny. It was common knowledge that one stopped short of killing in the act of robbery. A prison sentence could be dealt with – especially with a good lawyer – but being convicted of murder, which at that time included a reasonable chance of being electrocuted, was an altogether different matter. No doubt exists in my mind that the threat of the electric chair saved the lives of some of those who were robbed in my town. No doubt some crimes are committed in the heat of passion or by the temporally (or permanently) insane, but many are committed through a process of risk assessment. Burglars, kidnappers, traitors, and vindictive people will sometimes be restrained by the threat of death. We simply don't know how much capital punishment deters, but this sort of common-sense,

Louis P. Pojman

anecdotal evidence must be taken into account in assessing the institution of capital punishment.

John Stuart Mill admitted that capital punishment does not inspire terror in hardened criminals, but it may well make an impression on prospective murderers:

> As for what is called the failure of the death punishment, who is able to be judge of that? We partly know who those are whom it has not deterred; but who is there who knows whom it has deterred, or how many human beings it has saved who would have lived to be murderers if that awful association had not been thrown round the idea of murder from their earliest infancy. (1986: 97–104)

Mill's points are well taken: first, not everyone will be deterred by the death penalty, but some will; second, the potential criminal need not consciously calculate a cost-benefit analysis regarding his crime to be deterred by the threat. The idea of the threat may have become a subconscious datum "from their earliest infancy." The repeated announcement and regular exercise of capital punishment may have deep causal influence.

Gernstein quotes the British Royal Commission on Capital Punishment (1949–53), which is one of the most thorough studies on the subject and which concluded that there was evidence that the death penalty has some deterrent effect on normal human beings. Some of its evidence in favor of the deterrence effect includes:

1 Criminals who have committed an offense punishable by life imprisonment, when faced with capture, refrained from killing their captor though by killing, escape seemed probable. When asked why they refrained from the homicide, quick responses indicated a willingness to serve life sentence, but not risk the death penalty.
2 Criminals about to commit certain offenses refrained from carrying deadly weapons. Upon apprehension, answers to questions concerning absence of such weapons indicated a desire to avoid more serious punishment by carrying a deadly weapon, and also to avoid use of the weapon which could result in imposition of the death penalty.
3 Victims have been removed [by criminals] from a capital-punishment State to a non-capital-punishment State to allow the murderer opportunity for homicide without threat to his own life. This in itself demonstrates that the death penalty is considered by some would-be-killers. (Gernstein, 1960: 253)

Gernstein then quotes former District Attorney of New York, Frank S. Hogan, representing himself and his associates:

> We are satisfied from our experience that the deterrent effect is both real and substantial ... for example, from time to time accomplices in felony murder state with apparent truthfulness that in the planning of the felony they strongly urged the killer not to resort to violence. From the context of these utterances, it is apparent that they were led to these warnings to the killer by fear of the death penalty that they realized might follow the taking of life. Moreover, victims of hold-ups have occasionally reported that one of the robbers expressed a desire to kill them and was dissuaded from so doing by a confederate. Once again, we think it not unreasonable to suggest that fear of the death penalty played a role in some of these intercessions.

A Defense of the Death Penalty

On a number of occasions, defendants being questioned in connection with homicide have shown a striking terror of the death penalty. While these persons have in fact perpetrated homicide, we think that their terror of the death penalty must be symptomatic of the attitude of many others of their type, as a result of which many lives have been spared. (Gernstein, 1960: 253–4)

It seems likely that the death penalty does not deter as much as it could do, because of its inconsistent and rare use. For example, in 1949, out of an estimated 23,370 cases of murder, non-negligent manslaughter, and rape, there were only 119 executions carried out in the United States. In 1953, out of 27,000 murder cases, only 62 executions for those crimes took place. Few executions were carried out in the 1960s and none at all from 1967 to 1977. Gernstein points out that at that rate a criminal's chances of escaping execution are better than 100 to 1 (1960: 254). Actually, since Gernstein's report, the figures have become even more weighted against the chances of the death penalty. In 1993, there were 24,526 cases of murder and non-negligent manslaughter and only 56 executions, while in 1994 there were 23,305 cases of murder and non-negligent manslaughter and only 31 executions – a ratio of more than 750 to 1 in favor of the criminal. The average length of stay for a prisoner executed in 1994 was ten years and two months. If potential murderers perceived the death penalty as a highly probable outcome of murder, would they not be more reluctant to kill? Gernstein notes:

The commissioner of Police of London, England, in his evidence before the Royal Commission on Capital Punishment, told of a gang of armed robbers who continued operations after one of their members was sentenced to death and his sentence commuted to penal servitude, but the same gang disbanded and disappeared when, on a later occasion, two others were convicted of murder and hanged. (1960: 254)

Gernstein sums up his data:

Surely it is a common-sense argument, based on what is known of human nature, that the death penalty has a deterrent effect particularly for certain kinds of murderers. Furthermore, as the Royal Commission opined, the death penalty helps to educate the conscience of the whole community, and it arouses among many people a quasi-religious sense of awe. In the mind of the public there remains a strong association between murder and the penalty of death. Certainly one of the factors which restrains some people from murder is fear of punishment and surely, since people fear death more than anything else, the death penalty is the most effective deterrent. (1960: 254)

A retentionist is someone who advocates retaining the death penalty as a mode of punishment for some crimes. Given the retributivist argument for the death penalty based on desert, the retentionist does not have to prove that the death penalty deters *better* than long-prison sentences, but if the death penalty is deemed at least as effective as its major alternative, it would be justified. If evidence existed that life imprisonment were a *more effective* deterrent, the retentionist might be hard-pressed to defend it on retributivist lines alone. My view is that the desert argument plus the common-sense evidence – being bolstered by the following argument, the Best Bet Argument – strongly supports retention of the death penalty.

Louis P. Pojman

Ernest van den Haag (1968) set forth what he calls the Best Bet Argument. He argues that even though we don't know for certain whether the death penalty deters or prevents other murders, we should bet that it does. Indeed, due to our ignorance, any social policy we take is a gamble. Not to choose capital punishment for first-degree murder is as much a bet that capital punishment doesn't deter as choosing the policy is a bet that it does. There is a significant difference in the betting, however, in that to bet against capital punishment is to bet against the innocent and for the murderer, while to bet for it is to bet against the murderer and for the innocent.

The point is this: we are accountable for what we let happen, as well as for what we actually do. If I fail to bring up my children properly, so that they are a menace to society, I am to some extent responsible for their bad behavior. I could have caused it to be somewhat better. If I have good evidence that a bomb will blow up the building you are working in and fail to notify you (assuming I can), I am partly responsible for your death, if and when the bomb explodes. So we are responsible for what we omit doing, as well as for what we do. Purposefully to refrain from a lesser evil which we know will allow a greater evil to occur is to be at least partially responsible for the greater evil. This responsibility for our omissions underlies van den Haag's argument, to which we now return.

Suppose that we choose a policy of capital punishment for capital crimes. In this case we are betting that the death of some murderers will be more than compensated for by the lives of some innocents not being murdered (either by these murderers or by others who would have murdered). If we are right, we have saved the lives of the innocent. If we are wrong, we have, unfortunately, sacrificed the lives of some murderers. But say we choose not to have a social policy of capital punishment. If capital punishment doesn't work as a deterrent, we've come out ahead, but if it does work, then we've missed an opportunity to save innocent lives. If we value the saving of innocent lives more highly than we do the loss of the guilty, then to bet on a policy of capital punishment turns out to be rational. Since the innocent have a greater right to life than the guilty, it is our moral duty to adopt a policy that has a chance of protecting them from potential murderers.

It is noteworthy that prominent abolitionists, such as Charles Black, Hugo Adam Bedau, Ramsey Clark, and Henry Schwartzchild, have admitted to Ernest van den Haag that even if every execution were to deter 100 murders, they would oppose it, from which van den Haag concludes: "to these abolitionist leaders, the life of every murderer is more valuable than the lives of a hundred prospective victims, for these abolitionists would spare the murderer, even if doing so will cost a hundred future victims their lives." Black and Bedau said they would favor abolishing the death penalty even if they knew that doing so would increase the homicide rate by 1,000 percent.[2] This response of abolitionists is puzzling, since one of Bedau's arguments against the death penalty is that it doesn't bring back the dead: "We cannot do anything for the dead victims of crime. (How many of those who oppose the death penalty would continue to do so if, *mirabile dictu*, executing the murderer might bring the victim back to life?)" (Bedau, 1989: 190). Apparently, he would support the death penalty if it brought a dead victim back to life, but not if it prevented 100 innocent victims from being murdered.

If the Best Bet Argument is sound, or if the death penalty does deter would-be murderers, as common sense suggests, then we should support some uses of the death penalty. It should be used for those who commit first-degree murder, for whom no mitigating factors are present, and especially for those who murder police officers, prison guards, and political leaders. Many states rightly favor it for those who murder while committing another crime, e.g., burglary or rape. It should also be used for treason and terrorist bombings. It should also be considered for egregious white-collar crimes such as for bank managers who embezzle the savings of the public. The Savings & Loan scandals of the 1980s and the corporate scandals of 2002, involving wealthy bank officials and CEOs engaging in fraudulent business behavior, ruined the lives of many people, while providing the perpetrators with golden parachutes. This gross violation of the public trust may well warrant the electric chair.

Objections to the Death Penalty

Finally, let us examine four of the major objections to death penalty, as well as the retentionist's responses to those objections.

Objection 1

Capital punishment is a morally unacceptable thirst for revenge. As former British Prime Minister Edward Heath put it:

> The real point that is emphasized to me by many constituents is that even if the death penalty is not a deterrent, murderers deserve to die. This is the question of revenge. Again, this will be a matter of moral judgment for each of us. I do not believe in revenge. If I were to become the victim of terrorists, I would not wish them to be hanged or killed in any other way for revenge. All that would do is deepen the bitterness that already tragically exists in the conflicts we experience in society, particularly in Northern Ireland. (British Parliamentary Debates, 1982)

Response   Retributivism, as I argued above, is not the same thing as revenge, although the two attitudes are often intermixed in practice. Revenge is a personal response to a perpetrator for an injury. Retribution is an impartial and impersonal response to an offender for an offense done against someone. You cannot desire revenge for the harm of someone to whom you are indifferent. Revenge always involves personal concern for the victim. Retribution is not personal but is based on objective factors: the criminal has deliberately harmed an innocent party and so deserves to be punished, whether I wish it or not. I would agree that I or my son or daughter deserves to be punished for our crimes, but I don't wish any vengeance on myself or my son or daughter.

Furthermore, while revenge often leads us to exact more suffering from the offender than the offense warrants, retribution stipulates that the offender be punished in proportion to the gravity of the offense. In this sense, the *lex talionis* that we find in the Old Testament is actually a progressive rule, where retribution replaces revenge as the mode of punishment. It says that there are limits to what one may do to the offender. Revenge demands a life for an eye or a tooth, but Moses provides a rule that exacts a penalty equal to the harm done by the offender.

Objection 2

Perhaps the murderer does deserve to die, but by what authority does the state execute him or her? Both the Old and New Testament say, "'Vengeance is mine, I will repay,' says the Lord" (Deut. 32: 35 and Romans 12: 19). You need special authority to justify taking the life of a human being.

Response   The objector fails to note that the New Testament passage continues with a support of the right of the state to execute criminals in the name of God: "Let every person be subjected to the governing authorities. For there is no authority except from God, and those that exist have been instituted by God. Therefore he who resists what God has appointed, and those who resist will incur judgment. . . . If you do wrong, be afraid, for [the authority] does not bear the sword in vain; he is the servant of God to execute his wrath on the wrongdoer" (Romans 13: 1–4). So, according to the Bible, the authority to punish, which presumably includes the death penalty, comes from God.

But we need not appeal to a religious justification for capital punishment. We can cite the state's role in dispensing justice. Just as the state has the authority (and duty) to act justly in allocating scarce resources, in meeting the minimal needs of its (deserving) citizens, in defending its citizens from violence and crime, and in not waging unjust wars, so too it has the authority, flowing from its mission to promote justice and the good of its people, to punish the criminal. If the criminal, as one who has forfeited a right to life, deserves to be executed, especially if it will likely deter would-be murderers, the state has a duty to execute those convicted of first-degree murder.

Objection 3

Miscarriages of justice occur. Capital punishment is to be rejected because of human fallibility in convicting innocent parties and sentencing them to death. In a survey done in 1985, Bedau and Radelet found that 25 of the 7,000 persons executed in the United States between 1900 and 1985 were innocent of capital crimes (quoted in van den Haag, 1986: 1664). While some compensation is available to those unjustly imprisoned, the death sentence is irrevocable. We can't compensate the dead. As John Maxton, a British Member of Parliament puts it, "If we allow one innocent person to be executed, morally we are committing the same, or, in some ways, a worse crime than the person who committed the murder" (British Parliamentary Debates, 1982).

Response   Mr Maxton is incorrect in saying that mistaken judicial execution is morally the same or worse than murder, for a deliberate intention to kill the innocent occurs in a murder, whereas no such intention occurs in wrongful capital punishment.

Sometimes this objection is framed as follows. It is better to let ten criminals go free than to execute one innocent person. If this dictum is a call for safeguards, then

A Defense of the Death Penalty   117

it is well taken; but somewhere there seems to be a limit on the tolerance of society towards capital offenses. Would these abolitionists argue that it is better that 50 or 100 or 1,000 murderers go free than that one guilty person be executed? Society has a right to protect itself from capital offenses even if this means taking a tiny chance of executing an innocent person. If the basic activity or process is justified, then it is regrettable, but morally acceptable, that some mistakes are made. Fire trucks occasionally kill innocent pedestrians while racing to fires, but we accept these losses as justified by the greater good of the activity of using fire trucks. We judge the use of automobiles to be acceptable, even though such use causes an average of 50,000 traffic fatalities each year. We accept the morality of a defensive war even though it will result in our troops accidentally or mistakenly killing innocent people.

The fact that we can err in applying the death penalty should give us pause and cause us to build a better appeals process into the judicial system. Such a process is already in place in the American and British legal systems. That occasional error may be made, regrettable though this is, is not a sufficient reason for us to refuse to use the death penalty, if on balance it serves a just and useful function.

Furthermore, abolitionists are simply misguided in thinking that prison sentences are a satisfactory alternative here. It's not clear that we can always or typically compensate innocent parties who waste away in prison. Jacques Barzun has argued that a prison sentence can be worse than death and carries all the problems that the death penalty does regarding the impossibility of compensation.

> In the preface of his useful volume of cases, *Hanged in Error*, Mr Leslie Hale refers to the tardy recognition of a minor miscarriage of justice – one year in jail: "The prisoner emerged to find that his wife had died and that his children and his aged parents had been removed to the workhouse. By the time a small payment had been assessed as 'compensation' the victim was incurably insane." So far we are as indignant with the law as Mr Hale. But what comes next? He cites the famous Evans case, in which it is very probable that the wrong man was hanged, and he exclaims: "While such mistakes are possible, should society impose an irrevocable sentence?" Does Mr. Hale really ask us to believe that the sentence passed on the first man, whose wife died and who went insane, was in any sense *revocable?* Would not any man rather be Evans dead than that other wretch "emerging" with his small compensation and his reason for living gone? (Barzun, 162: 188–9)

The abolitionist is incorrect in arguing that death is different from long-term prison sentences because it is irrevocable. Imprisonment also takes good things away from us that may never be returned. We cannot restore to the inmate the freedom or opportunities he or she has lost. Suppose an innocent 25-year-old man is given a life sentence for murder and 30 years later the error is discovered and he is set free. Suppose he values 3 years of freedom to every one year of life. That is, he would rather live 10 years as a free man than 30 as a prisoner. Given this man's values, the criminal justice system has taken the equivalent of 10 years of life from him. If he lives until he is 65, he has, as far as his estimation is concerned, lost 10 years, so that he may be said to have lived only 55 years.

The numbers in this example are arbitrary, but the basic point is sound. Most of us would prefer a shorter life of higher quality to a longer one of low quality. Death prevents all subsequent quality, but imprisonment also irrevocably harms one by diminishing the quality of life of the prisoner.

Objection 4

The death penalty is unjust because it discriminates against the poor and minorities, particularly African Americans, over against rich people and whites. Former Supreme Court Justice William Douglas wrote that "a law which reaches that [discriminatory] result in practice has no more sanctity than a law that in terms provides the same" (*Furman* v. *Georgia*, 1972). Stephen Nathanson argues that, "in many cases, whether one is treated justly or not depends not only on what one deserves but on how other people are treated" (2001: 62). He offers the example of unequal justice in a plagiarism case: "I tell the students in my class that anyone who plagiarizes will fail the course. Three students plagiarize papers, but I give only one a failing grade. The other two, in describing their motivation, win my sympathy, and I give them passing grades" (2001: 62, 60). Arguing that this is patently unjust, he likens this case to the imposition of the death penalty and concludes that it too is unjust.

Response First of all, it is not true that a law that is applied in a discriminatory manner is unjust. Unequal justice is no less justice, however uneven its application. The discriminatory application, not the law itself, is unjust. A just law is still just even if it is not applied consistently. For example, a friend of mine once got two speeding tickets during a 100-mile trip (having borrowed my car). He complained to the police officer who gave him the second ticket that many drivers were driving faster than he was at the time. They had escaped detection, he argued, so it wasn't fair for him to get two tickets on one trip. The officer acknowledged the imperfections of the system but, justifiably, had no qualms about giving him the second ticket. Unequal justice is still justice, however regrettable. So Justice Douglas is wrong in asserting that discriminatory results invalidate the law itself. Discriminatory practices should be reformed, and in many cases they can be. But imperfect practices in themselves do not entail that the laws engendering these practices are themselves are unjust.

With regard to Nathanson's analogy with the plagiarism case, two things should be said against it. First, if the teacher is convinced that the motivational factors are mitigating factors, then he or she may be justified in passing two of the plagiarizing students. Suppose that the one student did no work whatsoever, showed no interest (Nathanson's motivation factor) in learning, and exhibited no remorse in cheating, whereas the other two spent long hours seriously studying the material and, upon apprehension, showed genuine remorse for their misdeeds. To be sure, they yielded to temptation at certain – though limited – sections of their long papers, but the vast majority of their papers represented their own diligent work. Suppose, as well, that all three had C averages at this point. The teacher gives the unremorseful, gross plagiarizer an F, but relents and gives the other two a D. Her actions parallel the judge's use of mitigating circumstances and cannot be construed as arbitrary, let alone unjust.

The second problem with Nathanson's analogy is that it would have disastrous consequences for all law and benevolent practices alike. If we concluded that we should abolish a rule or practice unless we treat everyone exactly by the same rules all the time, we would have to abolish, for example, traffic laws and laws against imprisonment for rape, theft, and even murder. Carried to its logical limits, we would also have to refrain from saving drowning victims if a number of people were drowning but we could only save a few of them. Imperfect justice is the best that we humans can attain. We should reform our practices as much as possible to eradicate unjust discrimination wherever we can, but if we are not allowed to have a law without perfect application, we will be forced to have no laws at all.

Nathanson acknowledges this latter response, but argues that the case of death is different. "Because of its finality and extreme severity of the death penalty, we need to be more scrupulous in applying it as punishment than is necessary with any other punishment" (2001: 67). The retentionist agrees that the death penalty is a severe punishment and that we need to be scrupulous in applying it. The difference between the abolitionist and the retentionist seems to lie in whether we are wise and committed enough as a nation to reform our institutions so that they approximate fairness. Apparently Nathanson is pessimistic here, whereas I have faith in our ability to learn from our mistakes and reform our systems. If we can't reform our legal system, what hope is there for us?[3]

More specifically, the charge that a higher percentage of blacks than whites are executed was once true, but is no longer so. Many states have made significant changes in sentencing procedures, with the result that, currently, whites convicted of first-degree murder are sentenced to death at a higher rate than blacks.[4]

One must be careful in reading too much into these statistics. While great disparities in statistics should cause us to examine our judicial procedures, they do not in themselves prove injustice. For example, more males than females are convicted of violent crimes (almost 90 percent of those convicted of violent crimes are males – a virtually universal statistic), but this is not strong evidence that the law is unfair, for there are biological/psychological explanations for the disparity in convictions. Males are on average and by nature more aggressive (usually linked to testosterone) than females; simply having a Y chromosome predisposes them to greater violence. Nevertheless, we hold male criminals responsible for their violence and expect them to control themselves. Likewise, there may be good explanations why people of one ethnic group commit more crimes than those of other groups, explanations that do not impugn the processes of the judicial system, nor absolve rational people of their moral responsibility.

As I write this, Governor Ryan of Illinois has just commuted the sentences of more than 167 death-row inmates. Abolitionists throughout the world celebrated this as a great victory. But they should have second thoughts. By summarily commuting the sentences of all of the condemned men, the Governor has undermined the stability and integrity of the law as a viable institution in his state, overturning years of work by the police, prosecutors, judges, and juries, and has turned his back on the right of the victims' families to see justice done. Apparently, some of those convicted were done so on insufficient evidence. If so, their sentences should have been commuted and the prisoners compensated. But such decisions should be taken on a case-by-case basis. Some of the convicts on death row were hardened unrepentant criminals, guilty of heinous crimes. If capital punishment is justified, its application should be confined to such clear cases in which the guilt of the criminal is "beyond reasonable

Louis P. Pojman

doubt." But to overthrow the whole system because of a few possible miscarriages of justice is as unwarranted as it is a loss of faith in our system of criminal justice. No one would abolish the use of fire engines and ambulances because occasionally they kill innocent pedestrians while carrying out their mission.

The complaint is often made by abolitionists that only the poor get death sentences for murder. If their trials are fair, then they deserve the death penalty, but rich murderers may be equally deserving. At the moment, only first-degree murder and treason are crimes deemed worthy of the death penalty. Perhaps our notion of treason should be expanded to include those who betray the trust of the public, corporation executives who have the trust of ordinary people, but who, through selfish and dishonest practices, ruin their lives. My proposal is to broaden, not narrow, the scope of capital punishment, to include businessmen and women who unfairly and severely harm the public. As I have mentioned above, the executives in the recent corporation scandals who bailed out with millions of dollars while they destroyed the pension plans of thousands of employees may deserve severe punishment and, if convicted, they should receive what they deserve. My guess is that the threat of the death sentence would have a deterrent effect in such cases. Whether it is feasible to apply the death penalty to horrendous white-collar crimes is debatable. But there is something to be said in its favor; it would certainly remove the impression that only the poor get executed.

Conclusion

While the abolitionist movement is gaining strength – due in part to the dedicated eloquence of opponents to the death penalty such as Hugo Adam Bedau, Stephen Nathanson, and Jeffrey Reiman – a cogent case can be made for retaining the death penalty for serious crimes. The case primarily rests on a notion of justice as desert, but is strengthened by utilitarian arguments involving deterrence. It is not because retentionists disvalue life that we defend the use of the death penalty. Rather, it is because we value human life as highly as we do that we support its continued use. The combined argument based on both backward-looking and forward-looking considerations justify use of the death penalty.

The abolitionist points out the problems in applying the death penalty. We can concede that there are problems and that reform is constantly needed, but since the death penalty is justified in principle, we should seek to improve its application rather than abolish a just institution.[5] If civilized society can reduce racism and sexism and send people to the moon, surely it can reduce the injustices connected with the criminal justice system. We ought not to throw out the baby with the dirty bath water.

Notes

1   Mike Royko, quoted in Moore (1995: 98–9).
2   Cited in Ernest van den Haag, "The Death Penalty Once More," unpublished manuscript. In "A Response to Bedau" (van den Haag, 1977: 798, n.5), van den Haag states that both Black and Bedau said that they would be in favor of abolishing the death penalty even if "they

knew that its abolition (and replacement by life imprisonment) would increase the homicide rate by 10%, 20%, 50%, 100%, or 1000%. Both gentlemen continued to answer affirmatively." Bedau confirmed this in a letter to me (July 28, 1996).

3 An example might be the abolition of large numbers of institutions for the mentally ill in New York which began in the 1960s, sought by reformers because of documented abuses related to both inadequate treatment and due regard for patients' rights. It was argued that prevailing conditions could not be reformed, but large-scale release of long-institutionalized persons without adequate planning for their follow-up led to new problems, including visibly increased homelessness. In hindsight, many believe that more work should have been done to reform the institutions. Sometimes it is the lesser of two evils to keep an imperfect institution than to abolish it for an unknown effect.

4 The Department of Justice's Bureau of Justice Statistics Bulletin for 1994 reports that between 1977 and 1994, 2,336 (5%) of those arrested for murder were white, 1,838 (40%) were black, and 316 (7%) were Hispanic. Of the 257 who were executed, 140 (54%) were white, 98 (38%) were black, 17 (7%) were Hispanic, and 2 (1%) were other races. In 1994, 31 prisoners – 20 white men and 11 black men – were executed, although whites made up only 7,532 (41%) and blacks 9,906 (56%) of those arrested for murder. Of those sentenced to death in 1994, 158 were white men, 133 were black men, 25 were Hispanic men, 2 were Native American men, 2 were white women, and 3 were black women. Of those sentenced, relatively more blacks (72%) than whites (65%) or Hispanics (60%) had prior felony records. Overall, the criminal justice system does not seem to favor white criminals over black, though it does seem to favor rich defendants over poor ones.

5 I have discussed these problems in Pojman (1998).

References

Barzun, Jacques (1962). "In favor of capital punishment." *The American Scholar*, 31: 181–91.
Bedau, Hugo Adam (1980). "Capital punishment." In Tom Regan (ed.), *Matters of Life and Death* (pp. 148–82). New York: Random House.
Bedau, Hugo Adam (1982). *The Death Penalty in America*. New York: Random House.
Bedau, Hugo Adam (1989). "How to argue about the death penalty." In Michael Radelet (ed.), *Facing the Death Penalty* (pp. 178–92). Philadelphia: Temple University Press.
British Parliamentary Debates (1982). Fifth Series, vol. 23, issue 1243, House of Commons, 11 May 1982.
Ehrlich, Isaac (1975). "The deterrent effect of capital punishment: a question of life and death." *American Economic Review*, 65 (June): 397–417.
Furman v. Georgia (1972). 408 US 238.
Gernstein, Richard E. (1960). "A prosecutor looks at capital punishment." *Journal of Criminal Law: Criminology and Police Science*, 51: 252–6.
Hentoff, Nat (2001). "The state closes our eyes as it kills." *The Village Voice* (May 1): 31.
Mill, John Stuart (1986). *Parliamentary Debates*. Third series, April 21, 1868. Reprinted in Peter Singer (ed.), *Applied Ethics* (pp. 97–104). New York: Oxford University Press.
Moore, Michael (1995). "The moral worth of retributivism." In G. Murphy Jeffrie (ed.), *Punishment and Rehabilitation* (pp. 94–130). Belmont, CA: Wadsworth.
Nathanson, Stephen (2001). *An Eye For An Eye: The Immorality of Punishing By Death*. Lanham, MD: Rowman & Littlefield.
Pojman, Louis P. (1998). "For the death penalty." In Louis P. Pojman and Jeffrey Reiman, *The Death Penalty: For and Against* (pp. 1–66). Lanham, MD: Rowman & Littlefield.

Louis P. Pojman

Reiman, Jeffrey (1998). "Why the death penalty should be abolished in America." In Louis P. Pojman and Jeffrey Reiman, *The Death Penalty: For and Against* (pp. 67–133). Lanham, MD: Rowman & Littlefield.

Sellin, Thorsten (1967). "Effect of repeal and reintroduction of the death penalty on homicide rates." In Hugo Bedau (ed.), *The Death Penalty in America* (pp. 339–43). Chicago: Aldine Books.

Stephens, James Fitzjames (1967). *Liberty, Equality, Fraternity.* Cambridge: Cambridge University Press.

Stephens, James Fitzjames (1863). *A History of Criminal Law in England.* New York: Macmillan.

van den Haag, Ernest (1968). "On deterrence and the death penalty." *Ethics*, 78: 280–8.

van den Haag, Ernest (1975). *Punishing Criminals: Concerning a Very Old and Painful Question.* New York: Basic Books.

van den Haag, Ernest (1977). "A response to Bedau." *Arizona State Law Journal*, 4: 797–802.

van den Haag, Ernest (1986). "The ultimate punishment: a defense." *Harvard Law Review*, 99: 1662–9.

Wilson, James Q. and Herrnstein, Richard J. (1986). *Crime and Human Nature.* New York: Simon and Schuster.

Further reading

Davis, Michael (1981). "Death, deterrence, and the method of common sense." *Social Theory and Practice*, 7: 145–78.

CHAPTER EIGHT

Why We Should Put the Death Penalty to Rest

Stephen Nathanson

My aim in this chapter is to make the strongest case that I can to show that punishing people by death is an unjust and immoral practice. Although we often think of the death penalty debate as one of those eternal, irresolvable issues, I believe that the arguments for the death penalty are extremely weak and that the practice of punishing by death is morally indefensible.

I know, of course, that not everyone sees things this way. The laws of 38 of the 50 states of the United States include death as a possible punishment, and public support in the US for the death penalty over the last 25–30 years has been very strong. This American consensus, however, is somewhat anomalous. The death penalty has been abolished in almost every modern, democratic country, and its abolition is now required of any country wanting to enter the European Union.

Still, in the US, many people strongly support the death penalty. Why is this? While it could be that death penalty supporters simply want vengeance and don't care about morality, I doubt that this is true. I believe that most death penalty supporters are people of good will who think that the death penalty is right or necessary. While some political leaders use the death penalty for political gain, most people have no vested interest in the death penalty. If they are wrong about it, this is the result of honest mistakes. They either have mistaken factual beliefs or are confused in their moral thinking. If I can show that the factual and moral beliefs on which death penalty support depends are mistaken, this should lead them to see that the death penalty ought to be abolished where it is used and left to rest in peace where it has already been rejected.

Whether I can do this remains to be seen. One reason for optimism is that the death penalty debate differs from some other controversial issues. Some controversies are hard to resolve because people on opposing sides differ in their fundamental values. In such cases, it is hard to find values that can serve as a basis for reaching agreement. The death penalty debate is not like this. Both death penalty supporters and opponents generally appeal to the same fundamental values: the pursuit of justice and respect for human life.

If I can show that a belief in the importance of justice and respect for human life is inconsistent with support for the death penalty, it would follow that people who hold these ideals and yet favor the death penalty are actually contradicting their own values. An argument that would show this would be very strong, both logically and psychologically. It would be logically strong because contradictory views are necessarily false, and psychologically strong because it appeals only to values that death penalty supporters themselves accept.

Of course, some people might reject the values of justice and respect for human life, but there would be a great cost to doing so. First, they would deprive themselves of some of the common arguments for capital punishment – such as that it is necessary for protecting human life and that it is a just punishment for murder. Indeed, they would be unable to say why murder is a serious crime since the condemnation of murder presupposes that human life has an especially high value. Second, rejecting these values would undermine their moral credibility. No one would listen to people who said that they were indifferent to justice and respect for human life because our society is publicly committed to these values (whether or not it actually takes the required steps to do achieve them).

We can assume, then, that all who support the death penalty and whose views we take seriously are committed to the values of justice and respect for human life. My goal is to show that the death penalty is inconsistent with these values. How can this be done?

My argument will proceed in two stages. First, a consideration of the death penalty in theory, followed by, second, an examination of the death penalty in practice. I will show that the principled bases for the death penalty are extremely weak. Then, I will show that even if the death penalty could be justified in theory, the actual practice of executing murderers violates both the values of justice and respect for human life. Even people who support the death penalty in theory should oppose it in practice.

The Death Penalty in Theory: Saving Lives and Doing Justice

The two basic arguments for the death penalty are (1) that it is the best deterrent of murders and thus saves people's lives and (2) that it is the punishment that justice requires for the crime of murder.

The argument from deterrence

According to this argument, the threat of execution is a more powerful deterrent than lesser punishments and therefore will lead to fewer deaths from homicide. If this is true, then anyone who values human life will be willing to support executing murderers because this will spare the lives of innocent people. Just as common-sense morality permits killing in self-defense or defense of others, so it permits the death penalty as a form of social self-defense, saving the lives of people who would otherwise be victims of murder.

In theory, this is a powerful argument. Anyone who values human life will want to diminish the number of people murdered, and if the death penalty is uniquely effective in preventing murders, then it cannot be dismissed as senseless violence or mere vengeance. Nor could it be said to be the same as murder, for while murders increase the number of innocent victims, the death penalty (according to this argument) diminishes the number of innocent victims.

The deterrence argument has been challenged on factual grounds, and the best evidence suggests that the death penalty is not a better deterrent than life imprisonment.[1] In general, countries and states that do not use the death penalty have lower homicide rates than countries that do. These are familiar points which I will not stress here because I want to consider the death penalty "in theory." I want to challenge the underlying moral principle, which is the idea that if a punishment deters more murders and thus saves more innocent lives, then it is justifiable. While this sounds plausible, it is false and thus fails to justify the death penalty. I offer two arguments to show this.

First, we can imagine punishments that have greater deterrent value than either the death penalty or imprisonment and yet would be wrong to inflict. Suppose we could deter more murders by executing not just the person who commits a murder but also the family or closest friends of such a person. If the idea behind the deterrence argument is that we deter more murders by threatening the most terrible punishments, then it is plausible to suppose that potential murderers who might be prepared to risk their own lives might be deterred by the loss of life to others that they care about – their husbands or wives, their children or parents, their closest friends. If, as it is often said, the death penalty is supposed to make potential murderers "think twice," this punishment would be likely to make them think three or four times. Its logic is the same as the argument used to support the death penalty over long-term imprisonment: the more terrible the punishment, the more powerful the deterrent.

Yet, even if this punishment succeeded, it would be an unjust, immoral punishment. It would save some innocent people's lives by killing other innocent people, and this is morally unacceptable.

Does this argument show that the death penalty is wrong? No, but it does show that the deterrence argument is not sufficient to justify it, even in theory. It shows that a punishment can be the best deterrent and still be morally wrong.

Someone might object to my use of a made-up example that involves a punishment that virtually no one supports. After all, they might say, the death penalty debate is about the execution of people who are guilty. No one defends the execution of innocent people to deter murders. But, of course, even in theory, death penalty supporters must acknowledge the risk that some innocent people will be executed and, even in theory, they must be willing to say that killing some innocent people is an acceptable price to pay for the saving of a greater number of innocent lives.[2] So my fanciful example shares an important feature with the actual death penalty for murderers: both involve a willingness to kill innocent people.

This is an issue that I will return to when considering the death penalty in fact. For now, I only want to show that even if the factual assumptions underlying the

Stephen Nathanson

deterrence argument were correct, the argument by itself cannot justify the death penalty. If deterrence were all that mattered, then we would be logically committed to executing the family and friends of murderers as well as the murderers themselves. This is scarcely something that people committed to justice and respect for human life should support.

The argument from justice and desert

Many people support the death penalty for a different reason. They think it is the only truly just punishment for murder, and they often feel that anything less than death is morally unacceptable. Why is this?

In explaining this view, many people cite the expression "an eye for an eye." This familiar saying is probably the most influential basis for the death penalty. It benefits from both the authority of the Bible and from its surface plausibility as a fair rule for punishment. The "eye for an eye" principle tells us how to treat those who commit crimes. It says that if one person harms another, then the perpetrator should suffer the very same harm as the victim. This is how the "eye for an eye" principle is generally understood: the punishment should equal the crime.

For those in the know, this principle gains additional credibility from the fact that it is affirmed by the great philosopher Immanuel Kant in a very famous passage about punishment. He writes:

> What kind and degree of punishment does public legal justice adopt as its principle and standard? None other than the principle of equality ... the principle of not treating one side more favorably than the other. Accordingly, any undeserved evil that you inflict on someone else ... is one that you do to yourself. If you vilify him, you vilify yourself; if you steal from him, you steal from yourself; if you kill him, you kill yourself. Only the Law of retribution (*jus talionis*) can determine exactly the kind and degree of punishment. (1965: 101)

And, he adds, if a person "has committed murder, he must die. In this case, there is no substitute that will satisfy the requirements of legal justice" (1965: 102).

There is, no doubt, something appealing about the "eye for an eye" principle and if it provides a general criterion for determining the appropriate level of punishment for crimes, the death penalty will be justified because it satisfies the test of doing to the criminal what the criminal has done to the victim.

In spite of its surface plausibility, it is easy to see that the "eye for an eye" principle is defective and cannot provide a solid basis for the death penalty. People are doubly mistaken about the "eye for an eye" principle. They are mistaken in thinking that it is correct and mistaken in thinking that they actually accept it as an adequate guide to punishment. The only reason that people think they believe it is that they have not really thought about it.

There are three serious problems for "an eye for an eye." First, it requires unjust and barbaric punishments in cases where people have acted barbarically. Second, it conflicts with many of our beliefs about punishment and its justification. Third, in many cases, it provides no real guidance in determining the appropriate punishments.

Why We Should Put the Death Penalty to Rest

Suppose that a person murders the entire family of someone that he regards as his enemy. If we describe his crime as "killing the family of his enemy," then the "eye for an eye" principle appears to require that we punish the killer by killing his entire family. Simply to execute the murderer alone would not satisfy the idea that the punishment should equal the crime. Yet no one would urge the death of the murderer's family as an appropriate punishment since they are innocent and should not suffer for the crimes of another.

Anyone who rejects this as a just punishment must reject the "eye for an eye" principle as well, and because virtually everyone would reject it, that shows that they do not really accept the "eye for an eye" principle. Even Kant, in spite of his strong affirmations of his version of "the eye for an eye" principle, departs from that principle for reasons very like the ones I have given. In a less famous passage than the one I quoted above, he asks: "[H]ow can this principle [of the equality of crime and punishment] be applied to punishments that do not allow reciprocation because they are either impossible in themselves or would themselves be punishable crimes against humanity in general?" (1965: 132). Just by asking this question, Kant acknowledges that the "eye for an eye" principle cannot be applied to all cases and that it sometimes recommends punishments that would be immoral to inflict. He follows his question with three examples in which the "eye for an eye" principle would lead to an immoral punishment, and then he suggests an alternative. He writes: "Rape, pederasty, and bestiality are examples of the latter. For rape and pederasty, [the proper punishment is] castration ... and for bestiality the punishment is expulsion forever from civil society since the criminal guilty of bestiality is unworthy of remaining in human society" (1965: 132). Kant believes that raping the rapist, forcing the pederast to have homosexual sex, or forcing the person guilty of bestiality to have sex with animals would be "crimes against humanity." Instead, he proposes castration for the rapist and exile for the person guilty of sex with animals.

These may or may not be sensible suggestions, but they are clearly not instances of the "eye for an eye" principle. The lesson here is important. When we actually think about the implications of the "eye for an eye" principle, we quickly come upon cases in which it provides us either with defective guidance in the setting of punishments or with no guidance at all.

These problems are directly relevant to issues about the death penalty for murder. A common feature of the criminal law is that acts with similar effects are treated quite differently because of various facts about the crime. Yet the "eye for an eye" principle focuses on only one aspect of the crime: the harm caused to the victim. It says that the punishment should match the effect of the crime and from this it follows that the taking of a victim's life should be followed by the killing of the murderer.

Yet there are many different types of action that can result in the death of a victim, and we tend to think that these different types of actions should not all be punished in the same way. Consider the following:

- A hired killer lies in wait and shoots the intended victim.
- An argument degenerates into a fight in which one person strikes the other and kills him.

Stephen Nathanson

- A person sets fire to a building, thinking that it is empty; several people in the building die in the fire.
- A drunken driver kills a pedestrian.

While all of these actions have dire effects, most of us would view the hired killer as more culpable than the others. His action would generally be classified as first-degree murder, and in states with the death penalty, he might be sentenced to die.

In none of the other cases is death intended, even though the people involved engaged in dangerous actions. The second case, depending on the circumstances, might be classified either as second-degree murder (which is not punishable by death) or manslaughter, a lesser charge. If the arsonist had taken steps to insure that there were no victims, he would most likely be charged with manslaughter, while the driver would be charged with vehicular homicide.

Most people agree that these actions should be dealt with differently. But anyone who believes this must reject the "eye for an eye" principle, since it requires us to treat them all in the same way. This supports both of the arguments I have put forward. First, because not all homicides should be punished in the same way, the "eye for an eye" principle is wrong. Second, if most people believe that we should treat homicides differently depending on the intentions and the circumstances, then those same people do not believe the "eye for an eye" principle. They might cite it in an argument, but they don't really believe it.

Whatever its customary force and initial plausibility, the "eye for an eye" principle is far from the last word on the appropriate punishment for particular crimes and cannot bear the burden of justifying death as a punishment for murder.

The Death Penalty in Practice

So far, I have considered the death penalty in theory. I have tried to show that the two most common reasons for supporting the death penalty – the "eye for an eye" principle and the argument from deterrence – are inadequate. Even in theory, the death penalty lacks a convincing moral justification.

But the death penalty debate is not merely an abstract moral issue. It is about actual institutions run by actual people in actual societies. Even if my arguments about the death penalty in theory had failed, there would still be a strong case against the death penalty in practice. To see this, consider the following: suppose that the deterrence argument worked in theory and that the "eye for an eye" principle provided an adequate principle for determining what punishment people deserve. It would still not follow that the death penalty should be adopted. Why? Because we need to consider how this punishment works out in practice.

Suppose that the death penalty deters more effectively than other punishments and suppose that murderers deserve to die. In addition, however, suppose that the legal institutions of a society that imposes the death penalty are not reliable. As a result, innocent people are often convicted of murder. Suppose, for example, that half of those convicted were innocent and that people know about the failings of the system. In this situation, even though the death penalty is justified in theory, it would be unjustified in practice. Indeed, it would be blatantly inconsistent for the death penalty to be retained by a society that is committed to the two values I emphasized at the start. It would not be respectful of human life because it would be killing innocent human beings, and it would not be consistent with a commitment to justice because it would be punishing innocent people. Any member of my imagined society who cares about justice and respect for human life should oppose the death penalty in that society even if they favor it in theory. To support the death penalty in that society would show that one had no genuine commitment to these values.

Whether the death penalty is justifiable or not, then, depends only partly on abstract beliefs about morality and justice. In addition, it depends on facts about a society and its institutions. Charles Black makes this point very effectively. He writes:

> We are not presently confronted, as a political society, with the question whether something called "the state" has some abstract right to kill "those who deserve to die." We are confronted by the single unitary question posed by reality: "Shall we kill those who are chosen to be killed by our legal process as it stands?" (1981: 166)

It is the practice of capital punishment – administered by real legal systems and real human beings – that kills people, and, we – as citizens of actual societies – have to decide if this practice should continue.

When I speak about an inconsistency in the pro-death penalty position, then, I mean an inconsistency between the values affirmed by death penalty supporters and the actual practice of capital punishment. My claim is that if death penalty supporters consider their own values, they will see that these values are violated by the institution of capital punishment, both as it exists now and as it is almost certain to exist for the foreseeable future.

Why the Death Penalty is Inconsistent with the Value of Justice

In order for the actual death penalty to be consistent with the value of justice, it would have to be true that people who are punished by death deserve the punishment. Since there is a widespread view that only some of those people who kill others deserve to die, a just system must be capable of two things: first, it must separate the guilty from the innocent and, second, it must be able to sort out the worst murderers – those who deserve to die according to the legal criteria of desert – from those who deserve a lesser punishment. If the system cannot do both of these reliably, then the results that it generates are unjust.

In fact, we know that the system in the United States is unreliable. We know this because a large amount of evidence shows that irrelevant features play a large role in determining the level of punishment that a person receives. In theory, the death penalty is imposed because of the terribleness of the specific crimes committed. In practice, actual death sentences are the result of arbitrary, irrelevant factors like race, socio-economic status, and the quality of legal representation. I will briefly cite some facts about the influence of the irrelevant factors.

Stephen Nathanson

Race

One of the most widely studied influences on sentencing is race. A large body of research has shown that sentencing in capital cases is very much influenced by both the race of the offender and the race of the victim.

- Between 1976 and 1996, 83% of the people executed in the United States were charged with the murder of a white victim (Hood, 1998: 745).
- In the 20 years after *Gregg* v. *Georgia* (1976), the Supreme Court case that reinstated the death penalty, only 1 percent of executions were imposed on a white person who had killed a black victim (Hood, 1998: 745).

Socio-economic status

A person's social and economic status also plays a role in determining the sentence for the crime of murder. A comprehensive study of the death penalty in Georgia yielded the following result:

- In Georgia, defendants classified as having low socio-economic status were 2.3 times more likely to receive a death sentence than defendants seen as having higher status (Baldus et al., 1990).

Quality of legal representation

Socio-economic factors are related to the ability of people to hire competent lawyers. When people lack money, they must accept court-appointed lawyers who are often less competent. The same Georgia study showed:

- Defendants with court-appointed attorneys were 2.6 times more likely to receive a death sentence than defendants who could afford to hire lawyers (Baldus et al., 1990: 158; Bright, 1997).

An investigation by the *Chicago Tribune* of 285 capital cases in Illinois concluded that the state's death penalty system was pervaded by "bias, error, and incompetence." It also cited poor legal representation, finding that 33 people sentenced to death had lawyers who were later disbarred or suspended (Armstrong and Mills, 2000).

A report by the American Bar Association on the death penalty in the United States shows this to be a national problem. According to the ABA, court-appointed lawyers for defendants charged with first-degree murder often have no criminal trial experience and do not know the special rules and procedures for capital cases. They often have insufficient funds to cover the cost of preparing and investigating cases and frequently fail to make relevant objections during a trial so that they can be considered on appeal. In addition, they often fail to introduce mitigating factors during the part of the trial devoted to determining the sentence (American Bar Association, 1997: 7–9).

The ABA report concluded that "in case after case, decisions about who will die and who will live turn not on the nature of the offense the defendant is charged with committing but rather on the nature of the legal representation the defendant receives" (American Bar Association, 1997: 6). This factual conclusion supports the following moral conclusion. If "decisions about who will die" do not depend on "the nature of the offense the defendant is charged with committing" but are determined by irrelevant factors such as race, social standing, and inadequate legal counsel, then the death penalty as it exists in our society cannot be relied on to produce just results.

Death penalty supporters claim that they want justice. Sometimes, in explaining why only some people guilty of homicide should be executed, they add that capital punishment should be restricted to people whose crimes are most terrible and whose culpability is greatest. What the evidence shows, however, is that the factors that determine whether people are executed or not differ from the factors cited in defense of the death penalty. Even if (in theory) justice would be achieved by executing the worst murderers, there is no reason to believe that this is what our system does.

Of course, these injustices would not support the abolition of capital punishment if the system could be reformed so as to eliminate the influence of these irrelevant factors. But there is no reason to believe that this can be done. The factors that interfere with the achievement of justice are too pervasive to be rooted out. Moreover, reforms have already been tried and have failed. In the United States, attempts to free capital sentencing from the influence of arbitrary factors have been ongoing since the 1972 case of *Furman* v. *Georgia*. Supreme Court Justice Harry Blackmun, who had supported the constitutionality of the death penalty in *Furman* and other cases, eventually argued that the defects in the system are unfixable. In the 1994 case *Callins* v. *Collins*, Blackmun announced:

> For more than 20 years I have endeavored ... along with a majority of this Court to develop procedural and substantive rules that would lend more than the mere appearance of fairness to the death penalty endeavor. ... I [now] feel morally and intellectually obligated to concede that the death penalty experiment has failed. (*Callins* v. *Collins*, 1994: 1145)

Anyone who is committed to the value of justice should follow Justice Blackmun's lead and reject the death penalty because of the injustices it has yielded in the past and is likely to yield in the future.

Why the Death Penalty is Inconsistent with Respect for the Value of Human Life

Having shown why support for the death penalty is inconsistent with a commitment to the value of justice, I will now show why it is inconsistent with respect for the value of human life and thus why it should be rejected by anyone who is committed to honoring that value.

When we examine how the death penalty system actually works, we see that it generates practices that show a callous disregard for human life. In fact, like the act of murder itself, the death penalty system embodies a lack of concern about the taking of human life.

In making this serious charge, I have a number of features of the death penalty system in mind. Consider the facts that I have cited about the injustice of the death penalty system. Since the quality of legal representation strongly influences the sentence imposed on a person, a system that tolerates inadequate representation for people who may be sentenced to death expresses indifference toward the value of these defendants' lives. There is no way that assigning incompetent lawyers to people in this position can be compatible with a commitment to take seriously the value of each person's life. Neither is the failure to provide court-appointed lawyers with the resources to investigate their clients' cases compatible with a commitment to take seriously the value of each person's life. Anyone concerned with the value of human life would be determined to insure that executions occur only after the most exacting procedures have proved beyond a reasonable doubt that death is the proper punishment. There is an obvious inconsistency between affirming the value of human life and tolerating the current level of legal representation for people who face the possibility of death.

Problems with our system can lead to two kinds of mistaken judgment. The first is that a person who is guilty of a crime may receive a more severe punishment than would have been received had he or she been a member of a different race, had a higher social status, or had been able to hire a better lawyer. The second is that the poor quality of legal representation may result in innocent people being convicted of murder and sentenced to die. While there has been a widespread impression that the legal system in the United States bends over backwards to give defendants every conceivable advantage, the facts are quite otherwise. In fact, for many defendants, the system is stacked against them, and the results of the process are not reliable indicators of guilt or innocence. Consider the following facts (Armstrong and Mills, 2000) that set the stage for the moratorium on executions in Illinois:

- Between 1977 and 2000, the state of Illinois executed 12 people for murder and also released 13 people from death row because they were shown to be completely innocent.
- In some of the cases of wrongful convictions, police used coercive measures, including torture, to extract confessions from innocent persons.
- In at least 46 cases, convictions for murder were based on testimony from jailhouse informants; these informants often benefited from their testimony and in some cases had long records of lies and deceit.

These kinds of occurrence are not limited to Illinois. According to James McCloskey, while 226 people were executed in the United States between 1973 and 1995, 54 people were released from death row because of innocence. "This means," McCloskey comments, "that during the last twenty years, for every five death row inmates executed, one has been released and exonerated. That points to a rather cracked system, one prone to serious and frequent mistakes" (1996: 70).

At the national level, the causes of error resemble those in Illinois. Hugo Bedau and Michael Radelet identified 350 instances of wrongful convictions in capital cases and found that 82 of them resulted from questionable actions by police officers and prosecutors (1987: 56–9). This is consistent with a general pattern in the causes of wrongful convictions. One study of wrongful convictions in general (i.e., not simply in homicide cases) concluded: "If we had to isolate a single 'system dynamic' that pervades large numbers of these cases [of erroneous convictions], we would probably describe it as police and prosecutorial overzealousness" (Huff et al., 1996": 64). The chance of convicting and executing innocent persons is substantial, and misconduct by officials in the criminal justice system is a frequent source of error.[3]

While these practices and the resulting convictions of innocent people are dreadful in connection with any crimes and punishments, they are especially horrifying in the case of the death penalty, since they can result in the killing of people for crimes of which they are entirely innocent. Moreover, the death penalty makes corrections of errors impossible.[4]

In reply, death penalty supporters may argue that the fact that innocent people were exonerated and released shows that the system works. This reply, however, is inconsistent with the facts. In many cases, people have been spared from death only by chance or through the intervention of people outside the system. In Illinois, one person on death row was released through the work of students at Chicago-Kent College of Law, while three others were exonerated after investigations by journalism students at Northwestern University. One of these people, Anthony Porter, came within two days of being executed (Armstrong and Mills, 2000). Such down-to-the-wire cases that depend on the fortuitous intervention of outsiders are no evidence for the reliability or self-correcting nature of the legal system.

Moreover, when claims of innocence arise, officials are often resistant to them. As McCloskey notes: "Once wrongly convicted and sentenced to death, the criminal justice system treats you as a leper. No one wants to touch you. In my view, those in authority seem to be more interested in finality, expediency, speed, and administrative streamlining than in truth, justice, and fairness" (McCloskey, 1996, p. 70). McCloskey's claim about the true interests of those in the system is supported by the American Bar Association report. It points out that the Supreme Court has ruled that "there is no constitutional right to counsel [i.e., representation by a lawyer] in post-conviction proceedings, even in capital cases" (American Bar Association, 1997: 9]. As a result, people who have new evidence or justified procedural claims may lack the professional assistance that is required to assert claims in a legally credible way.

The lack of interest in correcting mistakes is nowhere more evident than in the time limits set by states for the submission of new evidence and in the Supreme Court's upholding of such limits. In *Herrera* v. *Collins* (1993) the Court ruled that new evidence in support of a claim of innocence could be disregarded because it had been submitted too late to meet the Texas 60-day deadline. In other words, the Court ruled that a person could be executed even though there was now evidence that he or she is innocent. Why? Because the evidence came in too late. In defending this shocking view, the Court majority noted that these deadlines were quite common. It noted:

> Texas is one of 17 States that requires a new trial motion based on newly discovered evidence to be made within 60 days of judgment. ... Eighteen jurisdictions have time limits ranging between 1 and 3 years, with 10 States and the District of Columbia fol-

Stephen Nathanson

lowing the 2-year federal time limit. Only 15 States allow a new trial based on newly discovered evidence to be filed more than 3 years after conviction. ... [Only] 9 States have no time limits. (*Herrera* v. *Collins*, 1993: 409–11).

It is hard to see how the Court's judgment in this case or the state policies that are cited could be consistent with a commitment to respecting human life. What sort of commitment to the value of human life is shown by the 60-day deadline that Texas and 16 other states set for submitting new evidence of innocence? Or by the fact that only 9 states place no limit on the time period for making sure that people are guilty before we execute them? What sort of attitude toward human life is exhibited by a Supreme Court that places respect for deadlines ahead of a concern about the death of innocent human beings?

It is hard to see how anyone who is committed to the ideal of respect for human life could approve of such practices. And yet, these practices are completely understandable. They reflect the desire of a legal bureaucracy to bring time-consuming appeals to a halt. They reflect the desire of officials who resist the exposure of errors because they do not want to be seen as incompetent, misled, or over-zealous. They reflect the desire of citizens who want lower taxes more than they want to pay for competent lawyers for people charged with murder. They reflect the fact that it is easier to respect the value of human life in words than to do so in deeds.

Death penalty supporters ought to acknowledge that even if in their ideal world the values of justice and human life would be affirmed by executing murderers, in our actual world the actual practice of capital punishment violates these very same values. If consistency with the values of justice and respect for human life are the appropriate criteria for deciding the issue, then people who understand the death penalty system should oppose the practice of punishing by death. Opposition to the death penalty is consistent with these values, while support for the death penalty violates them.

A Final Point

I have tried to show that the death penalty fails in theory and is inconsistent in practice with the values that death penalty supporters claim to support and I think I have succeeded in showing this. Nonetheless, I know that many people will not shift their view the next time they read about a terrible murder or about a particularly vicious criminal. They will think, "Surely, this person deserves to die. Surely, the death penalty is justified in this case." What they overlook is that the death penalty is not about the treatment of a particular individual. Rather, as has been clear in my discussion, the death penalty is a system. It is a system that empowers prosecutors to seek death as a punishment, judges and jurors to sentence people to death, and prison officials to impose death. To favor the death penalty is *not* to favor the execution of a particular person whom you or I believe deserves to die. Rather, it is to authorize many different people – whose motives and attitudes are unknown to us – to seek and authorize death as a punishment. These people may well make judgments that you or I would disagree with and yet when we say we favor the death penalty we are authorizing people to act on these judgments. Moreover, we are authorizing them to do so in the context of a system that we know to be unfair and unreliable.

Our views about the death penalty, then, are views about an institution, not about individual murders or murderers. It is quite possible to believe that some murderers deserve to die and yet to oppose the death penalty because one knows that others who do not deserve to die will be executed. And we do know this. We know that death sentences will result from racial prejudice, poor legal representation, and misdeeds by police and prosecutors. We know that evidence of innocence will be rejected by courts because deadlines are missed. We know that the practice of capital punishment as it actually exists violates the principles of justice and respect for human life. Anyone who genuinely cares about justice and the value of human life should conclude that the death penalty should be put to rest.

Notes

1 For a discussion of both common-sense and statistical evidence concerning the deterrence argument, see Nathanson (2001: ch. 2). For a survey of research on deterrence, see Baily and Peterson (1997).
2 For one example of the claim that killing innocent people is acceptable, see van den Haag (1975: 219–21).
3 Official misconduct is not the only source of errors. For an analysis of a variety of sources of inaccuracy in criminal cases and proposals to increase accuracy, see Givelber (1997).
4 In a decision that was later overturned, Judge Jed Rakoff argued that the death penalty was unconstitutional because DNA evidence had definitively shown its imposition to be unreliable. For his decision, see *United States* v. *Quinones* (2002).

References

American Bar Association Report on the Death Penalty (1997). Available at ⟨http://www.abanet.org/irr/rpt107.html⟩.
Armstrong, K. and Mills, S. (2000). "Ryan: until I can be sure – Illinois is first state to suspend death penalty." *Chicago Tribune* (February 1): 1.
Baily, William and Peterson, Ruth (1997). "Murder, capital punishment, and deterrence: a review of the literature." In Hugo Adam Bedau (ed.), *The Death Penalty in America: Current Controversies* (pp. 135–61). Oxford: Oxford University Press.
Baldus, D., Woodworth, G., and Pulaski, C., Jr. (1990). *Equal Justice and the Death Penalty*. Boston, MA: Northeastern University Press.
Bedau, Hugo Adam and Radelet, M. (1987). "Miscarriages of justice in potentially capital cases." *Stanford Law Review*, 40: 21–179.
Black, Charles, Jr. (1981). *Capital Punishment: The Inevitability of Caprice and Mistake*, 2nd edn. New York: W.W. Norton.
Bright, Stephen (1997). "Counsel for the poor: the death sentence not for the worst crime but for the worst lawyer," In Hugo Adam Bedau (ed.), *The Death Penalty in America: Current Controversies* (pp. 275–309). Oxford: Oxford University Press.
Callins v. *Collins* (1994). 510 US 1141.
Furman v. *Georgia* (1972). 408 US 238.

Givelber, Daniel (1997). "Meaningless acquittals, meaningful convictions: do we reliably acquit the innocent?" *Rutgers Law Review*, 49: 1317–96.

Gregg v. *Georgia* (1976). 428 US 153.

Herrera v. *Collins* (1993). 506 US 390.

Hood, Roger (1998). "Capital punishment." In M. Tonry (ed.), *The Handbook of Crime and Punishment* (pp. 739–76). New York: Oxford University Press.

Huff, C. Ronald; Rattner, Arye, and Sagarin, Edward (1996). *Convicted But Innocent: Wrongful Convictions and Public Policy*. Thousand Oaks, CA: Sage Publications.

Kant, Immanuel (1965 [1785]). *The Metaphysical Elements of Justice*, trans. John Ladd. New York: Macmillan.

McCloskey, James (1996). "The death penalty: a personal view." *Criminal Justice Ethics*, 15: 70–6.

Nathanson, Stephen (2001). *An Eye for an Eye? The Immorality of Punishing by Death*, 2nd edn. Lanham, MD: Rowman & Littlefield.

United States v. *Quinones* (2002). 196 F. Supp. 2d 416 (SDNY).

Van den Haag, Ernest (1975). *Punishing Criminals*. New York: Basic Books.

Further reading

ACLU (1987). *The Case Against the Death Penalty*. Washington, DC: American Civil Liberties Union. Available at: ⟨http://www.aclu.org/DeathPenalty/DeathPenalty.cfm?ID=9082&tc=17⟩.

Amnesty International (1987). *United States of America: The Death Penalty*. London: Amnesty International Publications.

Bedau, Hugo Adam (1987). *Death is Different*. Boston, MA: Northeastern University Press.

Bedau, Hugo Adam (1999). "Abolishing the death penalty even for the worst murderers." In Austin Sarat (ed.), *The Killing State* (pp. 40–59). New York: Oxford University Press.

Bedau, Hugo Adam, Radelet, M., and Putnam, C. (1992). *In Spite of Innocence*. Boston, MA: Northeastern University Press.

Bentele, Ursula (1998). "Back to an international perspective on the death penalty as a cruel punishment: the case of South Africa." *Tulane Law Review*, 73: 251–304.

Berns, Walter (1979). *For Capital Punishment*. New York: Basic Books.

Bowers, William (1984). *Legal Homicide: Death as Punishment in America, 1864–1982*. Boston, MA: Northeastern University Press.

Bowers, William (1993). "Capital punishment and contemporary values: people's misgivings and the Court's misperceptions." *Law & society Review*, 27: 165–86.

Davis, Michael (1996). *Justice in the Shadow of Death*. Lanham, MD: Rowman & Littlefield.

Death Penalty Information Center. Available at ⟨http://www.deathpenaltyinfo.org/⟩.

McCleskey v. Kemp (1987). 481 US 279.

Nathanson, Stephen (1992). "Is the death penalty what murderers deserve?" In S. Luper (ed.), *The Moral Life*, 2nd edn. (pp. 380–9). New York: Harcourt Brace.

Nathanson, Stephen (1997). "How (not) to think about the death penalty." *International Journal of Applied Philosophy*, 11: 7–10.

Nathanson, Stephen (1999). "The death penalty as a peace issue." In D. Curtin and R. Litke (eds.), *Institutional Violence* (pp. 53–9). Amsterdam: Rodopi.

Pojman, Louis and Reiman, J. (1998). *The Death Penalty: For and Against*. Lanham, MD: Rowman & Littlefield.

Prejean, Helen (1993). *Dead Man Walking: An Eyewitness Account of the Death Penalty in America*. New York: Random House.

Sarat, Austin (ed.) (1999). *The Killing State*. New York: Oxford University Press.

Sorrell, Tom (1987). *Moral Theory and Capital Punishment*. Oxford: Blackwell.

Steffens, Lloyd (1998). *Executing Justice*. Cleveland: Pilgrim Press.

Supreme Court of South Africa: The State versus Makwanyane (1995). Anor [1995] ICHRL 34 (6 June). Available at ⟨http://www.worldlii.org/int/cases/ICHRL/1995/34.html⟩.

Van den Haag, Ernest (1978a). "In defense of the death penalty: a legal-practical-moral analysis." *Criminal Law Bulletin*, 14: 51–68.

Van den Haag, Ernest (1978b). "The collapse of the case against capital punishment." *National Review* (March 31): 395–407.

Woodson v. North Carolina (1976). 428 U.S. 280.

Zimring, F. and Hawkins, G. (1986). *Capital Punishment and the American Agenda*. Cambridge: Cambridge University Press.

Stephen Nathanson

CLONING

Why I Oppose Human Cloning

Jeremy Rifkin

Up to now, the cloning and stem cell debate has been viewed in Washington and the media as a classic struggle pitting social conservatives, right-to-life activists and the Catholic Church against the scientific community and progressive forces, with Republicans lined up on one side and Democrats on the other. In reality, many of us in the progressive left are equally opposed to both therapeutic and full birth cloning, although our reasons differ in some respects from social conservatives. Recently, 67 leading progressives lent their support to legislation that would outlaw therapeutic and full birth cloning. The signatories of the anti-cloning petition included many of the best-known intellectuals and activists in left circles today.

While the social conservatives' opposition is well understood, little or no attention has been given in the media or public debate to why some of us on the left oppose the cloning of human embryos for the specific purpose of using them to harvest stem cells for medical experiments or for giving birth to a baby. We worry that the market for women's eggs that would be created by this research will provide unethical incentives to undergo health-threatening hormone treatment and surgery. We are also concerned about the increasing bio-industrialization of life by the scientific community and life science companies and are shocked and dismayed that clonal human embryos have been patented and declared to be human "inventions." We oppose efforts to reduce human life and its various parts and processes to the status of mere research tools, manufactured products, and utilities. On the other hand, few, if any, on the left oppose research on adult stem cells, which can be taken from individuals after birth and have proved promising in both animal studies and clinical trials. This "soft path" approach to using the new science poses none of the ethical, social, and economic risks of strategies using embryo stem cells.

Moreover, many, if not most, of the diseases researchers hope to cure by using embryonic stem cells to produce body parts are the result of a complex choreography acted out between genetic predispositions and environmental triggers. By concentrating research almost exclusively on magic bullets in the form of gene replacements, the medical community forecloses the less invasive option of prevention – that is, using the sophisticated new scientific understanding of the relationship between genes and environments to develop medical therapies that keep people well.

We are also concerned about the slippery slope. If using a 12-day-old cloned embryo for producing cells and tissues is morally acceptable, what would preclude advocates in the future from championing the harvesting of more developed cells from, say, an 8-week-old embryo, or from harvesting organs from a 5-month-old cloned fetus if it were found to be a more useful medical therapy?

What about the question of cloning a full birth human being? Most members of Congress, on both sides of the aisle, would oppose a clonal birth. But for many in Congress, the scientific community, and the biotech industry, opposition is based solely on the fact that the cloning technique is still unsafe and could pose a risk of producing a malformed baby. Far fewer members of either party would be opposed to cloning a human baby were the procedure to become safe and reliable. After all, argue proponents, if an infertile couple desires to pass on their genetic inheritance by producing clones of one or both partners, shouldn't they be able to exercise their right of choice in the newly emerging biotech marketplace? Moreover, we are told not to be overly concerned because even though the clone will have the exact same genetic make-up as the original, he or she will develop differently because the social and environmental context within which his or her life unfolds will not be the same as the donor.

What both liberals and market libertarians miss is that the cloning of a human raises fundamental questions that go to the very nature of what it means to be a human being. From time immemorial we have thought of the birth of our progeny as a gift bestowed by God and/or a beneficent nature. We celebrate our generativity and revel in being participants in an act of creation. The coming together of sperm and egg represents a moment of utter surrender to forces outside of our control. We give part of ourselves up to another and the fusing of our maleness and femaleness results in a unique and finite new creation.

The reason most people have an almost instinctual revulsion to cloning is that, deep down, they sense that it signals the beginning of a new journey where the "gift of life" is steadily marginalized and eventually abandoned altogether. In its place, the new progeny becomes the ultimate shopping experience – designed in advance, produced to specification, and purchased in the biological marketplace.

Cloning is, first and foremost, an act of "production," not creation. Using the new biotechnologies, a living being is produced with the same degree of engineering as we have come to expect on an assembly line. When we think of engineering standards, what immediately come to mind are quality controls and predictable outcomes. That's exactly what cloning a human being is all about. For the first time in the history of our species, we can dictate, in advance, the final genetic constitution of the offspring. The child is no longer a unique creation – one of a kind – but rather an engineered reproduction.

Human cloning opens the door wide to the dawn of a commercial Brave New World. Already, life science companies have leapt ahead of the political game being played out in Congress and the media by patenting both human embryos and stem cells,

Jeremy Rifkin

giving them upfront ownership and control of a new form of reproductive commerce. Many on the left worry that human cloning, embryonic stem cell research, and soon designer babies lay the groundwork for a new form of bio-colonialism in which global life science companies become the ultimate arbiters over the evolutionary process itself.

We have good reason to be concerned. While heads of state and parliamentarians wrestle with the escalating struggle between right-to-life advocates and researchers, a far more menacing tale is unfolding behind the scenes with enormous potential consequences for society. US and British scientists and biotech companies are using embryo and stem cell technology to develop the framework for a commercial eugenics civilization with profound long-term implications for the human race.

"Eugenics" is a term coined by the British philosopher, Sir Francis Galton, in the nineteenth century. It means to use breeding both to eliminate undesirable genetic traits and to add desirable traits to improve the characteristics of an organism or species. When we think of eugenics, we think of Adolf Hitler's ghoulish plan to create the "master" race. Today, however, a new eugenics movement is being meticulously prepared in corporate boardrooms and far away from public scrutiny: a commercial eugenics, far different in nature from the kind of social eugenics hysteria that engulfed the world in the first half of the twentieth century.

Our story begins with a small biotech company, Roslin Bio-Med. The company was created in April 1998 by the Roslin Institute, a government-funded research institution outside Edinburgh, Scotland, where Dolly the sheep was cloned. The company was given an exclusive license to all the Roslin Institute's cloning technology for bio-medical research. A year later, Roslin Bio-Med was sold to Geron, a US firm headquartered in Menlo Park, California. Then, in January 2000, the British Patent Office granted a patent to Dr Ian Wilmut for his cloning technology. The patent – now owned by Geron – covers the cloning process and all the animals produced by the cloning process. What the public doesn't know – because it has received so little attention – is that the British Patent Office granted Wilmut and his company a patent on all cloned human embryos up to the blastocyst stage of development – that's the stage where pluripotent stem cells emerge. The British government, in effect, became the first in the world to recognize a human embryo as a form of intellectual property. The UK was also the first country to sanction the use of embryos, and even cloned embryos, for the harvesting of stem cells.

Despite British success in creating a favorable regulatory and commercial regime for the new research, it was the American company Geron that was quick to lock up the cloning technology. Even before securing the embryo patent, Geron had been quietly financing stem cell research conducted by two US researchers, Dr James A. Thomson of the University of Wisconsin and Dr John Gearhart of Johns Hopkins University in Baltimore, Maryland. In November 1998 both scientists announced that they had independently isolated and identified human stem cells. The breakthrough opened the door to the era of stem cell experimentation in medicine. The researchers' academic institutions immediately applied for patents and sold the exclusive licenses to use the patents to Geron. According to the terms of the Johns Hopkins agreement, Gearhart receives a share of the royalties collected on his patent. Gearhart and Johns Hopkins also own stock in Geron, and Gearhart serves as a consultant to the company.

Why I Oppose Human Cloning

Geron, once alone in the field, is now being challenged by a competitor. Geron's founder, Michael West, broke away from the company and now heads up Advanced Cell Technology in Massachusetts. West's new company has secured its own patents on non-human embryo cloning and is experimenting on alternative ways to create human stem cells.

By securing patents on the cloning process, as well as on cloned human embryos and stem cells, companies like Geron and Advanced Cell Technology are in a position to dictate the terms for further advances in medical research using stem cells. The mass production of cloned human embryos provides an unlimited source of stem cells. The stem cells, in turn, are the progenitors of all of the 200 or so differentiated cell types that make up the biology of human life. Researchers, institutes, and other companies from around the world will have to pay Geron and Advanced Cell Technology to access either the use of the embryos or the stem cells they produce, giving the companies unprecedented market advantage. If other researchers or companies actually succeed in making specific body cells from the stem cells, they will likely have to enter into commercial licensing agreements of various kinds with Geron and Advanced Cell Technology for the right to produce the products.

What does this portend for the future? To begin with, the granting of a patent for cloned human embryos raises a formidable political question. Can commercial institutions lay claim to a potential individual human life, in the form of intellectual property, at its early stage of development? The British Patent Office has said "yes." In the nineteenth century, we fought over the question of whether human beings after birth could be held as commercial property and eventually every nation abolished slavery. Now, however, we have technology that allows companies like Geron to claim potential human beings as intellectual property, at the developmental stage, between conception and birth. The question of whether commercial enterprises will be allowed to own potential human life at the developmental stage will likely be one of the seminal political issues of the Biotech Century.

Secondly, should companies like Geron and Advanced Cell Technology be allowed to own – in the form of intellectual property – the primary human cells that are the gateway to the entire biological composition that constitutes human life? Do we risk the dawn of a new era in human history where the creation of human life itself will increasingly fall under the control of commercial forces? Will global biotech companies own the designs, the parts, and the processes that produce a human life?

The commercial implications of embryo and stem cell research need to be examined in their entirety. Failure to do so could trap all of us into a commercial eugenics future we neither anticipated nor willingly chose.

The Poverty of Objections to Human Reproductive Cloning

John Harris

Dolly, the world's favourite sheep, was born on July 5, 1996 and died on February 14, 2003 (RIP). Since then, numerous objections have been made to the idea of using the cloning process that created her to create humans. While human reproductive cloning is probably of little scientific importance and, except in rare cases, of little use as a reproductive technology, suggestions that using cloning technology to create humans is in principle unethical are entirely without foundation.

When Dolly's birth was reported in *Nature* on February 27, 1997, amazement at the achievement and celebration of the science was overwhelmed by the comprehensively hostile reaction to the very idea of cloning. This hostility has lead to what is effectively a worldwide ban on reproductive cloning. Is such a ban justified? I do not believe so and in what follows I shall explain why.

I suggest that it is a fundamental principle of this society and all democracies worth the name, that human freedom should not be limited without good cause being shown. It should, I believe be disturbing to anyone that we have permitted our societies to be steamrollered into opposition to human cloning by a combination of what can only be considered to be hysteria and prejudice.

Is Anything Wrong with Human Cloning?

There are three principal types of argument against human reproductive cloning: it is claimed to be unsafe; it is claimed to be harmful to the resulting child; or it is claimed that duplicating a given genome is somehow a bad thing. Let's look briefly at these arguments.

Safety

The issue of safety, while by far the most important, need not detain us long. Of course we should not try to clone humans if doing so is unsafe or at least if it is sufficiently unsafe. It is important to notice that this is not an argument that gives any principled objections to cloning. It is an argument that would be good against the introduction of any new technology of whatever description. The appeal to safety, while for the moment cogent, could not conceivably justify the hysteria we have noted. We do not call for worldwide laws against vaccines against HIV, for example, although, so far as is known, there is as yet no thoroughly safe (or effective) vaccine available; nor do we campaign against the prospect of enabling humans to sprout wings, although we do not know whether that would be possible, safe, or effective. While safety is always a legitimate concern, there are important differences in the level of our concern depending on the degree of safety, or the lack of it, in question. We must remember that giving birth in the normal way is not a "safe" procedure for the mother or for the child; so unsafe is it for the mother that early abortion is known to be safer for her than childbirth. This notwithstanding, safety concerns are not normally considered powerful arguments against procreation. Thus, when the issue of safety is invoked as a concern relating to any medical procedure, let alone life choice, we need to ask detailed question about degrees of safety and possible alternatives. "Safety," *tout court*, is not the knockdown argument it is so often taken to be. Moreover, in so far as the degree of safety is unacceptable relative to the possible gains, it is not an argument against cloning per se, but against all and any procedures whatsoever with an unfavorable risk-benefit ratio. It is also of its nature contingent: solve the safety problems to a satisfactory degree and this objection fails.

The Welfare of the Child

The second type of argument against cloning concerns the welfare of the cloned child that might be born. All such arguments that do not refer to safety refer either to the burdens of expectation that might be placed on the child, or to the ambiguity of its status.

Expectations

Most parents have expectations of their children. Indeed, it might be thought that parents with no strong expectations of their children were highly irresponsible. Parents without strong expectations of their children are unlikely to be very concerned about their education, unlikely to provide the disciplined environment required for musical education, for example, or education in any of the other arts, let alone sports and physical training. The mother who spends hours at the piano with her son or the father who paces the touchline while his daughter practices hockey or football is not normally thought to be threatening the welfare of their child, yet they are likely to be motivated by strong expectations and hopes.

Many parents have children in the expectation that they will thereby have insured the future of the family business or the family farm; others may well have in mind the prospect of their children providing for them in old age or infirmity. Parental expectations are normal and normally disproportionate. But we do not panic, or seek regulation or legislation to control them. We accept them as normal or as within normal limits. There is no reason to suppose that the parents of cloned children will be radically different. They, like most parents, will in all probability see their expectations and hopes become transmuted to base metal in the cauldron of life and founder on the rock of individual autonomy. There is no reason to suppose that cloned children will be any the less rebellious or independent than other children, nor that those who parent such children will be any the more formidable in resisting such natural rebelliousness and independence than are the generality of parents. Of course there is here an assumption that those who would clone themselves are particularly unsuited to be parents perhaps because of the false expectations they are presumed to entertain and for the supposed neurotic strength of those expectations. Both these defects on prospective parents are possible, but we should note that we do not usually disqualify people from parenting on account of the false expectation about parenting and the likely virtues or capacities of the resulting children. Nor do we examine the strength of expectations in advance. Here, as in all other cases of allegations that parental states of mind are unacceptably harmful, we need more evidence that such states of mind will cause harm and, indeed, better evidence concerning the probability of the harm occurring and the degree of harm, before rushing to regulation or control.

Having ideals about the appropriate frame of mind for, and purposes of, procreation is a long way from evidence that those with other ideas are so immoral that legislation should prevent their procreative choices. We should not confuse our ideals and preferences for moral principles; nor should we imagine that we are entitled necessarily to enforce our preferences however strongly we hold them. The alleged "ambiguity" of the origins of possible clones and of the roles of their "parents" may be a valid reason for concern but hardly for condemnation. An adult who cloned herself would probably act as mother to the twin sister she had created; however, older siblings acting as parents to younger ones is a very common scenario and, while often not ideal, is not the sort of thing that causes widespread panic or outrage.

Onora O'Neill (2002) produces a new twist on some old arguments concerning child protection in the context of Human Reproductive Cloning (Cloning) and in doing so takes a swipe at some of my writings on the subject. Noting that I am on record as arguing that safe cloning would be morally acceptable, she insists that cloning is "something for which no responsible parents would plan." She suggests:

> Would-be parents by cloning who use reproductive tissue and genetic material from themselves or their relative aim to bring into existence a child with *confused* and *ambiguous* family relationships. Family relationships are confused when *several individuals hold the role of one*; they are ambiguous when *one individual holds the roles of several*. (2002: 67–8)

For O'Neill, such confusion and ambiguity are anathema. It is unclear why she is so worried about confusion and ambiguity. Evidence from divorce, adoption, fostering, and assisted reproduction suggests that children are able to cope with a great deal of ambiguity or confusion in family relationships without significant harm.[1]

Where it is rational to judge that an individual would not have a worthwhile life if he or she were to be brought into being in particular circumstances, then not only do we have powerful reasons not to make such choices ourselves, but also powerful moral reasons for preventing others from so doing if we can – by legislation or regulation if necessary. However, where we judge the circumstances of a future person to be less than ideal, but not so bad as to deprive that individual of a worthwhile existence, then we lack the moral justification to impose our ideals on others. This is particularly true when there is absolutely no empirical evidence of harms, simply a feeling that there "could be" such harms.

These are difficult matters on which to generalize and an example may help. We may all agree that poverty is a very good predictor of bad outcomes for children, and that ideally children should be brought up free from poverty and want. We may even think that if we ourselves were very poor, we would not want to have children, or not be justified in having them. It is quite another matter, however, to say that the poor should not be permitted to have children or should be denied assistance with reproduction. Nor does it seem good policy to permit those with power to use their discretion to deny assistance with reproduction on such general grounds.

We know that in the case of cloning, unless these technologies are used, the particular child in question will never exist (Burley and Harris, 1999; Harris, 2000a). A rational would-be child of cloning would regard the slight risk of confusion as a price well worth paying for existence, unless of course such confusion made life very terrible indeed.

The non-identity problem

This point was brought to philosophical attention by Derek Parfit (1984: ch. 16) and is often called "the non-identity problem." In this section I draw on some arguments I developed jointly with Justine Burley (Burley and Harris, 1999).

Consider the following two cases. The first is Parfit's and involves a 14-year old prospective mother. This girl chooses to have a child. Because she is so young, she gives her child a bad start in life. Though this will have bad effects throughout the child's life, his life will, predictably, be worth living. If the girl had waited for several years, she would have had a different child, to whom she would have given a better start in life (Parfit, 1984:358).

An analogue to this case is as follows. A woman chooses to have a child through cloning. Because she chooses to conceive in this way, she gives the child a bad start in life. Though this will have bad effects throughout the child's life, his life will, predictably, be worth living. If this woman had chosen to procreate by alternative means, she would have had a different child, to whom she would have given a better start in life.

In both cases, two courses of action are open to the prospective mother. In criticizing these women's pursuit of the first option available (i.e. conception at 14 and reproductive cloning respectively) people might claim that each mother's decisions will probably be worse for *her child* (Parfit, 1984: 359). However, as Parfit notes, while

John Harris

people can make this claim about the decisions taken, it does not explain what they believe is objectionable about them. It fails to explain this because neither decision can be worse for the particular children born; the alternative for both of them was to never to have existed at all. If the 14-year-old waits to conceive, a completely different child will be born. Likewise, if the woman chooses not to clone and instead conceives by natural procreative means, the child born will be a completely different one. Thus claims about the badness of pursuing the first option in both of the above cases cannot be claims about why *these* children have been harmed. It is better for *these* children that they live than not live at all.

Copying the Human Genome

Is it wrong or even bad to duplicate a human genome? Contrary to popular belief and the hysteria that has characterized discussions of cloning, human reproductive cloning is a process with which humanity has had vast and encouraging experience. Identical twins are nature's clones. They have been part of human nature and human experience from its earliest beginnings, and they are very common. Roughly three in every thousand births involve identical twins; that means that in a country the size of Britain there are about 200,000 such twins. Where is the evidence that it is cruel to produce such identical genotypes? Where is the evidence that twins lack individuality or are harmed by the existence of another with identical genes?

Genotype is not phenotype; genes influence, but do not determine, what traits people will have. Anyone who attempted to reproduce themselves by creating a clone would be mistaken because it simply can't be done. They might be foolish, but they are not necessarily wicked. We are entitled to prevent wickedness, but not, surely, naivety?

Human dignity

It is sometimes claimed that duplicating the human genome is contrary to human dignity. This idea is often also linked to Kantian ethics. A typical example is Axel Kahn's:

> The creation of human clones solely for spare cell lines would, from a philosophical point of view, be in obvious contradiction to the principle expressed by Immanuel Kant: that of human dignity. This principle demands that an individual – and I would extend this to read human life – should never be thought of as a means, but always also as an end. Creating human life for the sole purpose of preparing therapeutic material would clearly not be for the dignity of the life created. (1997a: 119)

This idea of using individuals as a means to the purposes of others is sometimes termed "instrumentalization" (McClaren, 1997), but it is very difficult to separate legitimate from illegitimate uses of others for one's own purposes. Respect for human dignity requires that an individual is *never* used *exclusively* as a means (see Harris, 1997: 754; Kahn, 1997b: 320) We can thus avoid instrumentalizing others if their parts in our plans are also parts of their own plans – i.e. if they have consented to their use by us.

Where, for example, a child is engendered to provide "a son and heir" or as "someone to take on the family farm or business" (as so often in so many cultures), it is unclear how or whether Kant's principle applies. Either other motives are also attributed to the parent to square parental purposes with Kant, or the child's eventual autonomy – and it's clear and substantial interest in or benefit from existence – takes precedence over the comparatively trivial issue of parental motives (Harris, 1998: 121–31, 145–57).

The preservation of the human genome

"The preservation of the human genome as common heritage of humanity" is deemed necessary by UNESCO (1997) and is used as an argument against cloning. Does this mean that the human genome must be "preserved intact" – that is, without variation – or does it mean simply that it must not be "reproduced asexually"? Cloning cannot be said to impact on the variability of the human genome; cloning simply repeats an existing genome, but this does not reduce variability, it simply does not increase it. Even if everyone in the world were to use cloning as his or her sole method of reproduction, this would not reduce the variety of the human genome, it would simply leave the variety exactly as it stands. However, because of the costs and the technical difficulty, not to mention the fact that sexual reproduction usually offers other incentives to those who use it, it is unlikely that cloning rates will ever be so high as to threaten the human gene pool or its variability.

It is sometimes feared that unless the human gene pool constantly changes through the random effects of sexual procreation, viruses and other diseases will become effective against a particular set of genotypes with disastrous consequences. This, if everyone were to reproduce only and forever via cloning, might well be a danger, but this is so unlikely, for reasons of cost, circumspection (or lack of it), and the attractions of alternative methods, that there is no real danger here.

A right to parents

It is sometimes claimed that children have "a right to have two parents" or "the right to be the product of the mixture of the genes of two individuals." If the right to have two parents is understood to be the right to have two social parents, then it is of course only violated by cloning if the family identified as the one to rear the resulting child is a one-parent family. This is not of course necessarily any more likely a result of cloning, than of the use of any of the other new reproductive technologies (or indeed of sexual reproduction). Moreover, if there is such a right, it is widely violated, creating countless "victims," and there is no significant evidence of any enduring harm from the violation of this supposed right. Indeed, the tragic existence of so many war widows throughout the world and the success most of them have in rearing their children is eloquent testimony to the exaggerated fears expressed concerning cloning.

John Harris

If, on the other hand, we interpret a right to two parents as the right to be the product of the mixture of the genes of two individuals, then the supposition that this right is violated when the nucleus of the cell of one individual is inserted into the de-nucleated egg of another is false in the way this claim is usually understood. There is at least one sense in which a right expressed in this form might be violated by cloning, but not in any way that has force as an objection. First, it is false to think that the clone is the genetic child of the nucleus donor. It is not. The clone is the twin brother or sister of the nucleus donor and the genetic offspring of the nucleus donor's own parents. Thus this type of cloned individual is, and always must be, the genetic child of two separate genotypes, of two genetically different individuals, however often it is cloned or re-cloned.

What good is cloning?

Reproductive cloning may help some people to have children genetically related to them who otherwise could not. This aside, the purely reproductive purposes of cloning are not obviously important or urgent; but that is not to say that it is a matter of indifference if cloning is banned. As I have suggested earlier, we should be reluctant to accept restrictions on human liberty, however trivial the purposes, without good and sufficient cause being shown. The argument of this chapter has shown such cause to be decidedly absent.

One major reason for developing cloning in animals is said to be to permit the study of genetic diseases and indeed genetic development more generally. Whether or not there would be major advantages in human cloning by nuclear substitution is not yet clear. Certainly, it would enable some infertile people to have children genetically related to them; it offers the prospect, as we have noted, of preventing some diseases caused by mitochondrial DNA; and could help "carriers" of X-linked and autosomal recessive disorders to have their own genetic children without the risk of passing on the disease. It is also possible that so-called therapeutic cloning could be used for the creation of "spare parts," by, for example, growing stem cells for particular cell types from non-diseased parts of an adult or by cloning stem cells for regenerative therapies and possibly for life-extending therapies (Harris, 2002a, 2002b, forthcoming).

Dolly collapses the divide between germ and somatic cells

There are some interesting implications of cloning by nuclear substitution (which have been clear since frogs were cloned by this method in the 1960s), which have not apparently been noticed.[2] There is currently a worldwide moratorium on the manipulation of the human germ line, while therapeutic somatic line interventions are, in principle, permitted. However, inserting the mature nucleus of an adult cell into a de-nucleated egg turns the cells thus formed into germ line cells. This has three important effects. First, it effectively eradicates the firm divide between germ line and somatic line nuclei because each adult cell nucleus is in principle "translatable" into a germ line cell nucleus by transferring its nucleus and creating a clone. Secondly, it permits somatic line modifications to human cells to become germ line modifications. Suppose you permanently insert a normal copy of the adenosine deaminase gene into the bone marrow cells of an individual suffering from severe combined immuno-deficiency (which affects the so called "bubble boy" who has to live in a protective bubble of clean air) with obvious beneficial therapeutic effects. This is a somatic line modification. If you were then to clone a permanently genetically modified bone marrow cell from this individual, the modified genome would be passed to the clone and become part of his or her genome, transmissible to her offspring indefinitely through the germ line. Thus a benefit that would have perished with the original recip-ient, and not been passed on for the protection of her children, can be conferred on subsequent generations by cloning.[3] The third effect is that it shows the oft-asserted moral divide between germ line and somatic line therapy to be even more ludicrous than was previously supposed.

Immortality?

Of course some individuals might wish to have offspring not simply with their genes, but with a matching genotype. However, there is no way that they could make such an individual a duplicate of themselves. So many years later, the environmental influ-ences would be radically different, and since every choice, however insignificant, causes a life-path to branch with unpredictable consequences, the holy grail of using cloning to achieve immortality would be doomed to remain a fruitless quest. We can conclude that people who would clone themselves might be foolish and ill-advised, but it is doubtful that they would be immoral and nor would their attempts harm society or their children significantly.

Therapeutic cloning coupled with stem cell research might enable the human body to repair itself indefinitely, leading eventually to a kind of immortality. Some people fear this; I for one believe the dangers have been exaggerated, but since this, at the moment remote, possibility does not involve reproductive cloning, I will not explore it further here.[4]

Jeremy Rifkin's Arguments

Jeremy Rifkin has produced two oblique arguments against cloning which merit some attention. The first is part of his general preference for one kind of biotechnology rather than another; and the second concerns the intrusion of intellectual property issues in general, and patenting in particular, into the cloning debate.

Curing disease versus preventive health

In *The Biotech Century*, Rifkin repeats his oft-asserted distinction between using biotechnology "to 'correct' disorders and arrest the progress of disease" between "efforts designed to cure people who have become ill," on the one hand, and the task of "exploring the relationship between genetic mutations and environmental triggers with the hope of fashioning a more sophisticated, scientifically based understanding

John Harris

and approach to preventive health" on the other (1998: 228). He concludes that it is wrong to pursue both methods, and judges rightly that the question we need to answer so as to know which is preferable is: "on balance, does it do more harm than good?" (1998: 232). Rifkin thinks he knows the answer to this one, and he sets out his answer as follows:

> "First do no harm" is a well-established and long revered principle of medicine. The fact is, the more powerful a technology is at altering and transforming the natural world – that is, marshaling the environment for immediate, efficient and short term ends – the more likely it is to disrupt and undermine long-standing networks of relationships and create disequilibrium somewhere else in the surrounding milieu. Which of the two competing visions of biotechnology – genetic engineering or ecological practices and preventive health – is more radical and adventurous and most likely to cause disequilibrium and which is the more conservative approach and least likely to cause unanticipated harm down the line? The answer, I believe, is obvious. (1998: 233–4)

A number of points need to be made here. The first is that I have no objections to Rifkin's preferred use of biotechnology; but I believe there are strong grounds for resisting any attempts to make it the only approach. We need both approaches, not just one. Why? First, because when Rifkin asks "Which of the two competing visions of biotechnology ... is ... least likely to cause unanticipated harm down the line?" he is begging a crucial question. Although he does not produce (and indeed could not produce) any evidence for this claim, the claim is tendentious in the extreme because it implies that it is only "down the line" harm that we have to worry about. Recall that the genetic engineering of which he disapproves is directed toward "efforts designed to cure people who have become ill." If such genetic engineering methods are not pursued, there is a grave danger that those who have already become ill will be neglected and will suffer and perhaps die as a result. These are real and present dangers, faced by real and present people who will suffer and die if their diseases are not treated and if research, which might help them, is not pursued. Rifkin's preferred strategy of "ecological practices and preventive health" is directed toward preventing people becoming ill in the future, not toward helping those who have already become ill. We do not know which strategy will save more people overall, but we should not choose between them because either that will condemn present people to suffer and die when they might be helped, or it will fail to make ecological changes that might prevent future disease. It is obvious that we must do both, not least because the rule of rescue requires that we do not abandon those in present need. It is normal good practice to meet real and present dangers before future and speculative ones; this idea is part of the so-called rule of rescue.

Secondly, we should notice that Rifkin makes another rather tendentious claim. He says (see above): "The fact is, the more powerful a technology is at altering and transforming the natural world – that is, marshaling the environment for immediate, efficient and short term ends – the more likely it is to disrupt and undermine long-standing networks of relationships and create disequilibrium somewhere else in the surrounding milieu." Rifkin calls this a "fact," but it is simply a piece of reckless (and only partially coherent) speculation; moreover, even if it were coherent and true, we would need to know whether the resulting "disequilibrium in the surrounding milieu"[5] caused harm that would not be compensated for by the good done by the powerful technology. Without these two crucial pieces of information we cannot hope to make a rational choice, and all that is left to us is the pursuit of prejudice (Harris and Holm, 2002).

Intellectual property

In a newspaper article Rifkin made some radical, and radically misleading, claims about intellectual property issues in the context of cloning. Here is what he says:

> The British patent office has just granted Wilmut's Roslin Institute patents on his cloning process and all animals cloned using the process. The patents have been licensed to Geron Corp., a California-based biotech company. There is something more, however. The patent also includes as intellectual property – i.e., patented inventions – all cloned human embryos up to the blastocyst stage, which is a cluster of about 140 cells. For the first time, a national government has declared that a specific human being created through the process of cloning is, at its earliest phase of development, to be considered an invention in the eyes of the patent office. The implications are profound and far-reaching.
>
> It was less than 135 years ago that the United States abolished slavery, making it illegal for any human being to own another human being as property after birth. Now the British patent office has opened the door to a new era in which a developing human being can be owned, in the form of intellectual property, in the gestational stages between conception and birth.
>
> Regardless of where people may stand on the question of abortion, one would think that everyone would be shocked at the idea that a company might be able to own a human embryo as an invention.
>
> Parents, when they read about this extraordinary patent decision, should ask themselves whether their children and future generations will be well served ethically if they grow up in a world where they come to think of embryonic human life as intellectual property, controlled by life science companies. What happens to our children's most basic notions about the distinctions between human life and inanimate objects when the former comes to be regarded by law as mere inventions, simple utilities to be bartered like so many commodities in the commercial arena?
>
> And, if cloned human embryos are, in fact, considered to be human inventions, then what becomes of our notion of God, the creator? What will future generations say when their children ask, where do babies come from? Will they say they are the inventions of scientists and the property of life science companies? (Rifkin, 2000)

This is a fascinating article for a number of reasons. The first is that even if a patent of the sort Rifkin describes had been granted,[6] it would imply neither slavery nor the possibility of physical ownership of a human individual. Had such a patent been granted, it would not have withstood challenge in the courts for precisely the reasons Rifkin gives: namely, its incompatibility with even basic notions of human rights and with normal notions of public morals and so on. Moreover, the operations of the UK Patent Office are not the workings of a national government any more than the rulings of the US mail come from the Oval Office. But "ownership" of intellectual property in something, including a human embryo, does not necessarily imply other instances of ownership. If a biotech company had patents on every cell in my body

John Harris

and every gene in my genome, it would not affect my humanity, nor yet my civil, political, and moral rights one jot or title. I would not thereby be a slave to the biotech company, nor yet in any sense personally "owned." This is a combination of scare-mongering and/or misunderstanding of a very high order. For Rifkin to invoke the parallel with slavery implies both a very shaky understanding of intellectual property issues or a high degree of panic.

In any event, the panic is premature. The Patents Act 1977 has been amended by the introduction of Schedule A2.[7] Schedule A2 was introduced as part of a set of amendments to the UK Act, which came into force on July 28, 2000 and which were intended to implement EU Directive 98/44/EC on biotechnological inventions. Schedule A2 provides, inter alia, as follows:

1 An invention shall not be considered unpatentable solely on the ground that it concerns:
   (a) a product consisting of or containing biological material; or
   (b) a process by which biological material is produced, processed or used.
2 Biological material which is isolated from its natural environment or produced by means of a technical process may be the subject of an invention even if it previously occurred in nature.
3 The following are not patentable inventions:
   (a) the human body, at the various stages of its formation and development, and the simple discovery of one of its elements, including the sequence or partial sequence of a gene;
   (b) processes for cloning human beings;
   (c) processes for modifying the germ line genetic identity of human beings.

As to Rifkin's final rhetorical flourish (as quoted above):

And, if cloned human embryos are, in fact, considered to be human inventions, then what becomes of our notion of God, the creator? What will future generations say when their children ask, where do babies come from? Will they say they are the inventions of scientists and the property of life science companies?

Here, I must confess that I for one would feel that future generations would have a better grasp of reality if they had a biological and social explanation of where children come from, a socio-legal explanation of who their parents are, and an ethical account of how they and their parents should be considered. As to the question "what becomes of our notion of God, the creator?" I hope this goes the way of all theories that are totally without foundation and are, moreover, manifestly implausible.[8]

Notes

I am indebted to Susan Golombok and Martin Richards for many sources cited in the "Further reading" section.
1   There is a vast literature on the risks of harm to children from various factors concerning their origins; most of them skeptical about the bad effects of ambiguity, confusion, use of

reproductive technologies, adoption, fostering, divorce, etc. See the "Further reading" section.

2 Except by Pedro Lowenstein, who pointed them out to me.

3 These possibilities were pointed out to me by Pedro Lowenstein, who is currently working on the implications for human gene therapy.

4 For more on immortality, see Harris (2000b, 2002c).

5 For the record, this is the incoherent bit! What counts as disequilibrium and when and why might it be bad to unbalance the milieu are good causes.

6 I have been unable to trace the history of this claim by Rifkin. It may be that a patent was initially and erroneously granted by the UK Patent Office but, as will be seen in the discussion that follows, such a patent is now illegal and must have been revoked if it ever existed.

7 Patents Act 1977, Schedule A2, Paragraph 3(a). I am grateful to my colleague David Booton for his invaluable advice on intellectual property law.

References

Burley, Justine and Harris, John (1999). "Human cloning and child welfare." *Journal of Medical Ethics*, 25: 108–13.

Harris, John (1997). "Is cloning an attack on human dignity?" *Nature*, 387: 754.

Harris, John (1998). *Clones, Genes and Immortality.* Oxford: Oxford University Press.

Harris, John (2000a). "The welfare of the child." *Health Care Analysis*, 8: 27–34.

Harris, John (2000b). "Intimations of immortality." *Science,* 288/5463 (July 4): 59.

Harris, John (2002a). "The ethical use of human embryonic stem cells." *Medicine and Philosophy*, 23: 6–14.

Harris, John (2002b) "The use of human embryonic stem cells in research and therapy." In Justine C. Burley and John Harris (eds.), *A Companion to Genethics: Philosophy and the Genetic Revolution* (pp. 158–75). Oxford: Blackwell.

Harris, John (2002c). "Intimations of immortality – the ethics and justice of life extending therapies." In Michael Freeman (ed.), *Current Legal Problems* (pp. 65–95). Oxford: Oxford University Press.

Harris, John (forthcoming). "Stem cells, sex and procreation." *Cambridge Quarterly of Ethics.*

Harris, John and Holm, Søren (2002). "Extended lifespan and the paradox of precaution." *The Journal of Medicine and Philosophy*, 27: 355–68.

Kahn, Alex (1997a). "Clone mammals ... clone man." *Nature*, 386: 119.

Kahn, Alex (1997b) "Cloning, dignity and ethical revisionism." *Nature*, 388: 320.

McClaren, Anne (1997). *Opinion of the Group of Advisers on the Ethical Implications of Biotechnology to the European Commission*, No. 9 (May 29). Available at: ⟨http://europa.eu.int/comm/european_group_ethics/gaieb/en/opinion9.pdf⟩.

O'Neill, Onora (2002). *Autonomy and Trust in Bioethics.* Cambridge: Cambridge University Press.

Parfit, Derek (1984). *Reasons and Persons.* Oxford: Clarendon Press.

Rifkin, Jeremy (2000). "Cloning: what hath genomics wrought?" *Los Angeles Times* (February 3): B9.

Rifkin, Jeremy (1998). *The Biotech Century.* London: Phoenix.

UNESCO (1997). *Universal Declaration on the Human Genome and Human Rights.* UNESCO pamphlet (December 3).

Further reading

Blyth, E., Crawshaw, M., and Speirs, J (1998). *Truth and the Child 10 Years On: Information Exchange in Donor Assisted Conception.* Birmingham: British Association of Social Workers.

Burley, Justine and Harris, John (1999). "Human cloning and child welfare." *Journal of Medical Ethics*, 25: 108–13.

Cook, Rachel and Golombok, Susan (1995) "A survey of semen donation: phase 2 – the view of donors." *Human Reproduction*, 10: 951–9.

Cook, Rachel, Golombok, Susan, Bish, Alison, and Murray, Clare (1995). "Disclosure of donor insemination: parental attitudes." *American Journal of Orthopsychiatry*, 65: 549–59.

Franklin, Sarah and McKinnon, Susan (2001) *Relative Values: Reconfiguring Kinship Studies.* Durham, NC: Duke University Press.

Freeman, M. (1996). "The new birth right?" *International Journal of Children's Rights*, 4: 273–97.

Giddens, Anthony (1991). *Modernity and Self-identity: Self and Society in the Late Modern Age.* Cambridge: Polity.

Golombok, Susan and Tasker, Fiona (1996). "Do parents influence the sexual orientation of their children? Findings from a longitudinal study of lesbian families." *Development Psychology*, 32: 3–11.

Golombok, Susan, Brewaeys, A., and Cook, Rachel et al. (1996). "The European study of assisted reproduction families: family functioning and child development." *Human Reproduction*, 11: 2324–31.

Golombok, Susan, Brewaeys, A., and Giavazzi, M. T. et al. (1996). "The European study of assisted reproduction families." *Human Reproduction*, 11: 2324–31.

Golombok, Susan, Brewaeys, A., and Giavazzi, M. T. et al. (2002) "The European study of assisted reproduction families: the transition to adolescence." *Human Reproduction*, 17: 830–40.

Golombok, Susan, Cook, Rachel, Bish, Alison, and Murray, Clare (1995). "Families created by the new reproductive technologies: quality of parenting and social and emotional development of the children." *Child Development*, 66: 285–98.

Golombok, Susan, Maccallum, F. M., Goodman, E., and Rutter M. (2002). "Families with children conceived by donor insemination: a follow up at age twelve." *Child Development*, 73: 952–68.

Golombok, Susan, Murray, Clare, Brinsden, Peter, and Abdalla, Hossam (1999). "Social versus biological parenting: family functioning and socioemotional development of children conceived by egg or sperm donation." *Child Psychiatry*, 40: 519–27.

Golombok, Susan, Tasker, Fiona, and Murray, Clare (1997). "Children raised in fatherless families from infancy: family relationships and the socioemotional development of children of lesbian and single heterosexual mothers." *Child Psychiatry*, 38: 783–91.

Harris, John (1997). "Goodbye Dolly: the ethics of human cloning." *The Journal of Medical Ethics*, 23: 353–60.

Harris, John (1998a). "Cloning and human dignity." *Cambridge Quarterly of Healthcare Ethics*, 7: 163–8.

Harris, John (1998b). "Rights and reproductive choice." In John Harris and Søren Holm (eds.), *The Future of Human Reproduction: Choice and Regulation* (pp. 5–37). New York: Oxford University Press.

Harris, John (1999a). "The concept of the person and the value of life." *Kennedy Institute of Ethics Journal*, 9: 293–308.

Harris, John (1999b). "Genes, clones and human rights." In Justine C. Burley (ed.), *The Genetic Revolution and Human Rights: The Amnesty lectures 1998* (pp. 61–95). Oxford: Oxford University Press.

Harris, John (2000). "Clones, genes and reproductive autonomy." In Raphael Cohen-Almagor (ed.), *Medical Ethics at the Dawn of the 21st Century. Annals of the New York Academy of Sciences*, 913: 209–18.

Harris, John (2001). "The scope and importance of bioethics." In John Harris (ed.), *Bioethics: Oxford Readings in Philosophy* (pp. 1–22). Oxford: Oxford University Press.

Harris, John (2003a). "Cloning." In R. G. Frey and Kit Wellman (eds.), *A Companion to Applied Ethics* (pp. 382–95). Oxford: Blackwell.

Harris, John (2003b). "Reproductive choice." *Encyclopaedia of the Human Genome*. London: Nature Publishing Group Reference.

Harris, John and Holm, Søren (eds.) (1998). *The Future of Human Reproduction*. Oxford: Clarendon Press.

Howe, David and Feast, Julia (2000). *Adoption, Search and Reunion*. London: The Children's Society.

McWinnie, J. (1996). "Families following assisted conception: what do we tell our child?" Dundee: Dept of Law, University of Dundee.

Modell, Judith S. (1994). *Kinship with Strangers: Adoption and Interpretation of Kinship in American Culture*. Berkeley: University of California Press.

O'Neill, Onora (unpublished manuscript dated 2002). "What is genetic identity?" Newnham College, Cambridge.

Tasker, Fiona and Golombok, Suan (1995). "Adults raised as children in lesbian families." *American Journal of Orthopsychiatry*, 65: 203–15.

EUTHANASIA

In Defense of Voluntary Active Euthanasia and Assisted Suicide

Michael Tooley

In this essay I shall defend the following two claims: first, given appropriate circumstances, neither voluntary active euthanasia nor assisting someone to commit suicide is in any way morally wrong; secondly, there should be no laws prohibiting such actions, in the relevant cases.

The discussion is organized as follows. First, I set out some preliminary concepts and distinctions. Then, in the next two sections, I offer two arguments in support of the thesis that assisted suicide and voluntary active euthanasia are not morally wrong. Finally, I ask whether there is any reason for thinking that, even if, as I have argued, voluntary active euthanasia and assisted suicide are not morally wrong, they should, nevertheless, not be legally permitted – and I argue that this is not the case.

Important Concepts and Distinctions

Writers on this topic define the term "euthanasia" in quite different ways. In the following discussion, I shall use the term "euthanasia" to refer to any action where a person is intentionally killed or allowed to die because it is believed that the individual would be better off dead than alive – or else, as when one is in an irreversible coma, at least no worse off. So understood, under what conditions, if any, is euthanasia morally acceptable, and should it ever be legally permitted?

Two familiar distinctions are important here. First, there is the threefold distinction involving voluntary euthanasia, non-voluntary euthanasia, and involuntary euthanasia. Thus, euthanasia is voluntary if the person who undergoes it has requested it. It is non-voluntary if the person is unable to indicate whether or not he or she wants to undergo euthanasia. (This will include, for example, cases involving infants, and adults who have permanently lost consciousness.) Finally, it is involuntary if the person in question wants to go on living.

The second important distinction is between active euthanasia and passive euthanasia. How this distinction is best drawn is controversial, and there are two slightly different ways of doing so, depending upon how cases involving the withdrawal of life-support systems are classified. Thus, one way of drawing the distinction is in terms of the contrast between acting and doing nothing at all: it is active euthanasia whenever anything at all is done – including the withdrawal of a life-support system – that facilitates the person's death, and passive euthanasia only if nothing is done that brings about the person's death.

A different way of drawing the distinction is in terms of whether what might be called the "primary cause" of death is some human action, or, instead, an injury or disease: one has a case of active euthanasia whenever the primary cause of death is human action, and a case of passive euthanasia whenever the primary cause of death is some injury or disease.

Precisely where the line should be drawn between active euthanasia and passive euthanasia is important if one holds, as a significant number of people do, that passive euthanasia is morally permissible, but that active euthanasia is not. Here, however, we can ignore this issue, given that my goal is to argue that voluntary *active* euthanasia is morally permissible.

Before turning to a defense of assisted suicide and voluntary active euthanasia, it should be noted that some opponents of voluntary active euthanasia and assisted suicide define the term "euthanasia" much more narrowly than I have done – indeed, often very narrowly indeed. This is especially so in the case of writers who are defending the Roman Catholic view on these issues. Thus, for example, Daniel Callahan offers the following definition: "By euthanasia I mean the direct killing of a patient by a doctor, ordinarily by means of a lethal injection" (2005: 189, n.1).

Notice that such a definition is narrower that what I have offered in three ways. First, cases where one allows a person to die do not get classified as euthanasia, even if one's intention is precisely the same as when one kills a person to enable that person to escape from the suffering that he or she is undergoing. Secondly, cases where, for example, a doctor administers a dose of morphine that it is known will cause death via respiratory failure do not get classified as cases of euthanasia, since it is held that the killing is not "direct": the doctor's intention is, it is said, merely to relieve the pain, not to kill, even though the doctor knows that the action will kill the patient. Finally, by incorporating the restriction to terminally ill persons, cases where a person is not terminally ill, but is suffering greatly from pain that cannot be relieved, are being defined as lying outside the scope of euthanasia.

Such a definition of "euthanasia" seems to me ill-advised in the extreme. In the first place, one is deprived of crisp and very useful expressions – such as "passive euthanasia" – for referring to cases where a terminally ill person is allowed to die. Secondly, and more seriously, the person who identifies euthanasia with the direct killing of a terminally ill person typically does so because he or she views the indirect killing of a terminally ill person as morally unproblematic, and similarly for an action of merely allowing a terminally ill person to die. If one holds, however, that such actions are morally permissible, but that the direct killing of a terminally ill person is morally wrong, then among the most crucial issues that one needs to address

Michael Tooley

are, first, why the direct versus indirect distinction has such moral significance, and, secondly, why the same is true in the case of the distinction between killing and letting die. If one defines euthanasia broadly, as I have done, those issues are immediately in front of one. By contrast, a narrow definition of euthanasia makes it very easy to pass over those crucial questions without even any comment, let alone careful discussion and argument.

A Fundamental Defense of Assisted Suicide and Voluntary Active Euthanasia

The argument

A very plausible argument in support of the claim that voluntary active euthanasia and assisted suicide are not morally wrong in themselves is as follows:

(1) If a person is suffering considerable pain due to an incurable illness, then in some cases that person's death is in his or her own interest.

(2) If a person's death is in that person's own interest, then committing suicide is also in that person's own interest.

(3) Therefore, if a person is suffering considerable pain due to an incurable illness, then in some cases committing suicide is in that person's own interest. (From (1) and (2).)

(4) A person's committing suicide in such circumstances may very well also satisfy the following two conditions:
   (a) it neither violates anyone else's rights, nor wrongs anyone;
   (b) it does not make the world a worse place.

(5) An action that satisfies conditions (a) and (b), and that is not contrary to one's own interest, cannot be morally wrong.

(6) Therefore, a person's committing suicide when all of above conditions obtain would not be morally wrong. (From (3), (4), and (5).)

(7) It could be morally wrong to assist a person in committing suicide only if (i) it was morally wrong for that person to commit suicide, or (ii) committing suicide was contrary to the person's own interest, or (iii) assisting the person to commit suicide violated an obligation one had to someone else.

(8) Circumstances may very well be such that neither assisting a person to commit suicide nor performing voluntary active euthanasia violates any obligations that one has to others.

(9) Therefore, it would not be wrong to assist a person in committing suicide in the circumstances described above. (From (3), (6), (7), and (8).)

(10) Whenever assisting a person in committing suicide is justified, voluntary active euthanasia is also justified, provided the latter action does not violate any obligation that one has to anyone else.

(11) Therefore, voluntary active euthanasia would not be morally wrong in the circumstances in question. (From (8), (9), and (10).)

This argument, progressing from suicide, through assisted suicide, and on to voluntary active euthanasia, is a very natural one, and the assumptions involved seem quite modest. But is the argument sound? Next, I shall argue that it is.

The soundness of the argument

Anyone who holds that assisted suicide and voluntary active euthanasia are never *in themselves* morally permissible must hold that the above argument is unsound. Can that contention be sustained? I shall argue that it cannot.

An argument can be unsound in two different ways. First, it may involve fallacious reasoning. Secondly, it may contain one or more false premises. Anyone who wishes to reject the conclusion of the above argument needs to show, therefore, that it is defective in one (or both) of these ways.

As regards the first possible shortcoming, the fundamental way of determining whether an argument contains any fallacious reasoning is to formulate the argument in a logically rigorous way, and then to determine whether each step in the reasoning is in accordance with some truth-preserving rule of inference. But one can also go back to the definition of validity, according to which a given inference is deductively valid if it is logically impossible for the conclusion to be false if all of the premises are true. In setting out the above argument, I have indicated, for each step in the reasoning, what earlier statements the conclusion is supposed to follow from. Readers can therefore ask themselves, in each case, whether the conclusion drawn could possibly be false if the relevant premises were true, and I suggest that, when this is done, it will be seen that the argument is deductively valid.

If this is right, then the argument can only be unsound if at least one of the premises is false. So let us consider whether any good reason can be offered for rejecting any of the premises.

The starting point of the argument is the following claim:

(1) If a person is suffering considerable pain due to an incurable illness, then that person's death may very well be in his or her own interest.

This claim is, I suggest, very plausible indeed. For one thing, the level of suffering that people undergo in connection with some incurable illnesses is such that they come to hope that death will occur sooner rather than later. In addition, when death does come in such cases, those who loved the individual who has died welcome death, and view it as in the interest of the individual in question.

Let us consider, then, the second premise:

(2) If a person's death is in that person's own interest, then committing suicide is also in that person's own interest.

Some would argue that this premise is false. In particular, Roman Catholic philosophers who accept the teachings of their church would argue that even if one is in a situation where one would be better off dead than alive, it is not in one's interest to *bring about* one's own death, since suicide is a mortal sin, and this means that someone

Michael Tooley

who makes a fully informed decision to commit suicide will wind up much worse off, since they will suffer eternal torment in Hell.

A full answer to this question would require a major detour through the philosophy of religion. A brief response, however, is as follows. The Catholic Church holds that many things, beside suicide, are mortal sins – including masturbation, any type of premarital sexual activity, homosexual sex, and the use of contraceptives within marriage. Anyone who wishes to appeal to the authoritative teachings of the Catholic Church in order to object to the second premise needs to be prepared, accordingly, to argue that the Catholic Church is right in holding that the other actions just mentioned also place one at serious risk of spending eternity in Hell. I would suggest that the chances of successfully doing this are not very great.

The third premise of my argument was this:

(4) A person's committing suicide in such circumstances may very well also satisfy the following two conditions:
   (a) it neither violates anyone else's rights, nor wrongs anyone;
   (b) it does not make the world a worse place.

This premise is, I suggest, very plausible. For while it is true that many people who are thus suffering have obligations to others – especially their husbands or wives, and their children – the obligations in question are typically ones that they could not possibly meet, given that they are in a state of extreme pain. In addition, most obligations are not of such a nature that one is morally obliged regardless of the cost to oneself, so that even if one could meet certain prima facie obligations by soldiering on in the face of extreme pain, it will rarely be the case that one acts wrongly if, in those circumstances, one does not meet the prima facie obligation. Finally, the ending of one's life, in such circumstances, will not only end one's own suffering; it will also end the emotional suffering experienced by those who love one. So, in general, the ending of a person's life in such circumstances will make the world a better place, not a worse one.

Some opponents of euthanasia would object, however, that although suicide may very well not violate the rights of other humans, it does not follow that condition (4a) is satisfied. Moreover, that condition, they would contend, is in fact never satisfied, since all lives belong to God, and so the destruction of anyone's life – including destruction by the person in question – violates God's right of ownership.

This 'divine ownership' objection is unsound for at least three reasons. First, it can be shown that many bad things that are present in the world, such as undeserved suffering, make it very unlikely that God, understood as an all-powerful, all-knowing, and perfectly good being, exists. Secondly, persons cannot be the property of others, since autonomy is a right that persons possess by virtue of their nature as beings capable of conscious experience, thought, and rational choice. Thirdly, consider sentient beings that are not persons. Such beings can be owned, but ownership does not make it permissible to compel such beings to suffer. Similarly, if, contrary to the second point, persons could be owned by others, that would still not render it permissible to prohibit persons from committing suicide when that was in their rational self-interest, and not morally wrong.

The fourth premise of the argument was this:

In Defense of Voluntary Active Euthanasia and Assisted Suicide

(5) An action that satisfies conditions (a) and (b), and that is not contrary to one's own interest, cannot be morally wrong.

The claim that this premise is plausible can be supported as follows. First of all, it initially seems plausible that for an action to be wrong, there must be some individual – either a person, or a sentient being that is not a person – who is wronged by the action. But if condition (a) is satisfied, then no one else is wronged, and so the only possibility is that in ending one's own life, one is wronging oneself. We are considering, however, a case where suicide is, by hypothesis, in one's own interest. But if an action is in one's own interest, how can one do wrong to oneself by performing that action? Surely one cannot. If so, then the upshot is that no one – either oneself or anyone else – is wronged by the action.

So far, so good. However, reflections concerning future generations have convinced many philosophers that an action may be wrong even if it wrongs no one (Parfit, 1984: 357–61). For consider two actions, one of which will lead to future generations that enjoy an extremely high quality of life, and the other of which will result in future generations that have lives worth living, but only barely so. Other things being equal, would not the second action be morally wrong? But notice that there may be no one who is worse off if the second action is performed, since it may be that none of the people who have lives worth living, but only barely so, when the second action is performed, would have existed if the first action had been performed, while the people who *would* have enjoyed lives of very high quality if the second action had been performed are not worse off, since they never exist. So it would seem that no one is wronged if the second action is performed, since no one is worse off.

What is true, however, is that the world is a worse place given the second action than it would have been if the first action had been performed. So if, as is generally thought, the second action is wrong, then a natural conclusion is that actions can be wrong if, even though they wrong no one, they make the world a worse place than it would otherwise be.

The reason for including condition (b) in statement (5), accordingly, is to address this possibility. This having been done, it would seem, then, that the fourth premise, thus formulated, is very plausible.

The fifth premise of my argument was this:

(7) It could be morally wrong to assist a person in committing suicide only if (i) it was morally wrong for that person to commit suicide, or (ii) committing suicide was contrary to the person's own interest, or (iii) assisting the person to commit suicide violated an obligation one had to someone else.

Here, the supporting line of thought is this. Suppose that someone is considering performing an action that is not morally wrong. How could it be wrong to help them to perform that action? Two possibilities come to mind. First, it could be that while it was not morally wrong for the other person to perform the action, it was an action that was very seriously contrary to that person's own best interests, and that, because of this, it would be wrong for one to provide the person with assistance in performing the action. Secondly, it could be that one has obligations to someone else that

Michael Tooley

one would violate if one helped the person to perform the action in question. One might, for example, belong to a religious group where it is a condition of membership that one does not provide assistance to someone in committing suicide.

In the absence of either of these circumstances, however, is there any way in which it could be wrong to help a person to commit suicide? It is, I suggest, very hard to see any other possibility here. It would certainly seem, then, that the fifth premise is justified.

The sixth premise was this:

(8) Circumstances may very well be such that neither assisting a person to commit suicide nor performing voluntary active euthanasia violates any obligations that one has to others.

The ground for accepting this premise is simply that, while one might have obligations to others that would make it wrong for one to assist someone to commit suicide, or for one to perform voluntary active euthanasia – obligations that arose, for example, from membership in some religious group, or professional union, that prohibited such actions – it will not in general be true that one has such obligations.

Finally, the concluding premise of my argument was this:

(11) Whenever assisting a person in committing suicide is justified, voluntary active euthanasia is also justified, provided the latter action does not violate any obligation that one has to anyone else.

Here the thought is simply this. Provided that one does not have any obligations to others that would make it wrong for one to provide someone with voluntary active euthanasia, then the difference between helping someone to end his or her life, and doing it for that person, cannot be morally significant. So the final assumption in the argument is justified.

Voluntary Passive Euthanasia versus Voluntary Active Euthanasia

The argument

My second argument in support of the thesis that voluntary active euthanasia and assisted suicide are not morally wrong in themselves focuses upon the relationship between active and passive euthanasia. To arrive at that argument, consider the following closely related, well-known argument:

(1) Voluntary passive euthanasia is not morally wrong in itself.
(2) Intentionally killing a person and intentionally letting a person die are, in themselves, morally on a par.
(3) The only intrinsic difference between voluntary active euthanasia and voluntary passive euthanasia is that the former is a case of killing, and the latter a case of letting die.

In Defense of Voluntary Active Euthanasia and Assisted Suicide

(4) Therefore, voluntary active euthanasia is not morally wrong in itself. (From (1), (2), and (3).)

Given that (3) is true by definition, and that few think that (1) is mistaken, the crucial premise in the argument appears to be (2). Is it true, then, that killing and letting die are morally on a par? The answer is not entirely clear. On the one hand, a number of philosophers have argued that intentionally killing and intentionally letting die have precisely the same moral status (Oddie, 1997, 1998; Rachels, 1975; Tooley, 1980). One very interesting way of attempting to establish this conclusion, for example, is by means of a "Bare Difference Argument," where the basic idea is to focus upon two cases, each involving a person's death, that differ only in that one is a case of killing, and the other a case of letting die, and where there does not appear to be any morally significant difference between the two cases. (See, for example, Rachels, 1975: 79.) If there are such cases, must it not follow that there is no intrinsic moral difference between killing and letting die?

The status of Bare Difference Arguments has been disputed, with many philosophers holding that this form of argument is sound (Malm, 1992; Oddie, 1997; Rachels, 1979), and others holding that it is not sound (Beauchamp, 1977; Foot, 1977: 101–2; Kagan, 1988). On the face of it, the argument certainly appears sound. The problem, however, is that there are cases where the intuitions of most non-consequentialists are that killing and letting die are not morally equivalent. One of the most famous cases, discussed at length by Harris (1975), involves the possibility of killing a healthy person in order to use that person's organs to save two people who need transplants if they are to survive. If killing and letting die are morally on a par, shouldn't killing one person to save two be not only permissible, but also commendable, and perhaps obligatory? Many people, however, feel that that is not so.

I think it can be shown that the Bare Difference Argument is sound. What I shall do here, however, is argue instead that one can avoid this controversial question by shifting from the above argument to a slightly different one.

To see how this can be done, consider the following, asymmetry principle:

(A) Both the property of killing a person and the property of allowing a person to die are wrong-making properties of actions, but the former is a weightier wrong-making property than the latter.

If this principle were correct, then statement (2) in the argument above would be false, and the argument itself would fail. But principle (A) is not sound. The reason is that, as David Boonin (2000: 160–1) has contended, any grounds for holding that there is a moral difference between killing and letting die must also be grounds for holding that a certain much more general principle is correct – the principle, namely, that intentionally causing a given harm is intrinsically more wrong than intentionally allowing that harm to occur. Or, to put it in terms of wrong-making properties:

(B) Both the property of intentionally *causing* a harm, and the property of intentionally *allowing* a harm to occur, are wrong-making properties of actions, but the former is a weightier wrong-making property than the latter.

Michael Tooley

But if this is right, then to the extent that the killing versus letting die distinction is morally significant, it is so *precisely because* it is just an instance of the more general distinction between intentionally causing harm and intentionally allowing harm to happen. But then the original asymmetry principle stated above cannot be an accurate formulation of what may be true in the killing versus letting die case, since it fails to distinguish between cases where killing and letting die are *harms* and cases where they are *benefits*. What is needed, then, is not (A), but the following, modified asymmetry principle:

(C) Both the property of killing a person, *when the killing harms the person*, and the property of allowing a person to die, *when allowing the person to die harms the person*, are wrong-making properties of actions, but the former is a weightier wrong-making property than the latter.

Next, given (B), the question naturally arises as to whether there is a corresponding principle dealing with *benefits*, and, in response, I would suggest that if (B) is plausible, then the following principle must also be plausible:

(D) Both the property of intentionally *causing* a benefit, and the property of intentionally *allowing* a benefit to occur, are right-making properties of actions, but the former is a weightier right-making property than the latter.

Or, at the very least, if (B) is plausible, then surely the following more modest variant on (D) must also be plausible:

(E) Both the property of intentionally causing a benefit, and the property of intentionally allowing a benefit to occur, are right-making properties of actions, but the former is *at least as weighty* a right-making property as the latter.

But then, finally, if (E) is plausible, then surely the following principle must also be acceptable:

(F) Both the property of killing a person, *when the killing benefits the person*, and the property of allowing a person to die, *when allowing the person to die benefits the person*, are right-making properties of actions, and the former is *at least as weighty* a right-making property as the latter.

Given principle (F), the argument that I want to advance is then as follows:

(1) Voluntary passive euthanasia is not morally wrong in itself.
(2) Both the property of killing a person, *when the killing benefits the person*, and the property of allowing a person to die, *when allowing the person to die benefits the person*, are right-making properties of actions, and the former is *at least as weighty* a right-making property as the latter.
(3) The only intrinsic difference between voluntary active euthanasia and voluntary passive euthanasia is that the former is a case of killing, and the latter a case of letting die.

In Defense of Voluntary Active Euthanasia and Assisted Suicide | 169

(4) Therefore, voluntary active euthanasia cannot be morally worse in itself than voluntary passive euthanasia. (From (2) and (3).)
(5) Therefore, voluntary active euthanasia is not morally wrong in itself. (From (1) and (4).)

An evaluation of the second argument

The argument just set out starts from the following premise:

(1) Voluntary passive euthanasia is not morally wrong in itself.

This is a claim that few would challenge, as the view that voluntary passive euthanasia is, in general, morally permissible is very widely accepted indeed. But it is not really a claim that should be taken for granted, especially given that many arguments offered against voluntary active euthanasia are in fact arguments against voluntary passive euthanasia as well (Tooley, 1995).

How, then, should one defend this premise? My own approach would be to defend this by the same line of argument that I used earlier to defend the view that suicide is not morally wrong, at least in certain circumstances. Those who hold that suicide is morally wrong would need, of course, to argue along different lines, but that is not something that we need to consider here.

The second premise of the argument is this:

(2) Both the property of killing a person, when the killing benefits the person, and the property of allowing a person to die, when allowing the person to die benefits the person, are right-making properties of actions, and the former is *at least as weighty* a right-making property as the latter.

How might this premise be challenged? The only challenge, I think, that deserves serious consideration is one that argues that the property of killing a person, when the killing benefits the person, cannot be a right-making property of actions, since the *direct killing* of an innocent person is always wrong in itself.

The proper response to this challenge to the second premise is, I suggest, to ask what basis can be offered for the claim that the direct killing of innocent persons is always morally wrong in itself. One possibility would be an axiological underpinning, according to which the existence of innocent persons is *valuable*, in the sense of making the world a better place. But this way of attempting to explain the principle in question is open to two serious objections. The first is that if this explanation of the wrongness of killing innocent persons were correct, then intentionally refraining from bringing innocent persons into existence would also be morally wrong, and to the very same degree, since the failure to create an object that would have a certain value makes precisely the same difference with regard to the overall value of the world as the destruction of an already existing object of the same sort, other things being equal. But the failure to bring an innocent person into existence is not morally on a par with destroying an innocent person who already exists. So the principle that the direct killing of innocent persons is always wrong in itself cannot be explained axiologically.

The second objection is this. Consider an innocent person who is suffering terribly from an incurable illness, and who would prefer to be killed, rather than to go on living. If one holds that killing such a person would be wrong because one would thereby be destroying something of value, then one should also hold that one would make the world a better place by creating an additional innocent person who one knew would suffer to the same degree as a result of the same incurable disease. But the latter, surely, is very implausible.

A second way of attempting to defend the claim that the direct killing of an innocent person is always wrong in itself is by appealing to the idea of rights, and by holding that such an action is wrong because an innocent person has a right to life. But this account is also open to at least two objections. The first is that people can, in general, waive their rights. Thus, for example, the fact that one has a right to some object does not mean that one does something wrong if one destroys it, or gives it to someone. Why, then, should the situation be any different with regard to the right to life? Why shouldn't it be permissible, for example, to commit suicide? Why should the right to life not be a right that, like other rights, one can waive?

A second, and deeper objection involves asking how rights function. A plausible view, I suggest, is that rights function in two ways. First, they function to protect an individual's interests. Secondly, they function to provide individuals with the freedom to make decisions concerning what they will do with their lives. But if this is correct, then when a person wants to die, helping her to do so will further that person's autonomy, while if it is in the person's interest to be dead, killing that person will further that person's interests. So if rights function to protect interests and autonomy, then, when both the relevant conditions are satisfied, so that it is in the person's interest to be killed, and the person asks to be killed, granting that request will not be contrary to either of the things that rights function to protect. Accordingly, the claim that the direct killing of an innocent person is always wrong in itself cannot be defended by appealing to the idea of rights. The conclusion that will be supported by an appeal to the idea of a right to life will be, at most, the much more limited one that the killing of an innocent person is wrong in itself if that action is either contrary to what the person really wants, or contrary to the person's interest.

The third and final premise of the second argument is this:

(3) The only intrinsic difference between voluntary active euthanasia and voluntary passive euthanasia is that the former is a case of killing, and the latter a case of letting die.

But this is unproblematic, since it follows from the relevant definitions.

In conclusion, then, the second argument also appears to provide a sound justification for the claim that voluntary active euthanasia is morally acceptable. It is then a straightforward matter to argue that the same is true of assisting a person to commit suicide, in the appropriate circumstances.

Should Assisted Suicide and Voluntary Active Euthanasia Be Legal?

If assisted suicide and voluntary active euthanasia are morally permissible, what should their legal status be? Certainly, the fact that an action is not morally wrong constitutes strong prima facie grounds for concluding that it should not be illegal. It is possible, however, for actions that are not morally wrong nevertheless to be such as should be prohibited, on the ground that allowing the actions in question would give rise to other actions that would harm individuals, or violate their rights. Further consideration is therefore necessary, and so, in this final section, I shall consider three important objections to the legalization of assisted suicide and voluntary active euthanasia.

The first argument, put forward by Yale Kamisar (1958), focuses upon possible harm to those who choose to undergo euthanasia. The thrust of Kamisar's argument is that if voluntary active euthanasia is available, some people will choose to be killed in circumstances where being killed is contrary to their interest.

Kamisar's argument is problematic in two ways. In the first place, if a person were tempted to choose euthanasia in a situation where that was contrary to that person's own interest, and where the person was not emotionally disturbed, it is hard to see why, if the person were presented with the reasons why it would be better to go on living, he or she would be unable to appreciate the force of those reasons.

In the second place, it can be shown (Tooley, 1995) that the possibilities for irrational choice that Kamisar proposes, whatever weight they have, generally have precisely as much weight in the case of voluntary *passive* euthanasia. So one cannot, as Kamisar does, hold that such possibilities constitute grounds for not legalizing active euthanasia without equally holding that they are also grounds for not allowing passive euthanasia.

The other two arguments against legalization deserve more careful consideration. First, there are what are often referred to as "wedge" or "slippery slope" arguments against voluntary active euthanasia. These come in two forms. Both maintain that legalizing active euthanasia would be a mistake because doing so would be likely to lead to undesirable consequences involving the legalization of other things. According to one version of the argument, these consequences would follow by virtue of a logical relation: if one legalizes voluntary active euthanasia, then logical consistency requires that one also legalize, for example, involuntary euthanasia (Sullivan, 1975: 24). The second version of the wedge argument, by contrast, maintains that the undesirable consequences would follow simply due to certain facts about human psychology.

The problem with the "logical consistency" version of the argument will be clear from the discussion in the previous section. For the present argument can be seen to rest upon the assumption that the relevant basic moral principle involved here is something along the lines of

(1) The *direct killing* of an innocent person (or, alternatively, an innocent human being) is always wrong in itself.

172   Michael Tooley

But as we in effect saw earlier, such a principle is not correct. It needs to be replaced, instead, by a principle such as

(2) Innocent persons have a right to life.

But then the point is that, while (2) does support a claim such as

(3) It is prima facie wrong to kill an innocent person if it is in that person's interest to go on living, or if the person has not given permission to have his or her life terminated.

It does not support a claim such as

(4) It is prima facie wrong to kill an innocent person who has a fixed and rational desire to be dead, and who has given permission to have his or her life terminated.

Thus, once the unsound claim that the direct killing of an innocent person is always wrong in itself is replaced by the sound principle that innocent persons have a right to life, the present argument collapses, since one can consistently hold both that voluntary active euthanasia is morally permissible and that involuntary euthanasia is not.

The second form of the wedge argument, by contrast, need not involve any unsound assumption about the relevant moral principles. For here it is granted, at least for the sake of argument, that voluntary active euthanasia is not wrong *in itself*. It is then argued, however, that acceptance of voluntary active euthanasia may lead to the acceptance of actions that *are* wrong in themselves – such as involuntary active euthanasia.

But what reasons are there for thinking that this will take place? Kamisar, in advancing this version of the wedge argument, offers three reasons. First, he claims that advocates of the legalization of voluntary active euthanasia often seem to hold that the case for legalizing certain types of non-voluntary euthanasia is at least as compelling as legalizing voluntary active euthanasia (1958: 1027–8). Secondly, he cites a poll that measured the amount of public support for, on the one hand, euthanasia for defective infants and, on the other hand, euthanasia for incurably and painfully ill adults, and where the result was that more people approved of the former than of the latter (45 percent versus 37.3 percent) (1958: 1029). Finally, Kamisar appeals (1958: 1031–2) to what happened under the Nazis, citing the description offered by Leo Alexander (1949; emphasis in original):

> The beginnings at first were merely a subtle shift in emphasis in the basic attitude of the physicians. *It started with the acceptance of the attitude, basic in the euthanasia movement, that there is such a thing as life not worthy to be lived.* This attitude in its early stages concerned itself merely with the severely and chronically sick. Gradually the sphere of those to be included in this category was enlarged to encompass the socially unproductive, the ideologically unwanted, the racially unwanted and finally all non-Germans.

In Defense of Voluntary Active Euthanasia and Assisted Suicide 173

But it is important to realize that the infinitely small wedged-in lever from which this entire trend of mind received its impetus was the attitude toward the non-rehabilitable sick.

How strong are the considerations offered by Kamisar? The problem with the first two types of support that he offers is that they concern attitudes toward *non-voluntary* euthanasia, and so they are not relevant to the claim that one is in danger of sliding down a slope that leads from voluntary active euthanasia to things that are morally wrong unless one holds that non-voluntary euthanasia – as contrasted with *involuntary* euthanasia – is morally wrong. But, in the first place, this is a deeply controversial claim, as is shown by one of the very facts that Kamisar cites – namely, that more Americans in the poll that he referred to approved of euthanasia in the case of "defective infants" than in the case of "incurably and painfully ill adults." Secondly, there are strong arguments that can be offered in support of the moral acceptability of euthanasia in the case of severely defective infants – arguments that Kamisar does not even address.

This leaves Kamisar's appeal to the case of Nazi Germany. Here there are at least two questions that need to be asked. The first is whether the claim that is advanced in the above passage is in fact correct. For some writers – such as Marvin Kohl (1975) and Joseph Fletcher (1973) – have argued that the Nazi mass murders, rather than growing out of attitudes toward the non-rehabitable sick, were based upon the idea of the protection and purification of the Aryan stock, and upon an intense anti-Semitism – and one that was long established in Europe (Hay, 1951). Moreover, if one examines Hitler's *Mein Kampf*, there appears to be very strong evidence for that view, and against Leo Alexander's claim. Consider, for example, the following passages:

> What we must fight for is to safeguard the existence and reproduction of our race and our people, the sustenance of our children and the purity of our blood, the freedom and independence of the fatherland, so that our people may mature for the fulfillment of the mission, allotted it by the creator of the universe. (Hitler, 1971: 214)
>
> The Jewish doctrine of Marxism . . . withdraws from humanity the premise of its existence and culture. As a foundation of the universe, this doctrine would bring about the end of any order intellectually conceivable to man. And as, in this greatest of all recognizable organisms [humans], the result of an application of such a law could only be chaos, on earth it could only be destruction for the inhabitants of this planet.
>
> If, with the help of his Marxist creed, the Jew is victorious over the other peoples of the world, his crown will be the funeral wreath of humanity and this planet will, as it did thousands of years ago, move through the ether devoid of men. (Hitler, 1971: 65)

In the light of passages such as these, Leo Alexander's claim that the starting point of the holocaust was "with the acceptance of the attitude, basic in the euthanasia movement, that there is such a thing as life not worthy to be lived" seems clearly untenable.

Secondly, even if Leo Alexander were right, one would still need to go on to ask to what extent the Nazi experience, which occurred in a dictatorship, is a good indicator of what is likely to happen in a democratic society such as the United States.

The answer, surely, is that it is not: if someone in the United States were to advocate such a program, the opposition would be overwhelming.

Finally, it is also possible to offer empirical evidence against the wedge argument, as is done, for example, by Rachels (1993: 62). He argues that there is "historical and anthropological evidence that approval of killing in one context does not necessarily lead to killing in different circumstances," and cites, as illustrations, the killing of defective infants in various societies, and the killing of people in self-defense in our own society. So there is good reason for thinking that people are perfectly capable of drawing clear and firm moral lines, and therefore are not in danger of sliding down what are claimed to be slippery slopes.

In addition, however, one can now offer empirical evidence of a very direct sort, since there is a society where voluntary active euthanasia has, for the past few years, been permitted – namely, the Netherlands. For while some who oppose legalization of voluntary active euthanasia have claimed that the Dutch experiment provides support for the slippery slope argument – on the grounds that there have been cases of involuntary euthanasia in the Netherlands – in fact the opposite is the case, as emerges if one compares the situation in the Netherlands with what obtains in societies where voluntary active euthanasia is not permitted. In particular, if one compares the results of surveys carried out in the Netherlands in 1990 and 1995, and in Australia in 1995–6, the following facts emerge. First, in the Netherlands, the percentage of active terminations without the patient's explicit consent fell from 0.8 percent to 0.7 percent over the period from 1990 to 1995, whereas, in Australia, the percentage of such cases in 1995–6 was 3.5 percent – that is, five times higher than in the Netherlands. Secondly, in the Netherlands, in 1995, 13.5 percent of all deaths involved a decision to withhold or withdraw treatment, whereas in Australia in 1995–6, this occurred in 30.5 percent of cases. Moreover, in Australia, in 22.5 percent of the cases, the decision to withhold or withdraw treatment was done without the patient's explicit consent (Kuhse et al., 1997; Oddie, 1998). The conclusion, accordingly, is that the rights of individuals are more likely to be violated when voluntary active euthanasia is illegal, than when it is permitted.

This brings me to the final objection that I shall consider to the legalization of voluntary active euthanasia. The thrust of this objection is that there are serious problems about how to implement the legalization of euthanasia. Should there be no laws at all concerning voluntary active euthanasia? That surely would lead to significant abuse. But if laws are needed, what form should they take? If the laws introduced complex and stringent procedures, then relatively few people who would benefit from voluntary active euthanasia might wind up being able to do so. On the other hand, if the procedures were very relaxed ones, wouldn't the likelihood of abuses re-emerge?

In response to this problem, Rachels (1993: 63–5) has suggested that one can bypass the problem of writing difficult and detailed legislation dealing with when voluntary active euthanasia is permissible by instead introducing a rule to the effect that, just as the fact that a killing has been done in self-defense may serve as a defense against a charge of homicide, so the fact that a killing was one of voluntary euthanasia could function in the same way – that is, as a satisfactory defense against a charge of homicide.

In Defense of Voluntary Active Euthanasia and Assisted Suicide

Rachels's proposal is an interesting one, and it would certainly appear to be a desirable change. It is unclear, however, how much access people would have to voluntary active euthanasia as a result. But perhaps one could combine Rachels's suggestion with the introduction of rather conservative legislation that would prescribe procedures under which voluntary active euthanasia, in certain clear-cut types of case, would be legally permissible. The combination of these two approaches might then both provide access to voluntary active euthanasia for those in need, while at the same time minimizing the likelihood of abuse, since anyone committing euthanasia in a borderline case would need to be prepared to prove that it was indeed a case of voluntary euthanasia.

One final important issue is this. It is usually assumed that if voluntary active euthanasia or assisted suicide were to be legalized, then such actions would be carried out by doctors. This assumption has led to strong opposition to legalization on the part of the American Medical Association, which has held that, in view of the basic orientation of the practice of medicine toward the saving of lives, doctors should not perform active euthanasia. Advocates of legalization have tended to respond by challenging the latter view – arguing, for example, that assisted suicide and voluntary active euthanasia are not really contrary to the Hippocratic Oath. But, even if this is so, one might very well ask whether it might not in fact be better if doctors were not involved, and if, instead, both the relevant counseling, and the carrying out of the actions in question, were in the hands of other trained professionals. For, in the first place, it may very well be psychologically difficult, for many people, to shift from attempting to do everything that can be done to save a person's life, to doing something to end that person's life. In the second place, would it not be better for euthanasia and assisted suicide to be carried out by people who have been specially trained to do this, people who are willing to step in when doctors have done all that they can, who are knowledgeable about the needs and the psychology of those who are dying, and who are therefore better able to provide the support and comfort that is needed at such a time?

References

Alexander, Leo (1949). "Medical science under dictatorship." *New England Journal of Medicine*, 241: 39–47.

Beauchamp, Tom L. (1977). "A reply to Rachels on active and passive euthanasia." In Thomas Mappes and Jane Zembaty (eds.), *Social Ethics: Morality and Social Policy* (pp. 67–76). New York: McGraw-Hill.

Boonin, David (2000). "How to argue against active euthanasia." *Journal of Applied Philosophy*, 17/2: 157–68.

Callahan, Daniel (2005). "A case against euthanasia." In Andrew I. Cohen and Christopher Heath Wellman (eds.), *Contemporary Debates in Applied Ethics* (pp. 179–90). Oxford: Blackwell.

Foot, Philippa (1977). "Euthanasia." *Philosophy & Public Affairs*, 6/2: 85–112.

Fletcher, Joseph (1973). "Ethics and euthanasia." In Robert H. Williams (ed.), *To Live and to Die* (pp. 113–22). New York: Springer Verlag. (Reprinted in Joseph Fletcher, *Humankind: Essays in Biomedical Ethics* (pp. 149–58). Buffalo, MA: Prometheus Books, 1979.)

Harris, John (1975). "The survival lottery." *Philosophy*, 50: 81–7.

Michael Tooley

Hay, Malcolm (1951). *The Foot of Pride*. Boston: Beacon Press. (Reprinted in 1960 as *Europe and the Jews*. Boston, NJ: Beacon Press.)

Hitler, Adolf (1971[1925–7]). *Mein Kampf*, trans. Ralph Manheim. Boston, MA: Houghton Mifflin Company.

Kagan, Shelly (1988). "The additive fallacy." *Ethics*, 99: 5–31.

Kamisar, Yale (1958). "Some nonreligious views against proposed 'mercy-killing' legislation." *Minnesota Law Review*, 42/6: 969–1042.

Kohl, Marvin (1975). "Voluntary beneficent euthanasia." In Marvin Kohl (Ed). *Beneficent euthanasia* (pp. 130–41). Buffalo, NY: Prometheus Books.

Kuhse, Helga, Singer, Peter, Baume, Peter, Clark, Malcolm, and Rickard, Maurice (1997). "End-of-life decisions in Australian medical practice." *Medical Journal of Australia*, 166: 191–6.

Malm, Heidi (1992). "In defense of the contrast strategy." In John Martin Fischer and Mark Ravizza (eds.), *Ethics: Problems and Principles* (pp. 272–7). New York: Harcourt Brace Jovanovich.

Oddie, Graham (1997). "Killing and letting-die: from bare differences to clear differences." *Philosophical Studies*, 88: 267–87.

Oddie, Graham (1998). "The moral case for the legalization of voluntary euthanasia." *Victoria University of Wellington Law Review*, 28: 207–24.

Parfit, Derek (1984). *Reasons and Persons*. Oxford: Oxford University Press.

Rachels, James (1975). "Active and passive euthanasia." *The New England Journal of Medicine*, 292/2: 78–80.

Rachels, James (1979). "Euthanasia, killing, and letting die." In John Ladd (ed.), *Ethical Issues Relating to Life and Death* (pp. 146–63). Oxford: Oxford University Press.

Rachels, James (1993). "Euthanasia." In Tom Regan (ed.), *Matters of Life and Death*, 3rd edn. (pp. 30–68). New York: McGraw Hill.

Sullivan, Joseph V. (1975). "The immorality of euthanasia." In Marvin Kohl (ed.), *Beneficent Euthanasia* (pp. 12-33). Buffalo, NY: Prometheus Books.

Tooley, Michael (1980) "An irrelevant consideration: killing versus letting die." In Bonnie Steinbock (ed.), *Killing and Letting Die* (pp. 56–62). Englewood Cliffs, NJ: Prentice-Hall.

Tooley, Michael (1995). "Voluntary euthanasia: active versus passive, and the question of consistency." *Revue Internationale de Philosophie*, 49/3: 305–22.

Further reading

'Ad Hoc' Committee of the Harvard Medical School (1968). "A definition of irreversible coma: report of the 'ad hoc' committee of the Harvard Medical School to examine the definition of brain death." *Journal of the American Medical Association*, 205/6: 337–40.

Den Hartogh, Govert (1998). "The slippery slope argument." In Helga Kuhse and Peter Singer (eds.), *A Companion to Bioethics*. Oxford: Blackwell.

Gay-Williams, J. (1979). "The wrongfulness of euthanasia." In Ronald Munson (ed.), *Intervention and Reflection: Basic Issues in Medical Ethics* (pp. 141–3). Belmont, CA: Wadsworth Publishing Company.

Hume, David (1985[1777]). "Of suicide." Reprinted in Eugene F. Miller (ed.), *Essays Moral, Political and Literary* (pp. 577–89). Indianapolis: Liberty Fund.

Kuhse, Helga and Singer, Peter (eds.) (1998). *A Companion to Bioethics*. Oxford: Blackwell.

Lamb, David (1988). *Down the Slippery Slope*. London: Croom Helm.

Maguire, Daniel C. (1975). "A Catholic view of mercy killing." In Marvin Kohl (ed.), *Beneficent Euthanasia* (pp. 34–43). Buffalo, NY: Prometheus Books.

Sacred Congregation for the Doctrine of Faith (1980). *Declaration on Euthanasia*. Available at: ⟨http://www.priestsforlife.org/magisterium/iuraetbona.htm⟩.

Tooley, Michael (1979). "Decisions to terminate life and the concept of a person." In John Ladd (ed.), *Ethical Issues Relating to Life and Death* (pp. 62–92). Oxford: Oxford University Press.

Walton, Douglas (1992). *Slippery Slope Arguments*, Oxford: Oxford University Press,

Williams, Glanville (1958). "'Mercy-killing' legislation – a rejoinder." *Minnesota Law Review*, 43/1: 1–12.

Michael Tooley

CHAPTER TWELVE

A Case Against Euthanasia

Daniel Callahan

Consider what I take to be a mystery. Life presents all of us with many miseries, sick or well. Why is it then that so few people choose to end their own lives in response to them? Why is it that when someone does commit suicide – even for reasons that seem understandable – the common reaction (at least in my experience) is one of sorrow, a feeling of pity that someone was driven to such a desperate extreme, particularly when most others in a similar situation do not do likewise? I ask these questions because, behind the movement and arguments in favor of euthanasia or physician-assisted suicide (PAS) – and I consider euthanasia a form of suicide – lies an effort to make the deliberate ending of one's life something morally acceptable and justifiable; and which looks as well to the help of government and the medical profession to move that cause along.[1]

It goes against the grain, I believe, of reason, emotion, and tradition, and all at the same time. If not utterly irrational, it is at least unreasonable – that is, it is not a sensible way to deal with the tribulations of life, of which a poor death is only one of life's horrible possibilities. Suicide generally provokes a negative emotional response in people, even if they can grasp the motive behind it. That response does not prove it is wrong, but it is an important signal of a moral problem. As for tradition, the doctor is being asked by a patient to go against the deep historical convictions of his discipline, to use his or her skills to take life rather than to preserve it, and to lend to the practice of euthanasia the blessing of the medical profession. I understand all of this to be opening the door to new forms of killing in our society, not a good development.

There have been, in Western culture, only three generally accepted reasons for taking the life of another, which is what euthanasia amounts to: self-defense when one's life is threatened, warfare when the cause is serious and just, and capital punishment, the ultimate sanction against the worst crimes. The movement to empower physicians legally to take the life of a patient, or help the patient take his own life, would then legitimate a form of suicide, but would also add still another reason by calling on medical skills to end a person's life.

Suicide: The Way (Rarely) Taken

Let me return to the first of my two questions. Why do comparatively few people turn to suicide as a way of dealing with awful lives? People die miserable deaths all the time, from a wide range of lethal diseases and other causes. While it may cross their minds from time to time, few seem to want euthanasia or physician-assisted suicide as a way out. Millions of people have been brutally treated in concentration camps, with many of them ultimately to die – and yet suicide has never been common in such camps. Many millions of others have undergone all kinds of personal tragedy – the death of children or a spouse, the end of marriage or a deep romance, failures in their work or profession – but most of them do not turn to suicide either. The disabled have been long known to have a lower suicide rate than able-bodied people.

Euthanasia is often presented as a "rational" choice for someone in great pain and whose prospects are hopeless. And yet rationality implies some predictability of behavior, that is, some reasonable certainty that people will act in a consistent and foreseeable way under certain familiar circumstances. Yet it is almost impossible, save for severe depression, to predict whether someone suffering from a lethal illness is likely to turn to suicide. It is far more predictable that, when faced with even the worst horrors of life, most people will *not* turn to suicide. It is no less predictable that, when gripped by pain and suffering, they will want relief, but not to the extent of ending their lives to get it.

We may of course say that people fear ending their own lives, lacking the nerve to do so, or that religious beliefs have made suicide a taboo, or that it has hitherto been difficult to find expert assistance in ending one's life. Those are possible explanations, but since some people do in fact commit suicide, we know that it is hardly impossible to overcome those deterrents. Moreover, to say that most of the great religions and moral traditions of the world have condemned suicide does not in the end explain much at all. *Why* have they done so, even when at the same time they usually do not condemn laying down one's life to save another? In the same vein, why has the Western medical tradition for some 2,500 years, going back to Hippocrates, prohibited physicians from helping patients to commit suicide?

My guess is that the answer to the first of those two questions is that suicide is seen as a particularly bad way to handle misery and suffering, even when they are overwhelming – and the behavior of most people in turning away from suicide suggests they share that perception. It is bad because human life is better, even nobler, when we human beings put up with the pain and travail that come our way. Life is full of pain, stress, tragedy, and travail, and we ought not to want to tempt others to see suicide as a way of dealing with it. We would fail ourselves and, by our witness, our neighbor as well, who will know what we did and be led to do so themselves some day.

I began by asking at the outset why most suicides are treated as unhappy events, even when they obviously relieved someone's misery, which we would ordinarily con-

Daniel Callahan

sider valuable. Those readers who have been to the funerals of suicides will know how rarely those at such funerals feel relief that the misery of the life leading up to them has now been relieved. They almost always wish the life could have ended differently, that the suffering could have been borne. My surmise is that those of us who are bystanders or spectators to such deaths know that a fundamental kind of taboo of a rational kind has been broken, some deep commitment to life violated, and that no relief of pain and suffering can justify that. To say this is by no means to condemn those who do so. We can often well enough comprehend why they were driven to that extreme. Nor do I want to imply that they must have been clinically depressed. I am only saying that it is very hard to feel good about suicide or to rejoice that it was the way chosen to get out of a burdensome life.

I present these considerations about suicide as speculations only, not as some kind of decisive arguments against euthanasia. But I think it important to see what sense can be made of a common revulsion against suicide, and sadness when it happens, that has marked generations of people in most parts of the world. Moreover, as I will develop more fully below, it turns out that the experience with the Dutch euthanasia laws and practice, as well as with the Oregon experience with physician-assisted suicide, indicates that it is not misery, pain, and suffering in any ordinary sense that are the motivation for the desire to put an end to one's life. It is instead in great part a function of a certain kind of patient with a certain kind of personality and outlook upon the world.

It is, I believe, important that we try to make sense of these background experiences and reactions. They tell us something about ourselves, our traditions, and our human nature. They offer an enriched perspective when considering the most common arguments in favor of euthanasia. On the surface those arguments are meant to seem timely, in tune with our mainstream values, commonsensical and compassionate, and of no potential harm to our medical practice or our civic lives together. I would like to show that they are indeed in tune with many of our mainstream values, but that they are misapplied in this case, harmful to ourselves and others if we accept them.

Three Arguments in Favor of Euthanasia

I want now to turn to the main arguments in favor of euthanasia, and to indicate why I think they are weak and unpersuasive. I will follow that with a discussion of the legal problem of euthanasia and physician-assisted suicide, and conclude with some comments on the experience with euthanasia and physician-assisted suicide in the Netherlands and the state of Oregon.

Three moral arguments have been most prominent in the national debate. One of them is that we ought, if we are competent, to have the right to control our body as we see fit and to end our life if we choose to do so. This is often called the right of self-determination. Another is that we owe it to each other, in the name of beneficence or charity, to relieve suffering when we can do so. Still another is that there is no serious or logical difference between terminating the treatment of a dying patient, allowing the patient to die, and directly killing a patient by euthanasia. I will look at each of these arguments in turn.

If there is any fundamental American value, it is that of freedom and particularly the freedom to live our own lives in light of our own values. The only limit to that value is that, in the name of freedom, we may not do harm to others. At least a hundred years ago the value of freedom was extended to the inviolability of our bodies – that is, our right not to have our bodies invaded, abused, or used without our consent. Even to put our hands on another without their permission can lead to our being charged with assault and battery. That principle was extended to participation in medical research and the notion of informed consent: no individual can use your body for medical research without your specific informed consent granting them permission to do so. In later years, many construed earlier bans on abortion as an interference with the right of a woman to make her own choices about her body and the continuance of a pregnancy.

It seemed, then, only a small and logical step to extend the concept of freedom and self-determination to the end of our life. If you believe that your pain and suffering are insupportable, and if there is no hope that medicine can cure you of a fatal disease, why should you not have the right to ask a physician directly to end your life (euthanasia) or to provide you with the means of doing so (physician-assisted suicide)? After all, it is your body, your suffering, and if there is no reason to believe others will be harmed by your desire to see your life come to an end, what grounds are there for denying you that final act of self-determination? As I suggested above, it is precisely because the claim of self-determination in this context seems so much in tune with our traditional value of liberty that it seems hard to find a reason to reject it.

But we should reject it, and for a variety of considerations, three of which seem most important. The first is that euthanasia is mistakenly understood as a personal and private matter only of self-determination. Suicide, once a punishable crime, was removed from the law some decades ago in this country. But it is one thing not to prosecute a person for attempting suicide and quite another to think that euthanasia is a private act, impacting on no other lives. On the contrary, with euthanasia as its means, it becomes a social act by virtue of calling upon the physician to take part in it. Legalizing it would also provide an important social sanction and legitimation of those practices. They would require regulation and legal oversight.

Most critically, it would add to the acceptable range of killing in our society, noted above, one more occasion for the taking of life. To do so would be to reverse the long-developing trend to limit the occasions of socially sanctioned killing, too often marked by abuse. Euthanasia would also reinstate what I would call "private killing," by which I mean a situation where the agreement of one person to kill another is ratified in private by the individuals themselves, not by public authorities (even if it is made legal and supposed safeguards put in place). Dueling as a way of settling differences was once accepted, a form of private killing, something between the duelists only. But it was finally rejected as socially harmful and is nowhere now accepted in civilized society. The contention that it was *their* bodies at stake, *their* private lives, was rejected as a good moral reason to legally accept dueling.

Daniel Callahan

Euthanasia as a Social, not Private, Act

A closely related objection is that what makes euthanasia and physician-assisted suicide social, and not individual, matters is that, by definition, they require the assistance of a physician. Two points are worth considering here. The first is whether we want to sanction the private killing that is euthanasia by allowing physicians to be one of the parties to euthanasia agreements. Since the doctor–patient relationship is protected by the long-standing principle of confidentiality – what goes on between doctor and patient may not be legally revealed to any third party – that gives doctors enormous power over patients.

Whatever the law might be, there will be no way of knowing whether doctors are obeying regulations allowing for euthanasia or physician-assisted suicide, no way of knowing whether they are influencing patient decisions in wrongful ways, no way of knowing whether they are acting with professional integrity. As Sir Charles Allbutt, a British physician, nicely put the problem a century ago:

> If all professions have their safeguards they also have their temptations, and ours is no exception. . . . Unfortunately the game of medicine is played with the cards under the table . . . who is there to note the significant glance, the shrug, the hardly expressed innuendo of our brethren. . . . Thus we work not in the light of public opinion but in the secrecy of the chamber. (Cited in Scarlett, 1991: 24–5)

To give physicians the power to kill patients, or assist in their suicide, when their actions are clothed in confidentiality is to run a considerable risk, one hard to spot and one hard to act upon. As will be noted below, the Dutch experience with euthanasia makes clear how easy it was for doctors to violate the court-established rules for euthanasia and to do so with impunity. There is just no way, in the end, for outsiders to know exactly what doctors do behind the veil of confidentiality; that in itself is a threat.

The second consideration is that the tradition of medicine has, for centuries, opposed the use of medical knowledge and skill to end life. Every important Western medical code of ethics has rejected euthanasia – and rejected it even in those eras when there were many fewer ways of relieving pain than are now available. That could hardly have been because earlier generations of doctors knew less about, or were more indifferent to, pain and suffering. Their relief was at the very heart of the doctor's professional obligation.

There was surely another reason. The medical tradition knew something of great importance: doctors are all too skilled in knowing how to kill to be entrusted with the power to deliberately use that skill. This is not to say that physicians are corrupt, prone to misuse their power; not at all. It is only to say, on the one hand, that the very nature of their profession is to save and protect life, not end it; and that they also, on the other hand, become inured much more than the rest of us to death. Ordinary prudence suggests that the temptation to take life should be kept from them as far as possible. To move in any other direction is to risk the corruption of medicine and to threaten the doctor–patient relationship.

But what of the duty to relieve suffering, to act out of compassion for another? Did the moral strictures against euthanasia and physician-assisted suicide in effect simply forget about, or ignore, that duty? Not at all, but the duty to relieve suffering has never been an absolute duty, overriding all moral objections. No country now allows, or has ever allowed, euthanasia without patient consent even if the patient is incompetent and obviously suffering. Nor are patients' families authorized to request euthanasia under those circumstances. Moreover, as time has gone on, the ability of physicians to relieve patients of just about all pain and suffering through good palliative care has shown that most suffering can be relieved without the ultimate solution of killing the patient. In any event, any alleged duty to relieve suffering has historically always given way to the considerations, noted above, about the nature of medicine as a profession whose principal duty is construed as the saving not the taking of life, and not even when the life cannot medically be saved.

The third argument against euthanasia I want to consider is based on the belief that there is no inherent moral difference between killing a patient directly by euthanasia and allowing a patient to die by deliberately terminating a patient's life-supporting treatment (by turning off a ventilator, for example). Since physicians are allowed to do the latter, it is said that they should be allowed to do the former as well – and indeed that it may be more merciful to carry out euthanasia than to stop treatment, perhaps increasing and prolonging the suffering before the patient actually dies. In effect, the argument goes, terminating treatment will foreseeably end the life of the patient, a death hastened by the physician's act; and that is no different, in its logic or outcome, from killing the patient directly by euthanasia (Rachels, 1975).

There are some mistakes in this argument. One of them is a failure to remember that patients with truly lethal, fatal diseases cannot be saved in the long run. The most that can be accomplished is, by aggressive treatment, to delay their death. At some point, typically, a physician will legitimately decide that treatment cannot bring the patient back to good health and cannot reverse the downhill course of the illness. The disease is in control at that point and, when the physician stops treatment, the disease takes over and kills the patient. It has been long accepted that, in cases of that kind, the cause of death is the disease, not the physician's action.

Moreover, how can it be said that a physician has "hastened" a patient's death by ending life-saving treatment? After all, but for the doctor's action in keeping the patient alive in the first place and then continuing the life-sustaining treatment, the patient would have died much earlier. Put another way, the doctor saves the patient's life at one point in time, sustains the patient's life through a passage of time, and then allows the patient to die at still another time. Since no physician has the power to stay indefinitely the hand of death, at some point or other, in any case, the physician's patient will be irreversibly on the way to death; that is, at some point, life-sustaining treatment will be futile. To think that doctors "kill" patients by terminating treatment is tantamount at that point to saying that doctors have abolished lethal disease and that they now die only because of a physician's actions. It would be lovely if doctors have achieved that kind of power over nature, with death solely in their hands. It has not happened, and is not likely ever to happen. To say this is not to deny that physicians can misuse their power to terminate treatment wrongly: they can stop treatment when it could still do some good, or when a competent patient

Daniel Callahan

wants it continued. In that case, however, the physician is blameworthy. It is still the underlying disease that does the killing, but the physician is culpable for allowing that to happen when it ought not to have happened.

Euthanasia and the Law

I have provided some reasons why, ethically speaking, euthanasia and physician-assisted suicide cannot be well defended. But what of the law? If we claim to live in a free country, and believe in pluralism, should not the law leave it up to us as individuals to decide how our lives should end? Many people will reject my arguments against euthanasia, and public opinion polls have consistently shown a majority of Americans to be in favor of it. A law that simply allowed those practices, but coerces no one to embrace them, would seem the most reasonable position.

Not necessarily. I noted earlier that the moral acceptance of euthanasia would have the effect of legitimating the role of the physician as someone now empowered to end life. It would also bring an enormous change in the role of the physician, changing the very notion of what it means to be one (Kass, 2002). Seen in that light, a law permitting euthanasia would have social implications far beyond simply giving patients the right to choose how their lives end. As in so many other matters, what on the surface looks like a narrowly private decision turns out, with legalization, to send much wider ripples through society in general and the practice of medicine in particular. It has been said that, in addition to its regulatory functions, the law is a teacher, providing a picture of the way we think people should live together. Legalized euthanasia would teach the wrong kind of lesson.

The actual enforcement of a law on euthanasia would be enormously difficult to carry out. The privacy of the doctor–patient relationship means that there is an area that the law cannot enter. Whatever conditions the law might set for legal euthanasia, there is in the end no good way to know whether it is being obeyed. Short of having a policeman sitting in on every encounter between a doctor and a patient, what they agree to will remain unavailable to the rest of us. All laws are subject to abuse, particularly when they are controversial in the first place. Not everyone will agree with the law as written, and we can be sure that some will bend it or ignore it if they can get away with it. But in most cases it is possible to detect the violation. We know when our goods have been stolen, just as we can know when someone has been brutally beaten.

It would be far more difficult to detect abuses with euthanasia. For one thing, two of the main reasons offered in favor of euthanasia – self-determination and the relief of suffering – do not readily lend themselves to the limits of law. Why should a right of self-determination be limited to those in a terminal state, which is what is commonly proposed and is required in Holland and Belgium? The Dutch law, which does not require a terminal illness, but only unbearable suffering, is in that respect much more perceptive about the logical and legal implications of the usual moral arguments in favor of euthanasia, which is why it rejected a terminal illness requirement.

The Dutch realized that the open-ended logic of the moral reasons behind euthanasia do not lend themselves well to artificial, legal barriers. Impending death is not the only horrible thing in life and, if an individual's body is her own, why should any interference with her choice be tolerated? The requirement of an impending death seems arbitrary in the extreme. As for the relief of suffering, why should someone have to be competent and able to give consent, as if the suffering of those lacking such capacities counts for less? In short, the main reasons given for the legalization of euthanasia seem, logically, to resist the kinds of limit built into the Oregon and Belgian laws. That reality opens the way to abuse of the law. All it requires is a physician who finds the law too narrow, the deed too easy, and a desperate patient all too eager to die.

The Dutch Experience

This is not speculation. The Netherlands offers a case study of how it happens. For many decades, until a formal change in the law only recently, the Dutch courts had permitted euthanasia if certain conditions were met: a free choice, a considered and persistent request, unacceptable suffering, consultation with another physician, and accurate reporting on the cause of death. Throughout the 1970s and 1980s euthanasia (and occasionally physician-assisted suicide) was carried out, with many assurances that the conditions were being met. But, curious to find out about the actual practice, the Dutch government established a Commission on Euthanasia in 1990 to carry out an anonymous survey of Dutch physicians (Van der Mass, 1992).

The survey encompassed a sample of 406 physicians, and two other studies, which, taken together, were eye-opening. The official results showed that, based on their sample, out of a total of 129,000 deaths there were some 2,300 cases of voluntary ("free choice") euthanasia and 400 cases of assisted suicide. In addition, most strikingly, there were some 1,000 cases of intentional termination of life without explicit request, what the Dutch called "non-voluntary euthanasia." In sum, out of 3,300 euthanasia deaths, nearly one-third were non-voluntary. Less than 50 percent of the euthanasia cases were reported as euthanasia: another violation of the court rules. Worst of all, some 10 percent of the non-voluntary cases were instances of euthanasia with competent patients who were not asked for their consent.

None of that was supposed to be happening – a clear abuse of the court-established rules. A number of doctors had obviously taken it upon themselves to unilaterally end the lives of many patients. If that could happen there, it could happen here. Since that time, the Dutch have officially established a legal right to euthanasia (replacing the early court-established guidelines), but the government there has recently found that only 50 percent of the physicians who carry it out report doing so, and that there continue to be 400 cases a year of voluntary euthanasia (Sheldon, 2003).

The American state of Oregon, which legalized physician-assisted suicide in 1994, but whose actual implementation was delayed until 1997 by a number of court challenges, offers a variety of further insights into the practice. To the surprise of many, the actual number of people to take advantage of the new law has been small. The number of prescriptions for physician-assisted suicide, written for the first four years, beginning in 1998, has been 24 (1998), 33 (1999), 39 (2000) and 44 (2001) – and the

Daniel Callahan

actual number of deaths from their use has been 16 (1998), 27 (1999), 27 (2000), and 21 (2001) (Oregon Death with Dignity, 2002: 24–5). While it is not wholly clear why there have been so few, or why all of those for whom lethal drugs were prescribed did not in the end use them, a possible reason is the high quality of pain relief care available in Oregon. Palliative care (that part of medicine that aims to reduce pain and suffering) has been particularly strong in Oregon, in great part because both proponents and opponents of the law worked hard to improve palliative care at the end of life, making it the most effective state in the country for doing so.

Has there been any abuse of the law in Oregon, as was the case in the Netherlands? One group supportive of the law, the Oregon Death with Dignity Legal Defense and Education Center, has flatly stated that "after four full years of legalized death with dignity in Oregon, there have been no missteps, abuses or coercive tendencies" (Oregon Death with Dignity, 2002: 24–5). That may possibly be true, but they can't possibly *know* it to be true. The experience of Holland, which uncovered abuses only after careful anonymous surveys of physicians, ought to raise a cautionary flag. Before that survey, Dutch euthanasia supporters issued equally confident statements about the purity of their practice. The underlying question, in the absence of such anonymous information, is whether there still exist incentives for physicians to violate the Oregon law. My surmise is that there are, simply because not all patients who want PAS will meet the legal standards and because not all physicians will agree with those standards. That is what happened in Holland and may quite possibly be happening in Oregon as well. We will only know after an anonymous survey.

Not Pain but Loss of Control

But for me the most interesting information to come out of the Oregon situation are the reasons given for wanting physician-assisted suicide. The standard argument, used frequently in getting the Oregon law changed to permit PAS, was that of the relief of unbearable pain and suffering. But as it has turned out, only a minority of those who availed themselves of the law cited inadequate pain relief. The pattern for 2001 was similar to that of the preceding year: the major motive (for about 80 percent of those wanting PAS) was "loss of autonomy and a diminished ability to participate in activities that make life enjoyable," to use the language of a major organizational supporter of the law (Oregon Death with Dignity, 2002: 24–5). No doubt that is a form of suffering for those for whom "loss of autonomy" is a grievous affliction. But of course that is one of the results of lethal disease and old age. We will all, eventually in our lives, lose our autonomy and see a reduction of our ability to do that which makes life enjoyable. Our bodies just give out at some point.

If that is our human fate – forestalled a bit by modern medicine, but not nullified – why is it that only a tiny fraction of the population wants euthanasia as the solution to the medical miseries of their lives even if they might let the law accept it with others? To refine that question a bit: why is it that PAS in Oregon seemed to attract people with a heavy focus on autonomy in their lives? From the clinical evidence, there seems to be no fixed response of human beings to suffering, and certainly no probability that people will typically see suicide as the way out. Much, if not everything, seems to depend on individual differences in values, not in bodily responses to pain or impending death. In reporting on the first year of the Oregon law, the state Oregon Health Commission noted that a majority of the 16 reported cases involved people with a particular fear of a "loss of control or the fear of loss of general control, and a loss of bodily function" (Chin et al., 1999: 580, 582). It was not the unbearable and unrelievable physical pain so often and luridly emphasized in the efforts to legalize PAS, or a fear of abandonment, or dependency on others (though some mentioned that), or a feeling of meaninglessness in suffering.

Worry about such a loss represents a particular set of personal (and idiosyncratic) values, by no means a widely distributed set. This was well brought out in the official state report. What the state officials did was to match those who received PAS (called the "case" group) with a group (called the "control" group) of patients with "similar underlying illnesses," and matched as well for age and date of death (Chin et al., 1999: 578). Their findings were striking: the PAS group was much more concerned about autonomy and control than the other group. Even more provocative was the fact that the PAS group was far more able to function physically than the control group: "21 percent of the case patients, as compared with 84 percent of the control patients . . . were completely disabled" (Chin et al., 1999: 580). In other words, the PAS group was far better off physically than the control group. It was their personal values that led them in one direction rather than another, not the objective intensity of their incapacities. Or to put it in terms we used earlier, PAS represents a legitimation of suicide for those who have a particular conception of the optimum life and its management, one of complete control.

Catering to a Small Minority

If it turns out, then, that PAS heavily attracts a particular kind of person, one very different from most terminally ill people, then much of the public policy argument on its behalf fails. It is not a general problem requiring drastic changes in law, tradition, and medical practice. Just as suicide in general, whatever the level of misery, is not the way most people seek to deal with it, so also are euthanasia and PAS the desire of a tiny minority. These results, it should be added, are much the same as those found in the Netherlands. At a 1991 conference there with the leaders of the Dutch euthanasia movement, I asked the physicians how it was possible reliably to diagnose "unbearable" or "untreatable" suffering as a medical condition and thus suitable for their euthanasia or PAS ministrations. They conceded that there is no reliable medical diagnosis, no way of really knowing what was going on within the mind and emotions of the patient, and – consistent with the findings of the Oregon state study – no correlation *whatever* between a patient's actual medical condition and the reported suffering.

Perhaps euthanasia is not, as many would like to put it, simply a logical extension of the physician's duty to relieve pain and suffering, an old obligation in a new garment. Perhaps it is just part of the drift toward the medicalization of the woes of life, particularly that version of life that regards the loss of control as the greatest of human indignities. Not only that, but even the fear of a loss of control is for many tantamount to its actual loss. I wonder if the voters of Oregon, and all of those who

Daniel Callahan

believe euthanasia a needed progressive move, mean to empower unto death that special, and small, subclass of patients uncommonly bent on the control of their lives and eager to have the help of doctors to do so. Somehow I doubt it, but it looks as if that may be what they got.

Underlying much of what I have written here are two assumptions, which need some defense. One of them is that good palliative care, a rapidly growing medical specialty, can relieve most pain and suffering. Some cases, I readily concede, may not be helped, or not enough, by even the best palliative care, but the overwhelming majority can be. My second assumption is this: it is bad public policy to abandon long-standing legal prohibitions, with important reasons and traditions behind them, for the sake of a very small minority, and particularly when the consequences open the way for abuse and a fundamental change in medical values. The fact, for so it seems, that the small minority reflects not some general human response to pain and suffering but a personal, and generally idiosyncratic, view of suffering is all the more reason to hesitate before legally blessing euthanasia. Human beings, in their lives and in their deaths, have long been able to see their lives come to an end without feeling some special necessity to have it ended of them, directly by euthanasia or self-inflicted by physician-assisted suicide.

What about the notion of "death with dignity," a phrase much used by euthanasia supporters? It is a misleading, obfuscating phrase. Death is no indiginity, even if accompanied by pain and a loss of control. Death is a fundamental fact of human biology, as fundamental as any other part of human life. If that human life has dignity as human life, it cannot be lost because death brings it to an end, even if in a disorderly, unpleasant fashion. It takes more than that to erase our dignity. Human beings in concentration camps did not lose their essential human value and dignity by being tortured, humiliated, and degraded. Euthanasia confers no dignity on the process of dying; it only creates the illusion of dignity for those who, mistakenly, believe a loss of control is not to be endured. It can be, and most human beings have endured it. No one would say that the newborn baby, unable to talk, incontinent, utterly unable to control her situation, and unable to interact with others, lacks dignity. Neither does the dying older person, even if displaying exactly the same traits. Dignity is not so easily taken from human beings. Nor can euthanasia confer it on someone.

Note

1   Unless there is a need to deal with the difference between euthanasia and physician-assisted suicide, I will hereafter refer only to euthanasia. By euthanasia I mean the direct killing of a patient by a doctor, ordinarily by means of a lethal injection. By physician-assisted suicide I mean the act of killing oneself by means of lethal drugs provided by a physician.

References

Chin, Arthur E., Hedberg, Katrina, Higginson, Grant K., and Fleming, David W. (1999). "Legalized physician-assisted suicide in Oregon – the first year's experience." *The New England Journal of Medicine*, 340: 577–83.

Kass, Leon Richard (2000). "'I will give no deadly drugs': why doctors must not kill." In K. Foley and E. Hendin (eds.), *The Case against Physician-assisted Suicide: For the Right to End-of-life Care*. Baltimore, MD: Johns Hopkins University Press.

Oregon Death with Dignity Legal Defense and Education Center (2000). *Oregon Death with Dignity*. Portland, OR: Oregon Death with Dignity Legal Defense and Education Center.

Rachels, James (1975). "Active and passive euthanasia." *The New England Journal of Medicine*, 292: 78–80.

Scarlett, Earle (1991). "What is a profession?" In B. R. Reynolds and J. Stone (eds.), *On Doctoring: Stories, Poems, Essays* (pp. 124–5). New York: Simon & Schuster.

Sheldon, Tony (2003). "Only half of Dutch doctors report euthanasia." *British Medical Journal*, 326: 1164.

Van der Maas, Paul J. (1992). *Euthanasia and other Decisions at the End of Life*. Amsterdam: Elsevier.

Further reading

Emanuel, L. L. (ed.) (1998). *Regulating How We Die: The Ethical, Medical, and Legal Issues Surrounding Physician-assisted Suicide*. Cambridge, MA: Harvard University Press.

New York State Task Force on Life and the Law. (1994). *When Death is Sought: Assisted Suicide and Euthanasia in the Medical Context*. New York: York State Task Force on Life and the Law.

Quill, T. E. (1996). *A Midwife Through the Dying Process: Stories of Healing and Hard Choices at the End of Life*. Baltimore, MD: Johns Hopkins University Press.

Weir, R. F. (ed.) (1997). *Physician-assisted Suicide*. Bloomington: Indiana University Press.

IMMIGRATION

Immigration:
The Case for Limits

David Miller

It is not easy to write about immigration from a philosophical perspective – not easy at least if you are writing in a society (and this now includes most societies in the Western world) in which immigration has become a highly charged political issue. Those who speak freely and openly about the issue tend to come from the far Right: they are fascists or racists who believe that it is wrong in principle for their political community to admit immigrants who do not conform to the approved cultural or racial stereotype. Most liberal, conservative, and social democratic politicians support quite strict immigration controls in practice, but they generally refrain from spelling out the justification for such controls, preferring instead to high-light the practical difficulties involved in resettling immigrants, and raising the spectre of a right-wing backlash if too many immigrants are admitted. Why are they so ret-icent? One reason is that it is not easy to set out the arguments for limiting immigration without at the same time projecting a negative image of those immi-grants who have already been admitted, thereby playing directly into the hands of the far Right ideologues who would like to see such immigrants deprived of their full rights of citizenship and/or repatriated to their countries of origin. Is it possible *both* to argue that every member of the political community, native or immigrant, must be treated as a full citizen, enjoying equal status and the equal respect of his or her fellows, *and* to argue that there are good grounds for setting upper bounds both to the rate and the overall numbers of immigrants who are admitted? Yes, it is, but it requires dexterity, and always carries with it the risk of being misunderstood.

In this chapter, I shall explain why nation-states may be justified in imposing restrictive immigration policies if they so choose. The argument is laid out in three stages. First, I canvass three arguments that purport to justify an unlimited right of migration between states and show why each of them fails. Second, I give two reasons, one having to do with culture, the other with population, that can justify states in limiting immigration. Third, I consider whether states nonetheless have a duty to admit a special class of potential immigrants – namely refugees – and also how far they are allowed to pick and choose among the immigrants they do admit. The third section, in other words, lays down some conditions that an ethical immigration policy must meet. But I begin by showing why there is no general right to choose one's country of residence or citizenship.

Can There Be an Unlimited Right of Migration Between States?

Liberal political philosophers who write about migration usually begin from the premise that people should be allowed to choose where in the world to locate themselves unless it can be shown that allowing an unlimited right of migration would have harmful consequences that outweigh the value of freedom of choice (see, for instance, Carens, 1987; Hampton, 1995). In other words, the central value appealed to is simply freedom itself. Just as I should be free to decide who to marry, what job to take, what religion (if any) to profess, so I should be free to decide whether to live in Nigeria, or France, or the USA. Now these philosophers usually concede that in practice some limits may have to be placed on this freedom – for instance, if high rates of migration would result in social chaos or the breakdown of liberal states that could not accommodate so many migrants without losing their liberal character. In these instances, the exercise of free choice would become self-defeating. But the presumption is that people should be free to choose where to live unless there are strong reasons for restricting their choice.

I want to challenge this presumption. Of course there is always *some* value in people having more options to choose between, in this case options as to where to live, but we usually draw a line between *basic* freedoms that people should have as a matter of right and what we might call *bare* freedoms that do not warrant that kind of protection. It would be good from my point of view if I were free to purchase an Aston Martin tomorrow, but that is not going to count as a morally significant freedom – my desire is not one that imposes any kind of obligation on others to meet it. In order to argue against immigration restrictions, therefore, liberal philosophers must do more than show that there is some value to people in being able to migrate, or that they often *want* to migrate (as indeed they do, in increasing numbers). It needs to be demonstrated that this freedom has the kind of weight or significance that could turn it into a right, and that should therefore prohibit states from pursuing immigration policies that limit freedom of movement.

I shall examine three arguments that have been offered to defend a right to migrate. The first starts with the general right to freedom of movement, and claims that this must include the freedom to move into, and take up residence in, states other than one's own. The second begins with a person's right to *exit* from her current state – a right that is widely recognized in international law – and claims that a right of exit is pointless unless it is matched by a right of entry into other states. The third appeals to international distributive justice. Given the huge inequalities in living standards that currently exist between rich and poor states, it is said, people who live in poor

David Miller

states have a claim of justice that can only be met by allowing them to migrate and take advantage of the opportunities that rich states provide.

The idea of a right to freedom of movement is not in itself objectionable. We are talking here about what are usually called basic rights or human rights, and I shall assume (since there is no space to defend the point) that such rights are justified by pointing to the vital interests that they protect (Griffin, 2001; Nickel, 1987; Shue, 1980). They correspond to conditions in whose absence human beings cannot live decent lives, no matter what particular values and plans of life they choose to pursue. Being able to move freely in physical space is just such a condition, as we can see by thinking about people whose legs are shackled or who are confined in small spaces. A wider freedom of movement can also be justified by thinking about the interests that it serves instrumentally: if I cannot move about over a fairly wide area, it may be impossible for me to find a job, to practice my religion, or to find a suitable marriage partner. Since these all qualify as vital interests, it is fairly clear that freedom of movement qualifies as a basic human right.

What is less clear, however, is the physical extent of that right, in the sense of how much of the earth's surface I must be able to move to in order to say that I enjoy it. Even in liberal societies that make no attempt to confine people within particular geographical areas, freedom of movement is severely restricted in a number of ways. I cannot, in general, move to places that other people's bodies now occupy (I cannot just push them aside). I cannot move on to private property without the consent of its owner, except perhaps in emergencies or where a special right of access exists – and since most land is privately owned, this means that a large proportion of physical space does not fall within the ambit of a *right* to free movement. Even access to public space is heavily regulated: there are traffic laws that tell me where and at what speed I may drive my car, parks have opening and closing hours, the police can control my movements up and down the streets, and so forth. These are very familiar observations, but they are worth making simply to highlight how hedged about with qualifications the existing right of free movement in liberal societies actually is. Yet few would argue that because of these limitations, people in these societies are deprived of one of their human rights. Some liberals might argue in favor of expanding the right – for instance, in Britain there has been a protracted campaign to establish a legal right to roam on uncultivated privately owned land such as moors and fells, a right that will finally become effective by 2005. But even the advocates of such a right would be hard-pressed to show that some vital interest was being injured by the more restrictive property laws that have existed up to now.

The point here is that liberal societies in general offer their members *sufficient* freedom of movement to protect the interests that the human right to free movement is intended to protect, even though the extent of free movement is very far from absolute. So how could one attempt to show that the right in question must include the right to move to some other country and settle there? What vital interest requires the right to be interpreted in such an extensive way? Contingently, of course, it may be true that moving to another country is the only way for an individual to escape persecution, to find work, to obtain necessary medical care, and so forth. In these circumstances the person concerned may have the right to move, not to any state that she chooses, but to *some* state where these interests can be protected. But here the right to move serves only as a remedial right: its existence depends on the fact that the person's vital interests cannot be secured in the country where she currently resides. In a world of decent states – states that were able to secure their citizens' basic rights to security, food, work, medical care, and so forth – the right to move across borders could not be justified in this way.

Our present world is not, of course, a world of decent states, and this gives rise to the issue of refugees, which I shall discuss in the final section of this chapter. But if we leave aside for the moment cases where the right to move freely across borders depends upon the right to avoid persecution, starvation, or other threats to basic interests, how might we try to give it a more general rationale? One reason a person may want to migrate is in order to participate in a culture that does not exist in his native land – for instance he wants to work at an occupation for which there is no demand at home, or to join a religious community which, again, is not represented in the country from which he comes. These might be central components in his plan of life, so he will find it very frustrating if he is not able to move. But does this ground a right to free movement across borders? It seems to me that it does not. What a person can legitimately demand access to is an *adequate* range of options to choose between – a reasonable choice of occupation, religion, cultural activities, marriage partners, and so forth. Adequacy here is defined in terms of generic human interests rather than in terms of the interests of any one person in particular – so, for example, a would-be opera singer living in a society which provides for various forms of musical expression, but not for opera, can have an adequate range of options in this area even though the option she most prefers is not available. So long as they adhere to the standards of decency sketched above, all contemporary states are able to provide such an adequate range internally. So although people certainly have an *interest* in being able to migrate internationally, they do not have a basic interest of the kind that would be required to ground a human right. It is more like my interest in having an Aston Martin than my interest in having access to *some* means of physical mobility.

I turn next to the argument that because people have a right to leave the society they currently belong to, they must also have a right to enter other societies, since the first right is practically meaningless unless the second exists – there is no unoccupied space in the world to exit *to*, so unless the right to leave society A is accompanied by the right to enter societies B, C, D, etc., it has no real force (Cole, 2000; Dummett, 1992).

The right of exit is certainly an important human right, but once again it is worth examining why it has the significance that it does. Its importance is partly instrumental: knowing that their subjects have the right to leave inhibits states from mistreating them in various ways, so it helps to preserve the conditions of what I earlier called "decency." However, even in the case of decent states the right of exit remains important, and that is because by being deprived of exit rights individuals are forced to remain in association with others whom they may find deeply uncongenial – think of the militant atheist in a society where almost everyone devoutly practices the same religion, or the religious puritan in a society where most people behave like libertines. On the other hand, the right of exit from state A does not appear to entail an unrestricted right to enter any society of the immigrant's choice – indeed, it seems that it can be exercised provided that at least one other society, society B say, is willing to take him in. It might seem that we can generate a general right to migrate by iteration: the person who leaves A for B then has the right to exit from B, which entails that C, at least, must grant him the right to enter, and so forth. But this move fails, because our person's right of exit from A depended on the claim that he might find continued association with the other citizens of A intolerable, and he cannot plausibly continue making the same claim in the case of each society that is willing to take him in. Given the political and cultural diversity of societies in the real world, it is simply unconvincing to argue that only an unlimited choice of which one to join will prevent people being forced into associations that are repugnant to them.

It is also important to stress that there are many rights whose exercise is contingent on finding partners who are willing to cooperate in the exercise, and it may be that the right of exit falls into this category. Take the right to marry as an example. This is a right held against the state to allow people to marry the partners of their choice (and perhaps to provide the legal framework within which marriages can be contracted). It is obviously not a right to have a marriage partner provided – whether any given person can exercise the right depends entirely on whether he is able to find someone willing to marry him, and many people are not so lucky. The right of exit is a right held against a person's current state of residence not to prevent her from leaving the state (and perhaps aiding her in that endeavor by, say, providing a passport). But it does not entail an obligation on any other state to let that person in. Obviously, if no state were ever to grant entry rights to people who were not already its citizens, the right of exit would have no value. But suppose states are generally willing to consider entry applications from people who want to migrate, and that most people would get offers from at least one such state: then the position as far as the right of exit goes is pretty much the same as with the right to marry, where by no means everyone is able to wed the partner they would ideally like to have, but most have the opportunity to marry *someone*.

So once the right of exit is properly understood, it does not entail an unlimited right to migrate to the society of one's choice. But now, finally, in this part of the chapter, I want to consider an argument for migration rights that appeals to distributive justice. It begins from the assumption of the fundamental moral equality of human beings. It then points out that, in the world in which we live, a person's life prospects depend heavily on the society into which she happens to be born, so that the only way to achieve equal opportunities is to allow people to move to the places where they can develop and exercise their talents, through employment and in other ways. In other words, there is something fundamentally unfair about a world in which people are condemned to relative poverty through no fault of their own when others have much greater opportunities, whereas if people were free to live and work wherever they wished, then each person could choose whether to stay in the community that had raised him or to look for a better life elsewhere.

The question we must ask here is whether justice demands equality of opportunity at the global level, as the argument I have just sketched assumes, or whether this principle only applies *inside* societies, among those who are already citizens of the same political community (see, for instance, Caney, 2001). Note to begin with that embracing the moral equality of all human beings – accepting that every human being is equally an object of moral concern – does not yet tell us what we are required to do for them as a result of that equality. One answer *might* be that we should attempt to provide everyone with equal opportunities to pursue their goals in life. But another, equally plausible, answer is that we should play our part in ensuring that their basic rights are respected, where these are understood as rights to a certain minimum level of security, freedom, resources, and so forth – a level adequate to protect their basic interests, as suggested earlier in this chapter. These basic rights can be universally protected and yet some people have greater opportunities than others to pursue certain aims, as a result of living in more affluent or culturally richer societies.

Is it nonetheless unfair if opportunities are unequal in this way? That depends upon what we believe about the *scope* of distributive justice, the kind of justice that involves comparing how well different people are faring by some standard. According to Michael Walzer, "the idea of distributive justice presupposes a bounded world within which distributions take place: a group of people committed to dividing, exchanging, and sharing social goods, first of all among themselves" (1983: 31). The main reason that Walzer gives for this view is that the very goods whose distribution is a matter of justice gain their meaning and value within particular political communities. Another relevant consideration is that the stock of goods that is available at any time to be divided up will depend on the past history of the community in question, including decisions about, for example, the economic system under which production will take place. These considerations tell against the view that justice at global level should be understood in terms of the equal distribution, at any moment, of a single good, whether this good is understood as "resources" or "opportunity" or "welfare" (Miller, 1999). The basic rights view avoids these difficulties, because it is plausible to think that whatever the cultural values of a particular society, and whatever its historical record, no human being should be allowed to fall below the minimum level of provision that protects his or her basic interests.

But what if somebody does fall below this threshold? Does this not give him the right to migrate to a place where the minimum level is guaranteed? Perhaps, but it depends on whether the minimum *could* be provided in the political community he belongs to now, or whether that community is so oppressive, or so dysfunctional, that escape is the only option. So here we encounter again the issue of refugees, to be discussed in my final section. Meanwhile, the lesson for other states, confronted with people whose lives are less than decent, is that they have a choice: they must either ensure that the basic rights of such people are protected in the places where they live – by aid, by intervention, or by some other means – or they must help them to move to other communities where their lives will be better. Simply shutting one's borders and doing nothing else is not a morally defensible option here. People everywhere have a right to a decent life. But before jumping to the conclusion that the way to respond to global injustice is to encourage people whose lives are less than decent to migrate elsewhere, we should consider the fact that this policy will do little to help the very poor, who are unlikely to have the resources to move to a richer country. Indeed, a policy of open migration may make such people worse off still, if it allows doctors, engineers, and other professionals to move from economically undeveloped to economically developed societies in search of higher incomes, thereby depriving their countries of origin of vital skills. Equalizing opportunity for the few may diminish opportunities for the many. Persisting global injustice does impose on rich states the obligation to make a serious contribution to the relief of global poverty, but in most instances they should contribute to improving conditions of life on the ground, as it were, rather than bypassing the problem by allowing (inevitably selective) inward migration.

Justifications for Limiting Immigration

I have shown that there is no general right to migrate to the country of one's choice. Does it follow that states have a free hand in choosing who, if anyone, to admit to membership? One might think that it does, using the analogy of a private club. Suppose that the members of a tennis club decide that once the membership roster has reached 100, no new members will be taken in. They do not have to justify this decision to would-be members who are excluded: if they decide that 100 members is enough, that's entirely their prerogative. But notice what makes this argument convincing. First, the benefit that is being denied to new applicants is the (relatively superficial) benefit of being able to play tennis. Second, it's a reasonable assumption that the rejected applicants can join another club, or start one of their own. It would be different if the tennis club occupied the only site within a 50-mile radius that is suitable for laying tennis courts: we might then think that they had some obligation to admit new members up to a reasonable total. In the case of states, the advantages that they deny to would-be immigrants who are refused entry are very substantial; and because states monopolize stretches of territory, and in other ways provide benefits that cannot be replicated elsewhere, the "go and start your own club" response to immigrants is not very plausible.

So in order to show that states are entitled to close their borders to immigrants, we have to do more than show that the latter lack the human right to migrate. Potential immigrants have a *claim* to be let in – if nothing else they usually have a strong *desire* to enter – and so any state that wants to control immigration must have good reasons for doing so. In this section, I shall outline two good reasons that states may have for restricting immigration. One has to do with preserving culture, the other with controlling population. I don't claim that these reasons will apply to every state, but they do apply to many liberal democracies that are currently having to decide how to respond to potentially very large flows of immigrants from less economically developed societies (other states may face larger flows still, but the political issues will be different).

The first reason assumes that the states in question require a common public culture that in part constitutes the political identity of their members, and that serves valuable functions in supporting democracy and other social goals. There is no space here to justify this assumption in any detail, so I must refer the reader to other writings where I have tried to do so (Miller, 1995 and 2000). What I want to do here is to consider how the need to protect the public culture bears upon the issue of immigration. In general terms we can say (a) that immigrants will enter with cultural values, including *political* values, that are more or less different from the public culture of the community they enter; (b) that as a result of living in that community, they will absorb some part of the existing public culture, modifying their own values in the process;

and (c) that their presence will also change the public culture in various ways – for instance, a society in which an established religion had formed an important part of national identity will typically exhibit greater religious diversity after accepting immigrants, and as a consequence religion will play a less significant part in defining that identity.

Immigration, in other words, is likely to change a society's public culture rather than destroy it. And since public cultures always change over time, as a result of social factors that are quite independent of immigration (participation in the established religion might have been declining in any case), it doesn't on the face of it seem that states have any good reason to restrict immigration on that basis. They might have reason to limit the *flow* of immigrants, on the grounds that the process of acculturation outlined above may break down if too many come in too quickly. But so long as a viable public culture is maintained, it should not matter that its character changes as a result of taking in people with different cultural values (Perry, 1995).

What this overlooks, however, is that the public culture of their country is something that people have an interest in controlling: they want to be able to shape the way that their nation develops, including the values that are contained in the public culture. They may not of course succeed: valued cultural features can be eroded by economic and other forces that evade political control. But they may certainly have good reason to try, and in particular to try to maintain cultural continuity over time, so that they can see themselves as the bearers of an identifiable cultural tradition that stretches backward historically. Cultural continuity, it should be stressed, is not the same as cultural rigidity: the most valuable cultures are those that can develop and adapt to new circumstances, including the presence of new subcultures associated with immigrants.

Consider the example of language. In many states today the national language is under pressure from the spread of international languages, especially English. People have an incentive to learn and use one of the international languages for economic and other purposes, and so there is a danger that the national language will wither away over the course of two or three generations. If this were to happen, one of the community's most important distinguishing characteristics would have disappeared, its literature would become inaccessible except in translation, and so forth. So the states in question adopt policies to insure, for instance, that the national language is used in schools and in the media, and that exposure to foreign languages through imports is restricted. What effect would a significant influx of immigrants who did not already speak the national language have in these circumstances? It is likely that their choice of second language would be English, or one of the other international languages. So their presence would increase the incentive among natives to defect from use of the national language in everyday transactions, and make the project of language-preservation harder to carry through. The state has good reason to limit immigration, or at least to differentiate sharply among prospective immigrants between those who speak the national language and those who don't, as the government of Quebec has done in recent years.

Language isn't the only feature to which the argument for cultural continuity applies. There is an internal relationship between a nation's culture and its physical

David Miller

shape – its public and religious buildings, the way its towns and villages are laid out, the pattern of the landscape, and so forth. People feel at home in a place in part because they can see that their surroundings bear the imprint of past generations whose values were recognizably their own. This doesn't rule out cultural change, but again it gives a reason for wanting to stay in control of the process – for teaching children to value their cultural heritage and to regard themselves as having a responsibility to preserve the parts of it that are worth preserving, for example. The "any public culture will do" position ignores this internal connection between the cultural and physical features of the community.

How restrictive an immigration policy this dictates depends on the empirical question of how easy or difficult it is to create a symbiosis between the existing public culture and the new cultural values of the immigrants, and this will vary hugely from case to case (in particular the experience of immigration itself is quite central to the public cultures of some states, but not to others). Most liberal democracies are now multicultural, and this is widely regarded as a source of cultural richness. But the more culturally diverse a society becomes, the greater need it has for a unifying public culture to bind its members together, and this culture has to connect to the history and physical shape of the society in question – it can't be invented from scratch (Kymlicka, 2001: esp. part IV; Miller, 1995: ch. 4). So a political judgment needs to be made about the scale and type of immigration that will enrich rather than dislocate the existing public culture.

The second reason for states to limit immigration that I want to consider concerns population size.[1] This is a huge, and hugely controversial, topic, and all I can do here is to sketch an argument that links together the issues of immigration and population control. The latter issue really arises at two different levels: global and national. At the global level, there is a concern that the carrying capacity of the earth may be stretched to breaking point if the total number of human beings continues to rise as it has over the last half century or so. At national level, there is a concern about the effect of population growth on quality of life and the natural environment. Let me look at each level in turn.

Although there is disagreement about just how many people the earth can sustain before resource depletion – the availability of water, for example – becomes acute, it would be hard to maintain that there is *no* upper limit. Although projections of population growth over the century ahead indicate a leveling off in the rate of increase, we must also expect – indeed should welcome – increases in the standard of living in the developing world that will mean that resource consumption per capita will also rise significantly. In such a world it is in all our interests that states whose populations are growing rapidly should adopt birth control measures and other policies to restrict the rate of growth, as both China and India have done in past decades. But such states have little or no incentive to adopt such policies if they can "export" their surplus population through international migration, and since the policies in question are usually unpopular, they have a positive incentive not to pursue them. A viable population policy at global level requires each state to be responsible for stabilizing, or even possibly reducing, its population over time, and this is going to be impossible to achieve if there are no restrictions on the movement of people between states.

At national level, the effects of population growth may be less catastrophic, but can still be detrimental to important cultural values. What we think about this issue may be conditioned to some extent by the population density of the state in which we live. Those of us who live in relatively small and crowded states experience daily the way in which the sheer number of our fellow citizens, with their needs for housing, mobility, recreation, and so forth, impacts on the physical environment, so that it becomes harder to enjoy access to open space, to move from place to place without encountering congestion, to preserve important wildlife habitats, and so on. It's true, of course, that the problems arise not simply from population size, but also from a population that wants to live in a certain way – to move around a lot, to have high levels of consumption, and so on – so we could deal with them by collectively changing the way that we live, rather than by restricting or reducing population size (De-Shalit, 2000). Perhaps we should. But this, it seems to me, is a matter for political decision: members of a territorial community have the right to decide whether to restrict their numbers, or to live in a more ecologically and humanly sound way, or to do neither and bear the costs of a high-consumption, high-mobility lifestyle in a crowded territory. If restricting numbers is part of the solution, then controlling immigration is a natural corollary.

What I have tried to do in this section is to suggest why states may have good reason to limit immigration. I concede that would-be immigrants may have a strong interest in being admitted – a strong economic interest, for example – but in general they have no obligation-conferring *right* to be admitted, for reasons given in the previous section. On the other side, nation-states have a strong and legitimate interest in determining who comes in and who does not. Without the right to exclude, they could not be what Michael Walzer has called "communities of character": "historically stable, ongoing associations of men and women with some special commitment to one another and some special sense of their common life" (1983: 62). It remains now to see what conditions an admissions policy must meet if it is to be ethically justified.

Conditions for an Ethical Immigration Policy

I shall consider two issues. The first is the issue of refugees, usually defined as people who have fled their home country as a result of a well-founded fear of persecution or violence. What obligations do states have to admit persons in that category? The second is the issue of discrimination in admissions policy. If a state decides to admit some immigrants (who are not refugees) but refuses entry to others, what criteria can it legitimately use in making its selection?

As I indicated in the first section of this chapter, people whose basic rights are being threatened or violated in their current place of residence clearly do have the right to move to somewhere that offers them greater security. Prima facie, then, states have an obligation to admit refugees, indeed "refugees" defined more broadly than is often the case to include people who are being deprived of rights to subsistence, basic healthcare, etc. (Gibney, 1999; Shacknove, 1985). But this need not involve treating them as long-term immigrants. They may be offered temporary sanctuary in states that are able to protect them, and then be asked to return to their original country

David Miller

of citizenship when the threat has passed (Hathaway and Neve, 1997). Moreover, rather than encouraging long-distance migration, it may be preferable to establish safety zones for refugees close to their homes and then deal with the cause of the rights-violations directly – whether this means sending in food and medical aid or intervening to remove a genocidal regime from power. There is obviously a danger that the temporary solution becomes semi-permanent, and this is unacceptable because refugees are owed more than the immediate protection of their basic rights – they are owed something like the chance to make a proper life for themselves. But liberals who rightly give a high moral priority to protecting the human rights of vulnerable people are regrettably often unwilling to countenance intervention in states that are plainly violating these rights.

If protection on the ground is not possible, the question then arises *which* state should take in the refugees. It is natural to see the obligation as shared among all those states that are able to provide refuge, and in an ideal world one might envisage some formal mechanism for distributing refugees among them. However, the difficulties in devising such a scheme are formidable (see Hathaway and Neve, 1997; Schuck, 1997). To obtain agreement from different states about what each state's refugee quota should be, one would presumably need to start with simple and relatively uncontroversial criteria such as population or per capita GNP. But this leaves out of the picture many other factors, such as population density, the overall rate of immigration into each state, cultural factors that make absorption of particular groups of refugees particularly easy or difficult, and so forth – all factors that would differentially affect the willingness of political communities to accept refugees and make agreement on a scheme very unlikely. Furthermore, the proposed quota system pays no attention to the choices of the refugees themselves as to where to apply for sanctuary, unless it is accompanied by a compensatory scheme that allows states that take in more refugees than their quota prescribes to receive financial transfers from states that take in less.

Realistically, therefore, states have to be given considerable autonomy to decide on how to respond to particular asylum applications: besides the refugee's own choice, they are entitled to consider the overall number of applications they face, the demands that temporary or longer-term accommodation of refugees will place on existing citizens, and whether there exists any special link between the refugee and the host community – for instance, similarities of language or culture, or a sense of historical responsibility on the part of the receiving state (which might see itself as somehow implicated among the causes of the crisis that has produced the refugees). If states are given this autonomy, there can be no guarantee that every bona fide refugee will find a state willing to take him or her in. Here we simply face a clash between two moral intuitions: on the one hand, every refugee is a person with basic human rights that deserve protection; on the other, the responsibility for insuring this is diffused among states in such a way that we cannot say that any particular state S has an obligation to admit refugee R. Each state is at some point entitled to say that it has done enough to cope with the refugee crisis. So the best we can hope for is that informal mechanisms will continue to evolve which make all refugees the *special* responsibility of one state or another (Miller, 2001).

The second issue is discrimination among migrants who are not refugees. Currently, states do discriminate on a variety of different grounds, effectively selecting the migrants they want to take in. Can this be justified? Well, given that states are entitled to put a ceiling on the numbers of people they take in, for reasons canvassed in the previous section, they need to select somehow, if only by lottery (as the USA began to do in 1995 for certain categories of immigrant). So what grounds can they legitimately use? It seems to me that receiving states are entitled to consider the benefit they would receive from admitting a would-be migrant as well as the strength of the migrant's own claim to move. So it is acceptable to give precedence to people whose cultural values are closer to those of the existing population – for instance, to those who already speak the native language. This is a direct corollary of the argument in the previous section about cultural self-determination. Next in order of priority come those who possess skills and talents that are needed by the receiving community.[2] Their claim is weakened, as suggested earlier, by the likelihood that in taking them in, the receiving state is also depriving their country of origin of a valuable resource (medical expertise, for example). In such cases, the greater the interest the potential host country has in admitting the would-be migrant, the more likely it is that admitting her will make life worse for those she leaves behind. So although it is reasonable for the receiving state to make decisions based on how much the immigrant can be expected to contribute economically if admitted, this criterion should be used with caution. What cannot be defended in any circumstances is discrimination on grounds of race, sex, or, in most instances, religion – religion could be a relevant criterion only where it continues to form an essential part of the public culture, as in the case of the state of Israel.

If nation-states are allowed to decide how many immigrants to admit in the first place, why can't they pick and choose among potential immigrants on whatever grounds they like – admitting only red-haired women if that is what their current membership prefers? I have tried to hold a balance between the interest that migrants have in entering the country they want to live in, and the interest that political communities having in determining their own character. Although the first of these interests is not strong enough to justify a right of migration, it is still substantial, and so the immigrants who are refused entry are owed an explanation. To be told that they belong to the wrong race, or sex (or have hair of the wrong color) is insulting, given that these features do not connect to anything of real significance to the society they want to join. Even tennis clubs are not entitled to discriminate among applicants on grounds such as these.

Let me conclude by underlining the importance of admitting all long-term immigrants to full and equal citizenship in the receiving society (this does not apply to refugees who are admitted temporarily until it is safe to return to their country of origin, but it does apply to refugees as soon as it becomes clear that return is not a realistic option for them). Controls on immigration must be coupled with active policies to insure that immigrants are brought into the political life of the community, and acquire the linguistic and other skills that they require to function as active citizens (Kymlicka, 2001: ch. 8). In several states immigrants are now encouraged to take citizenship classes leading up to a formal admissions ceremony, and this is a welcome development insofar as it recognizes that becoming a citizen isn't something that just happens spontaneously. Precisely because they aim to be "communities of character," with distinct public cultures to which new immigrants can contribute, democratic

David Miller

states must bring immigrants into political dialogue with natives. What is unacceptable is the emergence of a permanent class of non-citizens, whether these are guest workers, illegal immigrants, or asylum seekers waiting to have their applications adjudicated. The underlying political philosophy which informs this chapter sees democratic states as political communities formed on the basis of equality among their members, and just as this gives such states the right to exclude, it also imposes the obligation to protect the equal status of all those who live within their borders.

Notes

Earlier versions of this chapter were presented to the Nuffield Political Theory Workshop; the Politics, Law and Society Colloquium at University College London; and the Department of Government, University of Essex. I am very grateful to these audiences for their criticisms and suggestions, and especially to Clare Chambers, Matthew Gibney, Cecile Laborde, and Tiziana Torresi for their written comments on previous drafts.

1   For some reason this issue is rarely considered in philosophical discussions of immigration. An exception, albeit a brief one, is Barry (1992).
2   Another criterion that is often used in practice is having family ties to people who already have citizenship in the state in question, and this seems perfectly justifiable, but I am considering claims that have to do with features of the immigrants themselves.

References

Barry, Brian (1992). "The quest for consistency: a sceptical view." In B. Barry and R. E. Goodin (eds.), *Free Movement: Ethical Issues in the Transnational Migration of People and Money* (pp. 279–87). Hemel Hempstead: Harvester Wheatsheaf.

Caney, Simon (2001). "Cosmopolitan justice and equalizing opportunities." *Metaphilosophy*, 32: 113–34.

Carens, Joseph (1987). "Aliens and citizens: the case for open borders." *Review of Politics*, 49: 251–73.

Cole, Phillip (2000). *Philosophies of Exclusion: Liberal Political Theory and Immigration.* Edinburgh: Edinburgh University Press.

De-Shalit, Avner (2000). "Sustainability and population policies: myths, truths and half-baked ideas." In K. Lee, A. Holland, and D. McNeill (eds.), *Global Sustainable Development in the 21st Century* (pp. 188–200). Edinburgh: Edinburgh University Press.

Dummett, Ann (1992). "The transnational migration of people seen from within a natural law tradition." In B. Barry and R. E. Goodin (eds.), *Free Movement: Ethical Issues in the Transnational Migration of People and Money* (pp. 169–80). Hemel Hempstead: Harvester Wheatsheaf.

Gibney, Matthew J. (1999). "Liberal democratic states and responsibilities to refugees." *American Political Science Review*, 93: 169–81.

Griffin, James (2001). "First steps in an account of human rights." *European Journal of Philosophy*, 9: 306–27.

Hampton, Jean (1995). "Immigration, identity, and justice." In W. F. Schwartz (ed.), *Justice in Immigration* (pp. 67–93). Cambridge: Cambridge University Press.

Hathaway, J. C. and Neve, R. A. (1997). "Making international refugee law relevant again: a proposal for collectivized and solution-oriented protection." *Harvard Human Rights Journal*, 10: 115–211.

Kymlicka, Will (2001). *Politics in the Vernacular: Nationalism, Multiculturalism and Citizenship*. Oxford: Oxford University Press.

Miller, David (1995). *On Nationality*. Oxford: Clarendon Press.

Miller, David (1999). "Justice and global inequality." In A. Hurrell and N. Woods (eds.), *Inequality, Globalization, and World Politics* (pp. 187–210). Oxford: Oxford University Press.

Miller, David (2000). *Citizenship and National Identity*. Cambridge: Polity.

Miller, David (2001). "Distributing responsibilities." *Journal of Political Philosophy*, 9: 453–71.

Nickel, James (1987). *Making Sense of Human Rights*. Berkeley: University of California Press.

Perry, S. R. (1995). "Immigration, justice, and culture." In W. F. Schwartz (ed.), *Justice in Immigration* (pp. 94–135). Cambridge: Cambridge University Press.

Shacknove, Andrew (1985). "Who is a refugee?" *Ethics*, 95: 274–84.

Schuck, Peter A. (1997). "Refugee burden-sharing: a modest proposal." *Yale Journal of International Law*, 22: 243–97.

Shue, Henry (1980). *Basic Rights: Subsistence, Affluence, and US Foreign Policy*. Princeton, NJ: Princeton University Press.

Walzer, Michael (1983). *Spheres of Justice: A Defence of Pluralism and Equality*. Oxford: Martin Robertson.

Further reading

Barry, B. and Goodin, R. E. (eds.) (1992). *Free Movement: Ethical Issues in the Transnational Migration of People and Money*. Hemel Hempstead: Harvester Wheatsheaf.

Dummett, M. (2001). *On Immigration and Refugees*. London: Routledge.

Gibney, M. (ed.) (1988). *Open Borders? Closed Societies? The Ethical and Political Issues*. New York: Greenwood Press.

Joppke, C. (1999). *Immigration and the Nation-state*. Oxford: Oxford University Press.

Schwartz, W. F. (ed.) (1995). *Justice in Immigration*. Cambridge: Cambridge University Press.

Whelan, F. G. (1981). "Citizenship and the right to leave." *American Political Science Review*, 75: 636–53.

CHAPTER FOURTEEN

The Case for Open Immigration

Chandran Kukathas

People favor or are opposed to immigration for a variety of reasons. It is therefore difficult to tie views about immigration to ideological positions. While it seems obvious that political conservatives are the most unlikely to defend freedom of movement, and that socialists and liberals (classical and modern) are very likely to favor more open borders, in reality wariness (if not outright hostility) to immigration can be found among all groups. Even libertarian anarchists have advanced reasons to restrict the movement of peoples.

The purpose of this chapter is to make a case for greater freedom of movement or, simply, freedom of immigration. Its aim is to defend immigration against critics of all stripes, and also to defend immigration against some of its less enthusiastic friends.

To put a case for free immigration is not easy. Though it may be simple enough to enunciate political principles and stand doggedly by them, in questions of public policy coherence and consistency are merely necessary, but not sufficient, virtues. The feasibility of any policy proposal is also important, and political theory needs to be alive to this. "How open can borders be?" is an obvious question that it may not be possible to evade. The defense of free immigration offered here is, I hope, sensitive to this requirement. Nonetheless, it is an important part of its purpose to suggest that, in the end, political theory needs also to be suspicious of feasibility considerations, particularly when they lead us to morally troubling conclusions.

Before proceeding to the defense of free immigration, however, it will be important to understand what precisely immigration amounts to, and to recognize the nature of the *problem* of immigration as it exists in the world today. This is the task of the first section of this chapter. The second section defines and offers a short defense of free immigration. The three sections that follow then consider various challenges to the principle of free immigration coming from economic, national, and security perspectives, and argue that each challenge can be met. The final section offers some general reflections on the dilemmas of contemporary immigration policy, before restating more forcefully the case for the free movement of peoples.

The Problem of Immigration in the Modern World

More than 100 million people today live outside of the states of which they are citizens (Trebilcock, 1995: 219). But this figure does not come close to identifying the numbers of people who are moving about from country to country across the globe. Many people move between countries as tourists, businessmen, sportswomen or performers without ever stopping to "live" in a country – let alone with any intention to settle in a foreign land. Global human movement is a fact of life, as it has been for centuries, if not for all of human history. This has always had its own difficulties. But the problem of immigration is a problem of a particular kind, for immigrants are people who aim to stop rather than simply to pass through – though, as we shall see, the definition of "stopping" is not an easy one to establish. The migration of people is a problem in the modern world because that world is a world of states, and states guard (sometimes jealously) the right to determine who may settle within their borders. Immigration may be defined as the movement of a person or persons from one state into another for the purpose of temporary or permanent settlement (Kukathas, 2002a).

Modern states are reluctant to allow people to enter and settle within their borders at will for a variety of reasons. Security is one important consideration, though different states have different security concerns. The United States at present fears terrorist attacks and has tightened its immigration laws in part because of concerns for the safety of its citizens. China, on the other hand, has different security concerns since its political system does not permit much internal freedom of movement and could not tolerate an uncontrolled influx of foreigners into a population that harbors dissidents who would challenge the authority of the government. For states such as Israel, security is a prominent concern, but perhaps one no more important than the desire to preserve a certain cultural integrity. A state founded as a Jewish homeland cannot allow immigration to transform it into a multicultural polity.

For modern liberal democratic states, however, there are a number of important reasons why immigration is problematic. These states, including Canada, the United States, Australia, Britain, and several countries in Western Europe, are particularly popular destinations for immigrants, whether because they are refugees seeking safe havens, or simply people looking to improve their prospects of a better life. One important reason why immigration is a problem in these cases is that immigrants impose costs on society even as they bring benefits. While economists tend to agree that the consequences of free movement are generally positive, since competitive labor markets make for a more efficient use of resources (Simon, 1990; Sykes, 1995: 159–60), not all nations may benefit immediately from an influx of immigrants. Nor do the burdens of accommodating or adjusting to immigrants fall equally on all within a society – much will depend on who the immigrants are, where they settle, and with whom they end up competing for jobs, real estate, and public facilities. Even if the benefits of immigration outweigh the costs to the nation, those who are adversely affected by an

Chandran Kukathas

influx of settlers will object; and in liberal democratic states this will translate into electorally significant opposition.

Another important reason why immigration is a problem in liberal democratic states is that these states are, to varying degrees, welfare states. The state in such societies provides a range of benefits, including education, unemployment relief, retirement income, medical care, as well as numerous programs to serve particular interests. Immigrants are potential recipients of these services and benefits, and any state considering the level of immigration it will accept will have to consider how likely immigrants are to consume these benefits, how much they might consume, whether or not they are going to be able to finance the extra costs from the lifetime tax contributions of these immigrants, and what are the short-term implications of accepting immigrants who begin by consuming more in benefits than they pay in taxes. Consequently, such states are reluctant to accept immigrants who are infirm, or too old to contribute enough in taxes in their remaining working lives to cover the costs of medical care and retirement subsidies.

Under these circumstances liberal democratic governments will go to great lengths to limit immigration, though they will face pressures both to admit and refuse entry to applicants seeking to enter their countries. The pressures to admit will come from businesses looking for cheaper labor, from humanitarian groups calling for the admission of refugees, and from families and ethnic communities pressing to have relatives join them from their countries of origin. The pressures to refuse entry will generally come from labor unions, from "nativist" groups, and from conservatives concerned about the cultural and economic impact of settlers, particularly if the settlers are predominantly from ethnically different countries. The lengths to which liberal democratic states might go to discourage immigration is well illustrated by the reaction of the Australian government in August 2001 to the appearance near its coastal waters of a Norwegian merchant vessel, *The Tampa*, bearing refugees rescued at sea. The vessel was denied permission to enter Australian waters and to offload its human cargo, which was shipped to the island of Nauru to prevent the refugees from appealing for asylum in Australia (Marr and Wilkinson, 2003). More recently, the United States responded to the crisis in Haiti in February 2004 by intervening to encourage the departure of President Aristide, and to restore some degree of order, because it feared an exodus of Haitian refugees making their way to Florida.

Immigration is a problem largely because of the nature of the modern state. Most states, and certainly all liberal democratic states, regard their people as "citizens" or "members" of the state. Membership is not standard, and the nature of membership has a substantial bearing on the rights that individuals have within a state. Full membership might amount to citizenship and include the right to vote and stand for public office. (Though it is worth noting that in the United States, for example, even full citizenship does not entitle a member to stand for the office of President if he or she was not born in the country.) "Permanent resident" status might give one the right to work and to change employer at will, and also to draw on health, education, and welfare services, but not provide security against deportation. Status as a "guest-worker" or temporary resident might provide fewer rights still. Modern states restrict immigration because they must manage access to the goods for which immigrants and natives would compete. Modern states are like clubs that are reluctant to accept new members unless they can be assured that they have more to gain by admitting people than they have by keeping them out.

In Defense of Free Immigration

Given that immigrants will compete for goods and resources with natives, why should states open their borders when it is their task to manage affairs within their domains? Does the idea of open immigration not go against the principles of good husbandry?

There are many reasons why borders should be open and the movement of people should be free. But before considering these reasons more closely, it should be admitted that the prospect of states opening their borders completely is a remote one. Even as the European Union expands its membership and facilitates freer movement among its denizens, to take one possible counter-example to this claim, it continues to control entry into Europe – and is feeling the pressure from member states to tighten restrictions on entry from refugees and displaced people. "Open borders" is not a policy option currently being considered by any state. Nonetheless, the case for open borders should be considered, though in the end, as we shall see, it cannot be defended without rethinking the idea of the state.

There are two major reasons for favoring open borders. The first is a principle of freedom, and the second a principle of humanity.

Open borders are consistent with – and on occasion, protect – freedom in a number of ways. First, and most obviously, closed borders restrict freedom of movement. Borders prevent people from moving into territories whose governments forbid them to enter; and to the extent that they cannot enter any other territory, borders confine them within their designated boundaries. This fact is not sufficient to establish that so confining people is indefensible; but if freedom is held to be an important value, then there is at least a case for saying that very weighty reasons are necessary to restrict it.

Several other considerations suggest that such reasons would have to be weighty indeed. First, to keep borders closed would mean to keep out people who would, as a consequence, lose not only the freedom to move but also the freedom they might be seeking in an attempt to flee unjust or tyrannical regimes. The effect of this is to deny people the freedom they would gain by leaving their societies and to diminish the incentive of tyrannical regimes to reform the conditions endured by their captive peoples. Second, closing borders means denying people the freedom to sell their labor, and denying others the freedom to buy it. Good reasons are needed to justify abridging this particular freedom, since to deny someone the liberty to exchange his labor is to deny him a very significant liberty. Third, and more generally, keeping borders closed would mean restricting people's freedom to associate. It would require keeping apart people who wish to come together whether for love, or friendship, or for the sake of fulfilling important duties, such as caring for children or parents.

Now, to be sure, defenders of restricted immigration do not generally argue that borders should be completely sealed, or that no one should be admitted. Many concede that exceptions should be made for refugees, that some people should be allowed to come into a country to work, and that some provision should be made for admitting

Chandran Kukathas

people who wish to rejoin their families. Those who want restricted or controlled immigration are not indifferent to freedom. Nonetheless, even those who argue for generous levels of immigration by implication maintain that people should be turned away at the border. This in itself is a limitation of liberty, for which good reasons must be given. In the end, or so I will argue, the reasons that have been offered are not weighty enough to justify restricting freedom even to a limited degree.

The second reason for favoring open borders is a principle of humanity. The great majority of the people of the world live in poverty, and for a significant number of them the most promising way of improving their condition is to move. This would remain true even if efforts to reduce trade barriers were successful, rich countries agreed to invest more in poorer ones, and much greater amounts of aid were made available to the developing world. For even if the general condition of a society were good, the situation of particular individuals would often be poor, and for some of them immigration would offer the best prospect of improving their condition. To say to such people that they are forbidden to cross a border in order to improve their condition is to say to them that it is justified that they be denied the opportunity to get out of poverty, or even destitution. And clearly there are many people who share this plight, for numerous illegal immigrants take substantial risks to move from one country to another – courting not only discomfort and even death by traveling under cover in dangerous conditions, but also punishment at the hands of the authorities if caught.

A principle of humanity suggests that very good reasons must be offered to justify turning the disadvantaged away. It would be bad enough to meet such people with indifference and to deny them positive assistance. It would be even worse to deny them the opportunity to help themselves. To go to the length of denying one's fellow citizens the right to help those who are badly off, whether by employing them or by simply taking them in, seems even more difficult to justify – if, indeed, it is not entirely perverse.

Not all people who look to move are poor or disadvantaged. Nor do all of them care about freedom. But if freedom and humanity are important and weighty values, the prima facie case for open borders is a strong one, since very substantial considerations will have to be adduced to warrant ignoring or repudiating them. I suggest that no such considerations are to be found. But to show this, it is necessary to look more closely at arguments that restrictions of immigration are defensible, and indeed desirable.

Economic Arguments Against Open Borders

It is sometimes argued that there are strong economic arguments for limiting immigration. There are two kinds of concern here. The first is about the impact of migrants on the local market economy: large numbers of people entering a society can change the balance of an economy, driving down wages or pushing up the prices of some goods such as real estate – to the disadvantage of many people in the native population. The second is about the impact of migrants on the cost and availability of goods and services supplied through the state: education, healthcare, welfare, and the publicly funded infrastructure of roads, parks, and other non-excludable goods. Do these concerns warrant closing borders to immigrants?

In the end, the answer must be that they do not. But the reasons why are not as straightforward as might be anticipated. If our concern is the impact of migrants on the local market economy, one argument often advanced by economists is that, on balance, the net impact of immigrants is mildly positive. While immigrants do take jobs that might have gone to locals and drive down wages, while driving up some prices, they also have a positive impact on the economy. Migrants expand the size of the workforce and extend the division of labor, so society gains from the benefits this brings. As new consumers, they expand the size of the domestic market and help to lower prices for many goods. Measuring the precise impact of any cohort of immigrants is difficult; but the overall impact is, at best, positive and, at worst, only mildly negative – even with respect to employment. Moreover, the global effect of migration is positive, as it involves a movement of people from places where they are less productive and often unable to make a living to places where they are both more productive and better off – and in many cases no longer a burden on their societies.

The problem, however, is that whatever the overall impact of migration, particular persons will do badly out of it. An influx of cheap labor may be good for society overall, but bad for those who are put out of work or forced to accept lower wages. It is to these people that the critic of open borders will point to illustrate the economic costs of immigration. Why should *they* bear the costs? Equally, why should other societies be happy about the brain-drain that is also an aspect of immigration, as skilled people leave their native countries for better opportunities abroad?

While it is true that the burdens and benefits of immigration do not fall evenly or equitably on all members of a host society, open borders are defensible nonetheless for a number of reasons. First, it has to be asked why it must be assumed that locals are entitled to the benefits they enjoy as people who have immediate access to particular markets. As residents or citizens, these people enjoy the rents they secure by virtue of an arrangement that excludes others from entering a particular market.[1] Such arrangements are commonplace in every society, and indeed in the world as a whole. Often those who find a resource to exploit, or a demand which they are particularly able to fulfill, are unable to resist the temptation to ensure that they enjoy the gains to be had in exploiting that resource or fulfilling that demand by preventing others from doing the same. Yet it is unclear that there is any principle that can justify granting to some persons privileged access to such rents. To be sure, many of the most egregious examples of rent-seeking (and rent-protecting) behavior are to be found in the activities of capitalist firms and industries. But this does not make such activity defensible, since it serves simply to protect the well-off from having to share the wealth into which they have tapped with those who would like to secure a little of that same wealth for themselves.

If we are considering labor markets, there is no good reason to exclude outsiders from offering their labor in competition with locals. While it may disadvantage locals to have to compete, it is equally true that outsiders will be disadvantaged if they are forbidden to do so. Also, locals who would benefit from the greater availability of labor would also be disadvantaged by the exclusion of outsiders. To prevent, say, firms

Chandran Kukathas

from hiring outside labor would be no more justifiable on economic grounds than preventing firms from moving their operations abroad to take advantage of cheaper or more productive labor in other countries.

The same arguments hold if we are considering the case of people who wish to move to a different country to sell not their labor but their wares – perhaps by setting up a business. There is no more a justification for preventing them from doing this than there is for preventing them from trading their goods from abroad. Restricting access to markets certainly benefits some people, but at the expense of others, and generally to the disadvantage of all. If particular privileges should be accorded to some because of their state membership, the justification cannot be economic in the first of the two senses distinguished.

In the second sense of economic, however, the argument for restricting immigration is not that access to particular markets should be limited, but that the economic benefits dispensed by the state must be limited if economic resources and indeed the social system more generally are to be properly managed. Immigration dulls the edge of good husbandry. For some libertarians, the concern here is that open borders – or even increased immigration – will impose a greater tax burden on existing members of society as the poor and disabled move to states with more generous welfare provisions, as well as subsidized education and healthcare. Indeed, a number of libertarians have argued that until the welfare state is abolished, immigration will have to be tightly controlled in countries like the United States (Hoppe, 1998).

Here it would not be enough to point out that, to the extent that immigrants join the workforce, they would also contribute to the revenues of the state through taxes, even as they consume resources dispensed by the state. Open immigration might well encourage people to move with the intention of taking advantage of benefits that exceed their tax contributions. People on low incomes and with children or elderly or infirm dependents would find it advantageous to move to countries with generous public education and healthcare. This could impose a significant additional burden on taxpaying individuals and firms, or pressure a state with fiscal problems to reduce the quality of its services. Immigration is a problem for welfare states – understanding welfare in its broadest sense to include health and education services as well as unemployment relief and disability benefits.

The problem here is a significant one. But it should be noted that it is not a problem that results from the movement of the rich or able, only one that results from the movement of the poor. The independently wealthy, and the well-off moving into well-paying jobs, will contribute to the state's coffers through direct and indirect taxes, and may well pay for more than they consume. The poor will in all likelihood be net consumers of tax dollars – at least at the outset. An important purpose of closed borders is to keep out the poor.

If the concern is to preserve the integrity of the welfare state, however, the most that could be justified is restricting membership of the welfare system. The movement of people into a country could then be free. Such restricted forms of immigration would still impose serious disadvantages upon poorer people, for whom the attraction of immigration would diminish if they were obliged to fund their own healthcare and pay for the education of their children. Yet for many it would be better than no opportunity to move at all. Certainly, immigration with limited entitlements

The Case for Open Immigration

would be attractive to young and able people with dependents, since the opportunity to work abroad and remit money home might significantly improve all their lives.

Nonetheless, it would not do to be too sanguine about the possibility of such an arrangement. Most states would baulk at the suggestion of such arrangements, and even advocates of open immigration may reject the idea of different classes of membership. Moreover, immigrants paying taxes may feel disgruntled if their taxes do not buy them equal entitlements. In the end, it may be that the existence of the welfare state makes open borders, or even extensive immigration, very difficult – if not impossible. From the perspective of a principle of freedom, or a principle of humanity, I suggest, the standard of open borders should prevail. To defend closed borders a principle of nationality would have to take precedence. We should turn then to look more closely at the argument from nationality.

Nationality and Immigration

Implicit in most arguments for closed borders or restricted immigration is an assumption that the good or well-being of the members of a polity should take precedence – to a significant degree, even if not absolutely – over the good of outsiders. From this perspective, that one of my fellow countrymen is harmed or made worse off is a weighty consideration when assessing any policy, in a way that the impact of that policy on foreigners is not. Defenders of this perspective may disagree about the extent to which the interests of outsiders should be discounted; and indeed some may hold that rich nations owe substantial obligations of justice to the world's poor. But they are agreed that something more is owed to one's own country and its people. And this justifies protecting one's nation from the impact of open or substantial immigration. (For contrasting views see Miller, 1988; Goodin, 1988.)

Immigration, on this view, may be damaging for a number of different reasons. We have already considered some of the economic consequences of immigration; but there are other problems as well. First, immigration in substantial numbers, even if it takes place over a long period of time, "has the effect of changing the recipient area" (Barry, 1992: 281). The influx of Indian workers in the nineteenth century changed Fiji from an island of Polynesian people to one that is bicultural, just as the movement of Indians and Chinese to Malaya turned that society into a multicultural one. The fear of many people is that immigration will change a society's character, and perhaps undermine or displace an ancient identity (Casey, 1982). The cultural character of Britain or France cannot remain the same if substantial numbers of people move there from Africa or Asia.

Second, immigration from culturally different people may be damaging to wealthy countries to the extent that their wealth is dependent upon the existence of a political culture, and economic and social institutions, that are especially conducive to wealth-creation. Immigration from people who do not share the same values, and who would not help to sustain the same institutions, may ultimately undermine those institutions (Buchanan, 1995). If so, this may be good reason to restrict immigration not only by number but also by culture.

Third, immigration may make it very difficult for a society to develop or sustain a level of social solidarity that is necessary for a state to work well, and particularly for it to uphold principles of social justice. This argument has been developed especially forcefully by David Miller, who suggests that if immigration exceeds the absorptive capacities of a society, the bonds of social solidarity make break down. The nation is a natural reference group when people ask whether or not they are getting a fair share of society's resources. If people have different understandings of what their rights and obligations are and disagree about what they may legitimately claim, it may become impossible to establish and operate appropriate standards of social justice (Miller 1995, 1999a). For all of these reasons, then, open borders cannot be justified. Or so it is argued.

While all of these considerations are weighty, they do not suffice to warrant limitations on freedom of movement. First, while it is true that immigrants do change the character of a place – sometimes dramatically – it is not evident that this is necessarily a bad thing. More to the point, it is difficult to know how much change is desirable, partly because the results will not be known for some time and partly because different people – even in relatively homogeneous societies – want different things. It is perfectly understandable that some people want things to remain the way they have been during their lifetimes. Yet it is no less understandable that others want changes they regard as improvements. The Know-Nothings of nineteenth-century America were completely hostile to Catholic, and especially Irish, immigration; though Irish Americans were all too ready to welcome to the United States even more settlers from Ireland. In the end, our capacity to shape society or preserve its character may be as limited as our capacity to know how much (or how little) change is really desirable – even if we could agree on what sort of character we would like our societies to have.

It is also worth bearing in mind that many societies have experienced significant cultural or social transformations and not only survived but prospered. The United States in the nineteenth century welcomed immigrants from all over the world, incorporated large parts of what was once Mexico into its territory, overturned a three-century old tradition of slavery and yet began the twentieth century a prosperous and vibrant democracy. Canada and Australia have seen their societies transformed by postwar immigration into multicultural polities, while continuing to enjoy economic growth and social stability. And the European Union continues to expand its membership by admitting states from Eastern Europe – and perhaps, eventually, Turkey – in a way that makes it possible for peoples from diverse ethnic, religious, and political traditions to move freely from one end of the continent to the other, without fearing a loss in prosperity; though there can be no doubt that this development will bring with it significant cultural changes to many of Europe's communities.

Social and cultural change can be effected by large-scale immigration, and its significance should not be discounted. But neither should it be overestimated. Nor should too much weight be given to the possibility that immigration from poor nations to rich ones will undermine the institutions of wealth-creation – though it surely is a possibility. If anything, it is perhaps more likely that immigrants who move to wealthy countries will do so because they want to take advantage of the opportunities it offers, and that they will assimilate by adopting the practices that bring success to the natives. In any case, if our interest is in wealth-creation, it is more likely that this skill will be taught to those who enter a rich country than that it will be exported successfully to some countries that are poor.

The most challenging argument against open immigration, however, is that institutions of social justice can only be built if social solidarity is preserved – and that immigration may undermine that solidarity if it is not appropriately restricted. If we accept that social justice is an important concern, then Miller's analysis and argument are powerful and convincing. The only way to resist them is to question the very idea that the nation-state is the appropriate site for the settlement of questions of distributive justice. And indeed that is what we need to do.

There are a number of reasons why we should be suspicious of the idea that the nation-state is the site of distributive justice, but the most powerful have been advanced by Miller in his own critique of the idea of global social justice. Miller maintains that principles of social justice are always, "as a matter of psychological fact, applied within bounded communities" (1999a: 18). It is easier for us to make judgments of justice in small communities such as workplaces, but difficult in units larger than nation-states. We make such judgments by comparing ourselves with others. But it is difficult for us to compare ourselves with people who are remote from our own circumstances, such as people in other countries. We can more readily make judgments based on comparisons with people who belong to our own reference group – people with whom we are likely to share some common conceptions of value. When conceptions of the value of a resource differ, it becomes very difficult to establish common standards of distributive justice, since the very question of what counts as a resource to be distributed may be impossible to settle. And when we consider that different communities have conflicting views about how trade-offs should be made, for example, between the consumption of what the earth will produce and the preservation of the natural environment, it would be difficult for one community to demand a share of another's resources on the basis of its own determination of the "true value" of those resources (Miller, 1999b: 193–6). Global social justice is difficult to defend.

Yet all the things that make global justice problematic also go to make problematic social justice *within* the nation-state. Certainly, some nation-states are so large that it is difficult to see how they could really share a single conception of social justice. China and India between them hold more than a third of the world's population, and harbor different languages, religions, and customs. Even the United States, though much smaller, is sufficiently diverse that there are noticeable differences among significant groups about morality and justice – from California, to Utah, to Louisiana. Britain and France are smaller still, but are home to a diversity of religions and ethnicities. If the preservation of a shared ethos or sense of social justice is an important reason to restrict immigration, then, it might be defensible if we are considering small, homogeneous nations such as Iceland or Tahiti. It might also be defensible for a state such as Israel, though it might be more difficult to make this case the more it is a multicultural (or bicultural) state. But in larger states, which are diverse and already have a long history of immigration, the idea of a shared conception of social justice might be too much to hope for. Certainly, the vigorous debates among philosophers about social justice suggest that there is no substantial agreement on this question even among a group as homogeneous as the academy. Miller's point about the nature of social justice is a telling one; but it also tells against his own defense of restricted immigration. (For a fuller critique of Miller's view, see also Kukathas, 2002a.)

Even if states were plausible sites of social justice, however, there is another issue that has to be raised. Is it right that the preservation of local institutions of social justice take precedence over the humanitarian concerns that make open immigration desirable? As was noted earlier, immigration barriers operate largely to limit the movement of the world's poor. It seems odd to suggest that this can be defended by appeal to the importance of social justice. If the price of social justice is exclusion of the worst-off from the lands that offer the greatest opportunity, this may be a mark against the ideal of social justice.

To be fair, however, it should be acknowledged that defenders of social justice or the primacy of membership (Walzer, 1983) generally acknowledge the need to make special provision for the world's poor. In this regard, they suggest that refugees may have a special claim to be allowed to immigrate and resettle to escape persecution. But here a number of problems arise. First, the line distinguishing a refugee and what we might term an "economic migrant" is a very fine one. As it stands, the 1951 United Nations Convention relating to the Status of Refugees adopts a very narrow definition of refugee to include only persons with a well-founded fear of persecution for reasons of race, religion, nationality, membership of a particular social group or political opinion. Those people fleeing war, natural disaster, or famine are, on this definition, not refugees. Second, even on this narrow definition, there are more than 20 million people in the world who count as refugees who have yet to be resettled. The problem these two points pose is that making an exception for refugees requires a very significant increase in immigration – even if the narrow definition of refugee is used. If a more humane definition were adopted – one that recognized as refugees people fleeing war zones, for example – an even greater number of immigrants would have to be accepted. Yet then, if the standard of humanity is the appropriate standard, it is difficult to see why any sharp distinction should be made between the desperate fleeing war and the destitute struggling to make a living.

It would perhaps be too much to hope or expect that states – especially wealthy ones – will readily lower the barriers to the free movement of peoples. As it stands, the world of states has struggled to relocate the refugees for whom it has acknowledged responsibility. Indeed, it is sobering to remember that immigration controls were tightened with the invention of the passport during the First World War precisely to control refugee flows. Nonetheless, on this much at least, both the defenders of open borders and the advocates of restrictions can agree: that at present the borders are too securely sealed.

Immigration and Security

One reason for greater restriction of immigration, which clearly has assumed enormous significance in recent times, is the need for security. Can immigration be free in an age of terror?

Security from terrorist attack, it should be noted, is only one kind of security. Even before terror became a serious concern, modern states have been anxious about the security of political systems from foreign threats, and the security of society against international criminal organizations. Smugglers, traffickers in illegal goods (from drugs to rare wildlife to historical artifacts), and slave-traders of various kinds operate across boundaries to violate the laws of host states. Nonetheless, the threat of terror has added significantly to the security concerns of a number of Western states. Does this give us greater reason to restrict immigration, or show that the idea of open borders is simply untenable?

In the end, I suggest that security concerns do not do much to diminish the case for open borders. This is not to say that security concerns are unfounded or should not be addressed. But it is to say that immigration controls are not they key. There are a number of reasons why. First, while it is easy to restrict legal immigration, it is another matter to control illegal immigration. Limiting legal immigration is unlikely to deter either criminals or subversive agents from moving between states. Borders are porous even when they are closed. Second, limiting immigration seldom means limiting the movement of people more generally, since many more people move from one country to another as tourists, or students, or businessmen, or government officials than they do as immigrants intending to settle in a new land. If security is a concern, tourism should be more severely limited in many countries than it presently is. If a person is likely to pose a threat to a country's security, it would be odd to think it acceptable for him to be granted a tourist visa for one, three, or six months. Equally, if a person is considered safe to be awarded a three-month tourist visa, it is hard to see why he should be denied the right to permanent residence *on security grounds*. It might well be that in times of insecurity greater vigilance is necessary: greater scrutiny of many aspects of the behavior of people – including travelers – may be warranted, just as one would expect the police to establish road blocks and search cars when there is an escaped criminal in the vicinity. It is not evident, however, that this would justify further restrictions on immigration rather than simply greater effort to discover who poses a threat to society, to try avert the threat, and to apprehend the particular persons who are menaces.

There are, however, reasons not to place too much weight on the importance of security, for like all things, the search for security comes with costs of its own. In the case of the search for security through immigration controls, the cost is borne not only in the financial expense that is incurred but also in the impact that controls on immigrants and immigration have on society more generally. Immigration control requires the surveillance of people moving in and out of the country, and to some degree of people moving about within the country. But it is not possible to do this with immigrants or outsiders generally without also placing one's own citizens under surveillance. In dangerous times this may not be avoidable, at least to some degree. But the risks it brings are substantial. Even if the burdens imposed upon citizens and residents are trivial, they may be burdens all the same – and for some more than others. Furthermore, there is always a risk that impositions designed to meet a particular danger will remain in place long after the danger has passed. (Malaysia's Internal Security Act, which, among other things, sanctions arrest and detention without trial, was passed at the height of the communist insurgency in the 1960s, but remains in place 25 years after the emergency ended.) Liberal democracies, in particular, should be wary of state controls advocated in the name of national security – particularly since the trade-off is a loss of liberty.

Concluding Reflections

Whatever the merits of the case for open borders, it is highly unlikely that we will see an end to immigration controls at any time soon – for reasons that were canvassed at the beginning of this paper. In one important respect, free migration is entirely unfeasible: it is politically untenable.

One reason why it is politically untenable is that most voters in wealthy countries do not favor immigration, particularly by the poor. Another is that states themselves do not favor uncontrolled population movements. In a world order shaped by the Westphalian model of states operating within strict geographical boundaries, and dominated by the imperative to secure the welfare of members, the free movement of peoples is not a strong possibility. The inclination of most people to hold on to the advantages they possess also makes it unlikely that nations will open up their borders to allow others to come and take a greater share of what they control.

Yet if the free movement of peoples is not politically feasible, how can there be a case for open borders? Surely, political theory, in considering issues of public policy, should keep its focus on the world of the possible rather than on impossible ideals.

There is a good deal of truth to this. But there is, nonetheless, good reason for putting the case for open immigration. One important consideration is that many feasibility problems have their roots not in the nature of things but in our way of thinking about them. Many of the reasons open immigration is not possible right now have less to do with the disadvantages it might bring than with an unwarranted concern about its dangers. Even to the extent that the source of the problem for open immigration lies in the nature of things, however, it is worth considering the case for open borders because it forces us to confront the inconsistency between moral ideals and our existing social and political arrangements. One of the reasons why open immigration is not possible is that it is not compatible with the modern welfare state. While one obvious response to this is to say, "so much the worse for open immigration," it is not less possible to ask whether the welfare state is what needs rethinking.

Note

1 "Rent" is money someone pays to have access to some capital asset (such as land, a dwelling, or a means of transport) that she does not or cannot own outright. Persons who engage in "rent-seeking" seek money from rents instead of from profits or wage income.

References

Barry, Brian (1992). "The quest for consistency: a sceptical view." In Brian Barry and Robert E. Goodin (eds.), *Free Movement: Ethical Issues in the Transnational Migration of People and Money* (pp. 279–87). University Park, PA: Pennsylvania State University Press.

Buchanan, James (1995). "A two-country parable." In Warren F. Schwartz (ed.), *Justice in Immigration* (pp. 63–6). Cambridge: Cambridge University Press.

Casey, J. (1982). "One nation: the politics of race." *Salisbury Review*, 1: 23–8.

Goodin, Robert E. (1988). "What's so special about our fellow countrymen?" *Ethics*, 98/4: 663–86

Hoppe, Hans Herman (1998). "The case for free trade and restricted immigration." *Journal of Libertarian Studies*, 13/2: 221–33.

Kukathas, Chandran (2002a). "Immigration." In Hugh LaFollette (ed.), *The Oxford Handbook of Practical Ethics* (pp. 567–90). New York, Oxford University Press.

Kukathas, Chandran (2002b). "The nation-state: a modest attack." In Daniel A. Bell and Avner de-Shalit (eds.), *Forms of Justice* (pp. 107–22). Oxford: Oxford University Press.

Marr, David and Wilkinson, Marian (2003). *Dark Victory*. Crow's Nest, NSW, Australia: Allen & Unwin.

Miller, David (1988). "The ethical significance of nationality." *Ethics*, 98/4: 647–62.

Miller, David (1995). *On Nationality*. Oxford: Clarendon Press.

Miller, David (1999a). *Principles of Social Justice*. Cambridge, MA: Harvard University Press.

Miller, David (1999b). "Justice and global inequality." In Andrew Hurrell and Ngaire Woods (eds.), *Inequality, Globalization and World Politics* (pp. 187–210). Oxford: Oxford University Press.

Simon, Julian (1990). *The Economic Consequences of Immigration*. Oxford: Blackwell.

Sykes, Alan O. (1995). "The welfare economics of immigration law: a theoretical survey with an analysis of US policy." In Warren F. Schwartz (ed.), *Justice in Immigration* (pp. 158–200). Cambridge: Cambridge University Press.

Trebilcock, Michael J. (1995). "The case for a liberal immigration policy." In Warren F. Schwartz (ed.), *Justice in Immigration* (pp. 219–46). Cambridge: Cambridge University Press.

Walzer, Michael (1983). *Spheres of Justice: A Defence of Pluralism and Equality*. Oxford: Martin Robertson.

PORNOGRAPHY

The Right to Get Turned On: Pornography, Autonomy, Equality

Andrew Altman

Introduction

Debates over whether adults have a right to produce, distribute, and view pornographic materials have typically proceeded on the premise that freedom of speech is the central liberty at stake. Those who argue that there is a moral "right to pornography" contend that it is part of a person's freedom of speech. Those who argue that there is no such right contend that pornographic material is "low value" speech or more like conduct than speech. They proceed to claim that some other value such as sexual equality between men and women overrides an individual's claim to have access to pornography.

I believe that the premise behind this debate is mistaken. While there are certain respects in which freedom of speech is at stake in the matter of pornography, such freedom is not the central liberty relevant to the issue. Rather, the right to pornography should be understood primarily as an element of another form of freedom: sexual autonomy. Individuals ought to have a broad liberty to define and enact their own sexuality. Persons who view pornography are exercising their sexual autonomy, and the debate over pornography should be seen from the standpoint of that liberty.

When seen from such a standpoint, the claim that there is a right to pornography is analogous to claims that there is a right to use contraceptives, to engage in sexual relations outside of marriage, and to engage in homosexual activity. Freedoms that protect sexuality-defining decisions get closer to the heart of the pornography issue than freedoms that protect speech and other activities whose primary intent is to communicate ideas or attitudes.

The principle of sexual autonomy has its limits. The moral right to have sex without being married does not include the moral right to have sex with children or with a non-consenting adult. A moral right to pornography does not include the moral right to buy or possess photographs of children having sex, or of people who are actually being raped or sexually assaulted. However, I will argue that sexual autonomy does entail a moral right to buy and possess a wide range of pornographic materials, including those that depict sexual violence.

What is Pornography?

It is not realistic to think that there is a succinct definition of pornography that would prove acceptable to the different sides in the debate and capture all of the material that might reasonably be thought pornographic. This does not mean that we should remain content with Justice Potter Stewart's attitude: "I know it when I see it" (*Jacobellis* v. *Ohio*, 1964: 197). Rather, we can formulate a concise description of a class of materials that includes many, if not all, of the materials which the different sides in the debate could agree are reasonably described as pornographic. The description would be a kind of starting point that could be qualified and expanded in various ways as the debate proceeded. The point is that we need some reasonable starting point that can be accepted without unfairly tilting the debate over the existence of a moral right to pornography.

My suggestion for such a starting point is this: pornography is sexually explicit material, in words or images, which is intended by its creators to excite sexually those who are willing viewers of the material. By a "willing viewer," I mean a person who voluntarily pays something – in time, effort, or money – to view the material and who is willing to pay because he expects to become sexually aroused by viewing it. Thus, pornography is a commodity which represents a kind of sexual meeting of the minds between producer and consumer: the producer intends that the consumer be sexually aroused by the product and the consumer pays for the product in the expectation of becoming aroused by it.

The intention to cause sexual arousal is clearly not the only one for which a producer of pornography may be acting. Commercial producers intend to make money. However, the intent to cause sexual arousal is central, even in the commercial case. The producers intend to make money by creating a product which causes sexual arousal and the buyer expects to be aroused by viewing the product.

In contrast, consider the authors or publishers of a medical textbook which contains photographs of sexual organs and their various diseases. Such persons intend to make money. However, it is not their intention to make it by causing sexual arousal but rather by communicating medical information. Moreover, buyers of medical textbooks do not generally purchase them in order to stimulate themselves sexually: there is no sexual meeting of the minds between the authors or publishers and the consumers.

It is an important fact about human sexuality that different people are sexually excited by very different kinds of sexually explicit material. The makers of pornography know this fact well. Much hardcore pornography is explicitly addressed to the viewer's preference for particular types of sexual content: oral, anal, sadomasochist, gay, lesbian, and so on.

It seems clear that the vast majority of pornography in contemporary society is directed at males. Among all of the hours spent watching pornography, the vast major-

Andrew Altman

ity of those hours belong to men. However, even within the group of heterosexual men, there are differences in the pornographic content which they willingly seek out. In addition, empirical studies show that a significant percentage of willing viewers of pornography are women (Slade, 2001: 967).

Sexual Autonomy

Individuals have a right to a substantial degree of control over their own lives. This right does not mean that any individual has the liberty to do whatever she or he chooses: one person's liberty is limited by the duties that she has toward others. More-over, individual control is invariably exercised within a social context created by the choices and actions of other people who are exercising control over their own lives. Yet it would be mistaken to think that individual control is rendered factually impos-sible by the unchosen character of our social context or morally meaningless by the existence of duties we owe to others. Persons are not puppets of their social circum-stances, nor are they smothered by moral duties owed to others. Rather, they are agents who have the broad right to decide for themselves how to live their lives. Other individuals and the government have a duty to respect those decisions.

Under the rules of traditional sexual morality, a person's sexual life was, to a large extent, not his or her own: the rules imposed a highly confining set of duties on sexual choices and actions. In particular, sexual activity was condemned as "unnat-ural" if it was outside of heterosexual marriage or if the activities were undertaken for purposes of other than procreation. Traditional sexual morality looked askance on pornography because such materials excite passions that do not stay neatly confined within the narrow channels of sexual activity that traditional morality deemed the only natural and acceptable way of expressing human sexuality. Accordingly, pornog-raphy was seen as corrupting individual character and subverting the proper order of society.

The sexual revolution of the 1960s replaced the traditional sexual morality with a liberal one. This liberal morality located a person's sexual life much more within his or her own dominion than did traditional morality. One way of characterizing the liberal rules is to say that they left adults morally free to engage in the sexual activ-ities of their choice, so long as the activities had no direct unwilling victims. This characterization will require some qualification, but it does help to highlight the dif-ference between traditional and liberal sexual morality.

From the liberal viewpoint, traditional sexual morality violated the rights of the individual by treating a person's sexual choices as if they belonged to society. Where the traditional morality reigned, sexuality was conscripted by society to promote its interest in procreation and in preserving a certain model of the family. Individuals were expected to follow the "appropriate" social scripts, which were defined by gender and restricted a person to marital (heterosexual) intercourse without the use of con-traceptives. Liberal morality does not deny the importance of procreation or family, but it does assert that adult individuals have the right to decide for themselves when and whether to have children and when and whether to engage in sexual activity for purposes of other than procreation. And the liberal view is that this right of sexual autonomy is possessed equally by each adult. David Richards, a leading proponent of a liberal sexual morality, puts the central point plainly: "Legal enforcement of a particular sexual ideal fails . . . to accord due respect to individual autonomy" (1982: 99).

The new liberal principles cast a very different light on pornography than did the traditional morality. There is nothing inherent to the activities of producing or consuming pornography which raises a presumption that there is some direct unwilling victim of the activities. Pornography does not necessarily involve children or any unwilling adult. The sole participants in the production and use of pornographic materials may be consenting adults, and, in such a situation, the strong liberal presumption is that those adults have a moral right to do what they are doing. The basis of this presumption is the idea that the sexuality-defining decisions of adults are up to them, and those decisions include ones that involve voluntary association for purposes of sexual pleasure or for profit from the manufacture of materials that help produce sexual arousal.

Accordingly, on the liberal sexual morality, a right to pornography is akin to the right to use contraceptives: adults must be free to manufacture and use pornographic materials, just as they must be free to make and use contraceptive devices, and others must not interfere with those choices. Other sexuality-defining activities, such as the right to engage in homosexual activity, are also central to the liberal sexual morality.[1] Some people may be revolted by homosexuality and regard it as depraved, just as some are revolted by pornography and regard it as depraved. But such attitudes are not adequate grounds, on the liberal view, for restricting a person's sexual activities.

At the same time, it is important to understand that any reasonable version of liberal sexual morality must go beyond the idea that there is an absolute right to choose one's sexual activities as long as there is no direct unwilling victim. Some room must be left for the possibility that, in some circumstances, such choices are outside the boundaries of the person's right to sexual autonomy. In the next two sections, we will examine some possible circumstances that mark the limits of an individual's right. For the present, the key point is that, for a reasonable version of liberal morality, any restriction on the right of sexual autonomy must rest on considerations that possess considerable weight and are supported by clear and convincing evidence.

It is also important to note that the liberal claim that individuals have a broad right to define their own sexual identity is compatible with the idea that some of the activities which individuals have a right to engage in are, nonetheless, morally deficient. For example, one may agree that an adult has the right to view violent pornography but still contend that any adult who does seek sexual arousal by viewing violent sexual images has a morally deficient character. Put another way, it is consistent for a liberal to assert that a person who has an impeccable character would refrain from certain activities, even though people have a right to do those activities.[2]

Liberal sexual morality has become the dominant morality of contemporary society, although the traditional morality still survives and exerts some influence. Defenders of traditional morality claim that liberal "permissiveness" leads to social disintegration. Thus, Robert George, a contemporary proponent of the traditional view, asserts: "it is plain that moral decay has profoundly damaged the morally valuable institutions of marriage and the family" (1993: 36).

Andrew Altman

It is true that divorce rates are much higher than in past generations, and family life has taken on a very different shape. However, one cannot infer that profound moral damage has been done without making many unproven assumptions about how much better family was in "the good old days," when marriages were often forcibly held together by the economic dependence of the wife and the powerful social stigma of divorce. While it would be wrong for liberals to presume that liberal society is, in every aspect, better than traditional society was, there are two important respects in which liberals should insist that people are better off under the liberal morality. First, men and women are freer to define a central aspect of their existence, their sexuality, in ways that fit their individual character, and, secondly, women are freer and more equal participants in society. Without attempting any full-scale assessment of the traditional morality, in the sections below on 'Sexual Inequality' and "Sexual Identity," I will elaborate on these two considerations in favor of liberal sexual morality. However, the principal task of the remainder of this chapter is to examine critically several feminist arguments which, if sound, would show that any liberal right to pornography must be far more limited than I have suggested.

Sexual Violence

Suppose that the viewing of certain types of pornography has very harmful indirect effects on unwilling victims. For example, consider pornographic movies which depict the gang rape of a woman. Even assuming that all of the participants in such movies are consenting adults – so that the rapes are staged and not real – it is possible that the movies could lead some male viewers to "imitate" what they see and commit real rapes. Similar possibilities could obtain for other kinds of violent pornography.

Moreover, in contemporary society, there are many willing viewers of violent pornography: the material is commercially produced and widely distributed. Even if most viewers do not directly violate anyone's rights, some of them may be prompted to commit sexual violence as a result of their exposure to violent pornography. Accordingly, Helen Longino expresses the view of many feminist thinkers when she claims: "Pornography, especially violent pornography, is implicated in the committing of crimes of violence against women" (1995: 41). Longino proceeds to argue on the basis of her claim that the access of adults to pornography made by adults should be legally restricted. In the light of such an argument, it is important to address the question of whether the right to view pornography reaches its limit when sexual violence is depicted.[3]

It is true that a willing viewer of violent pornography who becomes sexually aroused does not necessarily harm any unwilling victim. Under liberal principles, this means that there is a presumption that the viewer is simply exercising his right of sexual autonomy. But we should not ignore the societal consequences of the availability of violent pornography in deciding whether that presumption is overridden by countervailing considerations.

If the availability of violent pornography led to substantial increases in sexual violence, then the victims of this increased violence would be paying the price for the availability of violent pornography to all adults. And it seems wrong to make those

Pornography, Autonomy, Equality | 227

victims pay such a steep price so that some can have ready access to violent sexual materials for purposes of sexually arousing themselves. In such a situation, it would appear that any presumptive right to violent pornography would be overridden by countervailing considerations.

Notice that the considerations here consist precisely of rights-based concerns to which a liberal sexual morality must give considerable weight. The victims of the criminals who commit pornography-inspired sex crimes have their basic liberal right to sexual autonomy violated egregiously by the perpetrators. However, there are obstacles that need to be surmounted before one can reasonably conclude that, in contemporary society, any right to pornography must stop short of including a right to pornographic materials depicting sexual violence.

First, there must be clear evidence of a causal connection between the production of violent pornography and sexual violence. In the absence of such evidence, there are insufficient grounds for limiting the right of sexual autonomy so as to leave out a right to make and view violent pornography. Yet, the evidence for the existence of a causal connection is, at best, mixed.

Experimental studies suggest that when males repeatedly view violence against women in films, they tend to undergo attitudinal changes that make them desensitized to such violence and more accepting of it.[4] However, the films used in the studies were R-rated "slasher movies," such as *Texas Chain Saw Massacre*, which lacked the sort of graphic depictions of sexual activity characteristic of paradigm cases of pornography. Moreover, the extrapolation from the experimental studies to conclusions about sexual crimes is rather tenuous: no one knows how long the attitudinal changes measured by the studies persist or whether they produce behavioral changes leading to the perpetration of sex crimes.

Since the 1960s, violent pornography has become much more readily accessible in many countries, including the United States. The incidence of sexual crime has also increased in those countries. However, data collected over many decades in the US show that the number of rapes rises in virtual lockstep with the rate of nonsexual assaults (Kutchinsky, 1991: 55). It is not plausible to think that violent pornography causes a rise in nonsexual violence.[5] Indeed, much more reasonable is the hypothesis that sociological variables such as poverty rates and the extent of alcohol consumption explain the equal increases in both sexual and nonsexual violence.

On the other hand, there are studies that provide some evidence for the conclusion that sexual crimes increase as a result of an increase in the availability of pornography. One such study found that the rise in rape rates around the world was traceable to pornography. However, other studies have found no correlation and some have even concluded that rape drops as a result of the availability of pornography (Slade, 2001: 997–8).

The existing state of the evidence, then, is quite far from clearly establishing any causal connection between violent pornography and sexual violence, and appears to weigh against any such connection. Yet, even if a causal connection between violent pornography and sexual violence were clearly established, it would still be insufficient to conclude that, in contemporary society, the production, distribution, and viewing of violent pornography lay beyond the limits of an adult's right of sexual

Andrew Altman

autonomy. Additionally, one would need to justify selecting out such pornography and distinguishing it from the myriad of other forms of media violence that have the potential to cause violence.

Consider the "slasher films" mentioned earlier. It is reasonable to suspect that such films and much else in the mass media cause at least some amount of violence against women, sexual and otherwise. However, it is unreasonable to deny that adults have a right to produce, distribute, and view such movies, even if we were to assume the existence of an established causal relation between the films and sexual violence. Adults who find the films entertaining are subject to criticism for getting enjoyment from watching depictions of terrified women inhumanely attacked. However, these adults do not violate anyone's rights by getting their enjoyment in that way. The situation with respect to viewing violent pornography is different only in the respect that watching such pornography is typically an exercise of sexual autonomy. To the extent that viewing "slasher films" is seen as nonsexual entertainment, the right to see them would actually be *less* strong than the right to view violent pornography.

Accordingly, it is unclear how one could justify selecting out violent pornography as setting a limit to the individual's right of sexual autonomy, while at the same time conceding that there is a right to view forms of media which, as far as we know, could contribute just as much to sexual violence as does violent pornography. It might be argued that violent pornography is a more powerful stimulus to sexual violence. However, we have seen that the evidence of any causal connection between pornography and violence is mixed. And there is simply no evidence indicating the relative contribution which different factors make to the overall level of sexual violence in society.

It may seem that liberal sexual morality is indifferent to the actual violence that may be caused by the production and viewing of the depictions of sexual violence found in films and other media. However, we must be careful in our understanding of what the liberal right of sexual autonomy involves. I have argued that it does include the right to produce and view violent pornography. But liberal sexual morality also holds that each adult has an equal right to sexual autonomy. If sexual violence is widespread in society, as it is in ours, then liberal morality cannot simply brush off that fact. Widespread sexual violence means widespread violation of the equal right of sexual autonomy. Liberal morality demands that something be done about it. But there are ways of reducing levels of sexual violence without placing the production and viewing of violent pornography – or any other media depictions of violence against women – beyond the bounds of the right of autonomy.

The most straightforward ways involve more vigorous prosecution of, and more serious punishments for, crimes of sexual violence. In a similar vein, laws regarding rape and sexual assault can and should be changed, so that the women who are the victims of such crimes are treated in a respectful manner by the criminal justice system. Additionally, efforts at educating individuals – especially young men – about sexual violence should be more seriously pursued.[6] In sum, then, subscribing to a liberal sexual morality does not require that one ignore or exhibit indifference to the level of sexual violence in society and its harmful impact on women.

Sexual Inequality

Even if we set aside the issue of whether violent pornography causes sexual violence, the question remains as to whether pornography in general helps to maintain many of the important social and economic inequalities that disadvantage females. Many feminists assert that pornography plays a pivotal role in maintaining such sexual inequalities, and they cast the issue of pornography as one that is "not a moral issue," but rather is a matter of the civil rights of women (MacKinnon, 1988: 146–62).

For example, Catherine Itzin claims that "women are oppressed in every aspect of their public and private lives," and she sees pornography as playing a central role in maintaining the system of oppression. Itzin proceeds to defend "civil sex discrimination legislation against pornography [that] would enable women to take action on grounds of harm done to them by pornography" (1992: 424). The legislation is seen as a kind of civil rights law for women.[7]

There is little doubt that the vast bulk of pornography willingly viewed by heterosexual men – whether violent or not – involves women in positions of sexual servility or subordination: the women are there to serve the sexual pleasure of the men. And serve it they do, not only to the men who are their "co-stars" in the movie or photograph, but also to the men who masturbate to the scene or who have sex with their partners while using the scene to help arouse them. These facts are what lead some feminists to argue that pornography is unique in its power to create a psychological nexus between the social subordination of women and the sexual pleasure of men, and so is unique in its power to create and sustain patterns of sex inequality that severely disadvantage females. Catharine MacKinnon puts the matter plainly: "Pornography is masturbation material. ... With pornography, men masturbate to women being exposed, humiliated, violated, degraded, mutilated, dismembered, bound, gagged, tortured and killed. ... Men come doing this" (1993: 17).

MacKinnon is right to take the focus off pornography as a form of speech and to look instead at its role in sexual behavior. However, there is a crucial consideration which renders her line of thinking problematic as a viable basis for rejecting a right to pornography. The evidence does not support the idea of any robust correlation, much less a causal relation, between the level of sex inequality in a society and the availability of pornography in it. Quite the opposite: the most repressive countries in the world for women are ones where pornography is least available. Compared to Saudi Arabia, the United States is awash in pornography. Indeed, MacKinnon herself insists that the United States is "a society saturated with pornography" (1993: 7) – a description which might be arguably applied to the US but clearly does not apply to Saudi Arabia. Nonetheless, on the indices of sex inequality developed by the United Nations Development Program, the United States and other Western countries where pornography circulates widely are the nations with the highest levels of *equality*, while Saudi Arabia and other sexually repressive regimes have among the highest levels of inequality (United Nations Development Program, 2002: 222–42). Thus, it is hard to credit the notion that pornography is a kind of causal linchpin in the creation and maintenance of large inequalities between males and females.

There is certainly an analogy between the ways in which much pornography depicts women in relation to men and the ways in which social practices actually treat women

Andrew Altman

in relation to men. In much pornography, there is a sexual hierarchy dominated by men; in much of society, there is a social hierarchy dominated by men. Moreover, it is plausible to think that pornography plays some causal role in the perpetuation of sexual hierarchy. But as with the matter of sexual violence, any limitation of the right of adults to sexual autonomy requires more than a plausible belief that some indeterminate degree of connection exists between pornography and sexual hierarchy.

Making Pornography

Much pornography depicts the subordination of women. Even though the symbolic representation of inequality is not the same as the inequality that is represented, it may be argued that in making pornography, women humiliate and subordinate themselves. They get on their knees and suck on men's cocks. They let men ejaculate into their mouth and on their face and breasts. They have several men simultaneously penetrating their anus, vagina, and mouth. They are tied up and gagged. The humiliation seems all the more acute because it is done before cameras that will circulate the images to untold numbers of men to view. One might claim that this means that making pornography is making female inequality, and not simply depicting it.

However, context counts in deciding whether a person's sexual conduct is a form of humiliation and subordination. It is difficult to see why fellatio is any more inherently degrading than cunnilingus, or why either form of oral sex has that feature. If the parties are adults and consent, the assessment of the activity as humiliating is highly contestable. Multiple penetration also seems inherently innocuous.

Nonetheless, the key point is this: even if we grant that much pornography does involve women performing humiliating or degrading sexual acts, it does not follow that the actors have no right to participate in making such material or that viewers have no right to see it. A willingness to sexually degrade oneself before a camera for commercial purposes may constitute a serious deficiency in one's character. A willingness to view such pornography may also reflect a character flaw. But the men and women who perform in such pornography have a right to make their choices, and consumers have a right to view the commercial product.

If women are intimidated by violent threats into performing in pornography, then their rights have been violated and their victimizers ought to be prosecuted and punished. But it is simply an ideological prejudice to assume a priori that any woman who performs humiliating or degrading sexual acts in pornography has been threatened or coerced in some way. Especially in matters of sex, the line between humiliation, on one side, and breaking the procrustean bed of traditional morality, on the other, is a very tricky one to draw.

Some feminist advocates of laws against pornography claim that physical threats, violence, and economic coercion against women pervade the actual operation of the pornography industry (Dworkin, 2000: 27–9). It may be said that the only way to stop such threats is by closing down the industry. But even if that were true, it would not justify closing down the industry. It does not make sense to think that the only industries that should be allowed are those that can operate without anyone abusing them by threatening violence. Such abuse can be found in any industry. Criminal prosecution of the perpetrators should be the main remedy for physical abuse and coercion in the pornography industry.

Moreover, there are less draconian ways of diminishing violence in the industry than shutting the industry down. For example, some feminists have argued for the unionization of women who work in pornography and other sex-related industries (Cornell, 2000: 552). While unionization efforts may not have good prospects at present, especially in the US, the prospects for banning pornography under a civil rights approach are no better. And the unionization strategy has the decided advantage of treating women in the pornography industry as agents who are capable of exercising their own right of sexual autonomy.

Some of the females who get caught up in the pornography industry are legal minors. The industry executives who intentionally, or negligently, hire minors ought to be prosecuted and punished. Legal minors may have some aspects of the right of sexual autonomy (for example, a 17-year-old girl has the right to purchase and use contraceptives), but the law should rest on the premise that minors are too easily manipulated by industry executives and other adults with vested interests to have a right to decide for themselves to perform in commercial pornographic films or pose for pornographic pictures.

Some feminists contend that women accede to make pornography only because they have no other economic options (except perhaps prostitution, a close cousin of pornography). This contention may have some truth in countries of the underdeveloped world, where educational opportunities for women are highly restricted, rampant sexism operates in all quarters of life, and economic opportunities even for many men are bleak at best. However, in the economically advanced liberal democracies, the situation of almost all women is drastically better, and claims of economic coercion are considerably less plausible as a result.

The clear conclusion seems to be that uncoerced adults have a right to be legally free to make, market, and view pornography. However, it might be objected that if some women voluntarily choose to make pornography in which they are engaged in humiliating or degrading conduct, then their actions affect all women in a detrimental way. The idea here is that the manufacture and circulation of such pornography shapes the sex-role expectations of men and women in society at large, and it does so by showing women as the sexual servants of men. The result is that individuals are not free to control their sexual identities: just as much as in a society ruled by traditional sexual morality, sexual identities are controlled by social forces which are beyond their control and which are hostile to their basic interests.

Sexual Identity

It must be admitted that, even in a society governed by a liberal sexual morality, the sexual autonomy of a person is significantly circumscribed. There is a built-in tension between living in a society and possessing the autonomy to define oneself sexually or in any other way. Without connections to other people in an organized and ongoing system of relations, the life-options of the individual would be radically limited. But those connections also mean that a person's life-defining choices are not entirely her

Andrew Altman

own. The patterns of behavior and attitude that other people adopt not only establish pathways through life which would not otherwise exist, but also create barriers and limits on the individual's exercise of her autonomy. The ability of the individual to shape her own identity is both enabled by, and held hostage to, the actions and attitudes of other people.

There is no solution to this problem. The conditions of meaningful autonomy are also conditions that can inhibit the exercise of such autonomy. Nonetheless, even though this conflict cannot be eliminated, it can be mitigated. And some kinds of society do a much better job of mitigating it than others. Societies with a liberal sexual morality are much better in this respect than those with a traditional sexual morality, and that is the decisive consideration in favor of the liberal morality. Individuals have many more meaningful options in living out the sexual aspects of their lives: their sexuality is not held hostage to what other people do and think to nearly the extent that is found in traditional societies. The grip of pre-existing social scripts that define a sexual identity for each person is dramatically weaker in liberal societies and the power of individuals to shape a centrally important aspect of their lives is correspondingly greater.

However, even in a liberal society, there is no escaping the fact that how other women act and think affects the opportunities and obstacles for any given woman's efforts to define her own sexual identity. The same is true, of course, for men, but the problem of concern here is the willingness of some women to participate in the creation of pornography in which they engage in conduct that is humiliating and servile. Such conduct may be voluntary on the part of the woman, but – the claim goes – it also makes it more difficult for other women to define their own sexual identities as the equals of men.

I think that it is reasonable to hold that the existence of such pornography makes it more difficult for women to live their lives as the sexual equals of men – i.e., more difficult relative to a society which was ruled by a liberal sexual morality and had fewer women, or none at all, who were willing to engage in humiliating conduct as part of the production of pornographic materials. However, women are far better off in societies where a liberal sexual morality dominates than they are in traditional societies, even when the liberal ones contain much pornography degrading to women. Although the freedom of women to humiliate or degrade themselves in making pornography creates costs that all women in a liberal society bear, the gains for women that have resulted from society moving to a liberal sexual morality from a traditional morality far outweighs the costs.

It might be argued that the costs are still too great, and I would not dissent. However, there are ways to lessen those costs without incursions on the right to sexual autonomy. Those ways are likely to be far more effective in promoting sexual equality than restricting the freedom of willing adults to view pornography made by willing adults.

Conclusion

The recognition of a right to sexual autonomy is critical in adequately addressing the issue of pornography. There are other important dimensions of the issue, including the levels of sexual violence perpetrated against women and the social inequalities that systematically disadvantage women. Also relevant is the question of whether there is some character defect in those who make and enjoy pornographic materials.

However, liberal sexual morality correctly places the right of sexual autonomy at the center of the pornography issue. In doing so, the liberal morality places a substantial burden on those who argue for legal restrictions on the access of adults to pornography made by consenting adults. Those who argue for such restrictions tacitly concede that the burden is theirs, as they make claims aimed at meeting it, for example, that pornography causes sexual violence, reinforces sexual hierarchy, and involves non-consenting women who are forced to perform.

When examined carefully, though, we find that the burden has not been met. The empirical claims are insufficiently verified, and some of the empirical assertions, even if substantiated, would be inadequate to justify restricting an adult's right of sexual autonomy. We are left, then, with the claim that the producers and viewers of pornography exhibit a defect of moral character. Such a claim is consistent with a liberal sexual morality. However, it is also inadequate to justify restrictions on adults who willingly create and view pornography.

Notes

1 Cf. Richards, 1982: 29 and 39.
2 Cf. Waldron, 1993: ch. 3; Driver, 1992.
3 Longino also contends that pornography defames women by communicating falsehoods about them and reinforces the societal oppression of women. The oppression argument is considered in the section "Sexual Inequality" below. The defamation argument would license sweeping restrictions on communication, including political expression.
4 See, for example, Linz et al. (1984).
5 Kutchinsky (1991) also found that in West Germany, Denmark, and Sweden, rape increased less than nonsexual assault, despite the greatly increased availability of violent pornography in those countries as well.
6 Many thinkers assert that pornography fosters the myth that women enjoy being forced to have sex (the rape-myth) and some studies support the assertion. However, other studies show that better educating young men can counteract their acceptance of the rape-myth. Moreover, mainstream movies in which rapes take place also appear to foster the rape-myth (see Slade, 2001: 992–3).
7 Catharine MacKinnon and Andrea Dworkin helped draft anti-pornography, civil rights laws in the United States, but the courts have found them to be unconstitutional on free-speech grounds (see *American Booksellers* v. *Hudnut*, 1985).

References

American Booksellers v. *Hudnut* (1985). 771 F.2d 323 (7th Cir.).
Cornell, Drucilla (2000). "Pornography's temptation." In Drucilla Cornell (ed.), *Feminism and Pornography* (pp. 552–68). New York: Oxford University Press.
Driver, Julia (1992). "The suberogatory." *Australasian Journal Of Philosophy*, 70: 286–95.

Andrew Altman

Dworkin, Andrea (2000). "Against the male flood." In Drucilla Cornell (ed.), *Feminism and Pornography* (pp. 19–44). New York: Oxford University Press.

George, Robert P. (1993). *Making Men Moral*. Oxford: Oxford University Press.

Itzin, Catherine (1992). "Legislating against pornography without censorship." In Catherine Itzin (ed.), *Pornography: Women, Violence, and Civil Liberties* (pp. 401–34). New York: Oxford University Press.

Jacobellis v. *Ohio* (1964). 378 US 184.

Kutchinsky, Bert (1991). "Pornography and rape: theory and practice." *International Journal of Law and Psychiatry*, 14: 47–64.

Linz, Daniel, Donnerstein, Edward, and Penrod, Stephen (1984). "The effects of multiple exposures to filmed violence against women." *Journal of Communication*, 34: 130–47.

Longino, Helen (1995). "Pornography, oppression, and freedom: a closer look." In Susan Dwyer (ed.), *The Problem of Pornography* (pp. 34–47). Belmont, CA: Wadsworth Publishing.

MacKinnon, Catharine (1988). *Feminism Unmodified*. Cambridge, MA: Harvard University Press.

MacKinnon, Catharine (1993). *Only Words*. Cambridge, MA: Harvard University Press.

Richards, David A. J. (1982). *Sex, Drugs, Death, and the Law*. Totowa, NJ: Rowman & Littlefield.

Slade, Joseph W. (2001). *Pornography and Sexual Representation*, vol. III. Westport, CT: Greenwood Press.

United Nations Development Program (2002). *Human Development Report 2002*. New York: Oxford University Press.

Waldron, Jeremy (1993). *Liberal Rights*. New York: Cambridge University Press.

CHAPTER SIXTEEN

"The Price We Pay"?
Pornography and Harm

Susan J. Brison

Defenders of civil liberties have typically held, with J. S. Mill, that governments may justifiably exercise power over individuals, against their will, only to prevent harm to others (Mill, 1978: ch. 1).[1] Until the 1970s, liberals and libertarians assumed that since producers and consumers of pornography clearly didn't harm anyone else, the only reasons their opponents had for regulating pornography were that they considered it harmful to the producers or consumers, that they thought it an offensive nuisance, and that they objected, on moral or religious grounds, to certain private sexual pleasures of others. None of these reasons was taken to provide grounds for regulating pornography, however, since individuals are considered to be the best judges of what is in their own interest (and, in any case, they cannot be harmed by something to which they consent), what is merely offensive may be avoided (with the help of plain brown wrappers and zoning restrictions), and the private sexual activities, of consenting adults anyway, are no one else's, certainly not the state's, business.

In the 1970s, however, the nature of the pornography debate changed as an emerging group of feminists argued that what is wrong with pornography is not that it morally defiles its producers and consumers, nor that it is offensive or sinful, but, rather, that it is a species of hate literature as well as a particularly insidious method of sexist socialization. Susan Brownmiller was one of the first to take this stance in proclaiming that "[p]ornography is the undiluted essence of anti-female propaganda" (1975: 443). On this view, pornography (of the violent degrading variety) harms women by sexualizing misogynistic violence. According to Catharine MacKinnon, "[p]ornography sexualizes rape, battery, sexual harassment, prostitution, and child sexual abuse; it thereby celebrates, promotes, authorizes, and legitimizes them" (1987: 171).

The claim that women are harmed by pornography has changed the nature of the pornography debate, which is, for the most part, no longer a debate between liberals who subscribe to Mill's harm principle and legal moralists who hold that the state can legitimately legislate against so-called "morals offenses" that do not harm any non-consenting adults. Rather, the main academic debates now take place among those who subscribe to Mill's harm principle, but disagree about what its implications are for the legal regulation of pornography. Some theorists hold that violent degrading pornography does not harm anyone and, thus, cannot justifiably be legally regulated, socially stigmatized, or morally condemned. Others maintain that, although it is harmful to women, it cannot justifiably be regulated by either the civil or the criminal law, since that would cause even greater harms and/or violate the legal rights of pornography producers and consumers, but that, nevertheless, private individuals should do what they can (through social pressure, educational campaigns, boycotts, etc.) to put an end to it. Still others claim that such pornography harms women by violating their civil right to be free from sex discrimination and should, for that reason, be addressed by the law (as well as by other means), just as other forms of sex discrimination are. But others argue that restricting such pornography violates the moral rights of pornography producers and consumers and, thus, restrictions are morally impermissible. Later in this chapter I will argue that there is no moral right to such pornography.

What is Pornography?

First, however, I need to articulate what is at issue, but this is hard to do, given various obstacles to describing the material in question accurately. (I have encountered the same problem in writing about sexual violence.) There is too much at stake to be put off writing about issues of urgent import to women because of squeamishness or fear of academic impropriety – but how can one write about this particular issue without reproducing the violent degrading pornography itself? (Recall the labeling of Anita Hill as "a little nutty and a little slutty" because she repeated, in public, the sexually demeaning language that Clarence Thomas had uttered to her in private.) However, if one doesn't write graphically about the content of violent degrading pornography, one risks being viewed as either crazy ("she must be imagining things!") or too prudish to talk frankly about sex. And what tone should one adopt – one of scholarly detachment or of outrage? There is a double bind here, similar to that faced by rape victims on the witness stand. If they appear calm and rational enough for their testimony to be credible, that may be taken as evidence that they cannot have been raped. But if they are emotional and out of control enough to appear traumatized, then their testimony is not considered reliable.

Any critic of violent degrading pornography risks being viewed not only as prudish (especially if the critic is a woman), but also as meddling in others' "private" business, since we tend not to see the harm in pornography – harm which is often made invisible and considered unspeakable. But "we" used not to see the harm in depriving women and minorities of their civil rights. And "we" used not to see the harm in distributing postcards depicting and celebrating lynchings. More recently, "we" didn't see the harm in marital or "date" rape, spousal battering, or sexual harassment. Even now, as Richard Delgado and Jean Stefancic point out:

[M]embers of the empowered group may simply announce to the disaffected that they do not see their problem, that they have looked for evidence of harm but cannot find it. Later generations may well marvel, "how could they have been so blind?" But paradigms change slowly. In the meantime, one may describe oneself as a cautious and principled social scientist interested only in the truth. And one's opponent, by a neat reversal, becomes an intolerant zealot willing to trample on the liberties of others without good cause. (1997: 37)

A further problem arises in critically analyzing violent degrading pornography, deriving from precisely those harmful aspects of it being critiqued, which is that descriptions of it and quotations from it can themselves be degrading, or even retraumatizing, especially for women who have been victimized by sexual violence. But one thing that is clear is that feminist critics of such pornography are *not* criticizing it on the grounds that it is erotic, or sexually arousing, or that it constitutes "obscenity," defined by the Court as "works which, taken as a whole, appeal to the prurient interest in sex, which portray sexual conduct in a patently offensive way, and which, taken as a whole, do not have serious literary, artistic, political or scientific value" (*Miller v. California*, 1973: 24). Those who work on this issue – and have familiarized themselves with the real world of the pornography industry – know all too well that pornography is not merely offensive. In contrast, here is how some of them define "pornography":

[T]he graphic sexually explicit subordination of women through pictures or words that also includes women dehumanized as sexual objects, things, or commodities; enjoying pain or humiliation or rape; being tied up, cut up, mutilated, bruised, or physically hurt; in postures of sexual submission, servility or display; reduced to body parts, penetrated by objects or animals, or presented in scenarios of degradation, injury, torture; shown as filthy or inferior; bleeding, bruised, or hurt in a context that makes these conditions sexual. (MacKinnon, 1987: 176)[2]

I define "pornography," for the purposes of this chapter, as violent degrading misogynistic hate speech (where "speech" includes words, pictures, films, etc.). I will argue that, if pornography unjustly harms women (as there is reason to suppose it does), then there is no moral right to produce, sell, or consume it. (I will not here be arguing for or against its legal restriction and no position on that issue is dictated by my arguments against the alleged moral right.)

Pornography and Harm

I cannot hope to portray adequately the harms inflicted on girls and women in the production of pornography (for the reasons given above), but there is plenty of research documenting them. One of the most powerful forms of evidence for such harms is the first-person testimony of "participants" in pornography. (Those who are interested in reading more about this are referred to the Attorney-General's Commission on Pornography, 1986; Itzen, 1992; Lederer, 1980; Lederer and Delgado, 1995; MacKinnon, 1987; MacKinnon, 1993; MacKinnon and Dworkin, 1997; Russell, 1993.)

Susan J. Brison

A not uncommon scenario in which a girl becomes trapped in the pornography indus-try is described by Evelina Giobbe in her testimony to the US Attorney-General's Com-mission on Pornography. After running away from home at age 13 and being raped her first night on the streets, Giobbe was befriended by a man who seemed initially kind and concerned, but who, after taking nude photographs of her, sold her to a pimp who raped and battered her, threatening her life and those of her family until she "agreed" to work as a prostitute for him. Her "customers" knew she was an ado-lescent and sexually inexperienced. "So," she testified, "they showed me pornogra-phy to teach me and ignored my tears and they positioned my body like the women in the pictures, and used me." She tried on many occasions to escape, but, as a teenager with no resources, cut off from friends and family, who believed she was a criminal, she was an easy mark for her pimp: "He would drag me down streets, out of restau-rants, even into taxis, all the while beating me while I protested, crying and begging passers-by for help. No one wanted to get involved" (quoted in Russell, 1993: 38). She was later sold to another pimp who "was a pornographer and the most brutal of all." According to her testimony, he recruited other girls and women into pornogra-phy by advertising for models:

> When a woman answered his ad, he'd offer to put her portfolio together for free, be her agent, and make her a "star." He'd then use magazines like *Playboy* to convince her to pose for "soft-core" porn. He'd then engage her in a love affair and smooth talk her into prostitution. "Just long enough," he would say, "to get enough money to finance your career as a model." If sweet talk didn't work, violence and blackmail did. She became one of us. (Quoted in Russell, 1993: 39)

Giobbe escaped the pornography industry by chance, after "destroy[ing] herself with heroin" and becoming "no longer usable." She considers herself one of the lucky ones – "a rare survivor" (quoted in Russell, 1993: 39–40). And this was *before* the AIDS epidemic.

More recently, according to an article in the *Sunday New York Times Magazine*, pornography – of an increasingly violent sort – has played an important role in the global sex trafficking of girls and women who, lured by promises of employment (for example, as nannies or waitresses), end up trapped in foreign countries, with no money, no (legal) papers, no family or friends, and no ability to speak the local lan-guage. Immigrations and Customs Enforcement (ICE) agents at the Cyber Crimes Center in Fairfax, Virginia are "tracking a clear spike in the demand for harder-core pornography on the Internet. 'We've become desensitized by the soft stuff; now we need a harder and harder hit', says ICE Special Agent Perry Woo." With ICE agents, the author of the article looked up a website purporting to offer sex slaves for sale: "There were streams of Web pages of thumbnail images of young girls of every eth-nicity in obvious distress, bound, gagged, contorted. The agents in the room pointed out probable injuries from torture" (Landesman, 2004: 72). "'With new Internet tech-nology', Woo said, 'pornography is becoming more pervasive. With Web cams we're seeing more live molestation of children'" (Landesman, 2004: 74).

It is not enough to say that the participants in pornography consent, *even* in the case of adult women who apparently do, given the road many have been led (or dragged) down, since childhood in some cases, to get to that point. Genuine autonomous consent requires the ability to evaluate critically and to choose from a range of significant and worthwhile options. Even if all the participants genuinely consented to their use in the pornography industry, however, we would need to consider how pornography influences how *other* non-consenting women are viewed and treated. Compare the (thankfully imaginary) scenario in which some blacks consented to act servile or even to play the part of slaves – who are humiliated, beaten, and whipped for the pleasure of their masters. Suppose a *lot* of whites got off on this and some people got a lot of money from tapping into (and pumping up) the desire for such films. And suppose the widespread consumption of such entertainment – a multi-billion-dollar industry, in fact – influenced how whites generally viewed and treated blacks, making it harder than it would otherwise be for blacks to overcome a brutal and ongoing legacy of hate and oppression. It is unimaginable that we would tolerate such "entertainment" simply because some people got off on it.

To give another analogy, the fact that scabs will work for less money (in worse conditions) than strikers harms the strikers. It makes it harder for the strikers to work under fair conditions. Sure, the scabs benefit; however, that's not the point. The point is that the strikers suffer. Suppose there were "slave auction" clubs where some blacks allowed themselves to be brutalized and degraded for the pleasure of their white customers. Suppose the black "performers" determined that, given the options, it was in their best interest to make money in this way. Their financial gain – imagine that they are highly paid – more than compensates for the social harm to them as individuals of being subjected to a slightly increased risk (resulting from the prevalence of such clubs) of being degraded and brutalized outside their workplace. Some of them even enjoy the work, having a level of ironic detachment that enables them to view their customers as pathetic or contemptible. Some, who don't actually enjoy their work, don't suffer distress, since they manage to dissociate during it. Others are distressed by it, but they have determined that the financial benefit outweighs the psychic and physical pain. For those blacks who did not work in the clubs, however, there would be nothing that compensated for their slightly increased risk of being degraded and brutalized as a result of it. They would be better off if the clubs did not exist. The work done by the blacks in the clubs would make it harder for other blacks to live their lives free of fear.

The harms caused by pornography to non-participants in its production – often called "indirect" or "diffuse" harms, which makes them sound less real and less serious than they actually are – include (1) harms to those who have pornography forced on them, (2) increased or reinforced discrimination against – and sexual abuse of – girls and women, (3) harms to boys and men whose attitudes toward women and whose sexual desires are influenced by pornography, and (4) harms to those who have already been victimized by sexual violence. The first three categories of harm have been amply documented (Attorney-General's Commission on Pornography, 1986; Itzen, 1992; Lederer, 1980; Lederer and Delgado, 1995; MacKinnon, 1987; MacKinnon, 1993; MacKinnon and Dworkin, 1997; Russell, 1993). That the proliferation of pornography leads to attitudinal changes in men, which, in turn, lead to harmful behavior, should not be surprising, especially given the high rates of exposure to pornography of pre-teen and teenage boys. On the contrary, as Frederick Schauer, Frank Stanton

Susan J. Brison

Professor of the First Amendment at the John F. Kennedy School of Government at Harvard University, testified at the Pornography Civil Rights Hearing in Boston, Massachusetts on March 16, 1992:

> I find it a constant source of astonishment that a society that so easily and correctly accepts the possibility that a cute drawing of a camel can have such an effect on the number of people who take up smoking, has such difficulty accepting the proposition that endorsing images of rape or other forms of sexual violence can have an effect on the number of people who take up rape. (cited in MacKinnon and Dworkin, 1997: 396)

One might object, though, that pornography is merely a symptom (of a misogynistic, patriarchal society), not a cause. Even if this were the case, however, that would not mean that we should not be concerned about it. The fact that there are so few female legislators in the US at the federal level (and that it's still inconceivable that a woman could be elected president) is a symptom, not a cause, of patriarchy. But this does not mean that we should not do anything about the political status quo. In any case, pornography is more than a mere symptom: it fosters and perpetuates the sexist attitudes that are essential for its enjoyment, even if it does not create them.

It should be noted here that the fact that the *point* of pornography (from the standpoint of the producers) is to make money by giving pleasure does not mean that it cannot also be harmfully degrading. On the contrary, it is pleasurable (and profitable) *precisely because* it is degrading to others. And it is reasonable to expect a spill-over effect in the public domain, since its enjoyment requires the adoption of certain attitudes. Compare the case of pornography with that of sexist humor. Until quite recently, it used to be maintained that women who were offended by sexist jokes were simply humorless. After all, it was held, one can laugh at a sexist joke (because it's funny) and not *be* a sexist. Now it is widely acknowledged that such jokes are funny only if one holds certain sexist beliefs: in other words, the humor is contingent upon the beliefs.[3] With regard to pornographic depictions, it would be difficult to argue that the degradation and subordination of women they involve are merely incidental to their ability to arouse. The arousal is dependent on the depiction of degradation, just as, in sexist humor, the humor is dependent on the sexism. I stress this in order to deflect the objection that the *point* of pornography is to give pleasure, not to defame or degrade women.

It might be argued that one could laugh at sexist jokes and enjoy sexist pornography *in private* without this having any effect on one's ability to view women as equals *in public* and to treat them accordingly. But are we really so good at keeping our private and public attitudes distinct? Suppose it became known that a white public official – say, a judge – privately relished racist humor, collected racist paraphernalia, and showed old racist films at home for the entertainment of his close friends and family. Although one might not want there to be laws against such reprehensible behavior (for their enforcement would require gross invasions of privacy), one would presumably consider such *private* behavior to compromise the integrity of the judge's public position. (Were this judge's pastime to be made public during his confirmation hearings for a seat on the Supreme Court, for example, it would presumably defeat his nomination.)

It is easier for us, now, to see the harm in the dehumanization of blacks and Jews in racist and anti-Semitic propaganda. We are well aware that the Nazis' campaign to exterminate the Jews utilized anti-Semitic propaganda which portrayed Jews as disgusting, disease-ridden vermin. In addition, "Nazis made Jews do things that would further associate them with the disgusting," making them scrub latrines to which they were then denied access (Nussbaum, 2001, p. 348). This in turn made them appear less than human. As Primo Levi observed in *The Drowned and the Saved*:

> The SS escorts did not hide their amusement at the sight of men and women squatting wherever they could, on the platforms and in the middle of the tracks, and the German passengers openly expressed their disgust: people like this deserve their fate, just look how they behave. These are not *Menschen*, human beings, but animals, it's as clear as day. (Quoted in Nussbaum, 2001: 348)

It is harder for us to see the same process of dehumanization at work when girls and women are routinely portrayed as being worthy of degradation, torture, and even death. But empirical studies have shown that exposure to such portrayals increases the likelihood that people will take actual sexual violence less seriously – and even consider it to be justified in some cases (see Lederer and Delgado, 1995: 61–112; MacKinnon and Dworkin, 1993: 46–60; Russell, 1993: 113–213).

There is another connection between the dehumanization of girls and women in pornography and their brutalization in rape, battering, forced prostitution, and sexual murder, which is that, in a society where women are victimized in these ways at an alarming rate, it shows a callous disregard for the actual victims to have depictions of sexual violence bought and sold as entertainment. For a short while, after 9/11, we empathized so much with the victims of the terrorist attacks that films of similarly horrifying attacks were withdrawn because they were no longer considered entertaining. But victims of sexual violence are given so little respect that many of us see nothing wrong with being entertained by depictions of what they have had to endure.

If we take seriously the harm of pornography, then we want to know what to do about it. Should the government intervene by regulating it? The standard debate over pornography has framed it as a free speech issue. The drafters of an anti-pornography ordinance adopted by the city of Indianapolis argued that pornography constitutes a violation of the civil rights of women. In response to those who asserted that the First Amendment protected pornography, they argued that pornography violated the First Amendment rights of women (by "silencing" them – depriving them of credibility and making "no" appear to mean "yes" in rape scenarios) as well as their Fourteenth Amendment rights to equal protection. In his opinion in *American Booksellers Association* v. *Hudnut*, which ruled unconstitutional the Indianapolis anti-pornography ordinance, Judge Frank Easterbrook acknowledged that pornography harms women in very significant and concrete ways:

> Depictions of subordination tend to perpetuate subordination. The subordinate status of women in turn leads to affront and lower pay at work, insult and injury at home, battery and rape on the streets. In the language of the legislature, "[p]ornography is central in

Susan J. Brison

creating and maintaining sex as a basis of discrimination. Pornography is a systematic practice of exploitation and subordination based on sex which differentially harms women. The bigotry and contempt it produces, with the acts of aggression it fosters, harm women's opportunities for equality and rights [of all kinds]." Indianapolis Code §16-1(a) (2). Yet this simply demonstrates the power of pornography as speech" (*American Booksellers Association, Inc. v. Hudnut*, 1985: 329).[4]

Easterbrook seems to take the harms of pornography seriously, but he then goes on to talk about its "unhappy effects" which he considers to be the result of "mental intermediation." He assumes that speech has no (or merely negligible) effects that are not under the conscious control of the audience, although this assumption is undermined not only by the widely acknowledged power of advertising, but also by recent work in cognitive neuroscience on the prevalence of unconscious imitation in human beings.[5] It might be argued, though, that, if we consider the producers of pornography to be even partially responsible for the violence perpetrated by some of its consumers, then we must consider the perpetrators *not* to be responsible or to be less than fully responsible for their crimes. But this does not follow. Even if the perpetrators are considered to be 100 percent responsible, some responsibility can still be attributed to the pornographers. (In fact, two or more people can each be 100 percent responsible for the same crime, as in the case of multiple snipers who simultaneously fire many shots, fatally wounding their victim.)

The courts have, for now, decided that even if serious harm to women results from it, pornography is, qua speech, protected (except for that material which also meets the legal definition of obscenity). That is, there is, currently, a *legal* right to it, falling under the right to free speech. But *should* there be?

A Moral Right to Pornography?

Of course we value freedom of speech. But how should we value it? What should we do when speech is genuinely harmful? Traditionally, in the US, the right to free speech is held to be of such high importance that it trumps just about everything else. For example, in the *Hudnut* case, discussed above, it was acknowledged that the pornography producers' and consumers' right to free speech was in conflict with women's right to equal protection, but it was asserted (without argumentation) that the free speech right had priority. Acceptance of this claim without requiring a defense of it, however, amounts to adopting a kind of free speech fundamentalism. To see how untenable such a view is, suppose that uttering the words "you're dead" caused everyone within earshot (but the speaker) to fall down dead. Would anyone seriously say that such speech deserved protection? Granted, the harms of pornography are less obvious and less severe, but there is sufficient evidence for them for it to be reasonable to require an argument for why the legal right to it should take priority over others' legal rights not to be subjected to such harms.

If we reject free speech fundamentalism, the question of whether pornography should be legally restricted becomes much more complicated. My aim here is not to articulate or defend a position on this question, but I do want to stress that whatever view we take on it should be informed by an understanding of the harms of pornography – the price some people pay so that other people may get off on it.

In his chapter in this volume, "The Right to Get Turned On: Pornography, Autonomy, Equality," Andrew Altman shifts the debate over pornography in a promising way by arguing that there is a *moral* right to (even violent misogynistic) pornography, falling not under a right to free speech, but, rather, under a right to sexual autonomy (which also covers the right to use contraceptives and the right to homosexual sex).[6] On this view, which Altman dubs "liberal sexual morality," whatever harm results from pornography is just the price we pay for the right to sexual autonomy. Sexuality is an important, arguably central, aspect of a flourishing human life. Sexual expression is one of the primary ways we define ourselves and our relations to others, and a healthy society should value and celebrate it. But what does it add to these claims to say that we have a moral *right* to sexual autonomy? And, if we do have such a right, does it include a right to produce, distribute, and consume pornography (defined, as above, as violent degrading misogynistic hate speech)?

Although philosophers disagree about the nature of rights (and, indeed, even about whether such things exist at all), most hold that to say that someone, X, has a moral right to do something, y, means that others are under a duty not to interfere with X's doing y. (Of course, X's right is limited by others' rights, as expressed by the saying "your right to swing your arm ends at my face.") But beyond this, there is little agreement. Some hold that rights are natural, inalienable, and God-given. Others hold that rights-talk is just short-hand for talk about those interests that are especially important to us (for example, because protecting them tends to increase our welfare). Some hold that we have positive rights, just by virtue of being human, such that other people are under an obligation to provide us with whatever we need to exercise those rights. (If there is a positive right to education, for example, then society has an obligation to provide free public education for all.) Others hold that we have only negative rights (unless individuals *grant* us positive rights by, for example, making promises to assist us), which require only that other people do not interfere with our exercising those rights. (The right to privacy, if taken to be simply a right to be left alone, is an example of a negative right.)

On any account, the concept of a right is diffuse. To say that X has a moral right to do y does not, by itself, say very much, unless we specify what others are required to do (or to refrain from doing) in order not to violate that right. There is a wide range of different responses to X's doing y, given that X has a right to do y – from complete acceptance (or perhaps even positive support) to something just short of physical restraint or intervention. Where is the alleged right to pornography located on this spectrum of moral assessment?

Altman considers the right to pornography and the right to sexual orientation to have the same foundation in a right to sexual autonomy. What should our (society's) attitude be toward the exercising of that right? Should we tolerate it, that is, have no laws against it, while allowing private individuals to lobby against it or to try to dissuade people from it? Or should we actively embrace it? Assimilating the right to pornography to the right to sexual orientation muddies the waters here. Presumably, according to liberal sexual morality, the right to sexual orientation requires more than mere tolerance. It requires society's complete acceptance (and, I would argue, posi-

Susan J. Brison

tive support, given that prejudice and violence against gays and lesbians persist in our society). It is wrong to hold that gays and lesbians have "bad characters" or to try to get them to "reform."

The right to pornography, however, does not lie on the same end of the spectrum, since Altman claims that getting off on pornography is a sign of a bad character. Some feminists and liberals who defend a legal right to pornography hold at the same time that all sorts of private pressure – protests, boycotts, educational campaigns – should be brought to bear on the pornographers. Altman's position is that there is not just a legal right, but also a *moral* right to pornography, even if there is something bad about exercising it. There are persuasive reasons for holding that we have legal rights to do some things that are morally wrong, in cases in which enforcement would be impossible or would involve gross violations of privacy. But Altman seems to hold that we have a *moral* right to do some things that are morally wrong. What does this mean? It cannot mean that people have a right to do things that are wrong in that they harm others. It might mean that people have the right to do things that other people consider wrong (but that are not harmful to others) – that is, people have the right to do harmless things that other people morally disapprove of. However, if the behavior, e.g. engaging in homosexual sex, is not unjustly harming others, then liberals who subscribe to Mill's harm principle have no grounds for considering it to be wrong.

So where should the right to pornography be located on the spectrum of moral assessment? There is no one answer to this question. We need to look at particular cases. Suppose I have a 21-year-old son – leaving aside the question of whether minors have a right to pornography – who is a heavy consumer of pornography (of the kind I've been talking about). What does his (alleged) right to pornography entail? Given my opposition to pornography, presumably I would not be under an obligation positively to support his pornography habit by buying it for him. But would I have to pretend that I'm not aware of it? Would I be under a duty not to try to dissuade him from viewing pornography? Would his sister be under a duty not to throw the magazines out when she saw them in common areas of the house? Would it be wrong for his buddies to try to talk him out of it? Would his teachers have a duty to refrain from arguing against it? Would it be wrong for his neighbors to boycott the local convenience store that sold it? Would his girlfriend (or boyfriend) who became convinced it was ruining their relationship be under a moral duty not to rip it out of his hands? If the answer to each of the above questions is "no," which I think it is, then it's not clear what, if anything, his right entitles him to.[7] What is clear is that, if a right to pornography exists, it is quite unlike a right to engage in homosexual sex or to use contraceptives, and is located at the opposite end of the spectrum of moral assessment.

Perhaps there is, nevertheless, something special about sexual arousal ("getting turned on") that gives it special moral status. But Altman has not said what makes sexual arousal different (in a morally significant way) from other forms of arousal – for example, that of racial animus. It makes sense to say that there is a right to be turned on – not a special right, but, rather, one falling under a general right to liberty, but this general right to liberty is delimited by the harm principle. There is no general right to have pleasurable feelings (of any sort, sexual or otherwise) that override others' rights not to be harmed. There is no moral right to achieve a feeling of comfort by unjustly discriminating against homosexuals on the grounds that associating with them makes you uncomfortable. Likewise, there is no moral right to achieve a feeling of superiority (no matter how pleasurable such a feeling might be) by discriminating against those of a different race. And it doesn't matter how central to one's self-definition the feeling in question might be. For parents, the satisfaction of ensuring the good upbringing and education of their children is of paramount importance, and yet this degree of importance does not give racist parents the right to racially segregated housing or schools.

It might be argued that sexual arousal is special in that it is a bodily pleasure and, thus, more natural, possibly even immutable. Even if this were so, it would not follow that one has a right to achieve it by any means necessary. To take an example of another kind of "bodily" pleasure, suppose that there are gustatory pleasures that can be achieved only in immoral ways – for example, by eating live monkey brains (which some people used to do), or organs or flesh "donated" by (or purchased from) living human beings, or food that has been stolen from the people on the verge of starvation. That there is a (general) right to enjoy eating what one chooses to eat – it would be (in general) wrong, for example, for me to force you to eat, or not to eat, something – does not mean that one has a right to eat whatever gives one pleasure.

But it is not the case that what people find sexually arousing is a simple biological fact about them, a given, something immutable. People can be conditioned to be aroused by any number of things. In one study, for example, men were conditioned to be aroused by a picture of a woman's boot (Russell, 1993: 129). Emotions, especially ones with strong physiological components, such as sexual arousal, *feel* natural. They don't seem to be socially constructed, because we don't (at the time) consciously choose them: they just *are*. But emotions are, at least to some extent, learned reactions to things. There are gender differences in emotional reactions; for example, men tend to get angry in some situations in which women tend to feel not angry, but hurt. But this does not mean that such differences are *natural*.

Given the wide variety of sexual fantasies and fetishes we know about, it's conceivable that just about *anything* could be a turn on for someone – looking at photos of dead, naked bodies piled in mass graves in Nazi death camps, for example, or looking at photos of lynched black men. According to liberal sexual morality, the only reason for supposing that there might not be a moral right to make a profit from and get off on such "pornography" would be that the photographed people are posthumously harmed by it (given that they did not consent to their images being used in this way). But suppose they had consented. Or suppose, more plausibly, that the images were computer-generated – completely realistic-looking, but not images *of* actual individuals. Liberal sexual morality would have to allow (some) people to make money by others' getting turned on by these images. Not only that, but, given that sexual desires are malleable, the pornographer also has a right to make money by acculturating others to be turned on by such images. (In other words, the pornographer has a right to turn the world into a place where people get turned on by such images.) And, if our attitude toward this is grounded in the right to sexual autonomy, it should be similar to our attitude toward homosexuality: we shouldn't merely tolerate it, we should come to accept and support it.

246   **Susan J. Brison**

While conceding that there are limits to the right to sexual autonomy – it is con-strained by the harm principle – Altman assumes (as most liberals do) that one cannot be harmed by something to which one consents. I argued earlier that the way many models get lured into the pornography industry should make us at least question the extent to which they are consenting to what is being done to them. But suppose they do consent. Does that mean that we must tolerate the production and use of whatever pornography results? Unfortunately, one doesn't have to construct a thought experiment to test our intuitions about this. According to *The New York Times*, Armin Meiwes, "[a] German computer technician who killed and ate a willing victim he found through the Internet" was recently convicted of manslaughter. His "victim," Bernd-Jürgen Brandes, had "responded to an Internet posting by Mr Meiwes seeking someone willing to be 'slaughtered'." " 'Both were looking for the ulti-mate kick'," the judge said. It was "an evening of sexual role-playing and violence, much of it videotaped by Mr Meiwes," enough to convince the court that the "victim" had consented (Landler, 2004: A3). Does the right to sexual autonomy include the rights to produce, sell, and get turned on by the videotape of this "slaughter" – a real-life instance of a snuff film? If we cannot *prove* that there is a causal connec-tion between the film and harm to others, the answer, according to liberal sexual morality, is "yes."

Altman claims that "even if a causal connection between violent pornography and sexual violence were clearly established, it would still be insufficient to conclude that, in contemporary society, the production, distribution and viewing of violent pornog-raphy lay beyond the limits of an adult's right to sexual autonomy" because *other* media – he cites "slasher films" – arguably "cause at least some amount of violence against women, sexual and otherwise. However, it is unreasonable to deny that adults have a right to produce, distribute, and view such movies" (2005: 229). Why, if one has established that, say, "slasher films" are harmful, we must hold that adults have a right to them is not explained. But even if we agree that adults have the right to produce/consume non-pornographic media even if it is as harmful as pornography, it does not follow that adults have the right to produce/consume pornography. To assume that it does would be like arguing against prohibiting driving while talking on cell phones on the grounds that this is not the *only* thing (or even the main thing) contributing to automobile accidents.

Altman accepts that "it is reasonable to hold that the existence of . . . pornography makes it more difficult for women to live their lives as the sexual equals of men – i.e., more difficult relative to a society which was ruled by a liberal sexual morality and had fewer women, or none at all, who were willing to engage in humiliating conduct as part of the production of pornographic materials," (Altman, 2005: 233), but he notes that women are better off in a society with liberal sexual morality than in a society with traditional sexual morality (for example, Saudi Arabia). I agree, but surely these are not the only two possibilities. I would advocate the alternative of a progressive sexual morality. What might that look like? We don't even know. Even our most deep-seated assumptions about sexuality may turn out to be mistaken. We used to view rape as being motivated purely by lust and battering as a way of showing spousal love. Some of us still do. Gradually, however, we are breaking the link between sexuality and violence. Perhaps some day we'll have reached the point where sexual violence is no longer arousing, where it makes no sense to talk of killing and being killed as the "ultimate" sexual "kick."

According to liberal sexual morality, the harms of pornography are the price we pay for having the right to sexual autonomy in other areas – e.g. the right to have sex (including homosexual sex) outside of marriage and the right to use contraceptives. But this view (of the right to sexual autonomy as an all-or-nothing package) is formed in response to legal moralism, and makes sense only if one considers all these rights to be rights to do harmless things that some people nevertheless morally condemn. In such cases, proponents of liberal sexual morality say: "If you don't like it, don't look at it (or hear about it or think about it)." This is a satisfactory response only if the behavior in question isn't harming anyone. But as our views about what constitutes harm have changed, our views of what is our business have also changed. Just as we no longer look the other way in response to marital or "date" rape, domestic violence, and sexual harassment, we should no longer accept pornography's harms as the price we pay for sexual autonomy.

Notes

I would like to thank Ann Bumpus, Christopher Wellman, and Thomas Trezise for helpful discussions of many issues in this article. My deepest thanks go to Margaret Little who gave me invaluable comments on several drafts.

1   Mill considered his harm principle to apply equally to governmental regulation and to "the moral coercion of public opinion." The harm principle states that ". . . the only purpose for which power can be rightfully exercised over any member of a civilized community, against his will, is to prevent harm to others" (1978: 9). Mill does not specify what counts as harm. Following Joel Feinberg (1984), I consider it to be a wrongful setback to one's significant interests.

2   This is the definition used in the anti-pornography ordinance drafted by Andrea Dworkin and Catharine MacKinnon, passed by the city of Indianapolis, but ruled unconstitutional by the courts.

3   For a persuasive argument to that effect, see de Sousa (1987). In comparing sexist fantasies with sexist and racist humor, one might reply, however, that we have less control over, and thus are less responsible for, our fantasies than our jokes. This seems right, to the extent that we can refrain from laughing at or telling certain jokes (even though we might not be able to resist finding them funny). But the same distinction applies to fantasies. We do not always choose the fantasies that occur to us, but we can choose whether or not to cultivate them (voluntarily return to them repeatedly, make or view films about them, etc.). Even in the case of dreams, over which we, at the time, anyway, have no control, a white male liberal would be alarmed if he often had pleasurable dreams of watching blacks getting lynched. This would presumably prompt some probing of his unconscious attitudes about blacks.

4   This view can't consistently be held, however, by liberals and feminists who support laws against sex or race discrimination and segregation in schools, workplaces, and even private clubs. One doesn't hear the argument that if segregation harms minorities' opportunities for equal rights this simply demonstrates the power of freedom of association, which is also protected by the First Amendment.

5 The recent research discussed in Hurley (2004) suggests that the imitation of others' behavior, including others' violent acts, is not a consciously mediated process, under the autonomous control of the viewers/imitators.

6 Since some theorists ground the right to free speech in a right to autonomy, however, there may not be such a sharp distinction between these two approaches. See Brison (1998).

7 I also mean for the above thought experiment to illustrate the fact that the nature of the duty one has with respect to the holder of the alleged moral right to pornography depends on one's relationship to the right-holder. Presumably a neighbor would be under a duty not to snatch pornography out of the right-holder's hands. But if someone *else*, the right-holder's lover, say, is under no such duty, then it's not clear what the right amounts to.

References

Altman, Andrew (2005). "The right to get turned on: pornography, autonomy, equality." In Andrew I. Cohen and Christopher Heath Wellman (eds.), *Contemporary Debates in Applied Ethics* (pp. 223–35). Oxford: Blackwell, 2005.

American Booksellers Association, Inc. v. *Hudnut* (1985). 771 F.2d 323.

Attorney General's Commission on Pornography (1986). *Final Report*. Washington, DC: US Department of Justice.

Brison, Susan J. (1998). "The autonomy defense of free speech." *Ethics*, 108: 312–39.

Brownmiller, Susan (1975). *Against Our Will: Men, Women and Rape*. New York: Bantam Books.

Delgado, Richard and Jean Stefancic (1997). *Must We Defend Nazis? Hate Speech, Pornography, and the New First Amendment*. New York: New York University Press.

de Sousa, Ronald (1987). "When is it wrong to laugh?" In *The Rationality of Emotion* (pp. 275–99). Cambridge, MA: MIT Press.

Feinberg, Joel (1984). *The Moral Limits of the Criminal Law*, vol. 1: *Harm to Others*. New York: Oxford University Press.

Hurley, Susan L. (2004). "Imitation, media violence, and freedom of speech." *Philosophical Studies*, 17/1–2 (January): 165–218.

Itzen, Catherine (ed.) (1992). *Pornography: Women, Violence and Civil Liberties*. New York: Oxford University Press.

Landesman, Peter (2004). "The girls next door." *Sunday New York Times Magazine* (January 25): 30–9, 66–74.

Landler, Mark (2004). "German court convicts Internet cannibal of manslaughter." *New York Times* (January 31): A3.

Lederer, Laura (ed.) (1980). *Take Back the Night: Women on Pornography*. New York: William Morrow and Co., Inc.

Lederer, Laura J. and Richard Delgado (eds.) (1995). *The Price We Pay: The Case Against Racist Speech, Hate Propaganda, and Pornography*. New York: Hill and Wang.

MacKinnon, Catharine A. (1987). *Feminism Unmodified: Discourses on Life and Law*. Cambridge, MA: Harvard University Press.

MacKinnon, Catharine A. (1993). *Only Words*. Cambridge, MA: Harvard University Press.

MacKinnon, Catharine A. and Andrea Dworkin (eds/) (1997). *In Harm's Way: The Pornography Civil Rights Hearings*. Cambridge, MA: Harvard University Press.

Mill, John Stuart (1978). *On Liberty*. Indianapolis, IN: Hackett Publishing Co. (Originally published 1859).

Miller v. California (1973). 413 US 15.

Nussbaum, Martha (2001). *Upheavals of Thought*. Cambridge: Cambridge University Press.

Russell, Diana E. H. (ed.) (1993). *Making Violence Sexy: Feminist Views on Pornography*. Buckingham: Open University Press.

Further reading

Dwyer, Susan (ed.) (1995). *The Problem of Pornography*. New York: Wadsworth.
Kappeler, Susanne (1986). *The Pornography of Representation*. Minneapolis: University of Minnesota Press.

PRIVACY AND CIVIL SOCIETY

The Limits of Privacy

Amitai Etzioni

Privacy, Neither Absolute nor Highly Valued

Ask almost any American or any citizen of many other nations if they cherish their privacy, or wish to have more privacy – from the government, corporations, or Peeping Toms – and most will say that they indeed cherish it and are keen to have more. A Harris poll conducted in March 2003 found that 79 percent of Americans think it is "extremely important" to control who can get information about you, while 69 percent said it is "extremely important" to control what information is collected about you. (And a study by Barrington Moore (1984) found that some kind of concept of privacy is appreciated in cultures all around the world.) But this and other such questions are false ones because they are cost-free. It is like asking someone if he or she wants to have better health or some other good without any costs attached. The same people who want to have more privacy often use their credit and debit cards, leaving a trail that tells what they purchased at Victoria's Secret and with whom they checked into a motel or with whom they flew to a beach resort. Even if these people are reminded that if they pay cash then their privacy will be much better protected, most of them will show you in the way they conduct their affairs that they would rather do with much less privacy than be even slightly inconvenienced.

Privacy is a good, but hardly the only one; and privacy must be and is regularly weighed against many other goods. A child is brought to the emergency room with cigarette burn marks on his arms. X-rays reveal that his bones were broken several times. The parents will be suspected of child abuse and they will be asked many privacy-violating questions – for a cause few would doubt outweighs their desire to remain unexamined: the well-being of a child. Similarly, I often ask my audiences whether they would like to know if the person entrusted with the care of their child is a convicted child molester. I mention that when such screening is done, thousands are found to have criminal records, including pedophilia (LaGrasse, 1998: 8–9).[1] I further ask: would they want to know if the staff in the nursing home in which their mother now lives have criminal records that include abusing the elderly? I note that 14 percent of such employees are found to have criminal records, including violent acts against senior citizens (LaGrasse, 1998: 8). And, should public authorities be entitled to determine whether drivers of school buses, pilots, and members of the police are zonked on drugs? Should the FBI be in a position to crack the encrypted messages employed by terrorists before they use them to orchestrate the next bombing?

In short, our behavior shows that there are numerous values that trump or take precedence over privacy. Nor are there any ethical principles to guide us otherwise. This does not mean that we should disrespect privacy, but merely recognize its place as one value amongst others.

Privacy as a Legal Right: A Recent Creation

But what about privacy as a legal right, as a constitutionally protected right? First, one should note that the US Constitution does not so much as even mention privacy. Not once. Privacy is a constitutional right that was fashioned only in the mid-1960s; that is, it is of very recent vintage. And it was forged around reproductive rights court cases, especially the right of married couples to use contraception (*Griswold* v. *Connecticut*, 1965) and a woman's right to abortion (*Roe* v. *Wade*, 1973), which have little to do with what most people consider privacy.

In searching for a reliable legal foundation for the conception of privacy, it is best not to draw on the stitched-together interpretation of a curious amalgam of sundry pieces of various constitutional rights – which is the way the constitutional right to privacy was concocted in the United States – but instead to rest squarely on the legal conception contained in the Fourth Amendment, which deals with protection from searches by the government. Searches are at the essence of the matter because privacy means a right to conceal from view and audibility some parts of our conducts, thoughts, and emotions. It is like a right to build a wall around ourselves, or wrap ourselves in a veil no one can legally penetrate. Hence, when a criminal conceals a murder weapon and the police find it, we do not hold that the criminal's privacy was violated – because he had no right to conceal the said weapon, to keep it private, so to speak.

The Fourth Amendment is very explicit that the right to privacy is a limited one – limited by the needs of the community. In this Amendment, the Constitution provides a clear and strong foundation for acts that serve the common good – safety from terrorists, for instance – and that take precedent over privacy considerations, by establishing a whole category of legitimate, "reasonable" searches. It outlaws only *unreasonable* searches. In effect, the Fourth Amendment contains an explicit qualification of a right. To see this point most clearly, one should contrast the texts of the First and Fourth Amendments. If the Fourth Amendment were to be written in the same strongly privileging language as the First, it would read: "Congress shall make no law . . ." legalizing searches and seizures. Instead, it states: "The right of the people to be secure in their persons, houses, papers, and effects, against unreasonable searches and seizures, shall not be violated . . . ." This is of great import because privacy advocates often argue that our rights have been violated when new security measures or anti-crime measures are introduced – for instance, cameras in public spaces. However, if these new measures are reasonable, then no one's right has been violated – no privacy has been lost or violated – in the legal sense. People cannot give up what they never had and they never had a legal right against all searches.

The Fourth Amendment's further requirement, that "no Warrants shall issue, but upon probable cause, supported by Oath or affirmation, and particularly describing the place to be searched, and the persons or things to be seized," can be read merely as providing a mechanism for sorting out when searches are unreasonable as opposed to reasonable, rather than further restricting them. Admittedly, if one applies the criterion of original intent, there can be little doubt that the Fourth Amendment was constituted as one of a list of rights meant to protect individuals from an overpowering government. The same holds for a fair number of historical interpretations and even a large number of court cases, which very much tended to put the burden of proof on those who sought to limit privacy rather than the other way around. However, the changed historical conditions we currently face – as threats to our security have increased, first from criminals and then from terrorists – have already led to a much more even-handed interpretation of the Fourth Amendment. There are more and more legal searches for which neither warrants nor even specific suspicion are required (Froomkin, 1995: 824–5). Examples include screening gates in airports, drug-testing of train engineers, and field sobriety checkpoints.

To take the first example: each day many hundreds of thousands of innocent Americans and their belongings are searched by security staff – using machines and searches by hand – before they are allowed to board an airplane. They are not suspected of anything. There is no evidence to suggest that they may pose a danger to the public. No warrants have been issued authorizing that they be searched. Nevertheless, our elected officials, courts, and most of the public consider these searches – and many like them – reasonable because the intrusion is minimal and the contribution to our safety is considerable.

After the 2001 Attack on the Homeland

What is considered reasonable changes as conditions change. When SARS zoomed across national borders as if those borders were made out of tissue paper, public authorities in Canada requested that those who could be infected be quarantined for 10 days, which basically amounts to house arrest. Normally, no free society would have tolerated such limitations on the movement of citizens not charged or suspected of any illegal activity, but – under the circumstances – it was considered reasonable. The same holds for a large number of measures introduced after 9/11 to enhance homeland protection, many of which are included in the 2001 USA PATRIOT Act. One of the new measures, passed as part of this Act, is "roving surveillance authority" (US Code, 2001a: 1.II.206). After obtaining authorization from a court, the government can wiretap not merely one instrument of a suspect who is being investigated for foreign intelligence purposes under the Foreign Intelligence Surveillance Act of 1978

(FISA), but all the instruments he or she uses. (Before 9/11, federal officials engaged in surveillance under FISA could not follow suspects as they changed the instruments they were using – unless they wanted to get a new court order for each communication device.) Another change in the law is that national tracing and recording orders for email are now permitted under FISA (US Code, 2001b). (Before 9/11 the regulations that allowed public authorities to record or trace email were interpreted by Department of Justice lawyers as requiring court orders from several jurisdictions, through which email messages travel – Department of Justice, 2001.) Walls which separated various intelligence and law-enforcement agencies before 9/11 are being torn down, thanks in part to a 2002 ruling by the Foreign Intelligence Surveillance Court of Review, which permitted information-sharing between intelligence agents and criminal investigators, under FISA (Lichtblau, 2002; Ashcroft, 2002). Also, since 9/11, under new "sneak and peak" legislation, a home can be searched without notifying the home-owner in the way that is required under traditional warrants (US Code, 2001c). Most of these new "violations" of privacy merely brought the law in line with new technologies available to terrorists and criminals. Arguably, these measures should have been undertaken well before 9/11, and even if there had never been an attack.

In contrast, privacy considerations quickly put an end to other programs seen as unreasonable. A case in point is Operation TIPS (Terrorist Information and Prevention System), which was initially proposed by President Bush as a part of Citizen Corps, a voluntary service introduced during the 2002 State of the Union Address. The Bush administration viewed Operation TIPS as "a nationwide mechanism for reporting suspicious terrorist activity"(USA Freedom Corps, 2002: 17), but to many it sounded as if all mail deliverers, UPS drivers, and meter readers were being asked to spy on one another. The program ended up being killed in a little-known provision of the Homeland Security Act, which states: "Any and all activities of the Federal Government to implement the proposed component program of the Citizen Corps known as Operation TIPS (Terrorism Information and Prevention System) are hereby prohibited" (US Code, 2002: 111).

About some other measures, reasonable people may differ. However, by and large, there is no evidence – as distinct from a storm of outcry, which may help keep the government from going overboard – that privacy has been significantly and unduly violated by public authorities since 9/11.

Less Privacy – Less Government

Beyond legal rights and individual preferences is the question of what is in the common good. For libertarians, who strongly oppose social formulations of the good, who believe that each person should be free to form and pursue his or her own good, and who thus seek to maximize private choice and privacy, the distinction between individual liberty and the common good matters little. For social conservatives, especially religious fundamentalists who would rely on the state to enforce their values – for instance, to suppress pornography – and who are willing to curtail both private choices and privacy, the difference between these two concepts is also of limited

Amitai Etzioni

import. In contrast, the distinction is crucial for communitarians (like myself) who hold that important social formulations of the good can be left to private choices – provided there is sufficient *communal* scrutiny. That is, *the best way to curtail the need for governmental control and intrusion is to have somewhat less privacy.* This point deserves some elaboration.

The key lies in the importance of the social realm, about which communitarians are particularly mindful. This realm is not the state or the market (or individual choices), but the community, which relies on subtle social fostering of good conduct by such means as communal recognition, approbation, and censure – processes that require the ability to have some behavior scrutinized not by police or secret agents, but by friends, neighbors, and members of one's voluntary associations,[2] which entails some limitations of privacy.

Crimes are best prevented when a community abhors the behavior that is considered criminal by lawmakers and one's neighbors, friends, and kin; and, conversely, law-enforcement works poorly when not supported by the community's moral and informal controls (Sampson, 1995). For instance, abuse of controlled substances and alcoholism are very rare in religious communities that object to such behaviors, such as in Mormon, Hasidic Jewish, Amish, and black Muslim communities, and are relatively rare in much of the Bible Belt and segments of small-town America. The reason is not simply that internalized values lead individuals to avoid the behaviors in question; these pro-social values also find much support in their communities, support that entails a measure of scrutiny by others. The extent to which many professionals, such as physicians and lawyers, conform to their ethical codes is largely determined by the values their particular community upholds, and mostly by informal enforcement mechanisms, which require social scrutiny but reduce the need for government control. The same holds true for honor codes among students in military academies and select colleges. The more people do not allow friends to drive while drunk, the less police and sobriety tests we need, and the fewer drunks there will be on the road.

Is Privacy Dead?

Popular books and articles decry the recent decline in privacy under titles such as "privacy is dead" and "the surveillance society" (Garfinkel, 2000; Stanley and Steinhardt, 2003; Sykes, 1999). Actually, in some ways privacy is better protected than it ever was. This is true because of both changes in technology and changes in law. I demonstrate my observation in these two areas, one at a time.

Technologically, much has been made about the increase in the means of surveillance, which include cameras, satellites (including GPS technology), wiretaps, email tracing orders, and heat censors. These indeed enable public authorities to eavesdrop or otherwise track or follow movements by individuals (or their goods and messages) much more effectively than was possible in the past. However, somewhat like in arms races, not merely the means of attack (on privacy) have increased, so too have the means of defense. Regrettably, those who claim that privacy is being lost tend not even to mention these new defenses.

The most important technological privacy-enhancing development is that of high-power encryption. Encryption of some sort has existed for many centuries. However, roughly around the early 1990s a new generation of hyper-encryption technologies was developed, one that is either unbreakable or at least extremely difficult to break. True, recently, as part of the continued "arms race," public authorities have found ways to obtain a suspect's computer password through the Key Logger System (KLS) and Magic Lantern, but these devices still do not enable authorities to read a massage caught en route (Etzioni, 2002). Anyhow, for all but those who have access to these very special tools of agencies, such as the CIA and the NSA, encrypted messages are extremely well protected – their privacy is unprecedented.

All one has to do is to compare messages previously sent by mail, carrier pigeon, fax, telegram, and messenger to see how much more private encrypted messages are. (Encryption is now routinely built into many computers and hence sending and receiving encrypted messages takes place automatically.) Moreover, information stored in encrypted files is many thousands of times better protected than when such data are stored in a locked cabinet or file drawer. In short, far from dead, privacy has a whole new and very powerful defense.

Other technological developments that should be of special interest to those concerned with the protection of privacy are access and audit trails. Access and audit trails are computer technologies that record the identity of people who access files. Generally, to access the information, a user must log in with his or her user name, ID number or code, as well as a password. Audit trails further enhance privacy by forming a record of the details of all accesses to a database. Such a record may include the dates and times of accesses, the information or particular record accesses and the identity of the people who examine the information (Brakeman, 1997: 36). These technologies are routinely used by hospitals and financial institutions, as well as by the FBI and CIA, to determine if any unauthorized party obtained access to data. Overall, audit trails deter snooping much better than paper records.

The second area in which privacy is better protected than it ever was is on the legal front. Here, the picture is more complicated than on the technological front, but the general direction of recent developments is nevertheless quite clear. The main sources of attacks on privacy in the last decades have been from the private sector. For instance, many corporations, such as Acxiom, maintain massive amounts of data about consumers and businesses. The data come from both public and private sources and allow companies to generate telephone and address information, mailing lists, and email information about potential customers. Many other corporations, from airlines to banks, from grocery stores to hospitals, also collect information about their current and potential customers. Until very recently there were federal laws (the 1973 Code of Fair Information Practices and the Privacy Act of 1974) that limited the information the *federal government* could collect on people and how that information could be used; but these laws did not apply to the private sector. In addition, there was a crazy quilt of state laws that some states enacted to protect various (but not the same) pieces of privacy of their residents and a few very narrowly crafted federal laws. One such law is the Video Protection Privacy Act of 1988 (US Code, 1988). The impetus for the law was the release of Judge Robert Bork's rental video records to a Washington-area newspaper during his confirmation hearing to the Supreme Court.

The Act prohibits video-tape rental-service providers from disclosing customer rental records without the written consent of the customer unless a warrant or other appropriate court order requests the information. Although this was and is a privacy-enhancing law, it and the few others like it cover only a small area of the data collected and used in the private sector.

A major strengthening of privacy came during the Clinton administration. At that time, one could buy medical records on the internet; banks used these records to call in loans when people had a heart attack or were diagnosed with cancer; and employers used them in order to avoid hiring employees with "bad" genes (Etzioni, 1999: 144–8). Here are just a few examples of how the privacy of medical records was being invaded. In Florida, a state health department worker, using state computers, compiled a list of 4,000 people who tested positive for HIV and forwarded it to a local health department and two newspapers, the *St Petersburg Times* and the *Tampa Tribune* (Siwicki, 1997;Palosky, 1996: 1). In Maryland, a state database which contained medical records of state residents was used illegally by state employees to sell confidential information about Medicaid recipients to HMOs, and it was also used by a banker to call in loans on bank customers whom he discovered had cancer. And the media obtained, and sometimes published, the detailed medical information of candidates for elected office and sports figures.[3]

These wanton violations of medical privacy led to an outcry from the public and the Clinton administration responded by issuing medical privacy regulations. Bush basically allowed them to stand and they took effect on April 14, 2003. The new regulations require hospitals, doctors, and health plans to provide the patient with information about how the patient's medical information may be used and what the patient's rights are. Doctors and nurses may share information needed to treat patients, but health information may not be used for non-healthcare purposes. Also, pharmacies and health plans must obtain an individual's authorization before patient information is disclosed for marketing purposes. Within entities covered by these regulations, a designated individual is charged with the responsibility of ensuring that proper privacy procedures are followed. The laws apply equally to government and private hospitals. Furthermore, if a state has more stringent laws dealing with medical privacy in place, then the federal guidelines will not pre-empt those of the state (Office for Civil Rights, 2003a, 2003b).

In addition, several laws have been enacted that better protect financial privacy. These laws are not flawless but no one can deny that privacy has been given a whole new set of federal laws, with teeth, that protect it.

Come a Hitler or a Stalin . . .

Privacy advocates, failing to find serious public harm from privacy violations that are still legal, have hence turned to the imaginary dangers: mainly what would happen if the United States were taken over by some tyrant who would find data banks stock-full of information about most Americans. First of all, such a development is extremely unlikely. Hence the question arises: what should one do now, "just in case"? Prohibit sellers from keeping tabs on customers' tastes and preferences? Prohibit credit bureaus from keeping information about who did not pay back loans? And so on. Second, if and when such a danger arises, much more would be at risk than our privacy: our whole way of life; all of our rights and liberties. Therefore, the best way to deal with such a danger is to shore up the American political system, citizen education, the free press, and so on – all measures that will protect our democracy, privacy included, rather than merely, or even mainly, privacy.

None of this is meant to disparage privacy. It is an important part of a good and free society. Privacy allows dissent to brew before it goes public; it fosters innovation; it protects those who deviate from the prevailing norms. Privacy has its place in our scale of values and should not be wantonly be limited. However, privacy needs to find its place among a whole host of values that are dear to us and which are not fully compatible. Hence we must constantly weigh how much importance we ought to accord privacy and how much importance we ought to accord other values, above all, the protection of our families, communities, and homeland.[4]

Notes

1   A Congressional law bars background checks from reporting criminal convictions that are more than 7 years old for positions that will earn less than $75,000, which includes most positions in childcare centers (Jones).
2   In a similar discussion, Steven Nock frames the issue in terms of *reputation*: "Reputation, I will argue, is a necessary and basic component of the trust that lies at the heart of social order. To establish and maintain reputations in the face of privacy, social mechanisms of *surveillance* have been elaborated or developed. In particular, various forms of credentials and modern ordeals produce reputations that are widely accessible, impersonal, and portable from one location to another. *A society of strangers is one of immense personal privacy. Surveillance is the cost of that privacy*" (1993: 1; emphasis in original). For additional discussion of this issue, see also Shoeman (1992).
3   For instance, Arthur Ashe had sought to keep his HIV-positive status private, but was forced to reveal it because *USA Today* was on the verge of printing the information (Deford, 1992). Nydia Vasquez, a candidate for New York's Twelfth Congressional District in 1992, had hospital records detailing a suicide attempt released to the press and published in the *New York Post* (Gorman, 1996).
4   I am indebted to Deirdre Mead for editorial assistance.

References

Ashcroft (2002). Attorney-General Ashcroft news conference transcript regarding decision of foreign intelligence surveillance court of review. Available at ⟨http://www.usdoj.gov/ag/speeches/2002/111802fisanewsconference.htm⟩. Accessed May 9, 2003.

Brakeman, Lynne (1997). "A physician leads the technology team." *Health Data Management*, February: 36–7.

Constitution of the United States of America. Text drawn from ⟨http://www.law.corncll.cdu/constitution/constitution.overview.html⟩.

Deford, Frank (1992). "Arthur Ashe's secret." *Newsweek*, April 20: 62–3.

Department of Justice (2001). *Field Guide on the New Authorities (Redacted) Enacted in the 2001 Antiterrorism Legislation*, section 216. Available at ⟨http://www.epic.org/privacy/terrorism/DOJ_guidance.pdf⟩. Accessed January 29, 2002.

Etzioni, Amitai (1999). *The Limits of Privacy*. New York. Basic Books.

Etzioni, Amitai (2002). "Implications of select new technologies for individual rights and public safety." *Harvard Journal of Law and Technology*, 15/2: 257–90.

Froomkin, Michael (1995). "The metaphor is the key: cryptography, the clipper chip, and the Constitution." *University of Pennsylvania law review*, 143: 824–5.

Garfinkel, Simon (2000). *Database Nation: Death of Privacy in the 21st Century*. Cambridge: O'Reilly.

Griswold v. *Connecticut* (1965), 381 US 479.

Gorman, Christine (1996). "Who's looking at your files?" *Time*, May 6, 1996, reprinted in Long (1997): 81–4.

Harris Poll (2003). Poll #17, by Humphrey Taylor: "Most people are 'privacy pragmatists' who, while concerned about privacy, will sometimes trade it off for other benefits." See ⟨www.harrisinteractive.com⟩.

Jones, Del (1998). "Background check rule change contains flaws." *USA Today*, February 24: 4B.

LaGrasse, Carol W. (1998). "Ex-con caregivers." *City Journal*, 7/3: 8–9.

Lichtblau, Eric (2002). "US acts to use new power to spy on possible terrorists." *New York Times*, November 24: A1.

Long, Robert Emmet (1997). *Rights to Privacy*. New York: H. W. Wilson Co.

Moore, Barrington, Jr. (1984). *Privacy: Studies on Social and Cultural History*. Armonk, NY: M. E. Sharpe.

Nock, Stephen L. (1993). *The Costs of Privacy: Surveillance and Reputation in America*. New York: Walter de Gruyter, Inc.

Office for Civil Rights (2003a). United States Department of Health and Human Services. Summary of the HIPAA Privacy Rule: OCR Privacy Brief, May 2003, pp. 1–25. Available at: ⟨http://www.hhs.gov/ocr/privacysummary.pdf⟩. Accessed September 5, 2003.

Office for Civil Rights (2003b). United States Department of Health and Human Services. Fact Sheet: Protecting the Privacy of Patients' Health Information, April 14, 2003. Available at ⟨http://www.hhs.gov/news/facts/privacy.html⟩. Accessed September 5, 2003.

Palosky, Craig S. (1996). "HIV tracked on unauthorized lists." *Tampa Tribune*, October 3: 1.

Roe v. *Wade* (1973), 410 US 113.

Sampson, Robert J. (1995). "The community." In James Q. Wilson and Joan Petersilia (eds.), *Crime* (pp. 193–216). San Francisco: Institute for Contemporary Studies Press.

Shoeman, Ferdinand David (1992). *Privacy and Social Freedom*. Cambridge: Cambridge University Press.

Siwicki, Bill (1997). "Health data security: a new priority." *Health Data Management*, 5 (September): 46–58.

Stanley, Jay and Steinhardt, Barry (2003). *Bigger Monsters, Weaker Chains: The Growth of an American Surveillance Society*. New York: ACLU.

Sykes, Charles J. (1999). *The End of Privacy*. New York: St. Martin's Press.

US Code (1988). Video protection privacy act of 1988, 18 USC §2710.

US Code (2001a). USA PATRIOT Act, 50 USC §1805 (c)(2)(B).

US Code (2001b). 50 USC §1842.

US Code (2001c). USA PATRIOT Act, 18 USC, §3103(a).

US Code (2002). Homeland Security Act. 6 USC, §460.

USA Freedom Corps (2002). Available at ⟨http://www.usafreedomcorps.gov/usafreedomcorps.pdf⟩. Accessed March 15, 2002.

Further reading

Etzioni, Amitai (1996). *The New Golden Rule: Community and Morality in a Democratic Society.* New York. Basic Books.

Sampson, Robert J., Raudenbush, Stephen W., and Earls, Felton (1997). "Neighborhoods and violent crime: a multilevel study of collective efficacy." *Science*, August 15: 918–24.

Amitai Etzioni

CHAPTER EIGHTEEN

The Case for Privacy

David D. Friedman

An old science fiction novel features a device that surrounds its bearer with an impenetrable bubble of force. The inventor rapidly discovers that every government and political faction on the planet wants what he has and is prepared to use any means, from persuasion to brute force, to get it. Our hero spends most of the book alternately listening to arguments, trying to decide who are the good guys and using his invention to help him escape attempts to capture him.

After about a hundred and fifty pages he realizes that he has been asking the wrong question. The answer to "What faction can be trusted with a monopoly over the shield?" is "No." The question he should be asking is how the shield will affect the world – how it will alter the balance between freedom and oppression, individual and state, small and big. The answer to that is easy. A world where the random individual is armored against anything short of an atomic explosion will be, on net, a better and freer world than the one he is currently living in. He writes out an explanation of how the shield works and spends two days distributing the information to people all over the world. By the time Military Security – the most formidable of his pursuers – catches up with him, it is too late. The cat is out of the bag.

Poul Anderson's (1982) *Shield* is fiction. The nearest real-world equivalent is privacy – my control over other people's access to information about me. Neither my government nor my neighbor can punish my thoughts, because neither can read my mind. That is why thoughts are free. However much other people are offended by what someone writes, they cannot retaliate unless they know who wrote it, what he looks like, where he lives. That is why Salmon Rushdie is still alive despite the death sentence passed on the author of *The Satanic Verses* more than 15 years ago by Iranian authorities.

Defensive weapons can be used for bad purposes; an impenetrable shield would be very useful for a bank robber. But it would be even more useful for the bank teller. Robbing banks would be harder in a world where everyone had the shield than in a world where nobody did.

The ability to control other people's access to information about you can be used for bad purposes too. That is the usual argument against privacy – "If you haven't done anything wrong, what do you have to hide?" The ability to conceal past crimes from the police and potential victims is useful to a robber. But the ability to conceal what I have that is worth stealing, where it is, how it is protected, is equally useful to the potential victim. Broadly stated, privacy gives each of us more control over our own life – which on average, if not in every case, is likely to lead to a freer world.

If I am a bad guy, the police are not the only people from whom I might want to keep secrets. When courting a wealthy widow, it helps if she does not know that my last three wives drowned in their bath tubs after taking out large life insurance policies. When borrowing money, it helps if the lender does not know that I have declared bankruptcy twice already.

But in a world of voluntary transactions – such as loans and marriages – my privacy does not require you to take me on faith. You have the option of not taking me. I have the power to keep my past defaults secret from a potential lender, but he has the power to refuse to lend to me if I do. Privacy is my ability to control other people's access to information about me. That does not mean that they cannot get the information – only that they cannot get it without my permission. Someone who offers to take care of my children but refuses to allow me access to the records that would show whether or not he has ever been convicted of child abuse has already told me all I need to know.

In some contexts I am willing to let other people know things about me. In others I am eager to. If only lenders knew a little more about my finances I would not be interrupted at dinner by phone calls from people offering to refinance my nonexistent mortgage. If sellers were better informed about what sort of things I am interested in buying, advertisements would be less of a nuisance and more of a service. Even in a world where I could keep information secret, I often would choose not to. Privacy provides me with protection when I want it and only when I want it.

Privacy and Government

> Government is not reason. It is not eloquence. It is a force, like fire: a dangerous servant and a terrible master.
>
> George Washington (1989)

Privacy includes the ability to keep things secret from the government. The better I can do that, the less able government is to help me – I might be keeping secret my weakness for alcohol, or heroin, or gambling, or pornography and so preventing the government from stepping in to protect me from myself. And the better other people can keep secrets from the government, the harder it is for the government to protect me from them. If you view government as a benevolent super-being watching over you – a wise and kindly uncle with a long white beard – you will and should reject much of what I am saying.

David D. Friedman

But government is not Uncle Sam or a philosopher king. Government is a set of institutions through which human beings act for human purposes. Its special feature – what differentiates political action from the other ways in which we try to get what we want – is that government is permitted to use force to make people do things. A firm can try to fool me into giving it my money. A tax collector uses more direct methods. A preacher can try to persuade me to renounce my sins. The Drug Enforcement Administration, with the help of the local police, can arrange to have me locked up until I do.

Part of the genius of American political culture is the recognition that making it hard for governments to control people is not always a bad thing. Political mechanisms, even in a democracy, give us only very limited control over what government can do to us. Reducing government's ability to do bad things to us, at the cost of limiting its ability to protect us from bad things done to us by ourselves or by other people, may not be such a bad deal. And since government, unlike a private criminal, has overwhelming superiority of physical force, control over what information it can get about me is one of the few ways in which I can limit its ability to control me.

I have defined what I mean by privacy and sketched the reasons why I think it is, on the whole, a good thing. The obvious next questions are where privacy comes from – what determines how much of it we have – and what we can and should do to get more of it.

Where Does Privacy Come From?

One of the things that determines how much control I have over other people's access to information about me is technology. If someone invents a mind-reading machine or a reliable truth drug, my thoughts will no longer be as private as they now are. Or as free.

Another is custom – systems of social norms. The more willing my friends and neighbors are to gossip about something, the easier it is for information about that something to get from those who have it to those who want it. That is one reason why Israelis are better informed about how much money their friends and relations make than Americans are – and modern Americans better informed about other people's sex lives than nineteenth-century Britons were.

A final factor is law. In the US, the Fourth Amendment to the Constitution prohibits "unreasonable searches and seizures" and requires that search warrants shall only be issued with probable cause. The more narrowly courts interpret that restriction, the easier it is to keep secrets from the police. One important example is the series of cases that applied the restriction to wiretaps as well as physical searches. Later cases have ruled on the extent to which high-tech devices may be used in figuring out what people are doing inside their houses — infra-red photographs to spot illegal greenhouses growing marijuana, for example — is a search and so requires a warrant.[1]

Law and technology interact in complicated ways. For your neighbor's nosy 15-year-old to use a scanner to listen to the phone calls you make on your wireless phone and then tell his friends about them is illegal. It is also easy, making that particular legal protection of privacy in practice unenforceable. The substitute is technology – encryption of the signal from the handset to the base station. Similarly with cell phones.

As these examples suggest, technological developments can both decrease and increase privacy. So can law. Legal rules that ban or limit technologies for learning things about other people, such as laws against wiretaps, increase privacy. Legal rules that ban or limit technologies for preventing other people from learning things about us, such as restrictions on the use of encryption, decrease it.

Privacy and Technology: The Dark Side of the Force

It used to be that one reason to move from a village to the big city was to get more privacy. Walls were no higher in the city, windows no less transparent. But there were so many more people. In the village, interested neighbors could keep track of who was doing what with whom. In the city, nobody could keep track of everyone.

That form of privacy – privacy through obscurity – is doomed. I cannot keep track of the million people who share the city I live in. But the computer on my desk has enough space on its hard drive to hold a hundred pages of information on every man, woman, and child in San Jose. With a few hundred dollars worth of additional storage, I could do it for everyone in California, for a few thousand, everyone in the country. And I can do more than store the information. If I had it I could search it – produce, in a matter of seconds, a list of those of my fellow citizens who are left-handed gun-owners with more than six children. Privacy through obscurity cannot survive modern data processing.

As it happens, I do not have a hundred pages worth of information on each of my fellow citizens. But with a little time and effort – too much for a single individual, but not too much for a government, a collection of police departments, or a large firm – I could. It is hard to pass through the world without leaving tracks. Somewhere there is a record of every car I have registered, every tax form I have filed, two marriages, one divorce, the birth of three children, thousands of posts to online forums on a wide variety of subjects, four published books, medical records, and a great deal more.

Much such information, although not all of it, was publicly available in the past. But actually digging it up was a lot of work. The result was that most of us went through life reasonably sure that most of the people we met did not know much about us beyond what we chose to tell them. That will not be true in the future.

Data processing is one technology with the potential to sharply reduce privacy. Another is surveillance. One form – already common in England – is a video camera on a pole. A video camera in a park connected to a screen with a police officer watching it is, at first glance, no more a violation of privacy than the same police officer standing in the park watching what is going on. It merely lets the officer do his watching somewhere warm and out of the wet. Add a video recorder and it is arguably an improvement, since the evidence it produces is less subject to mistake or misrepresentation than the memory of the policeman. And, judging by British experience, such surveillance cameras are an effective way of reducing crime. What's the problem?

David D. Friedman

To see the answer, add one more technology – face recognition software. Combine that with a database, put up enough cameras, and we have a record of where everyone was any time of the day and – with suitable cameras – night. The arresting officer, or the prosecuting attorney, no longer has to ask the defendant where he was at 8 p.m. of July 9. All he has to do is enter the defendant's social security number and the date and the computer will tell him. And, if the defendant was in a public place at the time, show him.

For a slightly lower-tech version of the same issue, consider the humble phone tap. In the past, the main limit on how many phones got tapped by police was not the difficulty of getting a court order but the cost of implementing it. Phone taps are labor-intensive – someone has to listen to a lot of phone calls in order to find the ones that matter.

That problem has now been solved. Voice recognition software originated by companies such as Dragon Systems and IBM allows computers to convert speech into text – a boon for computer users who are slow typists. The same technology means that the police officer listening to someone else's phone calls can now be replaced by a computer. Only when it gets a hit, spots the words or phrases it has been programmed to listen for, does it need to call in a human being. Computers work cheap.

In an old comedy thriller, *The President's Analyst* (1967), starring James Coburn, the hero, having temporarily escaped his pursuers and made it to a phone booth, calls a friendly CIA agent to come rescue him. When he tries to leave the booth, the door won't open. Down the road comes a phone company truck loaded with booths. The truck's crane picks up the one containing the analyst, deposits it in the back, replaces it with an empty booth and drives off.

A minute later a helicopter descends containing the CIA agent and a KGB agent who is his temporary ally. They look in astonishment at the empty phone booth. The American speaks first: "It can't be. Every phone in America tapped?" The response (you will have to imagine the Russian accent): "Where do you think you are – Russia?" A great scene in a very funny movie – but it may not be a joke much longer. The digital wiretap bill, pushed through Congress by the FBI a few years ago, already requires phone companies to provide law enforcement with the ability to simultaneously tap 1 percent of all phones in a selected area. There is no obvious reason why that cannot be expanded in the future. My current estimate is that the dedicated hardware to do the listening part of the job – for every phone call in the US – would cost less than a billion dollars. And it is getting cheaper.

So far I have been discussing technologies that already exist. Fast forward a little further and surveillance need no longer be limited to public places. Video cameras are getting smaller. It should not be all that long before we can build one with the size – and the aerodynamic characteristics – of a mosquito.

Here again, if we regard government law enforcement agents as unambiguously good guys, there is no problem. The better our record of where everyone is at a given time, the easier it will be to catch and convict criminals.

The same technology would make keeping track of dissidents, or political opponents, or members of an unpopular religion, or people with the wrong sexual tastes, or people who read the wrong books, or anyone else, a great deal easier than it now is. It is true that the random government is rather less likely to have bad intentions than the random criminal. But if it does have bad intentions it can do a great deal more damage.

The technologies I have been discussing so far – database and face recognition software, surveillance hardware – have the potential to make this a much less private world. So do other technologies that I have not covered: improvements in lie detectors and interrogation drugs to learn what we think, biometric identification by fingerprints, retinal patterns, DNA to learn who we are, with or without our permission. The future implications of such developments are sufficiently strong to have convinced at least one thoughtful observer that the best we can hope for in the future is a transparent society, a world without privacy where the police can watch us but we can also watch them (Brin, 1998). I would find the symmetry of that future more appealing if it did not conceal an important asymmetry: they can arrest us and we cannot arrest them.

But there are other technologies.

Encryption: A World of Strong Privacy

We start with an old problem: how to communicate with someone without letting other people know what you are saying. There are a number of familiar solutions. If worried about eavesdroppers, check under the eaves. To be safer still, hold your private conversation in the middle of a large, open field, or a boat in the middle of a lake. The fish are not interested and nobody else can hear.

That no longer works. The middle of a lake is still within range of a shotgun mike. Eaves do not have to contain eavesdroppers – just a microphone and a transmitter. Phone lines can be tapped, cordless or cell phone messages intercepted. An email bounces through multiple computers on its way to its destination – anyone controlling one of those computers can save a copy for himself.

The solution is encryption. Scramble the message. Provide the intended recipient with the formula for unscrambling it. Now it does not matter if someone intercepts your mail. He can't read it.

There is still a problem. In order to read my scrambled message, you need the key – the formula describing how to unscramble it. If I do not have a safe way of sending you messages, I may not have a safe way of sending you the key either. If I sent it by a trusted messenger but made a small mistake as to who he was really working for, someone else now has a copy and can use it decrypt my future messages to you.

About 25 years ago, this problem was solved. The solution is public key encryption. It works by using two keys, each of which decrypts what the other encrypts. One of the two – my public key – I make available to anyone who might want to send me a message. The other never leaves my hands. Someone who wants to communicate with me encrypts his messages with my public key. I use my private key to decrypt them.

Public key encryption provides a free bonus – digital signatures. In order to prove that a message was sent by me I can encrypt it using my private key. The recipient

David D. Friedman

decrypts it using my public key. The fact that what comes out is text rather than gibberish proves it was encrypted with the matching private key – which only I have. Hence, unless I have been very careless, the message is from me.

Imagine a world where public key encryption is in general use. Add in related technologies such as anonymous digital money to permit payments that leave no paper trail, and anonymous remailers to keep who I am talking to, as well as what I am saying, private – for details see Friedman (1996). In that world I can email someone – anyone – with reasonable certainty that nobody else can read the message. I can have telephone conversations without worrying about who may be listening. In that world I can, if I wish, establish an online persona – an identity defined by my digital signature – while keeping control over the link between that and my real-space persona. However much my online persona offends someone – even the rulers of Iran – there is very little anyone can do about it. It is hard to murder someone when you don't know his name, what he looks like, or what continent he is on.

I have been describing things we already know how to do. Most can already be done using free software that runs on the computers most of us have. I now take a small step forward to add one more element to the mix: virtual reality. Using goggles and earphones – if we are willing to step further into science fiction, direct links between mind and computer – we create the illusion of seeing, hearing, perhaps tasting and touching. The world of strong privacy expands from text messages and phone conversations to something very much like the real world we currently live in. Just let your fingers do the walking.[2]

Combine and Stir

I have described two clusters of technologies. One – database, voice and text recognition, surveillance – has the potential to reduce privacy to the point where those who control the technology know very nearly everything that everyone does. The other – encryption, online communication, virtual reality – has the potential to increase privacy to the point where individuals have nearly total control over other people's access to information about them. What if we get both?

It will be an interesting world. Everything you do in real space will be known to the authorities, perhaps to everyone – David Brin's Transparent Society. But most of the important stuff – all transactions involving information, ideas, arguments, beliefs – will have been moved to cyberspace, protected by the strong privacy of encryption. Freedom of speech will no longer depend on how the Supreme Court interprets the First Amendment. It will be protected, instead, by the laws of mathematics – which so far, at least, heavily favor defense over offense, encryption over cracking.

There will be – already have been – attempts to use law to block both futures. Supporters of privacy will try to get laws restricting the ability of law enforcement – and other people – to use technology to learn our secrets. Opponents of privacy will try to get laws restricting the ability of private individuals to use encryption to protect their secrets.

Technology and Law

There are two approaches to using law to preserve privacy in the face of technologies that threaten it. One is to use law to prevent other people from getting information – a database is of no use if there is nothing in it. The other is to permit other people to get information but use law to limit what they can do with it.

An example of the first approach is regulation of wire tapping and other forms of surveillance – both laws against private surveillance and laws restricting surveillance by law enforcement agents. Such restrictions can keep some information about me from getting to other people. But they do nothing to protect the vast amount of information that I generate by going about my daily life in the public view – buying and selling, marrying and getting divorced, writing and talking.

An example of the second approach is the web of restrictions, legal, contractual, and customary, on the use of confidential information. I cannot keep my doctor from having access to the medical information he creates when he examines me and uses when he prescribes for me. But I can, to some limited degree, prevent him from sharing that information with other people. Credit bureaus are free to collect information on people in order to advise other people as to whether to lend them money but, under current federal law, they are only permitted to release that information in response to requests from people who have a legitimate need for it.

As the example of credit bureaus suggests, there are practical difficulties with protecting privacy by letting other people have information and then controlling what they do with it. Credit agencies could not serve their intended purpose at any reasonable cost if they engaged in an extensive investigation of everyone who asked for information. And even if the agency limits itself to giving the information to people who can prove they are entitled to it, there is no way it can control who they then give it to. It is probably prudent to assume that what the credit agency knows about you anyone else can know if he really wants to. The forms you sign when you shift to a new doctor include an extensive list of people to whom and circumstances under which your medical information will be made available, so it might be equally prudent not to rely too much on your medical privacy.

As long as we limit our options to current technologies for protecting privacy, the outlook does not look good. We might succeed in restricting the use of surveillance, wiretapping, and similar technologies, although attempts to prevent their use by law enforcement face serious opposition by those concerned with the threat of crime and terrorism. But most information about us is public, and once information is out it is hard to control how other people use it or to whom they give it.

The technologies of strong privacy offer at least a partial solution. If I make a purchase with a credit card, I create a paper trail – someone, somewhere, knows what I bought. Even if I use cash, a purchase in real space requires me to walk into a store where someone sees me – the information about what I bought is now his as well as mine. In a world where the relevant software is a little better than it now is – say ten years in the future – that someone is a store video camera linked to facial recognition software linked to a database. Stores, after all, like to know who their customers are.

If, however, I buy something over the phone or over the internet, using the digital equivalent of cash – anonymous digital currency – only I know that I bought it. If

David D. Friedman

the something is not a physical object that must be delivered to me, but information – music, data, software – I can collect my purchase online without ever revealing my identity or location.

Thus the technologies of encryption and computer networking can permit us, to a considerable extent, to move through the world without leaving footprints. If I want to receive advertising based on my past purchases – as it happens I often do – I can choose to make those purchases under my real name and provide my real address. If I want to receive the advertising without making my acts publicly observable – perhaps I am purchasing pornography – I can do it via an online identity. The link that ties my real-space body to my cyberspace persona is under my control. I have privacy – control over other people's access to information about me.

If we go a little further into science fiction I could even have privacy from my doctor. He knows the information that an examination – via remote-controlled devices – revealed about me. He does not need to know what my name is, my face looks like, or where I live. It is not likely that I would want to carry my privacy that far – but I could.

So far I have been considering ways in which we might preserve privacy against the threat posed by technology. But there is another side to the story. For those who think that we already have too much privacy, what I view as the solution may look more like the problem. There have already been attempts to restrict the use of encryption to protect privacy. There will be more.

Suppose I concede, at least for the purposes of argument, that it is possible to have too much privacy as well as too little. Further, and less plausibly, suppose I believed that the strong privacy provided by encryption is a serious problem. How might one use law to solve it?

One difficulty is that encryption regulation poses the problem summed up in the slogan "when guns are outlawed, only outlaws have guns." The mathematics of public key encryption has been public for decades. The software to do it already exists in a variety of forms, some of them freely available. Given the nature of software, once you have a program you can make an unlimited number of copies. Keeping encryption software out of the hands of spies, terrorists, and competent criminals is not a practical option. They probably have it already, and if not they can easily get it. The only people affected by a law against encryption software are those who abide by the law.

What about banning or restricting the use of encryption – at least encryption that cannot be broken by law enforcement agents? To enforce such a ban, law enforcement agencies could randomly monitor all communication systems, looking for illegally encrypted messages. One practical problem is the enormous volume of information flowing over computer networks. A second and even more intractable problem is that while it is easy enough to tell whether a message consists of text written in English, it is very much harder – in practice impossible – to identify other sorts of content well enough to be sure that they do not contain encrypted messages.

Consider a three-million-pixel digital photograph. To conceal a million-character-long encrypted message – an average-sized novel – I replace the least significant bit of each of the numbers describing the color of a pixel with one bit of the message. The photo is now a marginally worse picture than it was – but there is no way an

FBI agent, or a computer working for an FBI agent, can know precisely what the photo ought to look like.

Short of banning communication over computer networks – or at least restricting it to text messages – there is no way that law enforcement can keep sophisticated criminals, spies, or terrorists from using encryption. What can be done is to put limits on the encryption software used by the rest of us – to insist that if AOL or Microsoft builds encryption into their programs it must contain a back door permitting properly authorized persons to read the message without the key.

This still leaves the problem of how to give law enforcement what it wants without imposing unacceptably high costs on the rest of us. Consider the description of adequate regulation given by Louis Freeh, at the time head of the FBI: the ability to crack any encrypted message in half an hour. The equivalent in real space would be legal rules that let properly authorized law enforcement agents open any lock in the country in half an hour. That includes not only the lock on your front door but also the locks protecting bank vaults, trade secrets, lawyers' records, lists of contributors to unpopular causes, and much else.

Encryption provides the locks for cyberspace. If all legal encryption comes with a mandatory back door accessible in half an hour to any police officer with a court order, everything in cyberspace is vulnerable to a private criminal with the right contacts. Those locks have billions of dollars worth of stuff behind them – money in banks, trade secrets in computers, and messages. If being a police officer gives you access to locks with billions of dollars behind them, in cash, diamonds, or information, some cops will become criminals and some criminals will become cops.

In one important way, the consequence for cyberspace is even worse than the equivalent in real space. If a police officer opens a safe and pockets a stack of cash or a bag of diamonds, the owner can see that something is missing and demand it back. When information is copied, the original is still there. If the officer who has decrypted your communications or stored data assures you that he found nothing relevant to his investigation and so took nothing away, there is no way to prove he is lying.

For encryption regulation to be useful it must either prevent the routine use of encryption or make it easy for law enforcement agents to access encrypted data and messages. Not only would that seriously handicap routine transactions, it would make computer crime easier by restricting the technology best suited to defend against it. And what we get in exchange is protection not against the use of encryption by sophisticated criminals and terrorists – there is no way of providing that – but only against its use by ordinary people and unsophisticated criminals. It does not look like a very attractive deal.

Privacy, Freedom and Government

Some years ago Amitai Etzioni, who has contributed a chapter to this volume, published a book (1999) arguing for some restrictions on privacy as ways of promoting the common good. In reading it, I was struck by two differences between our views that explain much of the difference in our conclusions.

David D. Friedman

The first was that I did, and he did not, define privacy within the context of freedom of association. Consider the question of airlines requiring their pilots to be tested for drugs and alcohol. Etzioni regards that as a (desirable) restriction on the pilots' privacy. I agree that it is desirable but not that it restricts privacy. In a society where privacy is protected, you have a right not to be tested. You do not have a right to be hired to fly airplanes – and, if you choose to exercise your right not to be tested, you should not be surprised if the airline exercises its right not to hire you. The background legal principle is not that I have a right to be hired as a pilot or that United Airlines has a right to have me fly their planes. The background principle is that they can hire me to fly their planes if and only if we can find terms that both they and I will agree to. Given that principle of free association, many – although not all – of the problems that Etzioni sees with privacy vanish.

The second difference has to do with our different views of government. While Etzioni (1999) makes occasional references to the risk of some future oppressive government misusing information, he does not take seriously similar concerns with regard to our current government. His implicit assumption is that government is to be viewed as a benevolent agent standing above the human struggle, not as a mechanism through which individuals seek to achieve their goals, often at the expense of other individuals. That is not a view that strikes me as realistic.

Conclusion

Privacy, like almost anything else, can be used for good or bad purposes. My thesis in this chapter is that, on net, more privacy makes the world a better place. It does so because it is an essentially defensive weapon, a way of reducing the ability of people to control each other.

Reducing the ability of other people to control us is not always a good thing – someone may, after all, want to control me for my own good or control you to keep you from hurting me. But we live in a world where too much control is more of a problem than too little. In the entire world over the past century, something on the order of ten million people have been killed by private murderers. Between one and two hundred million have been killed by the governments that ruled them (Rummel (1999) estimates about 170 million from 1900 to 1987). Quite a lot of individual pain, suffering, and injustice have been the result of the acts of private individuals; some could have been prevented by better law enforcement. But mass pain, suffering, and injustice has been very nearly a monopoly of governments. If governments were better able to control us, there would have been more of it. And at the individual level, while privacy can be used to protect criminals against police, it can also be used to protect victims against criminals.

It is tempting to try for the best of both worlds – to restrict the privacy of bad people while protecting that of good, to permit governments to collect detailed information about us but only allow it to be used for good purposes. But somebody must decide who are the good and bad people, what purposes are worthy or unworthy. Whoever that somebody is will have his own agenda, his own purposes. Angels are in short supply.

To put the matter differently, "cannot" is better protection than "may not." If we permit law enforcement agents to know everything about everybody but forbid them from using that information against individuals with unpopular views or political opponents of the party in power, we are protected only by a "may not." The same is true if private parties are able to collect information but are restricted in what they may do with it. If the law keeps the information from being collected in the first place, we are protected by a "cannot" – however corrupt or dishonest they are, or however convinced that they are working for a greater good, people cannot use information they do not have.

"Cannot" at one level sometimes depends on "may not" at another. You cannot use information that you do not have. You do not have it because you may not collect it. But even if the law forbids wiretaps or unauthorized surveillance, a sufficiently determined agency – or a sufficiently competent private criminal – can violate the law. That is where technologies that support privacy come into the picture. In a world where encryption is routine, it does you no good to tap my phone because you cannot understand what I am saying. It does no good to intercept my email because you cannot read it. "Cannot" is better than "may not."

We can and should fight a delaying action against the use of technology to restrict privacy. But in the long run, technology – useful technology – is hard to stop. In the long run, the real battle will be the one fought in defense of technologies that protect privacy. That one we might win.

Notes

1 The wiretap case is *Katz* v. *United States*, 389 US 347 (1967). It found that a wiretap was a search, reversing the result in *Olmstead* v. *United States*, 277 U.S. 438 (1928). A story on the marijuana case (the SC ruled that it was a search and so required a warrant) is available at ⟨http://abcnews.go.com/sections/us/DailyNews/scotus_thermal010611.html⟩. The case is *Kyllo* v. *US* (no. 99-8508. Decided June 11, 2001) and is available at ⟨http://www.law.umkc.edu/faculty/projects/ftrials/conlaw/kyllo.htm⟩.
2 In this section I have somewhat simplified the mechanics of public key encryption and digital signatures for expositional clarity. It could be done as I describe, but there are more complicated ways that let you do the same things faster.

References

Anderson, Poul (1982) *Shield*. Berkley: Berkley Publishing Group.
Brin, David (1998), *The Transparent Society: Will Technology Force us to Choose Between Privacy and Freedom?* Reading, MA: Addison-Wesley. The first chapter is available at ⟨http://www.kithrup.com/brin/tschp1.html⟩.
Etzioni, Amitai (1999). *The Limits of Privacy*. New York: Basic Books.
Friedman, David (1996). "A World of strong privacy: promises and perils of encryption." *Social Philosophy and Policy*, 13: 212–28. Available at ⟨http://www.daviddfriedman.com/Academic/Strong_Privacy/Strong_Privacy.html⟩.
The President's Analyst (1967). Theodore J. Flicker (Dir). Paramount Studio.

Rummel, Rudolph J. (1999). *Statistics of Democide: Genocide and Mass Murder Since 1900.* Piscatway, NJ: Lit Verlag.

Washington, George (1989). Quote attributed to George Washington. Available at ⟨http://www.bartleby.com/73/754.html⟩.

Futher reading

Paul, Ellen Frankel, Miller, Fred D., Jr., and Paul, Jeffrey (eds.) (2000) *The Right to Privacy.* Cambridge: Cambridge University Press.

⟨http://www.mega.nu:8080/ampp/rummel/20th.htm⟩ (detailed statistics on twentieth-century democide).

⟨http://www.daviddfriedman.com/future_imperfect_draft/future_imperfect.html⟩ (more detailed account of encryption, surveillance, and much else).

VALUES IN NATURE

CHAPTER NINETEEN

The Intrinsic Value of Nature in Public Policy: The Case of the Endangered Species Act

J. Baird Callicott

The distinction between instrumental and intrinsic value is both familiar and vener-able in Western ethical thinking. In familiar and venerable Western ethical thinking, however, the only beings believed to "have" intrinsic value – or the only beings worthy of being valued intrinsically – are human beings. Beginning in the 1970s, the new breed of environmental philosophers sought to build a case (or cases) for the intrin-sic value of some nonhuman natural entities and nature as a whole – in order to eth-ically enfranchise nonhuman beings (though just which ones is a matter of debate).

This project has been persistently criticized by a group of environmental philoso-phers identifying themselves as pragmatists, Bryan Norton most notable among them. Norton's general arguments against the case for the intrinsic value of nonhuman natural entities and nature as a whole are many and some of them are subtle. Among them is what I regard as the core pragmatist complaint: that the distinction makes no practical difference. If one values waterfowl, for example, instrumentally, as a recrea-tional resource, or if one values waterfowl intrinsically, for its own sake, the upshot, Norton believes, is more or less the same: one will support such public policies as waterfowl habitat conservation. Norton (1991) calls this "the Convergence Hypothe-sis." Not only is the distinction practically otiose, Norton frequently argues, it is also politically divisive and a deal breaker for policy makers. Waterfowl hunters, on the one hand, and deep-ecological waterfowl lovers, on the other, can mutually agree on a common public policy – waterfowl habitat conservation, in this illustrative case – but only if attention is focused on what to do about what they both value, albeit in very different ways, not on their polarized values per se.

I will not here recapitulate the many and various philosophical cases for the intrin-sic value of nature. Rather, I consider a signal public policy document based, implic-itly, on the intrinsic value of nature: the Endangered Species Act (ESA) of 1973 (US Code, 1973). Nowhere in the ESA is the intrinsic value of threatened and endangered species ever mentioned. So one important task for me is to show that the ESA does indeed implicitly affirm the intrinsic value of threatened and endangered species. Another is to show that the first of Norton's claims is false. How we value things – instrumentally or intrinsically – does make a big practical difference.

The value of something as a means to an end other than itself is instrumental. The value of something for itself, for its own sake, as an end in itself, is intrinsic. To bring out the difference between instrumental and intrinsic value in the context of endangered species, consider the following anecdote. Edwin P. Pister, a now-retired Associate Fishery Biologist with the California Department of Fish and Game, worked long and hard to save from extinction several species of desert fishes living in small islands of water in an ocean of dry land (Pister, 1987: 221–32). Pister was often asked – not only by laypersons, but also by members of his own department (dedicated as most were to providing anglers with game fish) – what good the Devil's Hole and Owens River pupfishes are anyway. He tried in vain to answer seriously such a smug, essentially rhetorical question – rhetorical, because the person who asked it assumed that they were good for nothing – by saying that while such fishes may be of little value instrumentally, they are nonetheless intrinsically valuable. And to the next (inevitable) question, he would explain the emerging distinction in academic environmental philosophy and ethics between the instrumental and intrinsic value of nonhuman natural entities and nature as a whole – to little avail. Ultimately, he hit on a simple, effective, and dramatic means of getting the questioner to grasp the value distinction he was otherwise discursively articulating. He answered their question with one of his own: "What good are you?" (Pister, 1985: 3–12).

Most of us hope to be of some use to others (family, friends, associates) and to be responsible, contributing members of society. But when age or infirmity reduces our instrumental value (to others and to society) to a degree approaching zero, we expect others and society to acknowledge our intrinsic value. Thus, we do not simply dispose of one another – when that time comes – as we do things that are of value solely instrumentally, such as broken tools, junk cars, and withered house plants. Therefore we can think of an entity's intrinsic value as the value that remains when all its instrumental value has been subtracted. Hence, in academic environmental philosophy and ethics intrinsic value is often equated with (and synonymous with) noninstrumental value.

Instrumental Values Appropriately Quantified by Means of a Monetary Metric

ESA Section 2(a)(3) explicitly identifies the following values of threatened and endangered species: aesthetic, ecological, educational, historical, recreational, and scientific. The order in which these values are stated appears to be alphabetical.

Taken together, the values of endangered species explicitly stated in the ESA seem to be largely instrumental. To the extent that they are, they may be quantified in a monetary metric in order to compare them with other things that have instrumental value – such as pasture for livestock, farmland, and shopping malls – for purposes of making rational choices between competing values (Freeman III, 1993).

J. Baird Callicott

Some environmental philosophers object to quantifying the value of nonhuman species (and other aspects of the natural environment) in the monetary metric because that would "reduce" such values as aesthetic, ecological, educational, historical, recreational, and scientific values to "economic" value (Hargrove, 2000: 1–20). From the point of view of contemporary economics, such objections are unwarranted. Human beings instrumentally value many things in many ways. A car may be instrumentally valued as a means of transportation, an object of aesthetic delight, and a symbol of status. To aggregate the several and quite diverse values represented by such a car, we need a common metric. Money is a convenient metric for the diverse values bundled in things like cars because it is quantitative and fungible. A car's market price is the sum of its several and quite diverse kinds of value expressed in a monetary metric. Its price is not an additional "economic" value of a car; rather, its price is the quantification of its transportation, aesthetic, and status symbol values. Thus, from the point of view of environmental economics, to quantify the instrumental aesthetic, ecological, educational, historical, recreational, and scientific values of endangered species in monetary terms is not to reduce these values to some other value – economic value. Rather, it is to express them in the same metric in which other competing instrumental values are expressed for purposes of comparison and rational choice (Freeman III, 1993). Discomfort with quantifying the values of endangered species in a monetary metric may suggest, instead, a feeling that the values of endangered species are not solely instrumental, but are also intrinsic.

Commodities such as lumber derived from natural capital are traded in markets and thus have a price. Recreation is sometimes a bundle of commodities and services for sale at a price. Take, for example, a "canned hunt" on a private parcel of land, in which, for a price, a paying customer gets guided to a confined game animal, the experience of killing it, and the animal itself partly mounted as a trophy and partly butchered for meat (Norris et al., 2001). The value of a wooded property clear-cut for lumber can thus be compared with its value preserved for canned hunts – because both register an unambiguous signal in a common monetary metric. Non-consumptive forms of recreation involving endangered species, such as searching the piney woods of East Texas for red-cockaded woodpeckers, also register a clear signal in the same metric – the amount of money people spend on transportation, food, and lodging pursuing this form of recreation – even though, unlike canned hunts, they have no market price. In addition to such so-called "implicit pricing methods," the aesthetic, ecological, educational, historical, and scientific values of the red-cockaded woodpecker – for which there is no market to determine their price – are expressible in the monetary metric by other, indirect methods, such as "contingent valuation" (Freeman III, 1993).

If the aesthetic, ecological, educational, historical, recreational, and scientific values of endangered species were solely instrumental, then their value would scarcely appear robust enough to successfully outweigh the instrumental value of their habitats converted to other uses. To be sure, the instrumental ecological value of ecosystem services and natural capital, quantified in the monetary metric, may be great enough to afford a robust utilitarian argument for preserving valuable endangered keystone species – "a species whose ecological impact is large and disproportionately large relative to its abundance" (Power et al., 1996: 609). For example, when the southern subspecies of sea otter was reduced in number to near extinction, the underwater kelp "forests" on the continental shelf off the west coast of the United States began to disappear – because their holdfasts were being eaten by irrupting populations of sea urchins – resulting in cascading ecological effects. Sea otters prey on shellfish, sea urchins included. When sea otter populations rebounded, sea urchin populations were reduced and the kelp forests regrew, and once again provided habitat for many other animal species (Van Blaricom and Estes, 1998). Because sea otters indirectly benefit other species and are vital to the persistence of kelp-dominated aquatic communities, their instrumental ecological value would seem to be robust enough to outweigh the value of their fur.

Unlike the southern sea otter, few threatened and endangered species are essential to the provision of ecosystem services. As David Ehrenfeld notes:

> [T]he species whose members are the fewest in number, the rarest, the most narrowly distributed – in short, the one's most likely to become extinct – are obviously the ones least likely to be missed by the biosphere. Many of these species were never common or ecologically influential; by no stretch of the imagination can we make them out to be vital cogs in the ecological machine. (1988: 215)

The red-cockaded woodpecker, for example, is not a keystone species nor does it play any other vital role in its ecosystem. The very fact that it has become endangered as a result of the lumber industry suggests that the red-cockaded woodpecker's aesthetic, ecological, educational, historical, recreational, and scientific values – understood to be purely instrumental – compete poorly on a level playing field with the various instrumental values (quantified in the same metric) of the forests where it lives, after such forests are converted to other uses.

The ESA Operationally Provides Legal Rights for Listed Species and Implicitly Recognizes their Intrinsic Value

As stated in Section 2(a)(1), the intent of the ESA is clearly to temper "growth and development" by "adequate concern" for species "in danger of or threatened with extinction," leading to "conservation" of them. But, as noted, the values identified in Section 2(a)(3), when quantified in the monetary metric, would not appear to be adequate to achieve conservation of such species by purely market forces and mechanisms, even when such forces and mechanisms are "corrected" by environmental economists with the aid of their full arsenal of valuation techniques. The Act thus provides de facto rights for listed species, effectively exempting their conservation from purely instrumental – and thus purely economic – considerations.

Christopher D. Stone (1974) identifies four criteria that, when met, "operationally" confer legal rights on some entity, irrespective of whether the discourse of rights is used or not:

1 The entity must have standing in a court of law.
2 Legal action may be commenced on its behalf.

282   J. Baird Callicott

3 In granting legal relief the court must take injury to it into account, not only to some other party.
4 Relief must run to the benefit of it, not only to some other party.

As to Stone's criteria (1) and (2) – the "standing" criteria – Section 11(c) of the Act provides for "the several district courts of the United States" to have "jurisdiction over any actions arising under this Act." And Section 11(g)(1) provides that "any person may commence a civil suit" (i) against any other private person, the United States, or any agency thereof who is alleged to be in violation of any provision of the Act or any regulation issued under its authority; (ii) to compel the Secretary of the Interior to apply the provisions of the Act; or (iii) against the Secretary for alleged failure to apply the provisions of the Act. Thus any person can bring suit on behalf of a listed species in a US district court without having to allege that he or she has been personally injured. In other words, the person authorized to bring suit is not required to have legal standing in federal district courts; the party that has standing is the listed species, and the person who commences suit does so on behalf of the listed species, not for him- or herself.

As to Stone's criteria (3) and (4) – the injury criteria – Section 4(a)(1) specifies injury to threatened and endangered species from (i) "destruction, modification, or curtailment of its habitat or range," or (ii) "over-utilization for commercial, recreational, scientific, or educational purposes" as warrant for granting it legal relief. And Section 4(d) directs the Secretary of the Interior to "issue such regulations as he deems necessary and advisable to provide for the conservation of such [listed endangered] species." Especially in the mandate of Section 4(b)(2) to conserve the "critical habitat" of endangered species, relief of injury to listed endangered species clearly runs primarily to their benefit.

When these criteria are met, an entity acquires "a legally recognized worth and dignity in its own right, and not merely to serve as means to benefit 'us'" (whoever the contemporary group of rights holders may be) (Stone, 1972: 458). In effect, legal rights recognize and are based on the intrinsic value of the entities to which such rights are accorded. In short then, the ESA operationally confers legal rights on listed threatened and endangered species and thus implicitly recognizes their intrinsic value.

Dispute rages in the large literature on intrinsic value in environmental philosophy about its ontological status.[1] Is intrinsic value – as its name would suggest – an objective property of something that has intrinsic value, like its length or weight? Or is intrinsic value subjectively conferred, like something being loved or hated? In 1973, did the US Congress ratify a new moral *discovery* that endangered species have intrinsic value – analogous to a new scientific discovery such as the discovery of new forms of life near volcanic vents on the ocean's floor? Or did the Congress *grant* endangered species intrinsic value – as it might grant a disenfranchised group of citizens the right to vote? There is an even larger literature in legal philosophy on the ontological status of rights.[2] Are rights natural and real or are they artificial and conventional? While these questions are philosophically interesting and important, their answers make no practical difference. Whether endangered species literally *have* intrinsic value (like birds have feathers and plants have chlorophyll), or they *are valued* intrinsically (like X is a target only when Y aims at it), and whether their rights are natural or artificial, the practical consequences are the same.

Why Intrinsic Value Should Not Be Quantified in the Monetary Metric

The *locus classicus* of the concept of intrinsic value is found in the immensely influential moral philosophy of Immanuel Kant, who wrote:

> [E]verything has either a *price* or a *dignity*. Whatever has a price can be replaced by something else as its equivalent; on the other hand, whatever is above all price, and therefore admits of no equivalent, has a dignity. That which is related to general human inclinations and needs has a *market price*. That which, without supposing any need, accords with a certain taste, i.e., with pleasure in the mere purposeless play of our faculties, has an *affective price*. But that which constitutes the condition under which alone something can be an end in itself does not have a mere relative worth, i.e., a price, but an intrinsic worth, a *dignity*. (1959: 53)

The distinction that Kant draws between a market price and an affective price is roughly the same distinction that economists make between a market price and a shadow price. Things that people want (the objects of "human inclinations") and need are traded in markets – thus they have a market price. By things that accord with certain tastes and involve pleasure in the mere purposeless play of our faculties, Kant means objects of aesthetic experience. Some of these – works of art – also have a market price. But those that do not – for example, many environmental amenities, such as wild and scenic rivers and clear view-sheds – have, according to Kant, an affective price. They have a value, that is, which can be expressed in the monetary metric. But it is, Kant thinks, inappropriate to price things that have intrinsic value – to value them in monetary terms.

Two schools of thought have dominated Western moral culture since the late eighteenth century – utilitarianism and Kantianism. In the former, the aim of both private persons and public policy should be to achieve "the greatest happiness of the greatest number" (of human beings) – "happiness" then being understood to consist in a greater balance of pleasure over pain (Bentham, 1970; Mill, 1863). Later, utilitarians substituted "welfare" for happiness and defined welfare in terms of "preference satisfaction" (Baumol, 1965: 2–48). Preferences are treated as in themselves neither good nor bad and they are aggregated among preference-satisfying individuals, who are themselves regarded as counting equally. Thus a preference for the music of Beethoven is not better than a preference for the "music" of LL Cool J. Nor are those who prefer Beethoven given more weight in welfare calculations than those who prefer LL Cool J. The "rational" aim of each private person is to maximize his or her own welfare and the aim of public policy is to maximize aggregate welfare, from the point of view of the contemporary utilitarian school.

Aggregate preference satisfaction or total welfare may, however, in some circumstances, be maximized at an extreme cost to a few individuals. One example might be slavery. The aggregate welfare of a pre-industrial slave-owning society may be greater than that of a pre-industrial egalitarian society. Ancient Athenian society might be a case in point. If so, no self-consistent utilitarian argument can be deployed against the institution of slavery. Amartya Sen's example is torture (1982: 344–51). It seems to me that the best example is gladiator shows. Thousands of Romans took great satisfaction in watching a few people fight to the death in the Colosseum and similar arenas (Kyle, 1998). The modest but significant welfare gain of a gladiatorial spectator multiplied by forty or fifty thousand might well outweigh the extreme welfare loss of a vanquished gladiatorial contestant multiplied by only five or ten. The Kantian conceptual constellation of intrinsic value, dignity, and rights counters the potentially repugnant outcome of the unbridled utilitarian welfare calculus.

According to Kant, rationality is the sole intrinsic-value-conferring property. And, although he held open the possibility that there may be other rational beings in the universe, human beings were the only rational beings of which he was aware. Thus human beings and various aspects of human being were, until recently, the only entities accorded intrinsic value, dignity, and rights in Western moral culture. The clearest and most unambiguous effect of the recognition of the intrinsic value, dignity, and rights of human beings is to make a market in human beings illegal and to prohibit such things as gladiator shows in which the lives of some human beings are sacrificed for the entertainment of others (Sawyer, 1986). As to aspects of human being, legally prohibiting prostitution and some mind-altering drugs suggests that human sexuality and chemically unaltered states of human consciousness are also accorded – by whom and how I will shortly explain – a dignity and intrinsic value (Decker, 1979; Inciardi, 1986). With the advent of organ-transplant techniques, a market in human organs is now prohibited in the United States and many other Western countries (Rothman et al., 1997).

Proposals to accord intrinsic value, dignity, and rights to various nonhuman beings dominate the animal liberation, animal rights, and environmental ethics literature. To argue that some nonhuman animals (such as primates and cetaceans) are rational – and thus should be accorded intrinsic value, dignity, and rights – least departs from the original Kantian paradigm.[3] To argue that some other intrinsic-value-conferring property should be substituted for rationality preserves the structure of Kant's ethic, but alters, to one degree or another, its content. Salient among the various substitutes that have been proposed are being a "subject of a life," being "sentient," being a "teleological center of life," having a good of one's own, and having interests (Goodpaster, 1978; Regan, 1983; Singer, 1977; Taylor, 1986; Varner, 1998). Some of these proposals have had limited success in making their way into public policy. While there are still robust markets in animals – everything from livestock markets to puppy mills to the zoo trade – the increasing body of law governing the humane treatment and care of animals in agriculture, biomedical research, and rodeos suggest that pleas for animal liberation and animal rights have had some measurable effect on public policy (Cohen, 2000). ESA is outstanding in this regard for two reasons. First, it accords listed species robust legal rights, as here noted. Second, the theoretical justification of such rights is less well developed than the theoretical justification of animal rights (Callicott, 1986: 138–72). There has been no success in translating into law or regulation the claim that *individual* plants and other subsentient organisms – except for specimens of listed endangered species – have intrinsic value.

It should be immediately clear why the ethical concept of intrinsic value should not be conflated with the economic concept of existence value, as some economists propose (Aldred, 1994). Existence value is a personal preference. Some people would, for example, prefer that black-footed ferrets remain in existence rather than suffer extinction (Vargas et al., 1966). This kind of preference, as any other, may be expressed in the monetary metric, either by contingent valuation (asking respondents how much they would be willing to pay to keep black-footed ferrets in existence), or by esti-mating what fraction of the total monetary support donated to such organizations as Defenders of Wildlife might be fairly allocated to black-footed ferrets (Aldred, 1994). To accord something intrinsic value, on the other hand, is to declare that it has a dignity and that it should not be subject to pricing of any kind, shadow or otherwise.

There is another, more intuitive, way of highlighting the difference between intrin-sic and existence value. In modern Western moral culture human beings are recog-nized to have intrinsic value. But for each of us only our respective family members, friends, neighbors, colleagues, and acquaintances have measurable existence value. How much would you be willing to pay to assure the existence of your next-door neighbor? I would personally be willing to pay all the money I could get my hands on to preserve my son (my only child), if his existence were threatened or endan-gered. Understandably, most readers of this chapter would – if they were entirely honest – be willing to pay a great deal less to assure the existence of *my* son. And when one factors in consideration of every other mother's son, the existence value that one can honestly set on individual human beings to whom one is unrelated and with whom one is unacquainted shrinks to infinitesimal amounts. (I can get my hands on only so much money and there are more than six billion human beings in exis-tence. So what honest answer could I give if I were asked how much I would be willing to pay to preserve the existence of an individual whom I've never met?) On the other hand, all human beings have intrinsic value and all have it equally in modern Western moral culture, as reflected in the concept of universal human rights (which was formally endorsed by the United Nations in 1948) and the US Constitution's Four-teenth Amendment provisions for equal protection under the law. But the existence value of any given human being varies wildly with circumstances. For example, the existence value of the scion of a very wealthy family may approach a billion dollars; that of a street urchin in Rio de Janeiro may approach zero. To conflate existence and intrinsic value is to think like a kidnapper, rather than as a member of Kant's idyllic Kingdom of Ends.

The Dual Democracy of Value Objectification: The Market and the Legislature

The domain in which our instrumental values are appropriately expressed is the market. As noted, the market is not perfectly efficient, in part because all the things we value instrumentally are not routinely bought and sold and thus do not have actual prices. And, also as noted, to partially correct such imperfections of the market, the

J. Baird Callicott

things we value instrumentally that are not traded are valued by industrious econo-mists in the monetary metric less directly – shadow priced – for purposes of com-parison and rational choice. The market, despite its imperfections, is, on the whole, quite democratic. People "vote," as it were, with their dollars (or units of other cur-rency) for such things as McDonald's fast food and Coca Cola. Those things for which people do not "vote" in the market soon disappear. Infamous examples are Edsel auto-mobiles and Beta videotape cassette players. When we look around ourselves we can literally see the democratic common denominator of aggregated individual prefer-ences in contemporary society (massaged of course in myriad ways by advertising): the world of fast-food chain stores, strip malls, gas-guzzling SUVs, cell phones, lite beer, Wal-Mart Superstores, and so on and so forth.

According to Mark Sagoff (1988), the appropriate democratic domain for the expression of our non-instrumental values is the legislature – in the United States, the bicameral Congress at the federal level of government, often similarly bicameral legislatures at the state level, and city councils at the municipal level of government. Both our instrumental and our non-instrumental values are arguably subjective. Cer-tainly, preferences – such as the preference for Coca Cola over RC Cola – are incon-testably subjective. The market and its surrogates, however, serve in a way to objectify preferences. Aggregate consumer preferences are quite literally objectified in the form of the fast-food chain stores, strip malls, gas-guzzling SUVs, cell phones, lite beer, Wal-Mart Superstores, and so on and so forth that we see everywhere around us. It would seem that the belief that some things have intrinsic value while others do not is also subjective. Certainly, differences of opinion about what has intrinsic value and what does not are easy to find, but difficult to resolve by any evidentiary hearing or peer review as disputed findings of fact and scientific discoveries are resolved. Some people – members of People for the Ethical Treatment of Animals, for example – believe that many kinds of individual animals have intrinsic value, while other people (who are still in the great majority) do not. Analogous to the way the market objec-tifies preferences, we may think of legislatures as objectifying non-instrumental values. Thus, in contemporary Western democratic societies the intrinsic value accorded human beings and certain aspects of human beings is legislatively objecti-fied by laws prohibiting murder, slavery, other forms of human trafficking, prostitu-tion, and the selling of human organs. Many other non-instrumental values that are objectified by legislation (or are so fundamental as to be institutionalized in the US Constitution) orbit the intrinsic value of human beings – freedom of expression, for example, property rights, and the right to privacy.

That preferences are not the same as moral values is indicated by the different way in which each is objectified. Preferences are objectified through aggregate choice. Moral values are objectified through public debate. Legalized segregation and racial discrimination in the South were not abandoned because they were no longer pre-ferred by a majority of Americans. (Indeed, the persistence of de facto segregation and racial discrimination suggests that they are still preferred by a majority of Amer-icans). Rather, we democratically decide to objectify – through legislation (and some-times through subsequent judicial interpretation) – moral values on the basis of principle and argument from principle, irrespective of our preferences and often in defiance of our preferences. The wider extension of intrinsic value by legislation – to human fetuses, for example – is the subject of intense and often acrimonious public debate. Quite remarkably, the ESA objectifies the intrinsic value of listed endangered species. Listed endangered species are in effect awarded legal rights and their intrinsic value is implicitly recognized by the democratically elected Congress of the United States. In that special sense, the intrinsic value of listed endangered species has become objective.

A Suggested Metric for the Quantification of Intrinsic Value

Recognition of dual and parallel domains – the market and the legislature – for the democratic objectification of instrumental values on the one hand and intrinsic values on the other (and, more generally, all those moral values that orbit intrinsic value) suggests there might be dual and parallel metrics for the quantification of instrumental values opposed to intrinsic values (and, more generally, all those moral values that orbit intrinsic value). A common monetary metric, once more, enables us to compare the relative value of different kinds of instrumentally valuable things that are of unequal utility – the value of a car, for example, in comparison with the value of a house. But, once more, the monetary metric is inappropriate for quantifying intrinsic value – things, as Kant put it, which should have a dignity, not a price.

So what is an appropriate common metric for quantifying dignity? The question itself may seem impious until we reflect that, when democratically objectified by legislative fiat, intrinsic value, like utility, is not distributed equally. A human being has greater dignity, greater intrinsic value than do most mere aspects of human being – chemically unaltered states of human consciousness, for example, or sex. How do we know? Because the relative quantitative difference in the distribution of intrinsic value or dignity – as objectified democratically by legislative action – is reflected in the penalties and other social consequences for violating the legislation (or legislatively mandated regulations) protecting things whose intrinsic value or dignity is objectified democratically by legislative action (see table 1). The penalties for murder and kidnapping are quite severe. The penalties for prostitution or soliciting a prostitute are quite modest (although they are sometimes supplemented by the less direct social consequences of publishing the names of convicted prostitutes and their clients in the newspaper). The penalties for possessing prohibited mind-altering drugs – called "controlled substances" – are usually less severe than for trafficking in such drugs, but more severe than for trafficking in sex (except when sex traffic involves minors). Thus it appears that chemically unaltered states of human consciousness have a greater degree of democratically objectified dignity than does sex (among adults). Section 11(b)(1) of the ESA specifies a fine of not more than $50,000 and a prison term of not more than one year for "any person who knowingly violates any provision of this Act." The penalty metric for quantifying intrinsic value is far less sensitive than the monetary metric for quantifying instrumental value, but it does seem to reflect, however crudely, the inequality in the distribution of intrinsic value as it is recognized through legislative action.

J. Baird Callicott

Table 1: Sample federal crimes and associated penalties as a (crude) metric for quantifying intrinsic value (Legal Information Institute, 2003).

Federal crimes	Associated penalties
First-degree murder	Death, life in prison
Second-degree murder	10 years–life in prison
Voluntary manslaughter	10 years maximum prison + unspecific fine
Kidnapping	20 years maximum prison
Wholesale distribution of controlled substance	10 years–life prison + up to $4,000,000 fine
Retail distribution of controlled substance	4 years maximum prison + up to $30,000 fine
Simple possession of controlled substance	1 year prison maximum + $1000 fine
Trafficking in human organs	5 year prison maximum + $50,000 maximum fine
Prostitution (not a federal crime)	6 months and/or $500 fine (California)
Taking listed endangered species	1 year maximum prison and/or $50,000 maximum fine

How the Penalty Metric and the Monetary Metric Interact in the Real World

While Sagoff and others draw a sharp boundary between the market and legislative domains for the democratic expression and objectification of instrumental and non-instrumental values, respectively, such values necessarily interact in a single arena – the real world (Sagoff, 1988). Money influences legislation/regulation and legislation/regulation has an economic impact.

Notoriously, legislative action is subject to monetary manipulation. In the United States the most common and ubiquitous way in which it does so appears to be through the system of legal bribery of elected officials called campaign contributions (Corrado, 2000). Thus, the democratic objectification of changes in the popular perception of what should or should not be accorded some degree of intrinsic value and dignity may be thwarted by wealthy individuals and corporations whose interests might be adversely affected by such changes. For example, David Bengston and his associates find that popular values regarding the national forests are gradually sliding away from the instrumental and toward the intrinsic end of the value spectrum (Bengston and Zhi, 1997; Bengston et al., 1999). However, members of the US Senate and House of Representatives and the politically appointed heads of federal agencies seem more responsive to the interests of the timber, oil and gas, and grazing industries than to this shift in popular values (Sierra Club, 2003).

If a thing's intrinsic value is democratically objectified by legislative or regulative action, then it has an impact on the market and its monetary metric that sometimes varies proportionately to the strength of the signal it registers on the penalty metric. Often the intent of legislation recognizing the dignity of something is to place it beyond the pale of the free market, and thus to try to ensure that it has no price. This is obviously the intent of legislation prohibiting the sale of mind-altering drugs (controlled substances), sex, and human organs. One consequence of such legislation is to create a black market in which, however, prices are generally higher than in a free market. For example, the relatively severe penalties for the sale of marijuana and cocaine have wildly inflated their prices on the black market (Desimone and Farrelly,

2003). The relatively inconsequential penalties for the sale of sex (among adults) have not created much difference in its illegal and legal market price. In the absence of uniform legislation banning such sales, an international gray market in very pricey human organs has emerged (Rothman et al., 1997). Also, of course, there is an international black market in endangered species, and parts of endangered species, such as Bengal tiger bones and African elephant tusks (Stuart and Stuart, 1996; Woods, 1996).

In a spirit of Kantian ethics and in the name of judicial restraint, the US Supreme Court decided in 1978 that the ESA provided the listed endangered species a dignity and utterly exempted them from valuation (by the federal courts, at least) on the monetary metric. When completion of the federally funded Tellico Dam in Tennessee – because it was then believed to threaten the snail darter with extinction – was stopped, the Court was "urged to view the Endangered Species Act 'reasonably,' and hence provide an interpretation 'that accords with some modicum of common sense and the public weal'" (*Tennessee Valley Authority* v. *Hill*, 1978). The majority opinion of Chief Justice Warren Burger found that the language of the ESA, Section 7, "admits of no exception," when it "affirmatively command[s] all federal agencies 'to insure that actions authorized, funded, or carried out by them do not jeopardize the continued existence' of an endangered species or 'result in the destruction or modification of the habitat of such species . . . '." Burger alludes more than once to the economic impact of this piece of federal legislation – its effect in the domain of the market. Strictly interpreted, the ESA "will produce results requiring *the sacrifice of the anticipated benefits of the project and of many millions of dollars* in public funds. . . ." And although

> the burden on the public through the loss of millions of unrecoverable dollars would [seem to] greatly outweigh the loss of the snail darter . . . *neither the Endangered Species Act nor Article III of the Constitution provides federal courts with authority to make such fine utilitarian calculations.* On the contrary, the plain language of the Act, buttressed by its legislative history, shows clearly that Congress viewed the value of endangered species as "incalculable." Quite obviously, it would be difficult for a court to balance the loss of a sum certain – even $100 million – against a congressionally declared "incalculable" value, even assuming we had the power to engage in such a weighing process, which we emphatically do not. (*Tennessee Valley Authority* v. *Hill*, 1978; emphasis added)

Congress immediately responded to this high-court decision by amending the ESA – with Section 7(e) – to create a cabinet-level Endangered Species Committee (irreverently known as the God Squad) invested with the very power that the Supreme Court abjured. The Committee consists of the Secretary of Interior, who serves as chair, the Secretaries of Agriculture and the Army, the Administrators of the Environmental Protection Agency and the National Oceanic and Atmospheric Administration, the Chairman of the Council of Economic Advisors, and one person from each affected state, nominated by the governors of such states and appointed by the President. In addition to creating the God Squad, the ESA, as amended in 1978, included references to benefits and costs – albeit sparingly, such words being used only a half dozen times each and "benefit–cost" analysis only once.

J. Baird Callicott

The procedures the ESA mandates, by which the God Squad reviews applications for exemptions to the Act, illustrate another fundamental, but easily overlooked, way in which legislatively objectified intrinsic value affects instrumental values objectified by the market. Legislatively objectified intrinsic value shifts the burden of proof onto competing instrumental values. If a state or the federal government, for example, wants to seize an intrinsically valuable human being's real property under the right of eminent domain, the burden of proof is on the governmental entity to show that the aggregate utility of doing so is clearly in the public interest (Ackerman, 1978). Obviously, the burden of proof rests with a state or federal government that is threatening the life of an intrinsically valuable human being by prosecuting him or her for committing first-degree murder or some other capital crime. On the other hand, a landowner can dispose of specimens of non-listed plant species and many kinds of non-listed wildlife and fish – the intrinsic value of which has not been legislatively objectified – on his or her property in accordance with his or her preferences. But because the intrinsic value of listed endangered species has been implicitly objectified, any application for an exemption to the ESA's provisions is certainly not regarded as prima facie worthy of such granting, unless the Fish and Wildlife Service can prove that it should not be granted. On the contrary, the applicant for an exemption must demonstratively meet very stringent, multiple criteria. Among these is, as specified in Section 7(h)(2), the necessity to show that "the benefits of any such action [that would violate any provisions of the Act] clearly outweigh the benefits of alternative courses of action consistent with conserving the species or its critical habitat." Moreover, the benefits at stake must not be merely private profit; the applicant must also demonstrate that "such action is in the public interest." Warwick Fox has identified and clearly explained the burden-of-proof-shifting effect of legislatively objectifying intrinsic value (Fox, 1993: 101).

Some economists, as noted, seem to deplore the concept of intrinsic value and wish to reduce it to existence value (Aldred, 1994). One might speculate that this is precisely because intrinsic value is not amenable to measurement by means of the monetary metric (Broome, 1991). And if some values were not measurable by means of the monetary metric, the totalizing ambitions of some economists would be thwarted. Fortunately, there is a familiar – albeit somewhat controversial – economic analog to the burden-of-proof-shifting pragmatic effect of legislatively objectified intrinsic value: the Safe Minimum Standard (SMS). Perhaps not so coincidentally, the SMS concept appears to have been first applied to the economic conundrum of endangered species conservation in 1978 (Bishop, 1978).

Standard benefit-cost analysis (BCA) applied to endangered species conservation compares the benefits of a listed endangered species with the benefits of some alternative use of such a species' critical habitat, both expressed in the monetary metric. As noted, on a species-by-species basis, the results of BCA will often conflict with the provisions of ESA. SMS assumes, to the contrary, consistent with ESA, that the benefits of nonhuman species are incalculable. They are not "incalculable" in the figurative sense of infinite, but literally incalculable. That is, how they may collectively be of benefit (to us human beings) is far less amenable to accurate measurement – calculation – than is the benefit of a dam or a shopping mall. According to Alan Randall: "The SMS approach starts with the presumption that the maintenance of the

SMS for any species is a positive good. The empirical economic question is ... How high are the opportunity costs of satisfying the SMS? The decision rule is to maintain the SMS unless the opportunity costs of so doing are intolerably high?" (Randall, 1988: 221). But how high is intolerably high? That's what the God Squad was charged to determine. "In other words," Randall continues, "the SMS approach asks, how much will we lose in other domains of human concern by achieving a safe minimum standard of biodiversity? *The burden of proof is assigned to the case against maintaining the SMS*" (Randall, 1988: 221; emphasis added).

Because the practical outcome is the same – the burden of proof is assigned to the case against preserving listed endangered species – the SMS approach is pragmatically equivalent to recognizing the intrinsic value and legal rights of listed endangered species. Those economists for whom the concept of intrinsic value is anathema may thus resort to the pragmatically equivalent SMS approach for purposes of policy formation without making any alterations in their neo-utilitarian notions of value – and without incorrectly reducing intrinsic value to existence value. We may regard this as an alternative Convergence Hypothesis. Clearly, contrary to Norton, instrumentally valuing nature and intrinsically valuing nature do not converge on the same policy, as the case of the ESA proves. On the other hand, the SMS economistic approach to biodiversity conservation converges on the same public policy as the legislative/regulative approach based – whether implicitly or explicitly – on intrinsic value and rights.

Finally, the intrinsic value of listed endangered species, implicitly accorded to them by the ESA, has created an emerging new legal market in conservation credits. For example, International Paper's habitat conservation plan for the red-cockaded woodpeckers in its forest holdings includes provisions for it to sell conservation credits to other private owners of red-cockaded woodpecker habitat. Under the terms of the agreement, IP will dedicate 1,300 acres (eventually expanding to 5,000 acres) to intensive management of red-cockaded woodpecker habitat. Intensive management includes burning the under-story of longleaf pine forests to clear encroaching hardwoods, allowing the pines to reach old-growth ages, and boring out artificial nest cavities (Environmental Defense, 2003). On those acres of prime habitat, IP will consolidate its total of 18 nesting "clusters" of red-cockaded woodpeckers. Some of these are found on other of its holdings – which it may, by agreement, then log without violating the ESA. As red-cockaded woodpecker nesting clusters rise to more than 18 on the consolidated IP-owned habitat, IP may sell red-cockaded woodpecker conservation credits to other private landowners who may then log their red cockaded woodpecker habitat without violating the ESA. As the February 19, 1999 US Fish and Wildlife press release stated:

> This plan also marks the establishment of the first mitigation bank for endangered species created in the Southeast on private land. *This concept enables International Paper to increase its red-cockaded woodpecker population by assuming red-cockaded woodpecker mitigation responsibilities of other landowners who desire timely land management flexibility at market-driven rates.* (US Fish and Wildlife Service, 1999)

J. Baird Callicott

A Precarious Future for ESA?

The Endangered Species Act may itself be endangered in the political climate of the late twentieth and early twenty-first centuries. A 1992 Supreme Court decision, *Lujan* v. *Defenders* (1992), potentially undercuts one criterion, as specified by Stone, of the operational legal rights and implicit intrinsic value that ESA accords listed threatened and endangered species – that of standing.

Defenders of Wildlife sued the Secretary of Interior to abandon a revised regulation – promulgated in 1983 by the Regan administration – exempting federally funded activities abroad from the provisions of ESA. The district court granted Secretary of Interior Hodel's motion to dismiss for lack of standing (*Defenders of Wildlife* v. *Hodel*, 1987). Defenders appealed to the Eighth Circuit court, which reversed. After all, ESA Section 11(g)(1) – the "citizen-suit" provision – plainly states that "any person may commence a civil suit" against the Secretary of the Interior to compel enforcement of the provisions of the Act. On further appeal by the Secretary, the case then went to the Supreme Court, and there, it seems, Defenders blundered. Instead of using the very well-known legal theory of Stone and the plain citizen-suit language of ESA to assert that it was not they but listed threatened and endangered species outside the United States who were the entities that would be liable to injury by the Hodel revision, they alleged that two members of Defenders – Joyce Kelly and Amy Skilbred, both conservation scientists – would be liable to injury. Putatively, Kelly's interest in making future observations of the Nile crocodile and Skilbred's in making future observations of the Asian elephant would be variously harmed by the new regulation. Opining for the majority, Justice Scalia argued that their alleged injuries do not rise to the level of standing as specified by Article III of the Constitution and numerous precedent cases. He did not even entertain the idea – doubtless because they had not advanced it – that it was endangered and threatened species themselves which had standing, and that Defenders of Wildlife was bringing suit not on behalf of its aggrieved members, but on behalf of such species. Justice Scalia, however, did not leave it at that. He effectively overturned ESA Section 11(g)(1) by means of fundamentalist constitutional interpretation:

> Vindicating the *public* interest (including the public interest in government observance of the Constitution and laws) is the function of Congress and the Chief Executive. The question presented here is whether the public interest in proper administration of the laws (specifically, in agencies' observance of a particular, statutorily prescribed procedure) can be converted into an individual right by a statute [ESA] that denominates it as such, and that permits all citizens (or, for that matter, a subclass of citizens who suffer no distinctive concrete harm) to sue. If the concrete injury requirement has the separation-of-powers significance we have always said, the answer must be obvious. (*Lujan* v. *Defenders*, 1992)

Ironically, as in *Tennessee Valley Authority* v. *Hill* (1978) – which affirmed and reinforced ESA – also in *Lujan* v. *Defenders* the decision was based on judicial restraint. In the former case, the Court refused to presume to calculate the "incalculable" value of an endangered species and weigh it against the benefits of a nearly completed dam. In the latter, the Court refused to protect the public interest, claiming that the Constitution only "established courts to adjudicate cases and controversies as to claims of infringement of individual rights whether by unlawful action of private persons or by the exertion of unauthorized administrative power" (*Lujan* v. *Defenders*, 1992). In sharp contrast, *TVA* v. *Hill* expressly states the following separation-of powers doctrine: "Once Congress, exercising its delegated powers, has decided the order of priorities in a given area, it is for the Executive to administer the laws and *for the courts to enforce them when enforcement is sought*" (1978; emphasis added).

TVA v. Hill represents ESA's high-water mark; *Lujan* v. *Defenders* effectively reversed the Court's earlier position on the power of the courts to enforce the laws enacted by Congress as well as nullified the powerful "citizen suit" provision of ESA – Section 11(g)(1). Nevertheless, citizen suits continued to be filed on behalf of endangered species under this section of the Act.[4] As of this writing, I do not know why the effect of the plain language of the majority opinion in Lujan has not prevented that happening.

While the overt language of the Act itself and that of *TVA* v. *Hill* is free of references to "rights" and "intrinsic value," deontological rhetoric occasionally bubbles to the surface in the latter. For example: "It is conceivable that the welfare of an endangered species may weigh more heavily upon the public conscience, as expressed by the final will of Congress, than the write-off of those millions of dollars already expended . . . for Tellico in excess of its present salvageable value" (*TVA* v. *Hill*, 1978). The loss of a potential natural resource, something of mere instrumental (option) value – something especially of as little potential utility as the snail darter – can be regrettable, but hardly a matter of *conscience*. And while the expert testimony before Congress quoted in *TVA* v. *Hill* focuses on the "incalculable" utility of threatened and endangered species, such rationales are characterized as "the most narrow possible point of view" – the non-anthropocentric point of view, presumably, being the more expansive one (*TVA* v. *Hill*, 1978). Further, while *TVA* v. *Hill* concludes, as noted, that "Congress was concerned about the unknown uses that endangered species might . . . have," it also goes on immediately to conclude that Congress was also concerned "about the unforeseeable place such creatures may have in the chain of life on this planet." That may simply express a risk-averse utilitarian concern for potential ecological services parallel to a risk-averse utilitarian concern for potential ecological goods – that is, natural resources. But it may, on the other hand, express a non-instrumental ecocentric concern for biodiversity and ecological integrity. In *Lujan* v. *Defenders*, in any case, there is no hint of concern of any sort for endangered species and Justice Scalia can barely conceal his contempt for the concerns for them evinced by Joyce Kelly and Amy Skilbred.

To quote once again the words of Christopher Stone, when legislation such as ESA creates "a legally recognized worth and dignity in its own right [for an entity], and not merely to serve as means to benefit '*us*' (whoever the contemporary group of rights holders may be)" (Stone, 1972: 458), then "*we*" (the contemporary group of rights holders) may come to resent it. ESA in effect created a legally recognized worth and dignity in its own right for each listed species by stealth – because the

J. Baird Callicott

discourse of intrinsic value, dignity, and rights does not appear in the Act. But when first tested in the courts, *TVA* v. *Hill* showed the effects to be the same. I am not sure what it means to be "politically conservative," but it seems that at least part of what being politically conservative means is to resist and when possible to roll back attempts to expand the group of rights holders. A contemporary example would be the conservative resistance to expand marriage rights to gay and lesbian couples. A counter-example might be the conservative zeal to expand the group of rights holders to include fetuses. But a more cynical interpretation would view the conservative zeal to expand the group of rights holders to include fetuses as only a ruse to roll back the rights of women to reproductive freedom and restore the patriarchal rights men once enjoyed to control women's sexuality. We should not then be surprised to discover that a conservative Congress, Administration, and Judiciary would try to roll back the rights of listed endangered species provided them by ESA.

Notes

1 See the essays in *The Monist*, 75 (1992): 119–276.
2 For a good summary, see Wellman (1985).
3 See also Savage-Rumbaugh et al. (1998).
4 Kieran Suckling, personal communication.

References

Ackerman, Bruce (1978). *Private Property and the Constitution*. New Haven, CN: Yale University Press.
Aldred, Jonathan (1994). "Existence value, welfare, and altruism." *Environmental Values*, 3: 381–402.
Baumol, William J. (1965). *Welfare Economics and the Theory of the State*. Cambridge, MA: Harvard University Press.
Bengston, David N., Fan, David P., and Celarier, Doris (1999). "A new approach to monitoring the social environment for natural resource management: the case of US national forests benefits and values." *Journal of Environmental Management*, 56: 181–93.
Bengston, David N., and Zhi, Xu (1997). "Trends in national forest values among forestry professionals, environmentalists, and the news media, 1982–1993." *Society and Natural Resources*, 10: 43–59.
Bentham, Jeremy (1970). *Introduction to the Principles of Morals and Legislation*. Oxford: Clarendon Press.
Bishop, R. C. (1978). "Endangered species and uncertainty: the economics of a safe minimum standard." *American Journal of Agricultural Economics*, 60: 10–18.
Broome, John (1991). *Weighing Goods*. Oxford: Blackwell.
Callicott, J. Baird (1986). "On the intrinsic value of non-human species." In Bryan G. Norton (ed.), *The Preservation of Species* (pp. 138–72). Princeton: Princeton University Press.
Cohen, Henry (2000). "Federal animal protection statutes." *Animal Law*, 1: 143–53.
Corrado, Anthony (2000). *Campaign Finance Reform: Beyond the Basics*. Washington, DC: The Century Foundation.

Decker, John F. (1979). *Prostitution: Regulation and Control*. Littleton, CO: F. B. Rothman.

Defenders of Wildlife v. *Hodel* (1987). 658 F.Supp. 43, 47–48 (Minn.).

Desimone, Jeff, and Farrelly, Matthew, C. (2003). "Price and enforcement effects on marijuana and cocaine demand." *Economic Inquiry*, 41: 98–115.

Ehrenfeld, David (1988). "Why put a value of biodiversity?" In E. O. Wilson (ed.), *Biodiversity* (pp. 212–16). Washington: National Academy Press.

Environmental Defense (2003). Red-cockaded woodpecker conservation bank (2/24/03). ⟨http://www.environmentaldefense.org/article.cfm?ContentID=2664⟩ (accessed October 2003).

Fox, Warwick. (1993). "What does the recognition of intrinsic value entail?" *Trumpeter*, 10/3: 101.

Freeman III, A. Myrick (1993). *The Measurement of Environmental and Resource Values: Theory and Methods*. Washington, DC: Resources for the Future.

Hargrove, Eugene C. (2000). "Toward teaching environmental ethics: exploring problems in the language of evolving social values." *Canadian Journal of Environmental Education*, 5: 1–20.

Goodpaster, Kenneth E. (1978). On being morally considerable." *Journal of Philosophy*, 75: 308–25.

Inciardi, James K. (1986). *The War On Drugs: Heroin, Cocaine, Crime, and Public Policy*. Palo Alto, CA: Mayfield.

Kant, Immanuel (1959[1785]). *Foundations of the Metaphysics of Morals*, trans. Lewis White Beck. New York: Bobbs Merrill.

Kyle, Donald, G. (1998). *Spectacles of Death in Ancient Rome*. New York: Routledge.

Legal Information Institute (2003). ⟨http://www.law.cornell.edu/statutes.html⟩ (accessed October 2003).

Lujan v. *Defenders* (1992). *Lujan, Secretary of the Interior*, v. *Defenders of Wildlife et al*. US Supreme Court No. 90–1424. 504 US 505.

Mill, John Stuart (1863). *Utilitarianism*. London: Longmans.

Norris, Diana, Phelps, Norm, and Schubert, D. J. (2001). *Canned Hunts: The Newest American "Sport."* Silver Springs, MD: Fund For Animals.

Norton, Bryan (1991). *Toward Unity Among Environmentalists*. Oxford: Oxford University Press.

Pister, Edwin P. (1987). "A pilgrim's progress from group A to group B." In J. Baird Callicott (ed.), *Companion to a Sand County Almanac* (pp. 221–32). Madison: University of Wisconsin Press.

Pister, Edwin P. (1985). "Desert pup fishes: reflections on reality, desirability, and conscience." *Environmental Biology of Fishes*, 12: 3–12.

Power, M. E., Tilman, D., Estes, J. A., Menge, B. A., Bond, W. J., Mills, L. S., Gretchen, D., Castilla, J. C., Lubchenco, J., and Paine, R. T. (1996). "Challenges in the quest for keystones." *BioScience*, 46: 609–20.

Randall, Alan (1988). "What mainstream economists have to say about the value of biodiversity." In E. O. Wilson (ed.), *Biodiversity* (pp. 217–23). Washington, DC: National Academy Press.

Rawls, John (1971). *A Theory of Justice*. Cambridge, MA: Belknap Press.

Regan, Tom (1983). *The Case for Animal Rights*. Berkeley, CA: University of California Press.

Rothman, D. J. et al. (1997). "Bellagio task force report on transplantation, bodily integrity, and the international traffic in organs." *Transplantation Proceedings*, 29: 2739–45.

Sagoff, Mark (1988). *The Economy of the Earth: Philosophy, Law, and the Environment*. Cambridge: Cambridge University Press.

Savage-Rumbaugh, S., Shanker, S. G., and Taylor, T. J. (1998). *Kanzi: The Ape at the Brink of the Human Mind*. New York: Oxford University Press.

J. Baird Callicott

Sawyer, Roger (1986). *Slavery in the Twentieth Century*. London: Routledge and Kegan Paul.

Sen, Amartya (1982). "Approaches to the choice of discount rates for social benefit-cost analysis." In R. Lind (ed.), *Discounting for Time and Risk in Energy Policy* (pp. 325–53). Washington, DC: Resources for the Future.

Sierra Club (2003). "Dirty money equals forest destruction." ⟨http://www.sierraclub.org/politics/clean_elections/logging.asp⟩ (accessed October, 2003).

Singer, Peter (1977). *Animal Liberation: A New Ethics For Our Treatment of Animals*. New York: Avon.

Stone, Christopher D. (1972). "Should trees have standing?: toward legal rights for natural objects." *Southern California Law Review*, 45: 450–501.

Stuart, Chris and Stuart, Tilde (1996). *Africa's Vanishing Wildlife*. Washington, DC, Smithsonian Institution Press.

Taylor, Paul W. (1986). *Respect for Nature: A Theory of Environmental Ethics*. Princeton: Princeton University Press.

Tennessee Valley Authority v. *Hill* (1978). 437 US 153.

US Code (1973). Endangered Species Act. 16 USC 1531–1544: ⟨http://epw.senate.gov/esa73.pdf⟩.

US Fish and Wildlife Service (1999). "US Fish and Wildlife Service approves International Paper's red-cockaded woodpecker habitat conservation plan." Press release February 19, 1999: ⟨http://southeast.fws.gov/news/1999/r99-021.html⟩.

Van Blaricom, G. R. and Estes, J. A. (1988). *The Community Ecology of Sea Otters*. New York: Springer-Verlag,

Vargas, A. M., Lockhart, P., Marinari, P., and Gober, P. (1966). "The reintroduction process: black-footed ferrets as a case study." *Proceedings: American Zoo and Aquarium Association Western Regional Conference*, May 15–19: 829–34.

Varner, Gary (1998). *In Nature's Interests*. New York: Oxford University Press.

Wellman, Carl (1985). *Theories of Rights*. Totowa, NJ: Rowman and Allanheld.

Woods, Michael (1996). "Tiger economics." *Geographical Magazine*, 69: 38.

Further reading

Costanza, Robert, et al. (1997). "The value of the world's ecosystem services and natural capital." *Nature*, 387: 253–60.

Values in Nature:
A Pluralistic Approach

Bryan G. Norton

Introduction: Theories of Value and the Value of Theories

Everybody values nature in some way, and most of us value nature in many ways. The agriculturalist values nature, however implicitly, as a source of genetic diversity for crops, and for the provision of nutrients to grow them. The hunter-gatherer uses natural products more directly, and choosing to take and use these products indicates expected value. As populations have moved to urban areas, natural places have gained value as refuges from the chaotic and pressured lives of urban dwellers. So, there is no question, speaking thus loosely, that nature has value to human beings, and that nature and natural systems are valued, and produce values of many types for humans.

Accordingly, the topic of this exchange, "values in nature," has a deceptively simple ring to it, seeming to invite respondents to list and explain the various values attributable to nature, and perhaps to provide a useful taxonomy of types of natural value. Indeed, the literature is replete with studies that, from some point of view or another, provide careful and well-thought-out categorizations of natural values. The problem is that these categorizations are expressed in many different disciplinary tongues, and often articulated in incommensurable vernaculars.

In fact, one cannot even begin to list, definitively, the types of value that nature has, until we first adopt a theory of value. Values are not the kind of thing we find pre-packaged and countable; the way we think about values is thus deeply affected by the theory of value we assume or choose. So, I begin by questioning whether the topic at hand can be answered simply by reference to a few categories or types of environmental and natural values. When environmental values are identified and measured within the framework of a theory, using the technical vocabulary of that theory to express those values, it is inevitable that the assumptions of the theory will implicitly limit and shape our thinking about those values.

In order to avoid unthinking commitments regarding the nature of environmental values, accordingly, I will begin my discussion with as few assumptions as possible, and with a brief discussion, in the next section, of the types of value theories in which environmental ethicists have expressed environmental values. Before proceeding to that step, however, I will complete this introduction by listing and explaining three broad types of criteria by which one might judge proposed theories of value. In the process, we can briefly introduce some of the controversies that have predictably occurred because various writers on the value of nature have emphasized different criteria, and have held different expectations in choosing and defending theories of value to apply to nature. In my final section, it will be possible to address the question of what values nature "has," and how best to talk about them.

Many writers in environmental ethics and related fields write as if environmental values can be readily observed. If, however, I am correct that environmental values are always filtered through a specific theory of value – that they can only be understood within the context of theoretical assumptions – then it is reasonable to take a step backwards and ask, "What can we expect of a theory of environmental value?" I suggest that environmental theorists, at least implicitly, choose a theory of environmental values in response to three general types of expectation – expectations that might result in criteria by which theories can be justified and explained. I will refer to these expectations as: (1) metaphysical expectations, (2) epistemological expectations, and (3) practical considerations.

Metaphysics and values

Many authors in environmental ethics apparently believe that a theory of environmental value should, above all else, resolve metaphysical disputes so as to place discourse about environmental values on a firm, metaphysical foundation. Interestingly, however, metaphysical reasoning can be either conservative or more radical. For example, John Passmore, author of the first book-length study of environmental ethics, argued for a human-centered, utilitarian approach to valuing nature, because this theory would square with the dominant worldview/metaphysics of Western thought, and requires no major shift in worldview and core ethical beliefs of the culture (Passmore, 1974: 101–26).

Today, however, philosophers, self-described "radical" environmental ethicists, calling themselves "biocentrists," or "ecocentrists," argue that – since current treatment of nature is unacceptable – we need a metaphysical revolution that will provide a new conceptualization of the human–nature relationship. For example, J. Baird Callicott, in an essay entitled "The Metaphysical Foundations of Ecology," states: "A consolidated metaphysical consensus thus appears to be emerging presently from twentieth-century science which may at last supplant the metaphysical consensus distilled from the scientific paradigm of the seventeenth century" (Callicott, 1989: 102). Passmore and Callicott, in their own ways, exemplify metaphysical approaches to environmental values – emphasizing the metaphysical expectation that a theory of value will clarify basic relationships between humans and nature. They differ only in that Passmore, committed to the traditional, human-centered view, takes human well-being to be the measure of value, and denies the need and the wisdom of a radical shift to a non-anthropocentric system of value. Callicott, on the other hand, embraces a radical shift, substituting a new, more holistic metaphysics and a new, more holistic and ecocentric ethic.

Whether one's appeal to metaphysics is conservative or radical, the implication is that an important aspect of understanding environmental values is to make these values "fit" into an acceptable, and deep, conception of the world – a metaphysic or a "worldview." What is of course problematic is whether one can, independently, decide what our metaphysical views "should" be (in order to derive from them an appropriate theory of value), or whether, alternatively, one should get one's values "right," and then choose a metaphysic to support them. Despite this bewildering quandary, many writers on environmental ethics have assumed that the key issue regarding environmental values is to associate one's theory of value with an appropriate metaphysical view of the world.

Epistemological considerations

When choosing a theory of values, on our way to developing a theory of *environmental* values, I – and many others – seek a theory that supports justification and reason-giving in deliberation about values. For both practical (see "Practical considerations" below) and theoretical reasons, it would seem that – other things being equal – we would prefer a theory of environmental values according to which at least some value statements can be verified and supported. Given that some form of a justificatory method seems necessary to generate any moral arguments, one would expect that most theorists of environmental values would insist that any theory they choose would make clear – or at least leave open – ways to justify or warrant value claims with some form of evidence. Nevertheless, theorists do place very different weight on epistemological criteria, and employ very different epistemological approaches to understanding and justifying value claims. Because of this latter problem, it may make sense to follow John Dewey, who eventually stopped talking about "truth," about "certainty," and about "justifications," preferring instead to insist on a minimal epistemological requirement: our theory of value should at least allow "warranted assertability" of value claims by offering progressively more experiential – in the best case, experimental – evidence to support them.

Practical considerations

Turning away from theoretical considerations, it is also important to evaluate a theory of environmental values for its practical impacts. Any theory of environmental values that passes the minimal and warranted assertability test mentioned above will have an important practical advantage over more subjectivist theories of value: activists must feel free to argue that their proposed policies are morally obligatory, a type of epistemological status that cannot be achieved within a purely subjectivist theory of value.

One might also judge a theory of value to be useful if that theory allows quantification, or other clear forms of measurement, so that values can be compared

Bryan G. Norton

– quantitatively, if possible – as communities discuss their goals and objectives for environmental management. Theories and models of economics, for example, have been favored in environmental policy analysis because they promise to provide an analysis of the costs and the benefits associated with protection of elements of nature. On this point, I agree with Callicott, who in chapter 19 in this volume argues that there are many important values that are not easily or accurately quantified as economic values. It is important that we not over-emphasize the measurable at the expense of the essential, and Callicott rightly argues that economic analysis fails to capture the full range of values attributed by humans. Later, it will be seen that I disagree with Callicott about how to (theoretically) characterize these "non-economic" values, but on the most important point – that the techniques available to environmental economists are not "complete" over the range of values humans attribute to nature – we are in complete agreement. If, however, we reject the economic framework of costs and benefits as incapable of providing comprehensive reasons for protection of nature, the question remains: what kinds of argument/reason – appeals to what values – can be offered to support policies for protecting nature?

There is another important aspect to evaluating the usefulness of theories of environmental value, one that may be underrated in current discussions. Theories of environmental value, and the languages associated with them, can either encourage or hinder dialogue, dispute resolution, and achievement of cooperative action. So, in evaluating theories of environmental value, it is also useful to assess the impact of adopting a given theory on the quality and effectiveness of environmental discourse it supports and encourages.

These three types of consideration – metaphysical, epistemological, and practical – can be deployed to explain and justify proposed theories of value and the application of these theories to natural values more generally. Since its beginning in the early 1970s, the field of environmental ethics has emphasized metaphysical considerations in proposing and defending theories of natural value. As noted, philosophers as disparate as Passmore and Callicott have used metaphysical or "worldview" arguments as guidance determinative of value theories; more recently, a group of philosophers sometimes referred to as "environmental pragmatists" – among whom I would count myself – have emphasized practical criteria in choosing a theory of environmental value. This change in emphasis reflects a shift from thinking of natural values as abstractions to thinking of values as the driving force in an action-oriented science of environmental management. Pragmatism also reflects a shift from a tendency toward "monism," the view that a single rule, principle, or theory will govern all cases, dictating a single environmental policy as "rational" and "moral" in all situations (Stone, 1987: 116). Instead, pragmatism leans toward a more pluralistic approach to understanding natural values as diverse and in need of balancing in particular situations.

Instrumental versus Intrinsic Values

Many environmental ethicists draw and emphasize a distinction between "instrumental" and "intrinsic" values, and take instrumental values derived from nature to be uncontroversial – who could deny that humans enjoy utilitarian benefits from use of, and interactions with, natural systems, their products and processes?[1] On this distinction, it is posited that objects can be valued either for the ends of another being – as when the worm is of nutritional value to the robin or the tree in my back yard is used to mount a basketball hoop – or they can be valued "in themselves" – in which case the valued object can end the chain of instrumental valuations because the fulfillment of the object's needs or desires is considered a good in itself. Given the non-controversial nature of instrumental values to humans, much writing in the field of environmental ethics – dominated by the instrumental/intrinsic distinction – has focused on the latter type of values, asking: "Do elements or processes of nature have, in addition to instrumental value to humans, intrinsic value – value that exists independently of humans and their motives?" This question, in turn, gives rise to the controversy, noted above, between conservative and radical valuers of nature, and to a number of other controversies.

I believe this distinction between instrumental and intrinsic values raises more problems than it resolves because it can only be understood in light of the value theory one uses to interpret it. If, like Rolston III, one believes that values are "objective," then adoption of the view that nature has intrinsic value is a discovery by a few people that there are values in nature inherent in nonhuman objects or processes, and independent of our attributions (1987: 91–117). Further, these values will be thought to confer upon their owners "moral considerability," and hence these values, exerting moral force, motivate morally obligatory actions to protect those elements of nature that have human-independent values.[2] Rolston, for example, speaks of nature as "a value-generating system able to generate value" (1994: 195). On this theory of environmental values, which we can call "strong intrinsic value theory," nature is understood to have value in its own right, value that is both discoverable and capable of projecting moral force. This human-independent value places limits on acceptable human behaviors from outside the realm of human values, much as God's will and law limited human behavior in less secular societies of the past. On Rolston's view, these intrinsic natural values serve as a counterpoise to human preferences and demands, placing limits on human consumption and disruption of the natural world.

If, however, this distinction is coupled with – or, rather, is "expressed in" – a subjectivist theory of value (the view that all value requires a valuer and that all value, including intrinsic value, is normally attributed to nature by humans), then the attribution of intrinsic value to nature simply adds to uncontroversial instrumental values another type of human value. Callicott believes we are going through a metaphysical/worldview change, and that, subsequent to this change, most humans will attribute intrinsic value to nature. On the subjectivist theory of human value, however, attributions of intrinsic value describe a way that humans value things, and do not represent a non-relational characteristic of the objects themselves. If, at a given time, no valuing agent values object x intrinsically, then x has no intrinsic value at that time. If, later, at least one person comes to value x intrinsically, then the object is said to have intrinsic value; but of course, if all persons who so value the object stop valuing it in this way at some future date, then the object would, apparently, lose its status as an "intrinsically" valued entity.

302　Bryan G. Norton

Callicott's explanation of the nature of this attribution has changed somewhat over the years. At one time, he likened intrinsic valuing of nature to the way parents value their children, and asserted that such values are "inherent" in the object in the sense that they are "virtual in nature actualized upon interaction with consciousness" (2002: 169–70).[3] On this view, one might be tempted to say that, at those times when nobody values object x intrinsically, it is a failing of humans: they have not actualized a potentiality in natural objects and that to fail to do so would be unreasonable or wrong. Willingness to make such a claim seems essential to the goal Callicott set for his philosophical work in the 1980s, describing his work as "an attempt to outline an environmental ethic according to which it would be clearly and indisputably wrong" for humans to destroy nature (1989: 64). More recently, however, Callicott has further weakened the connection between attributions of intrinsic value and the inherent characteristics of the objects valued, arguing that "it is logically possible to value intrinsically anything under the sun – an old worn out shoe, for example," emphasizing that intrinsic valuing is a function of what an individual valuer chooses to value, not a function of, or related to, the "virtual" characteristics of the objects in question (2002: 10).

It is difficult to overemphasize the importance of the theoretical differences between strong and weak intrinsic value attributions. The strong–weak ambiguity, here exemplified by the disagreements between Rolston and Callicott, has huge epistemological implications that affect the role that intrinsic values and attributions of them can play in environmental policy discourse. Rolston's strong theoretical view has the advantage that attribution of intrinsic value to any element of nature apparently provides, in and of itself, a rational, moral reason for protecting it, implying that everyone is morally obliged to act on its behalf. Since this reason is based on the objective characteristics of the natural object, and not upon a hypothetical human attribution, Rolston can claim to offer "objective" reasons for protecting nonhuman species from extinction and for morally blaming *anyone* who fails to act to do so.

On this strong view, the Endangered Species Act simply codified and added sanctions to back up rationally based, pre-existing, moral law. Rolston's strong view of intrinsic value, if accepted, allows environmentalists to claim objective reasons to back up the policies they advocate, and it gives an almost theological bite to the law. By contrast, in this volume (chapter 19), Callicott asserts: "Listed endangered species are in effect awarded legal rights and their intrinsic value is implicitly recognized by the democratically elected Congress of the United States. In that special sense, the intrinsic value of listed endangered species has become objective" (2005: 288). Notice that, on Callicott's theory, saying that the intrinsic value of nonhuman species is "implicitly recognized" is really no different from saying such value is "created" by the legislation. It is the act of the legislature that creates the value, and using the term "recognized" is misleading.

The difference is enormous. On Rolston's sense of "recognize," there is a prior moral law that "justifies" the action of the legislature and *demands* recognition. "Recognition" in Callicott's sense, on the other hand, is morally hollow: it is created *ex nihilo* by the subjective feelings of congressional representatives as they vote. If one disagrees with the legislature's action, one will, surely, also reject the law as bad law, representing not a moral prescription but an immoral imposition. Callicott's appeal to

Values in Nature: A Pluralistic Approach

intrinsic values may explain and encourage the behaviors and linguistic expressions of a small band of "radical" environmentalists, and it may provide one expression of the tendency, shared by Callicott and me, to argue against the completeness of economics. Callicott's subjectivist theory of value, however, scores very low on the criterion of moral supportability, a point to which I return below.

Unfortunately, Rolston's stronger approach suffers two serious flaws. A theoretical flaw is connected directly to its attractiveness to activists who wish to assert a strong, moral obligation to protect the environment. The moral strength they gain by adopting strong, Rolstonian intrinsic value objectively attributed to nature rests on a highly questionable notion of objectivity and on strong epistemological assumptions that are difficult to defend philosophically. Rolstonians thus face a dilemma when challenged as to how they know the objective fact of intrinsic values in nature. If they claim that their evidence is mainly sensory, then how can they explain why others cannot "see" it? To say that the existence of intrinsic value is known, independent of any sensory experience, however, seems to commit the advocate to belief in self-evident, a priori truths of morality. If the existence of intrinsic value in nature is self-evident, why has it taken Westerners thousands of years to see that evidence? Again, Rolston's strong version cannot even explain, much less understand, the viewpoint of those who do not accept his central tenet of objective value (Rolston III, 1992: 226–8).[4]

Speaking more practically, I also think Rolston's approach is unlikely, ultimately, to be helpful in public discourse. To make strong, moralistic assumptions and then to enter public discourse speaking in a moral tone, trying to legally "enforce" moral strictures, is not a useful mindset with which to enter negotiations if one hopes to achieve compromise and cooperative action in protecting the environment. The strength Rolston offers eventually proves, thus, to be a weakness; adopting this strong stance in policy deliberation is likely to lead to polarization, not cooperation and compromise.

Callicott's weaker view of intrinsic value as an expression of subjective values, on the other hand, while apparently requiring a less implausible epistemological stance, can provide no moral arguments that can be expected to be persuasive to those who have not yet accepted the "radical" proposal that nature has intrinsic value. Since value, even intrinsic value, is subjective in nature deriving from individual feelings, no appeal to such values can serve as an argument to those who have not yet been converted to the new metaphysic of value. Appeal to intrinsic value in nature, understood within a subjectivist theory of value, provides no true moral imperative to back up value assertions or to ground actions in rational, debatable terms. To the extent that all value commitments toward nature are merely arbitrary and capricious "attributions," one can hardly expect them to be given much weight in rational debate about what to do and why. We might call this the "old shoe" effect, in honor of Callicott's illustration, mentioned above. If intrinsic values in nature have no more status than someone's attachment to a worn-out shoe, how could appeal to them have any effect on rational evaluators of environmental policies? Either one feels that nature has intrinsic value or one does not; if not, the subjectivist can only resort to rhetoric as a means to persuade others to change policies.

This subjectivist/objectivist disagreement among advocates of the intrinsic value theory, leading to two competing and incompatible understandings, represents only

Bryan G. Norton

one of many ambiguities that infects any notion of intrinsic value, once a sharp dichotomy between instrumental and intrinsic value is exposed to the range of extant theories of value. Advocates of intrinsic value in nature differ also in what they take the object of intrinsic value to be – individuals? species? ecosystems? communities? Unless some consensus emerges to questions like this, references to intrinsic value will not help to answer difficult questions (for example, those that involve invasive management of wildlife populations). This feature of intrinsic value theories causes them to score low on an important practical consideration: attributing intrinsic value to nature in general tells us very little about how to manage a system, which is composed of many complex parts that exist in competition and in symbioses with each other. When the manager turns to the advocates of intrinsic value for more specific guidance that might suggest priorities and discriminations, application of the theory is impossible because no consensus exists whether intrinsic value is instantiated in individuals, in species, or in ecosystems.

Some advocates of non-anthropocentrism have attempted to counter my concerns about the impracticality of theories based on a sharp dichotomy between intrinsic and other valuing, and have answered that belief in – or at least public appeal to – intrinsic value in nature is in fact the most useful tool philosophers can offer to activists (Callicott, 1999: 27–43). For example, Callicott, citing the Australian non-anthropocentrist Warwick Fox, argues that appeals to intrinsic values in nature transform public discourse, shifting the burden of proof against despoilers of nature, calling them to account for destroying intrinsically valued features of nature. Arguing that, in the absence of such appeals, wetlands will be without any protection from cost-benefit reasoning that will favor development, Callicott says: "If the intrinsic value of wetlands were broadly recognized, then developers would have to prove that the value to the human community of the shopping mall was so great as to trump the intrinsic value of the wetland" (Callicott, 2002: 15).

This is an odd argument, to say the least. It raises several questions: What conclusion should we draw if Callicott has, indeed, shown that the burden of proof would be shifted by broad acceptance of his theory of intrinsic value? Does he mean to conclude that environmentalists "should" believe in intrinsic value, because it would be rational to do so? No, he seems only to have offered evidence that it will serve their purposes to so believe. No argument is offered that such values exist in any sense other than as a perhaps effective rhetorical device in contentious public debate. But even this claim of usefulness seems questionable, given Callicott's interpretation of such values. Since such attributions are merely subjective expressions of feeling, they provide no *reasons* that despoilers must respond to. On the subjectivist interpretation of intrinsic value as a value attributable on mere human whim, injection of such values into the argument cannot affect the burden of *proof*, as no proof can be offered if the sentiments involved are merely subjective feelings. At most, appeal to such values could provide a rhetorical roadblock, and would not affect the question of what is right and wrong, justified or unjustified.

Worse, if we must wait for "broad acceptance" of intrinsic value theory – clearly a minority position today – before the burden actually shifts due to broad acceptance at some point in the future, should we conclude that policy-makers are presently justified in acting without regard to such values or related environmental management goals, since the burden of proof would now, apparently, rest on the minority position?

Even if one overlooks all of these oddities of Callicott's burden of proof argument and admit that appeals to intrinsic value have proved useful in some cases, it *still* would not follow that we should embrace his theory for its practical effect on the rhetorical situation, since there may be other – more solid and less speculative – values that can achieve the same shift. For example, appeals to the widely endorsed public value of protecting natural systems for future people who will need and love them – a strong sustainability ethic – would achieve the same shifting of the argument against short-sighted despoilers. Even if appeals to intrinsic value represent a *sufficient* condition for the shifting of the burden, it is not *necessary* for environmentalists to make such appeals – other, less contentious ethical appeals can accomplish the same shift. His argument therefore provides no reason to adopt a speculative theory of value based in arbitrary individual feelings.

We have seen, so far, that attributing intrinsic value to nature helps us to resolve very little. Advocates of this theory cannot agree on what kinds of elements of nature are the carriers of intrinsic value, nor can they agree on what it means, morally, to make such attributions. As I said above, placing the distinction between intrinsic and instrumental value at the center of the discussion raises more questions than it answers. Some of these questions only arise because of a rigid "either/or" conceptualization of values. As we encounter values in nature in our lives, we do not place our values in these artificial, dualistic categories. Consider the many ways I value a natural, resilient, productive wetland – for its beauty, for its contribution to biological diversity, for its usefulness in filtering impurities from surface waters, etc. Must they all be parsed into either instrumental value or intrinsic value? Why must they be? A positive answer to this question, I fear, can only be developed by appeal to the partisan – and incompatible – theories by advocates of intrinsic value.

Of course we value nature in many ways and we express these values in many vernaculars, assuming different theories. These human values can better be seen as forming a continuum, ranging from purely acquisitive to altruistic and spiritual values. Trying to force all of these types of value into two categories only asks for ambiguity and confusion, especially when these categories are so sensitive to the theoretical assumptions and commitments associated with them. It makes much more sense, in my view, to recognize that human individuals value nature in multiple ways and that these ways form a continuum ranging from, at one end, consumptive and self-oriented values, to include aesthetic, spiritual, and other non-instrumental values at the other. The key point is that these are all *human* values, requiring integration and balancing. They imply no "non-anthropocentric," extra-human values from an extra-human source. We can recognize that humans value nature as having more than instrumental value, without reifying this value as something that exists independent of human valuing.

Along this continuum of human values, one encounters values – sometimes called "transformative" values – which are not clearly instrumental or non-instrumental, though they are clearly human-oriented (Norton, 1987: 185–213).[5] Consider an example: human action is often a function of the preferences individuals

Bryan G. Norton

feel; a highly consumptive lifestyle can thus be understood as a reflection of materialistic and consumptive personal values. But environmentalists have noticed that many individuals, once exposed to the wonders of natural areas and wild species, come to see higher value and deeper enjoyment from these things than in the materialistic values they are accustomed to. If exposure to natural areas causes a shift in human valuation from materialism and consumption to more contemplation and enjoyment of natural systems and processes, is it appropriate to describe the value of these experiences of nature as "instrumental"? While the value in question is a human value, it is not instrumental to the fulfillment of human preferences; it represents, rather, a transformation of preferences in accord with a higher ideal, that of a more contemplative and less consumptive life. Rather than calling these values "instrumental," it would be more accurate to say that these experiences of nature have transformed or "constituted" new ways of valuing nature, ways that transcend prior values.

Similarly, many environmentalists have thought of nature as having "spiritual" value, which is likewise a human value that would not normally be considered "instrumental." On this understanding of human valuing of nature, there are human valuings that can be described as both human-oriented and "intrinsic," meaning "non-instrumental." Experience of them is considered good in-itself, but the experiencer is clearly a human individual and the value in question is in no sense "independent" of humans or their valuing.

So, while many philosophers, including Callicott, take the distinction between instrumental and intrinsic valuation as the starting point for their theorizing, one can support the distinction as representing a sharp dichotomy – between competing human and non-human interests – only if one assumes a strong, Rolstonian conception upon which nonhuman aspects of nature have value quite independent of humans. If, however, following Callicott, one considers intrinsic value to be a way that humans value nature, to "exist" only because it is attributed by human, valuing agents, then the "distinction" represents little more than an artificial and arbitrary line drawn crudely across a continuum of multiple ways that humans do in fact value nature.

Environmental Values, in the Plural

Because there are so many types of environmental value, and values affect the way we understand and address problems, diversity of viewpoints and interests in a community will ensure that a range of values will be cited in support of proposed policies. If participants in debates about what to do cannot even agree on what the problem is – that is, what values are curtailed or threatened by the current situation – then it is highly unlikely that there will be one measure of value that will be satisfactory for all, and even less likely that there will be agreement on what variables ought to be optimized. I therefore advocate pluralism, the view that humans value nature in many ways, some of them practical and some of them non-instrumental, at least in any usual meaning of that term. Pluralism is a fact of life in environmental discourse; if we reject ideology and take people at their word, we find them expressing many values, using varied vocabularies. An example of this pluralism is embodied in the Preamble to the United States' Endangered Species Act of 1973, which mentions, "aesthetic, ecological, educational, historical, recreational, and scientific" values. Interestingly, the Preamble does *not* mention either economic or intrinsic values, but rather provides, in this ideology-free list, a collection of social values that are associated with wild species.

Similarly, if we listen to how values function in policy debate in a context where there are opportunities for public deliberation and debate about what to do – rather than listening to the cacophonous debates among ideologists and advocates of monistic, exclusionary theories – we will find participants interjecting multiple values, trying to find win–win policies and objectives that will serve multiple values, and compromising among these values when win–win policies are not available. If we do not try to force all of these diverse values into the straitjacket of a single, monistic theory, but rather express values in natural language, we can expect that citizens will articulate their everyday values and advocate their concerns by proposing policies that will serve the whole range of values advocated. Accepting value pluralism as a fact of life in environmental discourse thus signals a shift in the way we frame environmental problems. If there are no monistic, unitary measures of all value, then it may be better to see environmental quandaries as competitions among multiple, competing values and associated criteria, with the goal being the achievement of a reasonable balance among competing, human values, rather than one that seeks agreement on an optimal provision of a single type of good.

Indeed, embracing pluralism over ideological polarization opens up many opportunities for forming advocacy coalitions and for compromises involving overlapping interest groups. Polarization over ideology can now be replaced with a search for win–win policies where multiple human values are served simultaneously, and with attempts at compromise and a reasonable balance in the pursuit of competing values. This common-sense position, which recognizes the range and diversity of values humans derive from nature, as expressed in public discourse, can be tested and refined within the policy process. As we deliberate about what should be done to protect the wonders of wild species and natural systems, appeals to these many values can guide us toward a better understanding of what natural processes are associated with various human values, and disagreements about what is important enough to save will provide a laboratory for identifying and studying natural values. This approach, which can be called "experimental pluralism," accepts pluralism as its starting point, develops proposed policies to protect the full range of natural values as advocated by citizens, and proceeds to develop compromises and fair balances when not all values can be fully supported (Norton and Toman, 1997: 553–68). If participants in these deliberative processes were allowed to pursue their own course toward improved environmental policy by citing and comparing multiple and diverse values, rather than by being interrupted by those who wield pre-experiential, ideological commitments and insist that all values be expressed in a single vocabulary that is warranted by a single theory, environmental policy could proceed as a search for win–win policies adequate to protect all natural values, and continue as negotiations toward an acceptable compromise in cases where, despite best efforts, important values remain in competition with each other. For these reasons, I choose a pluralistic system of environmental values over monism, ideology, and endless theoretical debates that stand in the way of negotiation and compromise, in order to protect the many values we derive from nature.

Notes

1 Callicott's essay in this volume (see chapter 20) represents a good example of this very widespread trend.
2 But see John O'Neill's convincing argument that, once one distinguishes three different meanings of "intrinsic," it can be seen that most of the arguments given to establish that there is an obligation to protect intrinsic value in nature are based on a fallacy of equivocation – they infer from the existence of elements of nature with "goods of their own," to the conclusion that they must, morally, be treated as ends-in-themselves. See O'Neill (1993: ch. 2).
3 See also Callicott (1989: 133, 161).
4 This is a very compressed version of a much longer argument from Norton (1992) and *Constructing Sustainability: A Philosophy of Adaptive Management* (forthcoming).
5 See also Sahotra Sarkar, *Biodiversity and Environmental Philosophy: An Introduction to the Issues* (forthcoming).

References

Callicott, J. Baird (1989). *In Defense of the Land Ethic*. Albany: State University of New York Press.
Callicott, J. Baird (1999). *Beyond the Land Ethic*. Albany: State University of New York Press.
Callicott, J. Baird (2002). "The pragmatic power and promise of theoretical environmental ethics: forging a new discourse." *Environmental Values*, 11: 3–25.
Callicott, J. Baird (2005). "The intrinsic value of nature in public policy: the case of the Endangered Species Act." In Andrew I. Cohen and Christopher Heath Wellman (eds.), *Contemporary Debates in Applied Ethics* (pp. 279–97). Oxford: Blackwell.
Norton, Bryan G. (1987). *Why Preserve Natural Variety?* Princeton, NJ: Princeton University Press.
Norton, Bryan G. (1992). "Epistemology and environmental values." *Monist*, 75: 226–28.
Norton, Bryan G. (forthcoming). *Constructing Sustainability*. Chicago: University of Chicago Press.
Norton, Bryan G. and Toman, Michael A. (1997). "Sustainability: ecological and economic perspectives." *Land Economics*, 73: 553–68.
O'Neill, John (1993). *Ecology, Policy, and Politics*. London and New York: Routledge.
Passmore, John (1974). *Man's Responsibility for Nature*. New York: Charles Scribner's Sons.
Rolston III, Holmes (1987). *Philosophy Gone Wild*. Buffalo, NY: Prometheus Books.
Rolston III, Holmes (1992). "Epistemology and environmental values." *Monist*, 75: 208–28.
Rolston III, Holmes (1994). *Conserving Natural Value*. New York: Columbia University Press.
Sarkar, Sahotra (forthcoming). *Biodiversity and Environmental Philosophy*. New York: Cambridge University Press.
Stone, Christopher (1987). *Earth and Other Ethics*. New York: Harper and Row.

Further reading

Kellert, Stephen R. (1986). "Social and perceptual factors in the preservation of animal species." In B. G. Norton (ed.), *The Preservation of Species*. Princeton, NJ: Princeton University Press.

WORLD HUNGER

Famine Relief: The Duties
We Have to Others

Christopher Heath Wellman

In developing countries, 6 million children die each year, mostly from hunger-related causes.

Bread for the World Institute

Never doubt that a small group of thoughtful, committed citizens can change the world; indeed, it's the only thing that ever has.

Margaret Mead

Positive Duties

Any moral theory that requires one ceaselessly to sacrifice for the common good should be rejected as too demanding. In my view, we need not apologize for devoting the lion's share of our time and resources to our own self-regarding projects and the people we love. However, if another person is gravely imperiled and one can rescue her at no unreasonable cost to oneself, then one has a moral duty to do so.

Imagine, for instance, that you are lounging by the pool at the Hard Rock Hotel and Casino in Las Vegas. In one hand you have a frozen margarita, in the other you hold a copy of this book. Ordinarily, of course, the essays in this volume would hold your undivided attention. On this occasion, however, you find yourself reading the same few sentences over and over again, as you repeatedly lift your head to check out the scantily clad, hard-bodied men and women frolicking in and around the pool. As you survey the "beautiful people," you notice that an unattended infant has just fallen into the water and will surely drown unless someone immediately saves her (Singer, 1972). Are you morally required to jump in and rescue the baby? Does it matter that she is not your child and that you have no special relationship with her?

I presume that virtually everyone reading this would agree that you ought to rescue the child, even if doing so would involve spilling your margarita and ruining the book. Perhaps we would not be obligated to help if the baby were not imperiled (we need not come to the infant's aid if she merely needed another coat of sun screen or a long overdue diaper change, for instance) or if the assistance would be unreasonably costly (as it might be if one was holding the Mona Lisa, rather than a copy of this book). Because the baby is sufficiently imperiled and you could save her without sacrificing anything significant, however, it does not matter that you are in no way related to or especially responsible for the child.[1] Thus, it is no defense to callously protest: "It's not my baby," or "I never agreed to baby-sit that kid." These defenses might be relevant in some instances (if someone questioned why you had not changed the baby's diaper, for instance), but they are not germane in this case because all of us have positive moral duties to rescue even anonymous strangers when they are sufficiently imperiled and we can do so without significant cost to ourselves.[2]

I take the preceding analysis to be merely commonsensical, and thus I presume that most people reading this chapter will not seriously object to anything at this early stage. Notice, however, that surprising implications follow from granting that we have moral duties to rescue others when they are sufficiently imperiled and we can assist them at no unreasonable cost. This is because there are currently masses of children starving to death, and virtually everyone reading this book is wealthy enough to save some of them without sacrificing anything significant. Thus, for the very same reasons that you would be morally required to save the drowning infant at the Hard Rock pool, you are morally required to contribute a modest amount, say $100, to saving the lives of a few children who are currently starving to death.

At this point, one might object that there is a huge difference between saving a drowning child in your immediate presence and sending money to help anonymous foreign children who are starving in some unfamiliar place, thousands of miles away. I acknowledge that these two scenarios are likely to *feel* different to many of us, but I suggest that there is no morally relevant difference between them. In other words, whatever effect the difference in nationality, the physical distance, or the use of mediating devices might make in *motivating* us to rescue someone else, the moral relations between you and the starving distant foreigner are the same as those between you and the drowning infant (Singer, 1972).

To see that common nationality is not necessary to ground a duty to rescue, think again of the drowning infant at the pool. Suppose that you are American: does it matter whether or not the infant is also American? I presume not. Imagine, for instance, if an American who sat and watched the infant drown defended herself in the following fashion: "Ordinarily I would have leapt in to save the child, but I did not do so in this case because I knew she was Australian." Would this strike you as an adequate defense? I assume that most people reading this book would not accept this justification because the infant's nationality is irrelevant. As long as the infant is sufficiently imperiled and one can rescue her without sacrificing anything significant, it makes no difference what nationality the two parties are because Samaritan duties are owed to fellow *human beings*, not just to *compatriots*.[3] (Notice, for instance, that the biblical story from which Samaritan duties derive their name involves a gentleman from Samaria saving an imperiled stranger, not a fellow Samaritan.)

Christopher Heath Wellman

Moreover, it is worth adding that it is equally irrelevant whether the rescuer and the imperiled person are on the same country's soil. Imagine, for instance, that the pool in question is not in Las Vegas but is on a desert resort that straddles the US/Mexico border. Suppose that in order to create a "Swim to Mexico" gimmick, the resort designed the small pool so that one side is in the US and the other in Mexico. Would it make a difference whether the infant fell in the American or the Mexican portion of the pool? Presumably not. Combining these two points, a Canadian tourist lounging on the American side of the pool who saw an Australian infant fall in the Mexican portion of the pool would be just as morally obligated to perform the rescue as an American tourist on the American side of the pool who saw an American infant drowning in the American portion of the pool. In short, both the citizenship of the parties and the country in which the rescue must be performed are morally irrelevant. What is crucial is whether the rescuee is sufficiently imperiled and can be saved at no unreasonable cost to the rescuer; where both of these conditions obtain, neither nationality nor national location makes a difference.

At this point, one might object that while the national location of the two parties is irrelevant, their spatial location does make a difference because one can be bound only to assist those in one's close proximity. To appreciate the moral relevance of distance, this critic might ask us to imagine that one is lounging beside the ocean rather than a pool. Suppose that one sees (perhaps through binoculars) an infant fall off the back of a boat ten miles offshore. (And suppose that those on the boat did not notice the infant's fall and that there is no one else on the beach at the time.) Under these circumstances, when the imperiled person is no longer right under one's nose, so to speak, it is not so clear that one has a moral duty. And this is explained, the skeptic suggests, by the distance between oneself and the infant.

I acknowledge that there may be no Samaritan duty in this case, but I deny that this is due merely to the physical distance separating the two parties. In my view, the distance itself is not morally significant; if one has no duty to rescue a drowning infant ten miles offshore, it is either because one is unable to do so (since the infant would no doubt drown before one could swim out to it) or because doing so would be unreasonably costly (since the rescuer might reasonably fear drowning or being attacked by sharks). To see that the distance itself is morally irrelevant, though, imagine that one has freakishly long arms that enable one to pull the baby out of the ocean without even getting out of one's chair on the beach (Kamm, 2000). (Or, if such long arms are too difficult to fathom, imagine that one has a super speedboat, a jetpack, or even a giant crane that would enable one safely to retrieve the infant in a matter of seconds.) Under these circumstances, I suspect that most would agree that one has a duty to save the drowning infant. Thus, once we strip this scenario of the features that undermine one's capacity to perform the rescue at no unreasonable cost, we see that the issue of distance is not in itself morally relevant.

Finally, notice that it makes no moral difference whether one's rescue is mediated by devices or other people. Imagine, for instance, that after spending a couple of hours by the Hard Rock pool, you decide that you had better return to your hotel room before you get sun-burned. Fortunately, the hotel has closed-circuit television coverage of the pool, so you can continue to check out the lively scene from the comfort of your air-conditioned room. While watching on your room's television, you notice the infant fall into the pool. Because you are staying on the 30th floor, there is no way that you could make it down to the pool in time to save her yourself. Without getting out of your chair, however, you could pick up your cell phone and call the bartender at the poolside bar, who – once alerted – could easily rescue the infant herself. It seems to me that you are just as obligated to make that call (even if there would be a substantial charge on your cell bill) as you would be to dive into the pool yourself. It makes no difference, in other words, whether one can personally rescue the drowning child all on one's own, or whether one can merely play a part in the rescue by calling others who, once informed, can complete the rescue.[4]

But notice: once one recognizes that neither nationality, distance, nor the use of mediating devices and people in any way diminishes one's duty to rescue imperiled strangers, it is clear that one's duty to rescue starving infants on another part of the planet is just as pressing as the initial poolside rescue with which we began. Indeed, the last scenario of using one's cell phone to initiate a rescue of someone whom one sees drowning on a television monitor is very much like a situation that many of us routinely experience. We are watching something entertaining on television when a commercial alerts us that starving children desperately need our help. If we have a duty to jump in the pool to save the infant, and we have a duty to make a relatively expensive cellular phone call to the poolside bar, then why do we not equally have a duty to use our cell phone to make a modest donation (say, $100) to the institution saving the starving children? If (1) the fact that the children are citizens of another country is irrelevant, if (2) the physical distance between you and them makes no difference, if (3), like the loss of the margarita and the damage to one's book, the loss of $100 is not an unreasonable sacrifice, and if (4) the use of mediating devices like cell phones, credit cards, and international relief agencies is not important, then it is hard not to conclude that one's moral duty to send money to famine relief is just as strong as one's duty to jump in the pool to save a drowning child.

At this point one might protest that there remains a big difference between saving a single drowning infant and sending money to help masses of starving children: the number of people imperiled. Numbers might be thought to matter because when there is only one imperiled person, her peril becomes salient in a way that explains why you as a potential rescuer have no discretion but to help her. When there are numerous imperiled people (so many, in fact, that you could not possibly rescue all of them), no single individual's peril is salient, and thus one retains the discretion as to whether or not to help.

I agree that numbers can sometimes matter, but I do not think they can make the type of difference that this objection supposes. More specifically, I acknowledge that one enjoys some discretion when there are more imperiled people than one could possibly save, but it is not the discretion of whether or not to perform the rescue; rather, it is merely the choice of whom to rescue.

Most who believe that we have a duty to assist others do not couch their arguments in the language of rights, but I would explain this discretion in terms of the correlative rights to assistance. Thus, to return to our initial example, I would say that the drowning infant in Hard Rock pool has a Samaritan right that you rescue her. If the situation were altered slightly so that there were two babies in the pool,

Christopher Heath Wellman

and you could not possibly save both, would you say that you no longer have any duty to rescue at all? Presumably not. The more sensible conclusion, I think, is that you must still rescue one of the babies, and you may choose which to rescue. In terms of the infant's rights, obviously neither of the two drowning babies has a right that you save her in particular, but I would say that each has a right that you save one of them (Feinberg, 1984). Thus, just as a lounger by the Hard Rock pool could not justify rescuing neither of the infants with the lame excuse that "Once the second child fell in, I knew that I could not save both," the fact that we cannot save all of the world's people from starving to death provides no justification for not rescuing some.[5] In short, while the world's current situation is admittedly much more messy and heartbreaking than our imagined situation of a single drowning baby who is seen by a single sun-bather, there is nothing about the complexity of the actual world's crises that makes our duty to rescue any less stringent.

Finally, let me comment on my suggestion that each of us has a duty to donate $100 to famine relief. I suspect that virtually everyone reading this book could easily give substantially more than $100 without sacrificing anything significant, but I chose this conservative sum because it is a round number that is in the general neighborhood, at least, of what it would cost to replace the drink and book that I imagined might be ruined in the initial rescue situation. Let me quickly respond, however, to those who might object that $100 is too large an amount to expect people, especially students, to sacrifice.

There will invariably be exceptional cases, of course, of people who could not give up $100 without sacrificing something morally significant. Some students are working parents, for instance, who have too little money even to buy the assigned texts (they either check the books out of the library or routinely borrow them from patient classmates), and who could not part with $100 and still manage to pay for their children's health insurance. If that sounds something like your situation, then it seems only reasonable to conclude that you could not contribute to famine relief without sacrificing something morally significant. If we are being honest, however, the vast majority of us must admit that we could charge $100 to our credit card and still shop at A&F, buy our coffee at Starbucks, order our dinner from Domino's, watch MTV on cable television, and talk with friends on our cell phones. If so, then it is hard to say with a straight face that we have no duty to save the lives of starving children because doing so would require us to sacrifice something significant.

Before moving on, let me acknowledge that in the past there was a profound difference between our moral responsibilities to an infant drowning in our midst and a child starving to death in some distant land. This difference stemmed from our lack of information regarding, and capacity to save, the latter. Times have changed, however, and so has the scope of our moral responsibilities (Singer, 1972). We do not have freakishly long arms that enable us literally to reach out and feed people thousands of miles away, but we do have other instruments that are just as effective. We have an international media that can inform us about distant tragedies, we have international relief agencies dedicated to performing acts of rescue, and we have phones and credit cards that enable us conveniently to transfer our funds to these agencies. Thus, if you are unwilling to contribute money to help save the lives of several starving children, it is hard to see why there is any difference, morally speaking, between

Famine Relief: The Duties We Have to Others | 317

you and a lounger by the Hard Rock pool who cannot be bothered to put down her drink and book to save the drowning infant.

Negative Duties

One of the most frequent objections to sending money to the masses of famine-stricken people around the world is that these famines are not strictly accidents; rather, they are brought on at least in part by inefficient or corrupt political and business institutions.[6] The twofold thought behind this observation is: "Why should I have to bail out these people when they played a part in creating their own misfortune and are likely to do so again?" It is common to argue in response either that the specific famine in question was in fact an unforeseeable accident or that, however much political and/or business leaders might be to blame for the severity of the problem, surely those actually starving to death are no more responsible for the unforgiving conditions that caused their peril than we are for the favorable conditions that (largely) explain our wealth. Here I will pursue neither of these routes. Instead, I shall concede that much of the world's poverty is at least exacerbated and prolonged (if not outright caused) by national and international institutions, but I will argue that this fact only strengthens the case for the duty to offer assistance because it illustrates that we have negative as well as positive duties to assist the world's most needy.

Before exploring the relationship between political institutions and world hunger, I would like to suggest that we have a negative duty to neither support nor profit from institutions that wrongly harm others (Pogge, 2002).[7] The basic idea behind this claim is merely that, just as we should not personally harm others, nor should we either support or profit from institutions that do so. Imagine, for instance, that your parents own slaves and therefore are able to provide a comfortable life for you. Among other things, they pay for your college tuition with the profits they garner from the slave labor. Should you accept this money from them? What would you think of a daughter of slave-owners who defended her privileged life by saying: "I agree that owning slaves is morally repulsive, but that provides no reason to criticize me because *I* don't own any slaves!"

I can understand why someone might contend either that children should not accept money from slave-owning parents or even that adult children should have nothing to do with their slave-owning parents, but I would argue for a more modest claim. Because children have limited influence over their parents, and because it would be an enormous sacrifice for most college-age children to have nothing to do with, or perhaps even to accept no financial support from, their parents, I suggest merely the following: if one is going to accept money from one's slave-owning parents, then one must at least make a conscientious effort to persuade one's parents that owning slaves is wrong. In other words, accepting the benefits of an unjust institution like slavery requires one, at the very least, to work to eliminate the unjust institution.

As I indicated above, the rationale for this conclusion is the commonsensical position that one should not be an accessory to injustice. As an historical example of someone who took this moral directive to heart, consider Henry David Thoreau. Both because of its support for the practice of slavery and because of its engagement in

Christopher Heath Wellman

the Mexican War, Thoreau was convinced that the United States government was a powerful instrument for injustice. Not wanting to support such an institution with his actions or money, Thoreau retreated to Walden Pond, where he lived in relative isolation, refusing to pay any taxes to the US government. In my view, Thoreau is to be applauded for his concerns about supporting an unjust institution, but he went above and beyond the call of duty by completely divorcing himself from political society. According to the modest view I am advocating here, one could not have objected to Thoreau's enjoying the benefits of political life as long as he worked to reform US policy.

For a more recent example of how one might try to influence an unjust institution, consider the student activism during apartheid South Africa. When I was an undergraduate, South Africa had an oppressive system of apartheid, wherein the whites oppressed the blacks. Despite being a numerical minority, the whites were able effectively to exploit the blacks because they controlled the political and financial institutions. What is more, the international community effectively buttressed the whites' privileged position by investing in their businesses and recognizing their government as legitimate. At the University of North Carolina, where I was in school, there was a relatively small group of well-informed students who were disturbed by the injustices being perpetrated in South Africa. (I regret to say that I was not among their number.) Distraught that their university was contributing to the injustice by investing in some of the South African companies that played a part in this oppressive system, these students lobbied the relevant authorities to divest the university of all South African holdings. As you might imagine, however, a few students did not wield a great deal of influence over the University's investment portfolio. Rather than give up, however, these students built a "shanty town" in a prominent place on campus (on the main quad, right below the Chancellor's office, actually). The students lived in these makeshift huts for months to call attention to the plight of blacks in South Africa who were forcibly relegated to ghettos where they lived in similar conditions. Over time, these huts attracted more and more embarrassing attention until the university finally decided to divest itself of all South African companies.

In my view, this story provides a prime example of how one might work to make one's institutions more just. Had these students been more like Thoreau, they might have simply withdrawn from school, so as not to play a supporting role in the perpetuation of injustice. Leaving school is a huge sacrifice, though, especially when one considers that virtually all schools were invested in South African companies, and thus there was nowhere else that these conscientious students could have enrolled. Under these conditions, it is enough for these students to make a concerted effort to reform their university. (Indeed, I should think that living in makeshift huts goes well beyond what could reasonably be asked of an average student, and thus they could have stayed in school in good conscience even if they had done considerably less – such as merely sponsoring petitions and organizing rallies.) Notice also that it is too much to require that students continue their efforts until they prevail. Students typically exert very little influence over university policy, and thus all one can ask is that they make a concerted effort to get their school to stop supporting major injustices. Finally, I would suggest that remaining within an institution and working for its reform is in many ways preferable to completely withdrawing from the institution because the former involves being an agent for positive change. Therefore, while it is sometimes thought to be better to keep one's hands entirely clean of injustice, working from the inside to improve an unjust institution can often be the best way to fight the good fight. (Indeed, if no one worked from within to reform corrupt institutions, these institutions would be left under the exclusive control of those who were either ignorant of or indifferent to injustice. Thus, it is perhaps best if some fight from without and others fight from within.) With this in mind, let us now return to the objection that we cannot be expected to save the victims of famines that were at least partly caused by institutional mismanagement.

Recent research confirms that there is indeed a correlation between the quality of one's government and the degree to which one is protected from famine (Dreze and Sen, 1989). In particular, evidence indicates that effective democratic governance virtually insures that a country will not be ravaged by a widespread famine with which it cannot internally cope.[8] This might seem counter-intuitive to those of us who think of famines as natural disasters but, on reflection, this claim makes perfect sense. Most of us have various qualms with our governments, but those of us fortunate enough to live in liberal democratic states take it for granted that governments are designed to be mutually beneficial institutions that more or less serve their constituents. In far too many instances, however, political power is not democratically distributed, and the government is a powerful institution designed to serve the tiny elite who happen to wield the political power. Just as apartheid South Africa was designed maximally to benefit the politically empowered whites, for instance, some governments are ruled so as to work to the greatest advantage of the dictator and her closest friends and family. It does not take much imagination to see why a government designed to benefit just a small fraction of the population would be uninterested and/or unable effectively to prevent famines, but it does require some explanation as to how such a government can stay in power. Think of it this way: if people more than 200 years ago in France and the American Colonies were able to overthrow oppressive governments, why are there currently so many people in the world who are either uninterested in or unable to establish effective democratic governments?

The answer to this last question is simply "brute force." Dictators are often able to maintain their oppressive regimes simply because they control the military, and they ruthlessly use this power to suppress anyone who seeks democratic reform. Of course, staying in power requires a vicious circle because the dictators are typically able to retain the military's loyalty only as long as they have the money to pay them, and they can acquire the necessary funds only if they continue to exploit their political power. What I want to call attention to now, though, is more specifically how these dictators are able to use their political power to generate wealth. Part of the answer, of course, simply comes from taxes that (insofar as the funds are used to benefit the ruler rather than the people themselves) essentially enslave the political subjects. Another important part of the equation, however, is that dictators frequently amass huge sums of money by selling the country's natural resources to foreign companies and governments.[9] Thus, if a dictator's country has extensive oil reserves, for instance, then the dictator can sell this oil and use the money to secure her military stranglehold over her subjects.[10]

Christopher Heath Wellman

Here, two points clearly emerge. First and most obviously, the mere fact that a dictator effectively controls the country's natural resources does not make her *morally entitled* to those resources any more than a slave-owner's effective control over her slaves implies that she is morally entitled to the fruits of these slaves' labor. Secondly, and more importantly for our purposes here, foreign companies are an integral part of the problem because, in seeking to acquire natural resources as cheaply as possible, they are giving the undemocratic leaders the money necessary to continue their unjust domination over their political subjects. In a very real sense, it is as if these companies were buying cheap cotton from slave-owners who were using this money to buy more guns and slaves.

If all of this is right, where does it leave you and me? Where does it leave those of us who enjoy our clothes from A&F, our coffee from Starbucks, our dinners from Domino's, our cell phones from Sprint, and our MTV on cable television?[11] Certainly, part of the reason we are able to enjoy these luxuries is because we work extremely hard in order to be able to buy things for ourselves and those we love. But equally certainly, another part of the reason we enjoy these luxuries is because we benefit from an economic system that utilizes natural resources bought very cheaply from political leaders who have control over these resources only because they happen to have the military power to suppress their compatriots. Thus, you and I profit from an overall economic system that plays a prominent role in propping up military dictators who in turn create the political conditions that play a causal role in the world's worst famines. In the end, then, the role that political and business institutions play in contributing to famine does not undermine our duty to send money to famine relief; on the contrary, it explains why we have not only positive duties to help those who are currently starving to death, but also negative duties to work to change the system so that future famines do not occur. In other words, just as Thoreau felt the need to divorce himself from an unjust political institution and my fellow students felt compelled to reform an unjust university, you and I should recognize our obligation to either withdraw from or seek to reform the current political and economic environment.

Now, just as it was extremely costly for Thoreau to withdraw from political society and it would have been a huge sacrifice for my fellow students to withdraw from school, virtually none of us is willing entirely to divorce herself from the existing international economic system. But if we are going to continue helping ourselves to the spoils of an unjust political and economic environment, then we have a responsibility to work conscientiously to make this system a more just one. If we continue to participate in the system without working diligently for its reform, on the other hand, then we are morally no different from the daughter of slave-owners who defends her willingness to accept gifts made possible only via the exploitation of slaves by saying: "Don't blame me; I don't own any slaves." Just as it would clearly not be too much to ask this daughter to try to persuade her parents of the injustice of slavery, it is not too much to ask you and me to work to make the international economic and political order more just.

At this point, it is tempting to protest that there is nothing one can do. Calling one of the agencies I listed above and giving $100 on one's credit card is a relatively simple act that will make a real difference for people who would otherwise starve to death, but how in the world is one supposed to change the international economic and political order?

This worry is understandable, but it is important to remember that you are not morally required to change the system; you are merely obligated conscientiously to work to reform it. Even so, one might object, it is not even clear how to begin![12] I concede that it is hard not to feel impotent in the face of such enormous institutions, but notice that the world has already experienced wave after wave of moral reform, and each of these changes had to start somewhere. Think, for instance, of Henry David Thoreau. It is unrealistic to suppose that Thoreau thought he could single-handedly get the US to abolish slavery, but there is no question that the integrity with which he lived his life had a profound influence on others who, over time, were able successfully to abolish slavery. Similarly, my fellow college students who built the shanty town on campus were among those who raised awareness of the horrors of apartheid South Africa until the international community gradually ceased supporting and ultimately began placing reformist pressures on the relevant political and economic institutions. More recently still, think about what a profound change has occurred regarding recycling in the United States. Not very long ago, one could not help but think that there was nothing substantial one could do. Over a remarkably brief period of time, however, environmental and political activists were able to change the system so that municipalities now routinely provide services that make it easy (if not mandatory) for each of us to contribute to a large-scale recycling effort.

If these and countless other monumental reform movements can succeed, then there is no reason to suppose that each of us cannot do our part in a movement to change international business and politics so that military dictators are no longer able to oppress their constituents in ways that, among other things, contribute to the frequency and severity of famines. I am not the most imaginative person, but it strikes me that anyone reading this chapter for a class could begin by trying to raise awareness on her own campus. Perhaps with the help of the professor who teaches the class, one might begin by organizing a student forum to publicize the issue and form a group on campus that can subsequently come up with additional ideas to spread the word and inspire constructive action. I cannot promise that you will change the world, but I do know that the incentives to perpetuate the current system are strong, so the world will not change without people like you dedicating their time and energy to making it a more just place.

Conclusion

Virtually everyone agrees that we have negative and positive duties toward one another. Negative duties prohibit us from harming others, and positive duties require us to assist others when they are gravely imperiled and we can rescue them at no unreasonable cost to ourselves. In this chapter I have sought to show that each of these types of duty explains why we are morally bound to help those famine victims who are starving to death. The positive duty to provide easy rescues obligates us at the very least to send money to those international relief agencies which have assigned

Christopher Heath Wellman

themselves the task of ministering to those who are starving to death, and the negative duty not to benefit from an institution that wrongly harms others requires us to work to reform the current practice of international politics and business. In short, if you can make a positive difference without sacrificing anything morally significant, then you have a duty to do so. The proverbial operators are standing by at toll free numbers to accept your donation: CARE's number is 1-800-521-2273; Oxfam America's number is 1-800-693-2687; and UNICEF's number is 1-800-367-5437 (Unger, 1996; p.175). It's your call . . .

Notes

This chapter is inspired by, and draws heavily upon, the previous work of a number of authors, especially Peter Singer and Thomas Pogge. I am grateful to Andrew Altman and Hugh LaFollette for helpful comments on an earlier version of this chapter.

1 For the purposes of this chapter, I treat "insignificant costs" and "not unreasonable costs" as interchangeable. Readers familiar with Peter Singer's landmark article, "Famine, affluence, and morality," will recognize this language from Singer's second, less demanding principle that we should contribute to famine relief until we sacrifice something "morally significant." (I do not mean to defend Singer's more demanding principle that we ought to contribute until we are sacrificing something "morally comparable.")

2 "Positive" duties require us to assist others; they are to be contrasted with "negative" duties, which require merely that we not harm or interfere with others.

3 I do not deny that one might have more robust responsibilities to one's compatriots; I insist only that being a fellow citizen is not necessary for one to have a minimal Samaritan duty to another.

4 One reason that you may be less motivated to make the call than to personally save the drowning child is because the former act would be less public. Thus, whereas you would be publicly applauded for diving in to save the drowning child (and perhaps condemned for failing to do so), your relatively private decision to call the bartender need not have these same social consequences. But, while these types of considerations can no doubt affect one's motivations, they are clearly irrelevant to what morality requires. To see this, notice that we might have much less motivation to refrain from murdering an enemy when we can do so in private without any social repercussions, but clearly this does not mean that our moral duty against clandestine murder is any less weighty.

5 Indeed, not only does each imperiled person have no right that you save her in particular, it is not clear that the most gravely imperiled have a right that you help someone who is at least as imperiled. If (as some argue) we can sometimes make a greater marginal difference by contributing to those who are less imperiled, then it would not seem objectionable to do so.

6 A similar objection is that we should not all give our money away to save foreigners because this would ruin our national economy and, as a consequence, render us unable to help other foreigners (or perhaps even our compatriots) in the future. This objection need not be taken seriously. It is true that our economy depends upon a certain amount of spending, but this would counsel us against *saving* too much, not against spending our money *on others*. More importantly, the dire economic consequences invoked in this objection could only come to fruition if the great majority of us gave considerably more than the $100 I am advocating here. In short, there are many things about which it is legitimate to worry, but excessive altruism to foreigners is not among them.

Famine Relief: The Duties We Have to Others | 323

7   I should stress that this is separate from the Samaritan duty. Samaritan duties are positive (as is the general duty to make the world a more just place), but the duty to refrain from either supporting or benefiting from injustice is a negative one.

8   There is also considerable evidence that extreme poverty and various problems tied to population growth are directly related to the standing of women. Societies that give women control over their bodies as well as access to education, economic opportunities, and reproductive technologies tend to have reduced birth rates and higher standards of living.

9   Of course, buying natural resources is only one of the more obvious ways in which the international community can help a dictator strengthen her domination over a population. As Thomas Pogge explains: "Local elites can afford to be oppressive and corrupt, because, with foreign loans and military aid, they can stay in power even without popular support. And they are often so oppressive and corrupt, because it is, in light of the prevailing extreme international inequalities, far more lucrative for them to cater to the interests of foreign governments and firms than to those of their impoverished compatriots. Examples abound. There are, in the poor countries, plenty of governments that came to power and/or stay in power only thanks to foreign support. And there are plenty of politicians and bureaucrats who, induced or even bribed by foreigners, work against the interests of their people: *for* the development of a tourist-friendly sex industry (whose forced exploitation of children and women they tolerate and profit from), *for* the importation of unneeded, obsolete, or overpriced products at public expense, *for* the permission to import hazardous products, wastes, or productive facilities, *against* laws protecting employees or the environment, etc." (2002: 244).

10 One might protest that, while an illegitimate ruler undeniably has no right to her country's natural resources, neither do her compatriots. According to this objection, the world's natural resources are owned jointly by all of the world's population. I will not contest this claim here. Rather, I suggest that if everyone is equally entitled to the world's natural resources, then this constitutes an argument in favor of something like a "global resources dividend." This dividend, recommended by Pogge, would be paid for by those of us who use the world's natural resources and would be owed to the world's poor who are involuntarily not using their share of these natural resources (Pogge, 2002: 196–215).

11 Let me be clear: I am NOT alleging that A&F, Starbucks, Domino's, Sprint, and MTV are particularly corrupt companies; each may do absolutely nothing immoral on its own. My point is that companies like these are part of an international system that benefits from the inexpensive natural resources purchased from undemocratic, illegitimate rulers.

12 Notice how awkward it is to protest that those of us who are privileged cannot be obligated to change the system because we are impotent in the face of its enormity, while simultaneously suggesting that those who are starving to death are entitled to no assistance because *they* are responsible for the political and economic institutions which led to their ruin.

References

Bread for the World Institute: ⟨www.bread.org⟩.

Dreze, Jean and Sen, Amartya (1989). *Hunger and Public Action*. Oxford: Oxford University Press.

Feinberg, Joel (1984). *Harm to Others*. New York: Oxford University Press.

Kamm, Frances (2000). "Does distance matter morally to the duty to rescue?" *Law and Philosophy*, 19: 655–81.

Pogge, Thomas (2002). *World Poverty and Human Rights*. Cambridge: Polity.

Singer, Peter (1972). "Famine, affluence, and morality." *Philosophy and Public Affairs*, 1: 229–43.

Unger, Peter (1996). *Living High and Letting Die: Our Illusion of Innocence*. New York: Oxford University Press.

Further reading

Hardin, Garret (1974). "Lifeboat ethics: the case against helping the poor." *Psychology Today Magazine*.

LaFollette, Hugh (2003). "World hunger." In R. Frey and C. Wellman (eds.), *A Companion to Applied Ethics* (pp. 238–53). Oxford: Blackwell.

Shue, Henry (1996). *Basic Rights: Subsistence, Affluence, and US Foreign Policy*. Princeton, NJ: Princeton University Press.

Schmidtz David and Goodin Robert (1998). *Social Welfare and Individual Responsibility*. Cambridge: Cambridge University Press.

Singer, Peter (2002). *One World: The Ethics of Globalization*. New Haven, CT: Yale University Press.

Famine Relief and Human Virtue

Andrew I. Cohen

Much of the philosophical literature on world hunger draws on analogies to life-threatening emergencies. We are sometimes asked to imagine babies drowning in various bodies of water. Shouldn't we rescue them? – especially when it is easy to do so?

Such fanciful examples have a compelling appeal. Virtuous persons automatically help others in immediate and profound need when they are in a position to do so. We do whatever we can to help, without dwelling on, for instance, the nuances of the value of saving babies versus saving the perfect martini, a good hair-do, or a fine work of art. The morally mature person lifts drowning babies out of the water. And so, this well-intentioned argument continues, moral decency similarly has us alleviating world hunger when we can. There is suffering and death, we know about it, and we can do something about it at little cost to ourselves. More than that: we *ought* to contribute to famine relief. A failure to do so is blameworthy; we may even *owe* such relief to distant suffering peoples.

I believe, however, that there are important moral differences between famine relief and tending to easily fixed nearby suffering. While it might be true that we ought to provide easy rescue, it is not clear that we have any similar moral responsibilities to distant hungry persons. But even if we had some duties to aid distant hungry persons, such duties must not be *enforceable*.

In what follows, I argue that the drowning baby analogy tells us very little about duties of famine relief. I explore the place for charity in a good life, arguing that enforceable duties of charity are incompatible with the key moral concern that every person should have the best chance to define and live a life of her own. I discuss how a virtuous commitment to alleviate suffering should have us focusing more on local problems. I close with some general remarks about economic and political considerations, noting how breaking down barriers to free markets would be the best way to promote everyone's prosperity – especially for the world's poorest peoples.

Drowning Babies

Let us return to the type of example that launched this and many other discussions. Some writers, such as Singer (1972), Unger (1996), Wellman (2005), and others, argue that just as we ought to rescue nearby drowning babies when we can do so at little cost to ourselves, so too we have a duty to alleviate distant suffering when we can do so without incurring unreasonable costs. The moral reasons to alleviate suffering are the same in each case. You ought to help – especially when you might easily redirect resources from some more frivolous pursuits.

The appeal to drowning babies gives little guidance for our responsibilities to distant suffering peoples. There are significant moral differences between the two cases. The cases warrant different moral reasoning and different responses.

At stake here is whether there are any "positive duties" to provide aid (as opposed to mere "negative duties" to abstain from performing certain actions). Arguments about rescue take different forms depending on the moral requirements they impose on potential benefactors. To simplify matters, we can speak of three forms of argument:

1 *Weak* versions of such arguments say that rescue, though morally commendable, is at your *discretion*. Rescue is above and beyond the call of duty, so should you choose not to rescue, you are not blameworthy.
2 *Moderate* versions remove any moral discretion for rescue: rescue is morally *required*; a failure to rescue is blameworthy. Other persons may at most blame you should you choose not to rescue. They may not use physical force to compel you to rescue or to punish your failure to do so. The positive duties implied by such arguments may be called *moderate duties*.
3 *Strong* versions of the argument, like moderate versions, say that rescue is morally required. And like moderate versions, blame is fitting should you choose not to rescue. But unlike moderate versions, your responsibility to rescue is morally *enforceable*. Potential beneficiaries of your aid, or those acting on their behalf, may use physical force to compel your assistance or otherwise punish you for your failure to act. The positive duties implied by such arguments may be called *strong duties*.

The question is what sort of responsibilities, if any, we have regarding distant hungry people. Following many proponents of either moderate or strong duties of famine relief, let us then start by considering babies drowning at our feet. I think we might best understand appropriate responses here by considering what good persons do in such cases. Leaving off fanciful counterexamples, virtuous people rescue drowning babies when they can do so at little cost or risk. Notice too that they do so in a certain way. They *automatically* and unhesitatingly take steps to rescue. They take steps to rescue as an expression of a certain commendable character. Their character is marked by tendencies or dispositions to do the right thing in the right way at the right time and for the right reasons. For such persons, doing the right thing is second nature (Aristotle, 1984: II.4). And so, such persons automatically lend a hand in dire emergencies at their feet.[1] This is why there is (at least) a *moderate* requirement that a person provides easy rescue. Those who fail to do so are rightly regarded as despicable. We would understandably take their failure to rescue as a moral failing. Though I doubt there is a *strong* requirement of easy rescue – that physical force is appropriate to compel easy rescue or to punish the failure to do so – I will not argue the point.[2] This much nevertheless seems clear: such persons lack important virtues. To put it another way, their character is not sufficiently defined by dispositions to do the right thing in the right way at the right time and for the right reasons. We do not want to be such persons, nor, other things equal, do we want them as neighbors, colleagues, or friends.[3]

So far, I have claimed that a failure to provide easy rescue shows that a person lacks important moral virtues. Notice, though, that saying we should provide easy rescue is actually shorthand for saying that we have excellent moral reasons for *being the sort of persons* who would unhesitatingly take steps to rescue. Why then can we not say the same things about helping distant suffering peoples?

To start, notice that we do not believe requirements of aid are the same in each case. Typically, we think that there are moderate requirements to rescue babies drowning at our feet, but there are only weak requirements to alleviate world hunger. If our thinking is correct about this, then there would be neither moderate nor strong duties to provide aid to distant hungry people. Relieving distant hunger might then be commendable, but a failure to do so would not make us fitting objects of scorn – and it would certainly not make us candidates for being coerced by potential beneficiaries of our care or by people acting on their behalf.

Critics may respond in the spirit of Singer (1972) and say that this line of argument at best *reports* moral beliefs; it does not defend them as legitimate. This is true. Some critics may then defend a sort of moral revisionism: we should, they might say, revise our moral beliefs or otherwise be more consistent in a way that favors our treating world hunger just like we treat drowning babies. I believe, however, that we rightly treat world hunger differently.

Consider a key, morally relevant difference between babies drowning at our feet and distant peoples suffering from hunger. One is an *emergency* calling for immediate action; the other is a *chronic* condition calling for reflection on complex moral, political, and economic considerations. As Paul Gomberg argues, "Hunger raises issues of causation and remedy that are not present in our duty to rescue" (2002: 30). But an easily rescued baby drowning in a shallow puddle is quite different. Such a case is so exceptional and presents such immediate need that it would be vastly inappropriate to consider the relative costs and benefits of rescue (Gomberg, 2002: 37). It is inappropriate to *pause* to determine the cause of the drowning baby and all circumstances surrounding the drowning. Typically, none of these questions is appropriate beforehand, or even at all: was she left here deliberately? Where are her parents? How wet will I get by rescuing her? If I rescue her, will she fall in again next week? Will she grow up to have children of her own who might happen to fall into puddles along my path? Will she grow up to become a mass murderer, or profoundly depressed, or a Republican who drives an SUV? What are the pH and temperature of this water? And, how can I rescue her best to promote my career?

World hunger, however, is more complicated and calls for us to consider its causes and circumstances (Gomberg, 2002: 37). Given that world hunger is chronic, it is also a good idea to consider how best to alleviate it (Schmidtz, 1998). We might even understandably *fault* someone who *indiscriminately* attempts to alleviate world hunger, by, for instance, giving $100 to some self-described representative of a relief organization without doing a little reflection and background work first (Kekes, 1987: 27). Is this person a genuine representative of the organization and not some charlatan? Does the organization have low administrative costs, or is it just a make-work scheme under the pretense of charity? Are there better uses of my money? Does this organization do more harm than good to the people it claims to help?

In short, the "moral logic" of the two cases differs. Typically, a case of a drowning baby calls for us to act immediately; but typically, a case of distant starving people calls for us to pause to consider causes and consequences. Since the moral logic differs, we ought to reason about the situations differently. Since the situations call for different reasoning, the one cannot be a moral analogue for the other without much more argument. It is thus not enough to justify a duty to aid distant suffering people by pointing to our intuitions about drowning babies needing easy rescue.

Of course, this has only shown that cases of nearby drowning babies are not necessarily analogous to cases of distant suffering peoples. It is still possible that there is a moderate (or even a strong) requirement to alleviate the suffering of distant hungry peoples. To assess whether there is such a requirement, we need to consider the function, the place, and the proper target for charity in a good life.

Charity, Personal Autonomy, and the Right to Do Wrong

Charity as a virtue

I regard charity, in the sense relevant here, as a disposition to sympathize appropriately with and to aid persons in need. This is not the place for a full discussion of the nature and grounding of charity. Here we need only consider how charity is a virtue and what conditions are required for it to be a part of a good life. My arguments will address the possibility of *strong* duties of charity – that is, duties that are physically enforceable. Later in the chapter I raise some worries about moderate duties.

A charitable person is someone disposed to feel and act toward needy people in the right way, at the right time, and for the right reasons. Charity is a virtue mainly because it is a desirable character trait. Speaking quite generally, a person's life tends to go better if one is the sort of person who feels sympathy for others' suffering and is disposed to mitigate their neediness when possible. How much sympathy one feels, how one manifests concern, and how much aid one provides will all vary from one person to another for many reasons, such as different temperaments, different financial circumstances, different abilities to have insight into others' lives, and variable understandings of the conditions in which people live. Speaking again generally, we can still say that charitable people will be sympathetic and helpful toward the right other persons in the right way, at the right time, in the right amount, and for the right reasons.

A virtuous person determines how and when to be charitable after reflecting on particular circumstances and the personalities involved. She must consider her own situation and the situations of needy others. She must also reflect on alternative uses of her property and emotional energy in light of other moral demands. For this sort of particularized reflection to be effective, though, prospective benefactors need the space to explore and deliberate about how they will be charitable. They then have the best opportunity to feel the spontaneous and correctly targeted charitable impulses that are central affective components of the virtue of charity. Without such opportunities for reflection, deliberation, and affective response, they lose a key motivational basis for cultivating the virtue of charity. More sharply, if they lack the opportunity *not* to be charitable, they are deprived of the fullest chance to define themselves as charitable.

Suppose a morally mature person, Allie, lives in reasonable comfort, while Bryce does not. Suppose further that Allie does not enjoy any protected opportunity to withhold her property or her time when providing them might benefit some very needy persons. There might be various institutions or norms in place to insure that Allie provides aid to persons such as Bryce. Perhaps the state taxes Allie and sends the money to the "Bryce fund." Or maybe Allie could help out by preparing a sandwich and delivering it to Bryce, so imagine that she is required to do so. She is not free not to do so; if she withholds her money or her time, she can be physically forced to provide them or punished for her failure to do so.

When Allie complies with the requirement that she assist Bryce or others like him, there is very little charity involved. Allie lacks the fullest opportunity to feel spontaneous sympathy for Bryce. There is little point to her gathering information about the merits of Bryce's case because, after all, she has to give anyway. Reflection on how much to give (at least regarding what she *must* give) is irrelevant; she has little choice about the matter. But if she does not enjoy any protected opportunity to study Bryce's case, reflect on its merits, and decide how much, *if anything*, to give, then her acts of giving are morally cheapened or entirely emptied of virtue. We cannot coerce the virtue of charity.

Charity and the right to do wrong

Individual rights are special moral norms that define and protect certain opportunities to reflect, choose, and act. If Allie may not withhold her resources when providing them might help Bryce, then she does not enjoy a right not to give. The right to make a choice in this situation is crucial for Allie to have the chance to define and cultivate a charitable character. Self-definition and personal integrity demand self-directed practice with the possibility of failure (Cohen, 1997: 48).[4]

We might even suppose that a virtuous person in Allie's situation would have given to Bryce after learning about his plight and reflecting on the merits of his case in light of her circumstances. Suppose also that Allie would have freely given exactly what she had no choice but to give to Bryce anyway. Her failure to give in such a situation would then have been wrong: it would have manifested the vice of stinginess. But without a right to be uncharitable, Allie has little reason to discover this. She would lack the fullest opportunity to decide. Absent what we might then call a "right to do wrong," she is not in the correct moral position to study and reflect on Bryce's situation. Such research and reflection are key for Allie to experience

Andrew I. Cohen

appropriate sympathetic feelings and to determine whether giving is appropriate (and how much) in light of other possible uses and moral demands for her time and property.

This is not just an issue of facilitating virtuous self-development, but one of making it possible for individuals to live their own lives. If Allie is not entitled to her property or her time when there are others who might need such resources, then her life is not hers to define and live. Consider that it is not just Bryce's needs that are at issue. There is also Callandra. And Doris. And Eunice. And countless others. All such persons may be worse off than Allie, so they may have a stake in Allie's property or time. There is no point, however, in Allie's taking any steps to live her own life when her productivity is mortgaged to the bottomless needs of others (Schmidtz, 2000: 693). For Allie to have her own life to lead, she must enjoy the right to make choices – including some wrong ones.[5]

Critical rejoinders

Critics may raise at least three possible objections at this point.

REJOINDER 1: THERE IS NO SERIOUS DANGER TO LIBERTY FROM ENFORCEABLE POSITIVE DUTIES
A critic may say that the foregoing arguments exaggerate the threat to a potential benefactor's liberty from enforceable positive duties. For instance, Wellman only defends duties to give "a modest amount, say $100, to saving the lives of a few children who are currently starving to death" (2005: 314). But it is not clear why such a duty can only demand so little. Philosophers such as Singer believe a person is obligated to reduce herself to penury as long as others are worse off (1972: 231, 241). It is then difficult to see why a mere $100 absolves us of an obligation to aid distant starving people. There are always people starving, and, at least until we are dead, there is always something more we could give (Schmidtz, 2000: 693).

No matter what the amount, though, there are at least four sorts of moral cost involved in obligating a person to provide any portion of her time or wealth.[6]

1 Such compulsion may clash with other important moral values, such as respecting each person's freedom to live her own life. A person who is obligated to give to the needy is deprived of the fullest opportunity to decide whether to use that money for famine relief, for an AIDS research fund, for cancer research, for some books for her child, for a gift for her lover, or even to save it for a rainy day. The point is that if she is to have a protected opportunity to define and live a life of her own, these must be her decisions to make.
2 The compulsion may not be the best way to satisfy the relevant moral demands. Allie may, for instance, do a better job at being charitable if she is not forced to give money or time.
3 It may be hard for anyone to know how to do the right thing or to know what exactly is the right thing to do, so enforcing duties to give may be misguided.
4 Such compulsion hinders the development of the virtues that are important for personal moral development. When we obligate a person to give, she has less of a chance to be fully and authentically *charitable* with *that money*.[7] And for

reasons I discuss later, I believe facilitating such authentic charity is the best way to minimize the need for it.

REJOINDER 2: ENFORCING POSITIVE DUTIES MAKES A PERSON BETTER

This brings us to a second possible objection. Critics may agree that Allie should have some discretion to make choices, but they may draw the line at certain obviously wrong choices, such as, say, Allie's decision to use $100 not for famine relief efforts but on a new outfit from Abercrombie & Fitch (which duplicates three others she already has, but would be in a different color). Not only would it be better overall for Allie's money instead to go to charity, the argument may run, but it would be better *for Allie* if that money were redirected. Here Allie's rights would be constrained by what might make her a better person (or, by what might best help her to do the right thing).

In response, perhaps Allie is mistaken in devoting her money to seemingly frivolous purchases instead of other uses that might better enhance the condition of others. But the question is whether this is something for Allie to decide. There is an important difficulty in saying that a person's life goes better when others impose a certain plan on her. Unless that person is left to make these and other key choices, she is deprived of the fullest chance to learn about and understand just what moral reasons bind her. A person has the best chance for a good life only if she leads it according to her own values (Kymlicka, 1989: 12).

Critics may insist that forcing Allie to hand over her money for a better cause is something she *would* endorse if only she were to think long and hard about it. Perhaps taking the money from her would even give her the chance to reflect about how frivolous the A&F purchase would have been in light of how the money may have helped distant starving people. Taking her money without or despite her consent could then be morally edifying.

This might all be true. But the problem with this approach is that it is better suited to children than to mature adults. Mature adults are left to make their own choices – even if their choices might go wrong – precisely because we grant that they should define and live lives of their own. This does not mean we should always ignore someone's offensive choices. It is always open to us to persuade that person to change. We can also openly protest or repudiate someone's actions. But it is inappropriate to use physical force to compel someone to do something we think is right – even if it seems to be for her own good (Mill, 1978: 9).[8] Doubtless we want people to make better choices – especially when significant moral values are at stake. But the only way human beings can be in the right relationship with prospective moral truths is if they are free to explore and discover them on their own (Hampton, 2003: 224; Locke, 1993: 394–5).

There are three further reasons to reject strong duties of charity. The first has to do with reasonable differences about what counts as good. The second has to do with finding effective ways to reduce the need for charity. The third has to do with the danger of giving anyone the power to make such decisions for us. I discuss each in turn.

First, persons often disagree about morality. Such disagreement is not necessarily a sign of some vice or poor reasoning; reasonable and conscientious persons often

Andrew I. Cohen

differ on moral matters. This disagreement is a function of different life experiences, different perspectives, and different knowledge about the world. More often than not, such differences are *permanent* and track fundamentally different worldviews – not just about what is good, but even about what should be the *standard* of good (Rawls, 1993: 54–8). If we are committed to letting each person live her own life, a healthy humility about moral knowledge along with a constructive openness to reasonable differences provide strong reasons for guaranteeing each person a morally protected space in which to decide whether, how much, and how often to be charitable. Otherwise someone arrogates to herself an inappropriate moral authority, and the rest of us lose the chance to live our own lives.

Second,[9] reasonable people disagree about how best to solve the problem of chronic hunger. But coercing people to give a certain amount, in a certain way, at a certain time, just about guarantees that people will discover no better way to respond to hunger. Experience has shown that people are best able to come up with innovative solutions to problems when they have the freedom to experiment with and discuss alternatives. This freedom to experiment – which requires a freedom not to give according to some single formula – will produce institutions and norms that differ depending upon the context of need and the situations of prospective benefactors.[10]

Third, defenses of strong duties of charity suppose there are trustworthy and reliable moral experts whose dictates, if imposed, would help us better to do the right thing with regard to hunger. But I doubt there are such persons. Given political and psychological realities, no one should be trusted with such power. Even if someone may *seem* to deserve such trust, this should be something each person gets to decide for herself. Moreover, no one person has such extensive knowledge about your circumstances and the circumstances of others that she reliably knows *better than you* how it would be morally best for you to allocate your resources with regard to hunger. Perhaps there are then moral authorities whose *advice* we would do well to heed on such matters, but who to put in such a role is something we should each be free to decide for ourselves. Our lives do not go better if they are foisted on us.

REJOINDER 3: WELFARE IS MORE IMPORTANT THAN LIBERTY

Now we come up against an important third objection. So far, the arguments have shown that a right to do wrong – which may include a right not to give to needy people – is an important component of protecting each person's opportunity to define and live a life of her own. A critic may say that all this talk of self-definition is overblown. What should really count in a moral theory, the critic may claim, is well-being – and not just the individual's well-being, but the well-being of everyone *overall*. So a prospective benefactor's liberty must sometimes (or always?) give way to the greater benefits that would come from redistributing her resources to other persons who are seen as needier (where judgments about who is needier are made and enforced by some authority with political power).

In response, note that this view all but rejects the importance of individual self-definition and choice. On this view, Allie can do as she pleases provided her conduct complies with the calculations of overall well-being by someone in power. But this cuts against Allie's having a chance to live her own life.

Famine Relief and Human Virtue | 333

Admittedly, this will not persuade the critic who takes self-definition lightly. But then the critic has to explain what, if anything, limits the goal of advancing overall well-being. May innocent persons be killed to quell a bloodthirsty mob bent on lynching someone for a crime? May babies be drowned in mud puddles in order to use their tissues for lifesaving medical procedures? If the answers to such similar questions are "no" (as I hope), then we need to hear why.

Presumably some principles or policies are necessary to guide and limit just how we seek to promote overall well-being for everyone. Typically, individual rights serve this purpose: they "trump" the pursuit of net welfare. Though respecting rights may sometimes seem to close off gains to well-being overall, we can do better in the long run by letting rights define protected liberties (Schmidtz, 2000).

At least two possible sorts of critic may speak up here. One sort says that rights *are* important, and that what rights should protect is not just a domain of choice but human welfare. This sort of critic might then defend a positive *right* to famine relief. Such a right typically correlates with some enforceable positive duties. The other sort of critic may dismiss talk of rights and simply argue for an enforceable positive *duty* of famine relief. In either case, the critics defend strong duties of famine relief.

But such critics face an important challenge: they must show that the relevant positive duties do more good than harm. There is a danger that such duties may create what policy theorists sometimes call a "moral hazard." While intended to alleviate suffering, guaranteeing aid to people who suffer may in the long run create more suffering people (Schmidtz, 1998; Shapiro, 2002: 23).

Requiring famine relief undermines benefactors' chances to decide how they shall live their own lives, and this cuts against overall well-being. Forcing people to hand over money to famine relief also threatens to "crowd out" better directed (and better motivated) giving (Shapiro, 2002). At its worst, such compulsion threatens to create an oppressive state and an institutionalized network of busybodies – and these would also cut against overall well-being. Even more, allowing for involuntary transfers of money or time for famine relief may further entrench the corrupt persons and institutions that often directly or indirectly contribute to widespread famine in distant countries. But most important here is that the *beneficiaries* of such relief may lose incentives to live their lives as best as they can (Schmidtz, 2000: 684–8). The beneficiaries can fall into a culture of dependency that undermines the families, communities, and sense of personal responsibility that are crucial for human beings to live good lives.

Of course, none of this shows that duties of famine relief – especially moderate duties – do not on balance promote overall well-being. Nor is this a decisive argument against any *right* to famine relief. Here we merely see how much is required to establish that there are such positive rights or positive duties. Philosophers must await the data from scholars and researchers in fields as diverse as economics, public policy, social psychology, political science, agricultural technology, and many others. But there is still much room for philosophy before the data come in. We can argue (as I did above) that personal liberty is of sufficient moral importance that it warrants protection from fallible human beings acting on limited knowledge who believe they know better than we do how best to dispose of our money and time. They rarely do. Given reasonable disagreement about what properly counts as a standard for the "best"

Andrew I. Cohen

use of money and time, it is far from clear that anyone can ever properly be in a position to make these decisions for us.

Many readers may still worry that without enforceable positive duties of famine relief, distant starving peoples will be consigned to certain death. But this worry itself reflects a widespread concern for the suffering of others. Since wealthier people do care, they can be persuaded to create and/or support institutions to alleviate the suffering of distant hungry peoples.[11] Though we cannot rob Peter to feed Paul, each of us is free to take steps to teach Paul how to feed himself.

As many as 11 million children may die each year before their fifth birthday, mostly from diseases and conditions traceable to poverty and malnutrition (Cowley, 2003: 78). Note, though, that private, voluntarily funded relief efforts – especially when organized locally – have often been quite effective at helping people to get back on their feet (Beito, 2000; Shapiro, 2002: 21–31). So once again we confront important and complex empirical questions about how best to alleviate hunger in the long run. We need to find out about the political, economic, and moral causes of chronic hunger, and we need to consider whether certain sorts of relief effort do more harm than good. This is a vastly complicated issue, but given the empirical uncertainties, reasonable disagreements, and importance of personal liberty and moral virtue, it is something that each person should be left to decide for herself after reflection and research.

In this section I have discussed how enforceable duties of famine relief are morally inappropriate and require daunting empirical support. Readers may think there is yet much room for moderate duties of famine relief. Even if we cannot be forced to do so, perhaps we still *ought* to devote some or all of our available resources to distant famine relief. In the next section, I will argue that distant famine relief, while sometimes commendable, must often take second place to addressing more local needs.

Local Versus Distant Needs

As recently as 2001, more than three-quarters of a billion people in developing countries were undernourished. These are staggering numbers. But nearly 39 million people in Western countries were similarly malnourished (Wren, 2001). Even if they are not our neighbors, we sometimes pass such persons on the street. The problems we face extend beyond hunger. There are ghastly statistics about battered wives, illiteracy, healthcare for the poor, and innocent children who endure horrific illnesses. The numbers in these and other categories refer to far too many persons in our communities who are victims, who suffer, and who could benefit from a helping hand.

I argue that our charitable energies should be more constructively focused on local needs. This is not necessarily because our neighbors are any more deserving or needy than distant starving persons. There need not be anything morally significant, in and of itself, about the fact that some person is *your neighbor*. Because our knowledge of local conditions is typically deeper than that of distant contexts, and because the actual costs of administering aid locally is typically lower, our charitable impulses are usually (though certainly not always) more constructively directed toward local contexts.

Some needy persons live among us. We are more likely to know about their plight and to have better insight into how we might effectively help them while neither insulting their dignity nor fostering any "moral hazards." So it seems that typically (though again, certainly not always), our moral reasons to contribute to distant famine relief would be outweighed by moral reasons to contribute in some way to a *local* rape crisis center or a *local* children's cancer ward or a *local* soup kitchen or a *local* literacy campaign. Again, this is not because being *local* is in itself morally significant. But insofar as we are concerned with alleviating need, we are best in a position to do that for familiar people in familiar situations. Typically (though certainly not always), these are people who are near or dear to us.[12]

Of course, sometimes persons do have excellent knowledge of distant conditions – perhaps even more so than of local conditions. In today's age of global communication and easy travel, we are sometimes better positioned to address some distant needs than to address those that may be closer to us. The point here is that because there is so much local need, it is difficult to see why we can always fault someone for failing to contribute to distant famine relief.

Note, though, that addressing charitable need is not a person's sole moral function. There are many moral demands on us – demands that come from various sources. As intimacy increases in relationships, for instance, there are greater legitimate expectations for care, attention, and devotion. What forms these take will vary from one relationship to another and from one moment to the next. But our resources are finite. We have to decide how best to satisfy all the moral reasons that bind us. Being required to direct our resources to the suffering of distant people may then jeopardize our ability to do fully what we ought to do in nearer and dearer contexts about which we have better knowledge (Kekes, 1987). There is a danger of falling into the pattern of the Dickens character Mrs Jellyby, who focused her caring energies on the natives of Borrioboola-Gha at the expense of her own children (Dickens, 2002).

Each of us is involved in many relationships of different levels of intimacy. To various persons you might be a sibling, a parent, a child, a spouse, a dear friend, a neighbor, a colleague, a teammate, or a fellow citizen. Each of these relationships may impose demands on us. Meanwhile, each of us has commitments to various other personal projects that shape a life. You might be a painter, a runner, a dancer, or a musician. You might enjoy poetry, travel, science fiction, or basketball. Pursuing and cultivating such interests are also part of what gives richness and meaning to a good life. If we devote ourselves to relieving distant situations (about which we know little) at the expense of our own interests (about which we each have a privileged understanding), we do violence to ourselves and undermine our chances to live a good life. There is more to life than alleviating distant need.

Does this mean that contributing to famine relief is *wrong*? Certainly not. Sometimes we can do much good by helping a well-organized relief effort – especially one that has good insight into local conditions, has very low administrative costs, and has taken great pains not to unwittingly prop up corrupt governments or create a culture of dependency. But given how much each of us differs in our understandings of distant conditions, and given our reasonably different conceptions of how each of us might best fashion a good life, contributing to famine relief, assuming it is done

Andrew I. Cohen

conscientiously, is commendable at most but not morally required – even in the moderate sense.

Local Reform and Distant Suffering

Writers on world hunger sometimes defend duties of famine relief as a way to compensate for having benefited from supposedly unjust institutions. Certainly decent persons must not blithely enjoy the fruits of oppression. But we need to consider just what is oppressive.

It would be vastly inappropriate to support or benefit from an industry whose products were manufactured exclusively in Nazi concentration camps. The labor force would consist of brutally oppressed prisoners; the products might be drawn from the property or body parts of slaughtered captives. If there are contemporary analogues to such Nazi concentration camp industries, then we do indeed have a responsibility to withdraw our support from them. We may even have a compelling reason to take active steps toward reform. But it is unclear just what the contemporary analogues are.

Consider just one example of a disturbing Western practice that props up the rich at the expense of poor people in distant countries. It is hardly as ghastly as a concentration camp, but it still unjustly robs the poor of a livelihood. I am speaking of protective tariffs and domestic agricultural and industrial subsidies. US cotton subsidies are a fine example. From the mid-1990s through 2003, $1.7 billion went toward propping up the US cotton industry by providing low-cost water and grants to large cotton conglomerates. The upshot is that domestic cotton farmers have greater incentives to plant a crop that would be less expensively grown abroad in developing countries. The subsidies give an unfair advantage to wealthy American cotton growers. They also drive down global prices for cotton. This forces farmers in developing countries out of business (Sullum, 2003).

This is not an isolated phenomenon. Any time the government subsidizes or protects an industry, it bypasses the market mechanisms that would otherwise direct resources toward their most efficient use. More often than not, the people who lose most are those with the least to lose. So if we are concerned about helping distant persons rise out of poverty, one step is to disassociate ourselves from these American industries that benefit from unfair advantages. Since it is nearly impossible to sort out how to do this, perhaps we might simply work to eliminate such protective measures.

Well-meaning people sometimes unfavorably compare the working conditions in developing economies with those in the West. True, workers in much of the world earn a fraction of what is earned by those in the West. They often work longer hours. Sometimes they start working at a young age. Critics of such conditions sometimes call for boycotts or the closure of "sweatshops" as a way of ending what they take to be oppression.

This is certainly a complex and controversial topic in social and economic theory. But we might note that many workers in developing economies eagerly embrace work in "sweatshops" as a chance to improve their lives and the lives of their families.

Workers often complain that a patronizing, misguided elitism motivates Westerners who believe the developing world would be better without such industries (Langewiesche, 2000: e.g. p. 46). Here we speak not of inmates in Soviet gulags, but people for whom working at a factory manufacturing Nike running shoes would quadruple their family's income, increase their caloric intake, and give the children a chance to be literate. Low-wage industries overseas are often a key step in improving the lives of terribly poor peoples (Myerson, 1997).[13] If anything, often one of the kindest things we can do for the distant poor is to spend some of our money on a new outfit from A&F – especially if it or its components (the fabric, dyes, or fasteners) were manufactured in low-wage factories overseas. Doing so supports distant economies and gives workers there the opportunities to build better lives for themselves and their families. We show a lot more respect for a person by trading with her and treating her as a productive equal than by merely sending her grain and treating her as a helpless open mouth or outstretched hand.

Economists have repeatedly discovered that the easiest way to improve the condition of the world's poor is to eliminate barriers to free markets and establish a rule of law that respects property rights (Bray, 1996; Gollin et al., 2002; Lomborg, 2001: part II; Simon 1996; Simon and Moore, 2000). If we in the West do have any moderate duties to relieve distant suffering, then maybe we are responsible for *opposing* subsidies and other government price supports and *supporting* foreign aid policies reasonably calculated to foster markets and the rule of law in impoverished states.[14] What this duty means for any given person – especially with such a matter of public policy – will of course vary considerably depending upon circumstances. One possibility is that we ought to deepen and apply our understanding of the social, moral, political, and economic institutions that allow people to live successful lives here and abroad. In the meantime, the best thing we could do for others might be to have a productive career and a successful life.

To paraphrase Aristotle, it is not easy being good (1984: II.6). There are so many ways to go wrong, and only one or a few ways of doing the right thing. Living well requires a lot of practice, and it is something we must do for ourselves. Each of us must reflect on all the competing moral considerations that vie for our attention, and each of us must decide how best to allocate our energies and how to forge a life for ourselves. Whether and how charity fits in that life is a deeply personal decision that we must be free to decide for ourselves.

Notes

I am grateful to Andrew Altman, Harry Dolan, Eric Karch, Mark LeBar, George Rainbolt, and Kit Wellman, each of whom provided many helpful comments on an earlier version of this chapter.

1   I stress that, to simplify matters, I pass over possible exceptions here. We can suppose that there are no mitigating circumstances for the prospective benefactor – such as: she is closely chased by a homicidal maniac, or is rushing her own dying child to the hospital,

or is not able-bodied, or can only attempt rescue at grave risk to her life and limb, and so forth. Proponents of a duty to rescue distant starving peoples must grant this simplifying assumption in order to show the duty in its clearest light. Otherwise the drowning baby analogy never gets off the ground.

2   Good Samaritan laws, which punish those who fail to provide easy rescues, must be based on such strong requirements. (Thanks to Mark LeBar for pointing this out.)

3   Consider the disturbing 1997 case of the teenager David Cash, Jr., who did nothing to stop his friend Jeremy Strohmeyer from raping and murdering 7-year-old Sherrice Iverson in the bathroom of a Nevada casino. Cash apparently saw his friend assaulting Iverson and muffling her screams in a bathroom stall, but he took no effective steps to stop the assault. Strohmeyer now serves life without parole in a Nevada prison; Cash went on to study nuclear physics at UC-Berkeley. Cash's inaction and remarks to the press have repeatedly illustrated that he is, to put it mildly, morally underdeveloped. Neither his classmates at UC-Berkeley nor the law were able to use physical force to punish him. But he rightly met with the deep scorn of his classmates at Berkeley. For further details on the story, see, for instance, Bickell (2000) and McDermott (1998).

4   A person who does not enjoy the right not to be charitable might still express charity in the acts she is forced to perform. She might simply authentically identify with them anyway. She may also give (in the right way and for the right reasons) over and above what she is required to do. My point is simply that rights to choose must include a right to withhold, and such rights are important moral norms that facilitate self-definition by protecting opportunities to choose freely (see Cohen, 1997: 48).

5   Certain wrong choices could never be protected by right. For example, no one can enjoy a right to be *unjust* (Cohen, 1997: 44–5). Here I talk only about non-rights-violating wrongs, and I also wish to argue that no one can or should have a right to another person's charity.

6   My thanks to Mark LeBar and George Rainbolt for a discussion of the issues in this paragraph.

7   Much depends on whether the duty to provide aid is moderate or strong. Here I only speak of *strong* positive duties, i.e., physically enforceable obligations. Some proponents of duties of famine relief, however, are not committed one way or the other on this issue. Wellman, for instance, merely speaks of a positive duty to provide minimal aid (as if to suggest that people who fail to provide such aid deserve our scorn but no more). But at other times he speaks of prospective beneficiaries' "Samaritan right" to aid (2005: 316). I think saying that people have a right to such aid suggests a strong duty on others to provide it. Later I raise doubts about whether there are even grounds for a *moderate* duty of famine relief.

8   Here again I stress that this only applies to non-rights-violating wrongs. If a person's choices amount to initiating the use of force against someone else, then defensive or punitive force may be appropriate.

9   My thanks to Mark LeBar for suggesting a discussion of the issues in this paragraph.

10 There are countless examples of organizations and spontaneous norms that help needy people far better than centrally and coercively imposed policies. Consider the burgeoning private "microcredit" movement that has helped *very* small businesses get started in India, Pakistan, Vietnam, Mexico, and elsewhere, helping to lift millions of people out of poverty. Earlier "fraternal" societies also provided locally administered relief, medical care, and rudimentary insurance. See the "Further reading" section for some source materials.

11 Not only can they be persuaded, but they often are. The data on this is extensive and complex, but here's one snapshot: individuals in the United States give far more than corporations (and often several hours each week of their own time). Charitable giving

has remained constant at around 1.9 percent of personal income since the 1970s (Lang, 1998). Private donors from the United States give about $35.1 billion in oversees aid, which is three times what the US government provides in Official Development Assistance. And the United States (privately and publicly) provides the most direct foreign investment and foreign aid and generates the bulk of the world's research and development (Adelman, 2003).

12 Interestingly, Wellman, who defends Samaritan duties of famine relief, elsewhere (2000: 545–7) appeals to similar considerations when discussing "redistributive policies that favor compatriots" (2000: 545). Such policies, Wellman argues, can help us better to comply with other significant moral reasons that bear on our cases.

13 Honduran girls aged 14 and older worked 75 hour weeks at 31 cent hourly wages in factories manufacturing Kathie Lee Gifford branded clothes for Wal-Mart. When Gifford closed the factories in response to protests, the girls were out of jobs and were left with nothing. They reportedly blamed Gifford (Myerson, 1997).

14 Thanks to Andrew Altman for suggesting this point.

References

Adelman, Carol C. (2003). "The privatization of foreign aid: reassessing national largesse." *Foreign Affairs*, 82 (November/December): 9–14.

Aristotle (1984). *Nichomachean Ethics*. In Jonathan Barnes (ed.), *The Complete Works of Aristotle*, vol. 2 (pp. 1729–867). Princeton, NJ: Princeton University Press.

Beito, David (2000). *From Mutual Aid to the Welfare State: Fraternal Societies and Social Services, 1890–1967*. Chapel Hill: University of North Carolina Press.

Bickell, Bill (2000). "Murder in the casino." Updated September 19, 2000 on crime.about.com at: ⟨http://crime.about.com/library/weekly/aa091498.htm⟩.

Bray, Anna J. (1996). "Hunger's real cure? Freedom." *Investor's Business Daily* (November 22): 1.

Cohen, Andrew I. (1997). "Virtues, opportunities, and the right to do wrong." *Journal of Social Philosophy*, 28: 43–55.

Cowley, Geoffrey (2003). "Where living is lethal." *Newsweek* (September 22): 78–80.

Dickens, Charles (2002). *Bleak House*. New York: Modern Library (Original work published in monthly parts March 1852–September 1853.)

Gollin, Douglas, Parente, Stephen, and Rogerson, Richard (2002). "The role of agriculture in development." *American Economic Review*, 92: 160–4.

Gomberg, Paul (2002). "The fallacy of philanthropy." *Canadian Journal of Philosophy*, 32: 29–66.

Hampton, Jean (2003). "The liberals strike back." In James P. Sterba (ed.), *Justice: Alternative Political Perspectives*, 4th edn. (pp. 218–25). Belmont, CA: Wadsworth.

Kekes, John (1987). "Benevolence: a minor virtue." *Social Philosophy & Policy*, 4: 21–36.

Kymlicka, Will (1989). *Liberalism, Community and Culture*. Oxford: Clarendon Press.

Lang, John (1998). "In US, giving is a national pastime." *Washington Times* (September 24).

Langewiesche, William (2000). "The shipbreakers." *The Atlantic Monthly*, 286 (August): 31–49.

Locke, John (1993[1689]). "A letter concerning toleration." In David Wootton (ed.), *Political Writings of John Locke* (pp. 390–436). New York: Mentor.

Lomborg, Bjørn (2001). *The Skeptical Environmentalist*. Cambridge: Cambridge University Press.

McDermott, Anne (1998). "A silent friend, and a debate over good Samaritan laws." Posted

September 4 on cnn.com at: ⟨http://www.cnn.com/SPECIALS/views/y/1998/09/mcdermott. casino/⟩.

Mill, J. S. (1978[1859]). *On Liberty*. ed. Elizabeth Rapaport. Indianapolis: Hackett.

Myerson, Alan R. (1997). "In principle, a case for more 'sweathshops'." *New York Times*, sect. 4 (June 22): 5.

Rawls, John (1993). *Political Liberalism*. New York: Columbia University Press.

Schmidtz, David (1998). "Taking responsibility." In David Schmidtz and Robert Goodin, *Social Welfare and Individual Responsibility* (pp. 3–96). Cambridge: Cambridge University Press.

Schmidtz, David (2000). "Islands in a sea of obligation." *Law and Philosophy*, 6: 683–705.

Shapiro, Daniel (2002). "Egalitarianism and welfare-state redistribution." *Social Philosophy & Policy*, 19: 1–35.

Simon, Julian (1996). *The ultimate resource 2*. Princeton: University Press.

Simon, Julian and Moore, Stephen (2000). *It's Getting Better All The Time: 100 Greatest Trends of the Twentieth Century*. Washington, DC: Cato Institute.

Singer, Peter (1972). "Famine, affluence, and morality." *Philosophy and Public Affairs*, 1: 229–43.

Sullum, Jacob (2003). "The fabric of their lives: US cotton subsidies make the poor poorer." *Gwinnett (GA) Daily Post* (November 8): 6A.

Unger, Peter (1996). *Living High and Letting Die Our Illusion of Innocence*. New York: Oxford University Press.

Wellman, Christopher Heath (2000). "Relational facts in liberal political theory: is there magic in the pronoun 'my'?" *Ethics*, 110: 537–62.

Wellman, Christopher Heath (2005). "Famine relief: the duties we have to others." In Andrew I. Cohen and Christopher Heath Wellman (eds.), *Contemporary Debates in Applied Ethics* (pp. 313–25). New York: Blackwell.

Wren, Christopher S. (2001). "UN report maps hunger 'hot spots.'" *New York Times* (January 9): A8.

Further reading

⟨http://www.results.org/website/article.asp?id=244⟩ for information about Results Educational Fund Microcredit project.

Beito, David, Gordon, Peter, and Tabarrok, Alexander (eds.) (2002). *Voluntary City: Choice, Community, and Civil Society*. Ann Arbor: University of Michigan Press.

Den Uyl, Douglas J. (1995). "The right to welfare and the virtue of charity." In Tibor R. Machan and Douglas B. Rasmussen (eds.), *Liberty for the Twenty-first Century* (pp. 305–34). Lanham, MD: Rowman & Littlefield.

Den Uyl, Douglas J. and Rasmussen, Douglas B. (1995). "'Rights' as metanormative principles." In Tibor R. Machan and Douglas B. Rasmussen (eds.), *Liberty for the Twenty-first Century* (pp. 59–75). Lanham, MD: Rowman & Littlefield.

Gilder, George (1981). *Wealth and Poverty*. New York: Basic Books.

Hasnas, John (1995). "From cannibalism to caesareans: two conceptions of fundamental rights." *Northwestern University Law Review*, 89: 900–41.

Hayek, F. A. (1945). "The use of knowledge in society." *American Economic Review*, 35: 519–30.

Lomasky, Loren (1987). *Persons, Rights, and the Moral Community*. Oxford: Oxford University Press.

Murray, Charles A. (1994). *In Pursuit of Happiness and Good Government*. San Francisco: ICS Press.

Murray, Charles A. (1994). *Losing Ground: American Social Policy, 1950–1980*. New York: Basic Books.

Nozick, Robert (1974). *Anarchy, State, and Utopia*. New York: Basic Books.

Semple, Kirk (2003). "Tiniest of loans bring big payoff, aid group says." *New York Times* (November 3): A6.

Smith, Tara (1995). *O*. Lanham, MD: Rowman & Littlefield.

Andrew I. Cohen

Index